Hardship and Force Majeure in International Commercial Contracts

Dealing with unforeseen events in a changing world

INTERNATIONAL CHAMBER OF COMMERCE
The world business organization

Edited by
Fabio Bortolotti
Dorothy Ufot, SAN

Hardship and Force Majeure in International Commercial Contracts
Dealing with unforeseen events in a changing world

ICC Services
Publications Department
33-43 avenue du Président Wilson
75116 Paris
France

ICC Publication No. 796E
ISBN: 978-92-842-0482-3

Contents

Foreword

by Yves Derains

After many years of Conferences dealing with issues related to the resolution of disputes, the 38th Annual Conference of the ICC Institute of World Business law reverts to contractual practice. This should not be a surprise as the Institute has always been deeply involved in training practitioners to negotiating and drafting contracts. The seminars on international contracts organized and conducted by Kristine Karsten, an Institute Council Member, are models of the kind.

What may surprise some of the usual readers of the *Dossiers of the Institute* is the fact that this 17th issue is available before the Annual Conference and not after. Indeed, the Council of the Institute has decided to adopt a new approach concerning the publication of its *Dossiers*: instead of publishing the works of the Annual Conference several months after the event, it was found more appropriate to ask the Council Members in charge of the scientific program of the Conference, in this case Prof Fabio Bortolotti and Dorothy Ufot, SAN, to regroup in a book prepared in advance of the event significant papers by some of the key speakers on the subject of the Conference, in order to be able to remit this book to the participants with the Conference documents as a basis for discussions. This is the genesis of this Dossier of the Institute.

Force majeure and hardship were not chosen at whim as a theme illustrating the Institute interest for contractual issues. These two institutions are at the heart of the very notion of contract, as they allow to maintain a balance between two basic old principles: "*pacta sunt servanda*" and "*rebus sic stantibus*" which have traditionally controlled the effects of the passing of time on the performance of contractual obligations.

Time is one of the challenges of contract drafters. An old peasant told me once that only dishonest persons need written contracts because honest people would keep their word in any case. This would be true if all transactions were instantaneous, like buying bread at the baker's shop: the customer does not need a written contract of sale in order to be able give its money to the baker before receiving the precious "*baguette*". He or she knows that the principle "*pacta sunt servanda*" will be respected within the following second.

The time factor changes everything and requires a careful drafting which covers the expected future conduct of the parties. This is not an answer to the need to be protected from dishonest parties as few people would enter into contract with the knowledge that their contracting partner is dishonest. The contract expresses the will of the parties to organize carefully the future of their relations, in terms of the substance of their respective obligations, their duration and the dates of their performance. Force majeure and hardship clauses are the tools which allow the contracting partners to foresee the reasonably unforeseeable. They deal with impossibility of performance and excessively onerous performance. However, they have a very different historical status in contractual practice.

Everybody is supposed to know what force majeure is. Sometimes translated in English as "Acts of God" when referring to fire, flood, earthquake, etc., it is commonly understood to be an event exonerating a party from liability. Before its 2016 reform, the French Civil Code, stated in its article 1148 that force majeure was exonerating a party who had not fulfilled an obligation from paying damages but it had not been felt necessary to provide any definition of force majeure. A new article 1218 felt that gap with a precise definition in 2016, but it is telling that the country of the codification of the law could wait for a definition of force majeure in its Civil Code for more than 200 years.

In international contractual practice, force majeure is too often left to boilerplate clauses with lists of events of force majeure which raise difficult problems of interpretation: is the list exhaustive or does it show examples of events with characteristics which may be used to admit as force majeure unlisted events which share the same characteristics. This difficulty is increased when the law applicable to the contract is not very familiar with the legal concept of force majeure, such as English law where the doctrine of frustration established in 1863 in *Taylor v Caldwell* is grounded on very different premises. Moreover, complicated issues of notification of the force majeure event as well as clear definition of their consequences, from suspension of the contract to its termination, requires the guidance of case law, mostly international arbitration case law.

Although they are an avatar of the *rebus sic stantibus* clause, hardship clauses are relatively new since they started to play a significant role in contractual practice in the last part of the 20th century. They do not contemplate the impossibility of performance but the onerous consequences for a party of the change of external circumstances on the performance of the contract, in particular in long term contracts. Many national law dealt with this problem, such as French law with the concept of *imprévision* applicable only to administrative contracts, Italian law with its *eccessiva onerosità*, some Latin American laws or the 1948 Egyptian Civil Code and the laws of all the Arab states which had been inspired by the works of Abd el-Razzâq el-Sanhourî. However, the conditions laid down by these national laws were not always adapted to the needs of modern trade and appropriate solutions had to be found in contract clauses, international arbitration case law, soft law and to some extent, international conventions. More recently, several national laws have taken the problem of hardship into consideration.

The above remarks show the practical importance of force majeure and hardship clauses. The effect on the performance of international contracts of the imposition of economic sanctions, which may be characterized as force majeure events or hardship according to the circumstances, is, among others, an illustration of this importance.

ICC has a great experience in this respect. It offered to practitioners a model for force majeure clauses since 1985. This model was revised in 2003, when a model for hardship clauses was issued as well. A revised version of that clause is currently under discussion and should be approved and published in 2019 and a number of the experts who have contributed to that work are responsible for the content of this Dossier.

A special tribute must be paid to Prof Fabio Bortolotti and to Dorothy Ufot, SAN who, thanks to their knowledge of the subject matter and their impressive efforts have produced another impressive Dossier of the Institute.

Yves Derains

Introduction

by Fabio Bortolotti and Dorothy Ufot, SAN

Force majeure and hardship are commonly invoked in international trade in case of occurrence of unforeseen events which make performance impossible or impracticable (force majeure) or which substantially upset the equilibrium of the contract (hardship). In the first case the party successfully invoking force majeure will be relieved from performance, while in the second case the party subject to hardship will be entitled to renegotiate the contract and in certain cases to obtain its adaptation to the changed circumstances.

While in the past the events to be considered in this context were mainly "acts of god" (fire, flood, earthquake, etc.), in recent years the growing complexity of trade in a globalized world has substantially increased the number of situations where a party can invoke force majeure and hardship, and consequently put into discussion the basic principle of *pacta sunt servanda*.

Most national legislators provide rules dealing with these issues, but the specific solutions adopted in domestic laws substantially vary from one country to the other, and consequently offer little certainty to negotiators, who are looking for precise and foreseeable rules governing these crucial issues.

This is why traders who are aware of the risks arising out of unforeseen events tend as far as possible to prepare for their occurrence by negotiating appropriate force majeure and/or hardship clauses. Parties frequently include in their contracts standard clauses, which, however, do not necessarily correspond to their actual needs (especially when copied from other contracts, without verifying their quality).

To deal with the impact of unforeseen circumstances which make performance impossible or excessively burdensome, parties need not only analyse the nature and characteristics of force majeure and hardship, as regulated in domestic laws and soft law instruments, but must also look for contractual clauses which can regulate these issues in conformity with their actual needs.

Most of the cases decided by courts and arbitrators imply (at least with respect to force majeure) the application and interpretation of contractual clauses governing these issues. This is why it is particularly appropriate to include the topic of the revision of the ICC 2003 force majeure and hardship clauses.

This *Dossier XVII* of the ICC Institute of World Business Law, which is edited in view of the 38th Institute Annual Conference on Hardship and Force Majeure in International Commercial Contracts, contains only the presentations provided by the key speakers of the conference, which could be provided by their authors before the conference, in order to make it possible to have the dossier ready to be distributed at the conference. We have made a choice of the presentations in order to cover most of the crucial issues and to provide an updated view of recent trends in this field.

HARDSHIP

In the first presentation Marcel Fontaine describes the evolution of the rules on hardship, from their "discovery" in 1976 to the enactment, in recent years, of a growing number of international soft law instruments and domestic laws regulating this issue. When the study group on international contracts, chaired by Marcel Fontaine, published its study on hardship clauses, such clauses were almost unknown outside some very specific trades. Thereafter the subject matter became an actual issue which was included in the UNIDROIT Principles and in several domestic laws.

At present many domestic laws contain rules on hardship, which, however, follow different types of approach, especially regarding the crucial issues regarding the obligation to renegotiate the contract and the right to request its adaptation by a judge or arbitrator.

In order to overcome the uncertainty due to the non-uniformity of domestic rules, parties are inclined to replace such rules with specific clauses, adapted to their actual needs, which specify the prerequisites of hardship in relation to their business, as well as the solutions to be applied: renegotiation, adaptation, etc. Regarding the option of contract adaptation, the point of view of business is divided. Some businessmen consider the possibility of having the contract conditions modified by a third party (judge, arbitrator) as an unacceptable risk; others, on the contrary believe this is to be considered as an indispensable tool for overcoming certain situations, particularly in long term contracts.

Concerning the role of arbitrators in adapting contracts in case of hardship, the presentation by Pascale Accaoui Lorfing examines a number of interesting issues, such as in particular the extent of contract adaptation, the methodology to be applied, as well as possible limits to the arbitrators' power.

FORCE MAJEURE

The section on force majeure opens with the presentation of Christoph Brunner, who gives an overview of recent arbitral case law regarding the various aspects of force majeure (impediment beyond sphere of control and risk of the obligor; foreseeability; insurmountable and temporary impediments, causation; notice requirement). Christoph Brunner concludes that in the context of international commercial contracts the impact of force majeure events is mostly regulated by the terms of a force majeure clause and that notwithstanding the different applicable laws and the different wording of the clauses, arbitral case law shows a rather uniform approach to their interpretation and application.

Considering the importance of a well drafted force majeure clause, the following two presentations deal with the ICC model clause. Filip De Ly, member of the task force which drafted the ICC 2003 Force Majeure Clause, analyses the main aspects of the clause and the approach followed by the working party when drafting the clause. Ercüment Erdem gives a short overview of the present stage of the revision of the ICC force majeure and hardship clauses, which should be approved and published in 2019. Readers will have the opportunity to consult the annexed text of the clauses as they are in the present stage of discussion

The Dossier concludes with two important contributions regarding other topical aspects of force majeure.

The first issue, examined by Klaus Peter Berger, looks at the relationship between force majeure and applicable law, general principles of law and trade usages. Are force majeure clauses self-sufficient or should they be interpreted in view of the applicable rules of law? What is the role of the applicable law with respect to unclear or insufficiently precise force majeure clauses?

Finally, Mercédeh Azeredo da Silveira, concludes with a theme of growing importance: the impact of economic sanctions on contracts as force majeure and/or hardship.

Fabio Bortolotti Dorothy Udeme Ufot, SAN

Chapter 1

The Evolution of the Rules on Hardship

From the First Study on Hardship Clauses to the Enactment of Specific Rules

by Marcel Fontaine*

INTRODUCTION

1. We are in April 1975. A few academics and corporate counsel are meeting at the University of Liège, in Belgium. The participants come from France, Belgium and Switzerland. It is the first gathering of the initial members of a working group intending to elaborate regular chronicles on the practice of international contracts, that was going to be known as the *Working Group on International Contracts*. Publications will appear in a new periodical created at the initiative of Professor Henry Lesguillons and entitled *Droit et pratique du commerce international—Law and Practice of International Trade*. The method has been decided; individual types of clauses will be successively discussed, on the basis of actual clauses found by members of the group in their own files.

2. When the concrete issue of choosing the subject of the first chronicle came up, several suggestions were made, but none of them seemed to be sufficiently attractive for an inaugural publication. A participant with a long experience at a Belgian company deeply involved in international trade, the regretted Jean-Marie Deleuze, then raised his hand and suggested *"Why not hardship clauses?"*.

A distinctive moment of silence and perplexity followed. Obviously no one else in the room had ever heard of *"hardship clauses"* and had any idea of what they could be... Some embarrassment. Our friend explained, and assured us that such clauses were quite frequent in certain types of contracts. As it sounded quite interesting, the subject was selected.

According to the working method we had agreed upon, I wrote to all members of the group (which had been enlarged in the meantime) to ask if they could provide me with examples of such clauses to be discussed in the group—and the outcome was miraculous. Very soon, every morning I found thick envelopes in my mailbox (yes, as some readers may still remember, that was the way information circulated then), with several samples of hardship clauses already accompanied by explanatory comments. When the first meeting came with hardship on the agenda, participants had a file of more than fifty clauses to discuss.[1]

---

* Professor emeritus at the University of Louvain (UCL). Marcel Fontaine has a substantial experience as a national and international arbitrator (CEPANI, ICC, LCIA, ad hoc). He is the author of several publications, and was the Leader of the Working Group on International Contracts (1974-1992). He was a member of the group that elaborated the UNIDROIT Principles of International Commercial Contracts and was the expert in charge of drafting the OHADA Uniform Act on International Contracts.

3. Discussions took place in a series of meetings in France and in Belgium during 1975 and 1976. The chronicle was published in 1976,[2] then included in a book gathering twelve other chronicles elaborated by the Working Group (some of them, since the second French edition, written by my successor as chairman of the Group, my excellent colleague Professor Filip De Ly). This book initially appeared in French,[3] and was later translated into English,[4] Italian[5] and Spanish.[6] Each chapter, including the one on hardship clauses, was updated at the occasion of each new book publication (in particular, to take into consideration the constantly growing number and larger variety of clauses available to the Group). The most recent version is the Spanish edition.[7]

4. We will summarise the contents of the Group's analysis of hardship clauses (I). We will then turn to the enactment of specific rules on the issue in several international (II.A.) and domestic (II.B.) codifications[8]. Finally, we will briefly comment on the ICC Clause on hardship in the context of the evolution described, in anticipation of the special attention this Clause will receive in later interventions (III), before offering a few concluding thoughts.

I. THE 1976 STUDY ON HARDSHIP CLAUSES

5. The chronicle on hardship clauses was initially published in 1976, and several times updated until 2013.[9]

We will of course not repeat the contents of this study, which can easily be consulted in one of the successive versions. Let us just briefly recall the main points that have been addressed.

6. An introduction presented the issue at stake (significant changes of circumstances upsetting the equilibrium of the contract) and the ways it was already treated in some legal systems, by case law or statutory provisions. Hardship clauses appeared as contractual solutions; they were compared to certain more or less similar clauses.

The main part of the study consisted in a systematic analysis of the drafting of hardship clauses in practice, with their many possible variations (together with critical comments and advice to negotiators).

As any other legal rule, a hardship clause contains two main parts, the "hypothesis" and the "regime".

7. The first task of the drafter is to describe the hypothesis, i.e. the situation that will be considered; in this case, a substantial change of circumstances, leading to considerable prejudice to one party. On the basis of the wide variety of hardship clauses that had been collected, the chronicle presented a detailed analysis of the different ways these two elements of the definition could be expressed (e.g. general definitions and/or enumerations of events, objective or subjective criteria to qualify the impact of the change of circumstances).

When considering the national provisions already existing about the phenomenon (cf. *infra*, no. 39-40), as well as the more recent international and national rules (cf. *infra*, nos. 15-37 and 42-57), we will see that there are two main approaches, one centered on the case where performing contractual obligations had become excessively onerous for one party (a situation frequently designated by its French appellation *"imprévision"*), and a broader approach which more generally considers situations where the *"foundations of the contract"* have been destroyed or substantially modified (in German law, the *"Wegfall der Geschäftsgrundlage"*) or where the contract has been *"frustrated"* (the English law approach). Definitions of the *"hypothesis"* in the hardship clauses analysed reflected one approach or the other, under the influence of the law applicable to the contract.

8. Then the *"regime"*, i.e. the rules that will be applicable if the hypothesis is verified. After imposing on the aggrieved party a duty of notification of the alleged occurrence of the event, the clause typically requires the parties to enter into renegotiation, with the view to agree on adaptations of the contract. Criteria are often given to qualify the purpose of the renegotiation, either objective (e.g. *"restore the initial equilibrium"*) or subjective (e.g. *"abate such unfairness"*).

However, such negotiations will not necessarily lead to a mutually acceptable solution (the non-aggrieved party may have an opposite interest as it may find the new circumstances to be particularly advantageous). While some of the clauses that were examined failed to provide for a way out in such a case (an omission due to lead to inevitable problems), we found that most hardship clauses gave *"teeth"* to their provisions on renegotiation (as nicely expressed by the regretted Clive Schmithoff), by allowing the aggrieved party, in case of failure, to terminate the contract—an incentive for the other party to accept an adaptation of the contract.

Some of the clauses, but a distinct minority, provided for another procedure: in case of lack of agreement, the matter would be referred to a third party, an expert or an "arbitrator".[10] However, that third party was often invited to give a mere recommendation, not a binding opinion, and in our sample of clauses, not a single one provided for the intervention of a judge.

The discussions in the Working Group revealed that this was one of the most important issues concerning the regime of hardship clauses, due to the obvious reluctance of practitioners to let a third party interfere with the contents or the existence of the contract. We will frequently come back to this issue below, when examining the different attempts to regulate this aspect of hardship.

9. The chronicle ended with some more general thoughts, such as the importance of hardship clauses for long-term contracts in an increasingly changing environment, or the interest of such clauses with regard to the absence or inadequacy of solutions to be found in the law applicable to the contract.

10. A last remark about the study of the Working Group. In spite of what could be inferred from the title of this contribution, the evolution of the rules on hardship of course did not begin with the chronicle that has just been described. The large sample of more than fifty clauses that were then assembled were not all recent. Hardship clauses had already been around for many years, and they were well known by negotiators of international contracts in many sectors (though they seem to have become more and more common in the 1970s).

The exercise was not done to attempt to date the oldest clause in the collection (a complicated task since most clauses were submitted individually, extracted from the whole contract where the date could have been found), but it was often not too difficult to guess the approximate "age" of a specific clause. The Working Group could easily see great differences in the degree of sophistication of the clauses which were provided, thus suggesting that there had been a significant evolution between early attempts to draft a rudimentary hardship clause (e.g. *"In case of change of circumstances causing undue hardship to ..., both parties agree to attempt to adapt the contract in a spirit of fairness"*) and some obviously more recent clauses, extremely detailed, which could take several pages—with all possible degrees of elaboration in between. The evolution of hardship clauses had already been impressive in the hands of contract drafters and negotiators much before academics discovered them, and later legislators started to take inspiration when drafting new provisions—or modernizing existing rules.

11. Obviously, this evolution continued after the first publication of the study in 1977. At each of the later publications (in the two editions of the book in French, and in the English, Italian and Spanish versions), the chapter on hardship clauses was updated and enriched with new clauses that had been received in the meantime. An example is the sophisticated *"Market Disruption Event"* clause which was first quoted and commented in the English edition of the book, published in 2006.[11]

It is true that the same English edition had noted that *"in the recent past, hardship clauses seem to have attained a certain state of stabilization"*.[12] After all, it is probably normal that after the important development which took place in the 1970s, hardship clauses had reached a certain stage of maturity. Yet, another systematic gathering of hardship clauses today would certainly reveal new trends in their drafting, or new varieties of clauses. More recently, for instance, *"Material adverse change clauses"*, especially frequent in corporate merger and share purchase agreements, have drawn much attention.[13]

It will presently be shown that the discovery of the actual practice of such clauses has gradually influenced, to various extents, several national and international recent codifications, which is a positive development. But such rules, happily, are not mandatory, and they should not, and do not hinder creativity in contract negotiations.

II. HARDSHIP REGULATED

12. The issue of change of circumstances is certainly not new for jurists. It was already a subject of discussion in the Middle Ages, in relation to the *clausula sic stantibus* doctrine.[14] In more recent times, in different legal systems, positions were taken on the issue, in legal theory, but also in either case law or Civil codes. Sometimes the principle was affirmed that the binding force of contract could in no way be affected by a change of circumstances, more frequently adaptation or termination of the contract could be envisaged under strict conditions and with judicial intervention. In certain legal systems, the issue is met from the angle of excessive onerosity (*"imprévision"*); in others in the wider perspective of changes upsetting the foundations of the contract (cf. *supra*, no. 7).

13. When the study by the Working Group was published, it contributed to a better knowledge (and for many, to the discovery) of the ways the impact

of change of circumstances on contract performance was actually handled by negotiators and drafters, in provisions very often called *"hardship clauses"*. A large number of further publications confirmed and enriched these new perspectives.[15]

It seems obvious that these new contributions were taken into consideration, admittedly to various extents, in the drafting of several new regulations that came out on the issue in recent years, both at the international and domestic levels.

We will now comment on several of these new texts, and attempt to evaluate the extent to which they seem to meet the expectations of practitioners.

14. Such a discussion, in our view, has a major practical interest. To our knowledge, general rules on changes of circumstances are never mandatory. They can always be replaced by different provisions negotiated between the parties, which is illustrated by the widespread presence of hardship clauses. However, the first task of a contract drafter should be to verify what the solution would be under the law applicable to the contract, in the absence of a specific clause. This solution may prove to be satisfactory, and then no hardship clause would be needed. Otherwise, in the drafting of such a clause (as for any other clause in the contract), awareness of the legal rule from which it intends to deviate is certainly not without interest.

We will start by examining some international instruments before presenting several recent reforms in domestic law, since some of the former (mainly the UNIDROIT Principles, and to a lesser extent, the Principles of European Contract Law) have often inspired the latter, at various degrees.

II.A. Hardship regulation in international instruments

15. Several important international instruments intending to harmonise the law of contracts have appeared in the recent past, usually containing provisions on hardship (or explaining the absence of such provisions). We will successively consider the *UNIDROIT Principles of International Commercial Contracts*, the *Principles of European Contract Law*, the European *Draft Common Frame of Reference*, the *OHADA Draft Uniform Act on Contracts* and the *OHADAC Principles on International Commercial Contracts.*

In the first place, however, we will refer to the Vienna *Convention on the International Sale of Goods*, where the question of whether its Article 79 concerns hardship is the subject of much debate.

II.A.1. The Vienna Convention on International Sale of Goods

16. The Vienna *Convention on Contracts for the International Sale of Goods of 1980* (CISG) has become one of the major success stories of contract law harmonisation, having by now been adopted by 89 countries and having become a basic reference for comparative lawyers.

At first sight, CISG does not contain any provision concerning change of circumstances. However, Article 79, in a section entitled *"Exemptions"*, states that

> A party is not liable for a failure to perform any of his obligations if he proved that the failure was due to an impediment beyond his control and

that he could not reasonably be expected to have taken the impediment into account at the time of the conclusion of the contract or to have avoided or overcome it or its consequences.

This seems to cover *force majeure* without using the expression (even though the terms are commonly used in practice, in contracts drafted in other languages than French). Failure to perform is due to an impediment beyond the control of a party, which could not have been avoided (nor its consequences) and which it could not reasonably have taken into consideration; this appears to meet the traditional conditions of having been unavoidable and unforeseeable.[16]

17. Yet, the circumvoluted language of the provision gave rise to controversy. Even though the term *impediment* had been chosen by drafters to replace the wider term *circumstances* which was used in the earlier Hague Convention, in the deliberate intent to express the condition for exemption a more restrictive way,[17] some commentators argued that the newly chosen term remained imprecise enough to apply not only to force majeure, but also to hardship.[18]

An important development had come with the publication in 2008 of Opinion No. 7 of the CISG Advisory Council, a group of eminent scholars forming a sort of *"think tank"* on issues related to CISG. Point 3.1 of this Opinion states that *"A change of circumstances that could not reasonably be expected to have been taken into account, rendering performance excessively onerous (hardship), may qualify as an 'impediment' under Article 79 (1). The language of Article 79 does not expressly equate the term 'impediment' with an event that makes performance absolutely impossible. Therefore, a party that finds itself in a situation of hardship may invoke hardship as an exemption of liability under Article 79."*[19]

However, in this document, the experts had to admit that *"at the time of the drafting of this opinion, no court has exempted a party from liability on the grounds of economic hardship"* (point 31).

18. In 2009, the gap was filled by an unexpected decision of the Belgian *Cour de cassation*. It was about an international contract for the sale of steel tubes, and the price of steel had increased sharply. Though there was no price adjustment clause in the contract, the seller raised the price. The buyer refused and sued the seller, who invoked Article 79 of CISG. After two successive decisions of lower courts, the case was submitted to the *Cour de cassation*. The Court recalled the text of Article 79 (1), and went on in the following terms: "*Changed circumstances that were not reasonably foreseeable at the time of the conclusion of the contract and that are unequivocally of a nature to increase the burden of performance of the contract in a disproportionate manner, can, under certain circumstances, form an impediment in the sense of this provision of the Convention."*[20]

It could hardly be less explicit. Among its justifications, the Court refers to Articles 7 (1) and (2) of CISG (dealing with interpretation of the Convention) and to the UNIDROIT Principles, but it gives no indication as to what these *"certain circumstances"* could be.

In any case, we are not convinced that if this solution were correct, it would adequately meet the issues related to hardship. The remedies provided in Article 79 are obviously adapted to force majeure situations, not to hardship circumstances. If the seller is exempted from liability under Article 79, *"nothing in this article prevents the other party from exercising any right other than to claim damages under this Convention"* (para. 5), i.e. in case of hardship invoked by the seller, the buyer could still, for instance, require delivery, cure by the seller or price reduction. We are far from a regime adapted to hardship, which usually gravitates around renegotiation and adaptation of the contract (price reduction is sometimes a possibility of adjustment, but if the seller is under undue hardship, price increase might on the contrary be the adequate solution—and CISG does not provide for price increase). The right to terminate in hardship circumstances should be organised in context, not by the application of rules designed for situations of breach of contract.

Personally we do not consider that the language of article 79 could be stretched to cover hardship cases. Force majeure and hardship require different regimes, as attested in contractual practice,[21] in the publication of separate clauses by the ICC (cf. *infra*, no. 59) and (to our knowledge) in all codifications dealing with both issues, as exemplified in the UNIDROIT Principles, which will now be discussed.

II.A.2. The UNIDROIT Principles of International Commercial Contracts

19. Since its first edition in 1994, Chapter 6 (Performance) of the *UNIDROIT Principles of International Commercial Contracts* (PICC) includes a Section 2 entitled *"Hardship"* (Force majeure is dealt with in Article 7.1.7 of the chapter on Non-performance). Having been fortunate enough to be a member of the Group that elaborated the first three editions of the Principles (1994, 2004, 2010), I have taken part in the discussions of the UNIDROIT Working Group when this section was prepared, under the masterful chairmanship of Prof Joachim Bonell. From the start, there was general agreement that provisions on change of circumstances should be included in the codification. The Reporter for this Section was Prof Dietrich Maskow, then Director of the *Institut für ausländisches Recht und Rechtsvergleichung* in Potsdam.

Several models of possible approaches to the matter were already available in some national codes, but one explicit concern of UNIDROIT was to take actual contractual practice in international contracts into consideration. This is very apparent in the deliberate choice of the term *"Hardship"* to qualify the issue, expecting that this would immediately be understood by practitioners (as compared to more abstract terminology, such as *"change of circumstances"*, *"basis of the transaction"* or *"imprévision"*).[22]

20. The following provisions were adopted:

Section 2—Hardship

Article 6.2.1—Contract to be Observed
Where the performance of a contract becomes more onerous for one of the parties, that party is nevertheless bound to perform its obligations subject to the following provisions on hardship.

Article 6.2.2—Definition of Hardship
There is hardship where the occurrence of events fundamentally alters the equilibrium of the contract either because the cost of a party's performance has increased or because the value of the performance a party receives has diminished, and

a. the events occur or become known to the disadvantaged party after the conclusion of the contract;

b. the events could not reasonably have been taken into account by the disadvantaged party at the time of the conclusion of the contract;

c. the events are beyond the control of the disadvantaged party; and

d. the risk of the events was not assumed by the disadvantaged party.

Article 6.2.3—Effects of Hardship

1. In case of hardship the disadvantaged party is entitled to request renegotiations. The request shall be made without undue delay and shall indicate the grounds on which it is based.

2. The request for renegotiation does not itself entitle the disadvantaged party to withhold performance.

3. Upon failure to reach agreement within a reasonable time either party may resort to the court.

4. If the court finds hardship it may, if reasonable,

   a. terminate the contract at a date and on terms to be fixed; or

   b. adapt the contract with a view to restoring its equilibrium.

21. This is not the place to offer a detailed analysis of the provisions, which have inspired several excellent commentaries.[23] In the present context, we will briefly recall the structure and content of these three articles and comment on their contribution, or lack of contribution, to what could appear to be the needs and expectations of practice (judging from the experience of the study of contractual clauses examined above).

The Section on Hardship begins with a very appropriate reminder that as a principle, "*Where the performance of a contract becomes more onerous for one of the parties, that party is nevertheless bound to perform its obligations subject to the following provisions on hardship*" (art. 6.2.1). Hardship rules should be applied only in exceptional circumstances, since they interfere with the basic principle that parties are bound by the contract they have entered.

Therefore, Article 6.2.2 defines hardship in a very restrictive way, subjecting it to several cumulative conditions (we refer to the text) and addressing the issue from the angle of excessive onerosity (cf. *supra*, nos. 7 and 12).

22. More difficult was the elaboration of Article 6.2.3, providing for the effects of hardship. Previous statutory models, it will be seen (cf. *infra*, no. 41), usually provided that in case of change of circumstances, the aggrieved party could ask the judge to terminate the contract. In the Working Group on International Contracts, this was abundantly discussed and confronted with the expectations of practitioners as revealed in the hardship clauses which were on the table. It has been pointed out how reluctant parties are to voluntarily let a third party interfere with their agreement—certainly not a judge, not even an arbitrator (cf. *supra*, no. 8).

Article 6.2.3 of the UNIDROIT Principles quite satisfactorily meets the practitioners' expectations when providing for renegotiations between parties as the normal first step to be taken in case of hardship: "*In case of hardship the disadvantaged party is entitled to request renegotiations. The request shall be made without undue delay and shall indicate the grounds on which it is based.*"

However, unhappily in our view, in case of failure to reach agreement within a reasonable time, Article 6.2.3. (4) and (5) provide that *"either party may resort to the court"*, and that the court may then terminate or adapt the contract.[24]

This has often been considered as a regrettable choice, which may have dissuaded some practitioners from referring to the UNIDROIT Principles in their contract. Due to the obvious merits of the PICC in general, a more proportionate reaction has been suggested to refer to these Principles with the exception of the provisions on hardship, a selective solution specifically admitted by Article 1.5 of the Principles.[25] An appropriate hardship clause in the contract could then provide for a more satisfactory outcome should renegotiations fail.

II.A.3. The Principles of European Contract Law

23. The *Principles of European Contract Law* (PECL), like the *UNIDROIT Principles*, are a codification of contract law prepared by a Working Group and published as a soft law instrument. This Group worked under the competent chairmanship of Professor Ole Lando. The two sets of Principles are largely similar in many ways (they were elaborated almost simultaneously, and the respective Groups could share experiences along the way as several specialists took part in both projects), though there are many differences. The UNIDROIT Principles deal with international contracts, on a worldwide basis, while the European Principles also concern domestic and consumer contracts, and are meant to be applied in the European Union. More generally, decisions were made independently on all issues.

24. The European Principles include the following provision on *"Change of circumstances"*:

Article 6:111: Change of Circumstances

1. A party is bound to fulfil its obligations even if performance has become more onerous, whether because the cost of performance has increased or because the value of the performance it receives has diminished.
2. If, however, performance of the contract becomes excessively onerous because of a change of circumstances, the parties are bound to enter into negotiations with a view to adapting the contract or ending it, provided that:
    a. the change of circumstances occurred after the time of conclusion of the contract,
    b. the possibility of a change of circumstances was not one which could reasonably have been taken into account at the time of conclusion of the contract, and
    c. the risk of the change of circumstances is not one which, according to the contract, the party affected should be required to bear.
3. If the parties fail to reach agreement within a reasonable period, the court may:
    a. end the contract at a date and on terms to be determined by the court; or

b. adapt the contract in order to distribute between the parties in a just and equitable manner the losses and gains resulting from the change of circumstances.

In either case, the court may award damages for the loss suffered through a party refusing to negotiate or breaking off negotiations contrary to good faith and fair dealing.

25. One immediately apparent difference with Articles 6.2.1 to 6.2.3 of the UNIDROIT Principles is that the European Principles preferred to use the concept of *"Change of circumstances"* instead of the reference to *"Hardship"*—this is understandable as the PECL, unlike the PICC, do not especially address practitioners engaged in international trade, for whom the latter term is very familiar.

On the substance, both provisions are very close, in their focus on excessive onerosity (cf. *supra*, nos. 7 and 12), in their initial affirmations that in principle, a contract remains binding even when performing has become more onerous for one party (cf. *supra*, no. 21), as well as in their respective definitions of *"hardship"* or *"change of circumstances"* (except that the European Principles omit the condition, included in the UNIDROIT Principles, that the events are beyond the control of the disadvantaged party).

The regimes are quite similar. In case of change of circumstances, the European Principles provide in the first place that *"the parties are bound to enter into negotiations with a view to adapting the contract or ending it"* (in the UNIDROIT Principles, only the disadvantaged party is entitled to request renegotiations). Both instruments provide that in case of failure to reach agreement within a reasonable time, either party may resort to the court. The court may either terminate the contract or adapt it *"with a view to restore its equilibrium"* (PICC), or, in more elaborate terms, *"in order to distribute between the parties in a just and equitable manner the losses and gains resulting from the change of circumstances"* (PECL).

The European Principles finally include an additional rule, allowing the court to *"award damages for the loss suffered through a party refusing to negotiate or breaking off negotiations contrary to good faith and fair dealing".*

26. Globally, Article 6.111 of the European Principles, in our view, inspires the same compliments (mainly the priority given to renegotiation) and regrets (mainly, the direct resort to courts in case renegotiations fail) as the UNIDROIT Principles.

II.A.4. The Draft Common Frame of Reference

27. In 2009, the promoters of a large project entitled *Study Group on a European Civil Code*, chaired by Prof Christian von Bar, made public a *Draft Common Frame of Reference*, a codification meant to contribute to the harmonisation efforts of contract law then undertaken by the European Commission. The rules on contract law were initially inspired by the European Principles, but many changes were introduced by the Study Group.

The difference is spectacular concerning change of circumstances. Article III.-1:110 of the DCFR provides the following;

III.—1:110: Variation or termination by court on a change of circumstances

1. An obligation must be performed even if performance has become more onerous, whether because the cost of performance has increased or because the value of what is to be received in return has diminished.
2. If, however, performance of a contractual obligation or of an obligation arising from a unilateral juridical act becomes so onerous because of an exceptional change of circumstances that it would be manifestly unjust to hold the debtor to the obligation a court may:
   a. vary the obligation in order to make it reasonable and equitable in the new circumstances; or
   b. terminate the obligation at a date and on terms to be determined by the court.
3. Paragraph 2. applies only if:
   a. the change of circumstances occurred after the time when the obligation was incurred;
   b. the debtor did not at that time take into account, and could not reasonably be expected to have taken into account, the possibility or scale of that change of circumstances;
   c. the debtor did not assume, and cannot reasonably be regarded as having assumed, the risk of that change of circumstances; and
   d. the debtor has attempted, reasonably and in good faith, to achieve by negotiation a reasonable and equitable adjustment of the terms regulating the obligation."

This provision corresponds to Article 6:111 of the PECL which has just been commented, and there are still resemblances in the focus on excessive onerosity, in the reaffirmation of the binding force of obligations and in the conditions required for a change of circumstances to be taken into consideration (cf. *supra*, no. 25).

However, the DCFR has considerably increased the part of court intervention to the detriment of renegotiation between parties. In itself, the title of Article III.-1:110 calls the tune: *"Variation or termination by court on a change of circumstances"*. In case of excessive onerosity due to an exceptional change of circumstances, the regime immediately refers to possible court intervention in order to adapt or terminate the obligation. Renegotiation is only mentioned, as if reluctantly, as one of the conditions for court intervention, and only as a pre-requirement for the debtor to appeal to the court, not as an obligation for both parties: *"the debtor has attempted, reasonably and in good faith, to achieve by renegotiation a reasonable and equitable adjustment of the terms regulating the obligation"* (Art. III.-110, (3) (d).

28. Since these European efforts of harmonising contract law were not pursued, at least for the moment,[26] the *Draft Common Frame of Reference* did not have any success and we will not comment more extensively on the proposed rule on change of circumstances. Let it suffice to say that from the point of view of meeting the expectations of practitioners, we feel that Article III.-1:110, with its stress on court intervention, was a major step backwards.

II.A.5. The OHADA Draft Uniform Act on Contracts

29. An important project of law harmonisation has developed in Africa, among the 17 States belonging to the *Organization for the Harmonization of Business Law in Africa* (known by its French acronym, OHADA). Instituted by Treaty in 1993, OHADA has since then adopted Uniform Acts relating to arbitration, mediation, general commercial law, commercial companies and economic interest groups, cooperatives, accounting law and financial reporting, security interests, simplified debt collection procedures and enforcement proceedings, bankruptcy and road freight agreements. When a draft, after having been subject to a procedure of consultation with member states and the OHADA Court of Justice, is adopted by the Council of Ministers of the institution, the new Uniform Act enters into force, to be immediately applicable in and binding on all member states.

30. In 2002, the Council of Ministers mandated the Permanent Secretariat to approach UNIDROIT with a view to securing its assistance in preparing a draft Uniform Act on contract law, which would be based on the UNIDROIT Principles. The choice was motivated by the wide recognition already received then by the Principles. In this way, the Organisation's own harmonised contract law would reflect the solutions offered by a modern instrument developed by legal scholars from the different legal systems, and already well recognised around the world. Local African specificities would of course have to be taken into account, but it was generally felt that they should not be a major concern since the aim was to equip OHADA with a modern contract law apt to reassure and attract potential investors.

After extensive consultations of the expert in charge with representatives of the different legal professions in nine OHADA member states, a draft Uniform Act on the law of contracts was prepared, which was largely based on the UNIDROIT Principles.[27]

31. This was the case about hardship, where Articles 6/22 to 6/24 of the draft were largely identical to Articles 6.2.1 to 6.2.3 of the Principles. It is interesting to note that during the preparatory interviews, most interlocutors had strong views on the subject of hardship. The majority welcomed the idea of introducing the suggested rules; it was often mentioned how useful such rules could have been a few years before, when a devaluation of the common currency (the *"franc CFA"*) had caused so much turmoil. Admittedly, however, a minority had fears that the introduction of rules permitting adaptation or termination of a contract in case of changed circumstances could be a dangerous source of insecurity in a part of the world where arguing and palavers are so much part of the local traditions.

The draft Uniform Act was never adopted, for different reasons,[28] including the argument that aligning the rules of contract law on the UNIDROIT Principles would mean a departure from the French legal tradition, shared by the majority (but not all)[29] of the member states. It was perhaps a missed opportunity for OHADA, considering that little more than 10 years later, France itself modernised its contract law with provisions counting the UNIDROIT Principles among their sources of inspiration.[30]

II.A.6. The OHADAC Principles on International Commercial Contracts

32. In the Caribbean, an ambitious project of law harmonisation has also been undertaken by an institution inspired by the OHADA example, as reflected in its name: OHADAC, for *Organisation pour l'harmonisation du droit des affaires dans la Caraïbe*. The name in English is *Organization for the Harmonization of Business Law in the Caribbean.*

The area covered by OHADAC includes around thirty independent States and forty different territories, mainly insular. There is a large variety of cultural heritages and spoken languages. On the legal field, civil law systems are the most frequent, mainly influenced by French or Spanish law, but also by Dutch law since the new Dutch civil code. The *common law* is also present in the territories still subject to UK rule or belonging to the Commonwealth, as well in territories linked to the United States.

Such a large diversity explains the particular difficulties of the harmonisation efforts that have been undertaken.

33. This is apparent in the *OHADAC Principles on International Commercial Contracts*, adopted in 2015.[31] The introduction to the draft explains that the aim was to find harmonisation formulas that could be easily acceptable in the different legal cultures present. Contrary to the OHADA Uniform Act method, OHADAC rules are merely proposed as soft law, as models from which legislators and individuals could take inspiration—i.e. the same approach as that of the UNIDROIT Principles. Though the introductory presentation expresses much criticism about these Principles and some other previous similar instruments (the European *Principles* and *Draft Common Frame of Reference*), it is apparent that the OHADAC Principles have taken much inspiration from these earlier texts.[32]

34. However, to come now to our main concern, the OHADAC Principles depart from these models and also stand out among other recent codifications of the law of contracts in their approach to *"hardship"*:

Article 6.3.1. Hardship

1. A party is bound to perform its contractual duties even if events have rendered performance more onerous than could reasonably have been anticipated at the time of the conclusion of the contract.
2. Notwithstanding paragraph 1 a party is entitled to terminate the contract where this party proves that:
   a. the performance of its contractual duties has become excessively onerous due to an event beyond its reasonable control which it could not reasonably have been expected to have taken into account at the time of the conclusion of the contract; and that
   b. it could not reasonably have avoided or overcome the event or its consequences; and that
   c. it did not assume the risk of the event.
3. The party alleging any event rendering performance excessively onerous shall notify the other party in writing without delay, together with sufficient evidence of such event certified by a relevant body, and it is under an obligation to take all reasonable means to limit the effect of the event invoked upon performance of its contractual duties.

4. Where either contracting party has, by reason of anything done by another contracting party in the performance of the contract, derived a benefit before the termination of the contract, the party deriving such a benefit shall be under a duty to pay the other party a sum of money equivalent to the value of such benefit.

The rule is clearly inspired by the UNIDROIT model in its initial reminder of the binding force of contract as a principle, in its choice of using the term *"hardship"* and in its definition of the notion, based on excessive onerosity (cf. OHADAC Principles, Art. 6.3.1, points 1. and 2. with UNIDROIT Principles, Art. 6.2.1 and 6.2.2).

However, in order to meet the expectations of common lawyers, the following article provides that the same rules will apply in the case of *"frustration"*:

Article 6.3.2. Frustration of the purpose of the contract

The rule of the preceding article will also be applied to the cases where the events in question lead to a substantial frustration of the contract's purpose, when both parties have assumed such purpose.

Then, on the assumption that the OHADAC Principles should not include rules that would be unacceptable in some legal traditions of the area, the applicable regime is significantly different from the UNIDROIT Principles; in case of hardship (and frustration), the only possibility is for the aggrieved party to terminate the contract. There are no longer any references to an initial obligation for the parties to enter renegotiations, nor to any possibility to ask a judge to adapt or terminate the contract should the parties fail to agree. The right to terminate is stated in Article 6.3.1, point 2.; the party invoking it must notify its intention to the other party and attempt to mitigate the effects on performance of its obligations (Art. 6.3.1, point 3.); benefits obtained before termination due to performance of the contract by the aggrieved party are subject to restitution (Art. 6.3.1, point 4.).

This approach is very restrictive, unilateral termination of the contract being the only available remedy for the aggrieved party in case of hardship. Even though it could make the provision more acceptable in some legal systems, it is doubtful that it will satisfy practitioners, even the aggrieved party, who would probably prefer to attempt in the first place to adapt the contract—as reflected in the majority of hardship clauses (cf. *supra*, no. 8) and implemented in most other recent codifications (cf. *supra*, nos. 22, 25 and 31, and *infra*, nos. 44, 45, 47, 51 and 55).

35. However, the authors of the OHADAC draft, certainly aware of these last considerations, suggest another approach. The OHADAC Principles only provide for termination as a single remedy. But the comments accompanying the draft suggest that the parties could decide to discard Article 6.3.1 by agreeing on a specific hardship clause. After expressly quoting and commenting the *ICC Hardship clause*, several models of clauses are offered: a *"Termination option"* (clause A), an *"Option for renegotiation and mediation"* (clause B), *"Option for adaptation by a third* (party)" (clause C) and an *"Option for renegotiation and adaptation by a third* (party)" (clause D)[33]. These very detailed clauses cannot be analysed within the limits of the present contribution, but certainly, this original OHADAC approach deserves some attention.

36. In recent years, several international codifications of contract law have appeared. Even though they have been published as soft law instruments, or still as mere drafts, some of them have become regular sources of reference for law reform (as will be shown below, when examining recent reforms in domestic law)[34].

All of them include provisions on hardship, which is already remarkable (such provisions still do not exist in some domestic codes). They all opt for the *"excessive onerosity"* approach (cf. *supra*, nos. 7 and 12), but the OHADAC Principles explicitly assimilate *"frustration"* (cf. *supra*, no. 34). The experience of hardship clauses in practice has obviously inspired these rules in international instruments, admittedly to various degrees.

The *UNIDROIT Principles* and the *Principles of European Contract Law* initiated this new generation of rules on hardship taking actual practice into consideration. These two sets of Principles paved the way for more recent international instruments such as the European *Draft Common Frame of Reference*, the OHADA draft and the OHADAC Principles.

Renegotiation of the contract, particularly, appears in the PICC, the PECL and the OHADA draft as a necessary first stage when a situation of hardship arises; in the OHADAC Principles, model clauses are instead submitted, some of which also provide for initial renegotiation. Only the European *Draft Common Frame of Reference* shows obvious reluctance to renegotiation, though reference is made to it (cf. *supra*, no. 27).

37. As to the crucial issue of what to provide in case renegotiation is refused or fails, we remember that practice varies, but is generally reluctant to let a third party interfere with the contract (cf. *supra*, no. 8). Practice is taken into consideration in one of the OHADAC optional clauses, when in such circumstances, the right to terminate the contract is given to both parties (this threat could be an incentive for a constructive renegotiation). However, less satisfactory in that respect and in our view, is the solution leaving it to the judge to intervene in case of refusal or failure of renegotiation, as provided in the PICC, the PECL, the DCFR and the OHADA draft. The DCFR appears to be even more favourable to judicial review, which is presented as the normal remedy (cf. *supra*, no.27).

II.B. Hardship regulation in domestic legislation

38. Rules on hardship have been present for a long time in the laws of several national jurisdictions. However, in recent years, important reforms have been enacted (or are planned to be) in certain countries, which partly reflect the experience of hardship clauses in practice. We will first describe the situation in 1976 (the date when the chronicle on hardship clauses was initially published), before commenting on some recent reforms.

II.B.1. The situation in 1976

39. When the Working Group was discussing the large sample of hardship clauses it had gathered, it found out that such clauses had been around for quite some time in the practice of international contracts (cf. *supra*, no. 10). On the other hand, the Group was well aware that in many (but not all) national legal systems, there were already rules concerning changes of circumstances.

In 1977, statutory provisions already existed on the issue in several countries. Poland was perhaps a precursor with Article 262 of its Civil code of 1933 (this Code was later abrogated). Provisions on change of circumstances were present in countries such as Greece (Civil code, art. 388), Italy (*Codice civile*, art. 1467), Egypt (Civil code, art. 147), Ethiopia (Civil code, art. 3.183), Czechoslovakia (Code of international trade, art. 212) and Hungary (Civil code, art. 241), as well as in the already influent draft new Civil code of the Netherlands (then art. 6.5.3.1, now art. 6-259)[35]. On the other hand, significant case-law solutions had developed in countries such as Germany (theory of *Wegfall der Geschäftsgrundlage*, related to the principle of *Treu und Glauben*), Switzerland (several legal bases, including the very interesting *mistake on future circumstances*) or Italy (with the concept of *presupposizione*). In England, courts had developed the *doctrine of frustration*, partly through the famous *Coronation cases* (what was to be done about the rent of the balconies located along the route of the procession due to take place for the coronation of King Edward VII, when the ceremony was cancelled?[36]) The concept of *frustration* also belonged to American law, where one also found the notion of *impracticability*, codified in the *Uniform Commercial Code* (art. 2, § 615a) and retained by the *Restatement Second on Contracts* (§ 261)[37].

40. At that time, France and Belgium stood out as countries where the approach was very restrictive. There, the issue of change of circumstances was treated in the context of the theory of *imprévision*, which concerns only the case when the change of circumstances leads to unbalanced obligations. In both countries, courts then traditionally refused in principle to readapt the contract, except in French administrative case law or under particular legislation.

It was already apparent, in 1977, that the *imprévision* approach (also to be found in article 1467 of the Italian *Codice civile,* dealing with *eccessiva onerosità*) was too narrow. The issue of change of circumstances is often broader; it also includes situations when the change deprives the contract of all economic utility for one party, without necessarily rendering the respective obligations unbalanced (cf. a contract for the supply of some raw material for a still normal price, but which the buyer cannot use any more due to a technological change). Such was the approach of the German notion of *Wegfall der Geschäftsgrundlage* (disappearance of the contract foundations), of the Italian *presupposizione,* of *frustration* and *impracticability* under the *common law* (the *Restatement Second* refers to *"the occurrence of an event the non-occurrence of which was a basic assumption on which the contract was made").* The Dutch *N.B.W.* uses a very broad formula; Article 6-259 concerns the occurrence of unforeseen circumstances *"of such a nature that under the criteria of reason and equity, the other party cannot expect that the contract remains fully unchanged"* (cf. already on this, *supra,* no. 7).

41. Comparative law then already revealed many major differences between legal systems. In countries where substantial change of circumstances was taken into consideration, the legal basis was either statutory or case law. Each legal system had taken position in favour either of the narrow approach of excessively onerous performance or of the broader notion of disappearance of the foundations of the contract (sometimes, both, as in Italy). Original concepts had developed in the different jurisdictions.

Remedies offered were not identical; adaptation of the contract, or termination, or a combination of both, with different variations (but most frequently with judicial intervention).

II.B.2. Recent Regulation in Domestic Law

42. Since 1977, there have been important legislative developments in several countries. We will now examine some of them. Following the political changes that occurred after 1989, many Central and Eastern European countries adopted new Civil Codes, which often contained provisions on change of circumstances. In Western Europe, major reforms of the law of obligations in Germany (2002) and in France (2016) also dealt with the issue; we will also refer to the Belgian draft currently being discussed in Parliament. Obviously this is a choice, as similar attempts to regulate hardship have probably been made in other reforms of Civil codes around the world.

a. Eastern Europe (Russia, Estonia)

43. In Eastern Europe, Russia and Estonia will be our two examples. Further research would certainly reveal the presence of corresponding provisions in other new Civil codes.

44. In the new Russian Civil code of 1996, Article 451 deals with *"Change and Dissolution of Contract in Connection with Material Change of Circumstances"*. This elaborate provision will be briefly summarised[38].

A change of circumstances is deemed to be material when the change is such that *"if the parties could reasonably foresee this, the contract would not have been concluded at all by them or it would have been concluded on significantly different conditions"*. The formula is phrased in very general terms, not limited to situations of excessive onerosity (cf. *supra*, no. 7).

As to the applicable regime, the text refers to renegotiation between parties, but in an indirect way, while not imposing it: *"If the parties have not reached agreement concerning the bringing of the contract into conformity with the materially changed circumstances or the dissolution thereof..."*, then a court may intervene, either to dissolve the contract, or to adapt it (subject to a list of conditions enumerated in the provision). Adaptation by the court is permitted *"only in exceptional instances when dissolution of the contract is contrary to social interests or entails damage for the parties which significantly exceed the expenditures needed to perform the contract on the conditions changed by the court"*.

45. The new Estonian Law of obligations, in force since 2002, includes a § 97 concerning *Alteration of balance of contractual obligations;*

> **§ 97. Alteration of balance of contractual obligations**
>
> 1. If the circumstances under which a contract is entered into change after the entry into the contract and this results in a material change in the balance of the obligations of the parties due to which the costs of one party for the performance of an obligation increase significantly or the value of that which is to be received from the other party under the contract decreases significantly, the injured party may demand amendment of the contract from the other party in order to restore the original balance of the obligations.
>
> 2. Amendment of a contract under the circumstances specified in subsection (1) of this section may be demanded if:

(1) at the time of entry into the contract, the injured party could not have reasonably expected that the circumstances might change, and

(2) the injured party could not influence the change in the circumstances, and

(3) the risk of a change in the circumstances is not borne by the injured party pursuant to the law of the contract, and

(4) the injured party would not have entered into the contract or would have entered into the contract under significantly different terms if the party had known of the change in the circumstances.

3. Amendment of a contract may also be demanded if the circumstances under which the contract was entered into had already changed before the contract was entered into but became known to the injured party after the contract was entered into.

4. The injured party may also demand amendment of the contract retroactively, but not as of a time earlier than the time when the balance of the obligations changed.

5. If the bases for amendment of a contract exist but, due to the circumstances, amendment of the contract pursuant to subsection (1) of this section is not possible or would not be reasonable with respect to the other party, the party aggrieved by alteration of the balance of the obligations may withdraw from the contract or, in the case of a long-term contract, cancel the contract pursuant to the procedure provided for in § 196 of this Act".[39]

The change of circumstances under consideration is the situation where a material change occurs *"in the balance of the obligations of the parties"*, due to an increase of the costs to perform or a decrease in the value of the counterpart to be received from the other party. This is the *"imprévision"* approach (cf. *supra*, nos. 7 and 12).

In such a case, the aggrieved party may demand[40] amendment of the contract from the other party *"in order to restore the original balance of the obligations"*, under a number of conditions listed in the article (where the influence of Article 6.2.2 of the UNIDROIT Principles is very apparent). If amendment is not possible, or would not be reasonable with respect to the other party, the aggrieved party may withdraw from the contract.

Quite remarkable is the fact that in this Estonian provision, no reference is made to court intervention in adapting or terminating the contract.

b. **Germany**

46. It has been said above (cf. *supra*, no. 39) that the issue of change of circumstances was already recognised in German case law when the chronicle was prepared. In the past, there had been much theoretical discussion on the subject among scholars. The dramatic inflation that the country experienced in 1923 was the cause of much contractual litigation before the courts, and the *Reichsgericht* came to rely on the notion of *Wegfall der Geschäftsgrundlage* (disappearance of the contract foundations), which Örtmann had formulated in 1921. Every contract is based on general grounds agreed upon. Should these grounds disappear, the contract must be modified or terminated. This approach does not only cover alteration of the equilibrium between the parties' respective obligations (the French notion of *"imprévision"*—cf. *supra,* nos. 7 and 12), but also mistake on the motives or on circumstances which were essential in the formation of the parties' agreement (provided both parties were aware of them). More recently, the notion was also applied in many situations where substantial changes occurred due to the reunification of Germany.[41]

47. This was only case law. In 2002, the reform of the German civil code (BGB) introduced a new § 313 which, under the title *Störung der Geschäftsgrundlage* (disturbance of the contract foundations), codified the solutions which courts had developed:

> **§ 313. Interference with the basis of the transaction**
>
> 1. If circumstances which became the basis of a contract have significantly changed since the contract was entered into and if the parties would not have entered into the contract or would have entered into it with different contents if they had foreseen this change, adaptation of the contract may be demanded to the extent that, taking account of all the circumstances of the specific case, in particular the contractual or statutory distribution of risk, one of the parties cannot reasonably be expected to uphold the contract without alteration.
> 2. It is equivalent to a change of circumstances if material conceptions that have become the basis of the contract are found to be incorrect.
> 3. If adaptation of the contract is not possible or one party cannot reasonably be expected to accept it, the disadvantaged party may revoke the contract. In the case of continuing obligations, the right to terminate takes the place of the right to revoke.[42]

The first paragraph states the conditions under which the regime can be applicable. Circumstances must have changed after the contract was concluded, in a significant way, i.e. such that the parties would not have entered into the contract or would have entered into it under different terms if they had foreseen the change; one of the parties could not reasonably be expected to uphold the contract without an alteration (considering all circumstances, including the contractual or statutory distribution of risk). The second paragraph assimilates the situation when the parties' initial conceptions which became the foundations of the contract appear to have been incorrect.

In such cases, adaptation of the contract may be demanded. If it is not possible, or if one party cannot reasonably be expected to accept it, the aggrieved party may revoke or terminate the contract.[43]

48. This new § 313 certainly has the virtue of including in the BGB explicit provisions about a important aspect of the German law of contracts that had so far only developed in case law. From our main point of concern in this contribution, i.e. confronting codified rules to the needs of practice (as reflected in hardship clauses), the text inspires some critical comments.

Without entering into details, we are satisfied with this broad approach of *Störung der Geschäftsgrundlage*, which is not limited to *imprévision*, while covering it (cf. *supra*, no. 46). A good point is also that adaptation of the contract comes in the first place, before revocation or termination of the contract which may be resorted to only if adaptation turns out not to be possible, or if *"one party cannot reasonably be expected to accept it"*. And the right to revoke or terminate is directly given to the aggrieved party, without requiring court intervention.

49. However, we are less content when the text of § 313 states that adaptation can be *"demanded"* (*"… so kann Anpassung des Vertrags verlangt werden"*). Hardship clauses typically provide that in case of change of circumstances, parties will enter into negotiations with a view of adapting the contract if possible. Taking obvious inspiration from practice, the UNIDROIT Principles provide that in case of hardship, *"the disadvantaged party is entitled to request renegotiations"* (art. 6.2.2, cf. *supra*, no. 22). The right granted to the aggrieved party by § 313 of the BGB probably amounts to a request for renegotiation of the contract, but it may not be very appropriate to formulate such a request in the form of a *"demand"* for adaptation. The UNIDROIT Principles, as well as the new Article 1195 of the French civil code and Article 77 of the Belgian draft, to be discussed below (cf. *infra*, nos. 51 and 55), are phrased in more diplomatic terms, which should encourage the other party to enter such negotiations.

c. France

50. Until recently, France had been standing out with its rejection of the *"théorie de l'imprévision"*, condemned by a famous decision rendered in 1876 by its *Cour de cassation* (the case of the *Canal de Craponne)*. The Supreme Court had then invoked the binding force of contracts to refuse admitting adaptation of a royalty, the amount of which had been agreed in the 16th century!

51. It had been a long time since this position was generally criticized, and gradually assorted with an increasing number of exceptions. Still the *Cour de cassation* held to its principle position.[44]

The recent reform enacted by the *Ordonnance* of 10 February 2016 introduced a new Article 1195 in the French Civil code, which provides as follows;

> **Article 1195**
>
> If a change of circumstances that was unforeseeable at the time of the conclusion of the contract renders performance excessively onerous for a party who had not accepted the risk of such a change, that party may ask the other contracting party to renegotiate the contract. The first party must continue to perform his obligations during renegotiation.
>
> In the case of refusal or the failure of renegotiations, the parties may agree to terminate the contract from the date and on the conditions which they determine, or by a common agreement ask the court to set about its adaptation. In the absence of an agreement within a reasonable time, the court may, on the request of a party, revise the contract or put an end to it, from a date and subject to such conditions as it shall determine".[45]

It immediately appears that the new text is still only concerned with *imprévision* (excessive onerosity), which had been the key issue of earlier discussions in France, as opposed to the wider approach of *"foundations of the contract"* or similar formulas, present in some other legal systems (cf. *supra*, nos. 40 and 46).

The regime is obviously influenced by the developments described above, the *"discovery"* of the way hardship was usually handled in contractual practice, and some of the earlier recent examples of codifying the issue.

Renegotiation of the contract is the first step envisaged; the aggrieved party may *"ask"* the other party for it (not *"demand"*).[46]

Should renegotiation be refused or fail, the initiative is still offered to the parties; they may then commonly decide to terminate the contract (at the date and under the terms they determine); they may also agree to ask a judge to adapt the contract.

In case the parties cannot agree on either solution within a reasonable time, one of them may ask the judge to adapt or terminate the contract, at the date and under the terms he or she determines.

52. We feel that this is an interesting regime, which gives preference to renegotiation, and still suggests that the parties agree on further steps should renegotiation be refused or fail. Unilateral appeal to the judge is presented as a final remedy. Yet nothing obliges a party to attempt to enter into such an ultimate discussion with the other party before calling on the judge. It is then quite possible that under the new French regime also, a party could also unilaterally ask a judge to adapt or terminate the contract, the very perspective that practitioners are usually much afraid of. But having this in mind will probably incite the parties to renegotiate in a constructive way—this seems to be the intention of the legislator in this provision which gives obvious priority to solutions found by the parties themselves.

d. Belgian draft

53. The Belgian law of contracts used to be very similar to its French counterpart, since it had the same basis, the Napoleonic Civil code of 1804. Differences have certainly appeared in more than two centuries of separate evolutions, but this was not the case about *imprévision*. In 1921, a decision of the Belgian *Cour de cassation* took the same position as its French counterpart did in the Craponne case. Comparative studies used to point out that on that issue, two countries were isolated in their strict attachment to the binding force of contract, France and Belgium.[47]

As it did in France, a trend to reexamine its position became apparent in Belgium in recent years. It was more and more the case in legal literature, while lower courts often tried to circumvent the obstacle by relying on a broad approach to force majeure, on abuse of right or on good faith.[48] Even the *Cour de cassation*, with its remarkable decision of 2009 concerning Article 79 of the Vienna Convention on international sales (cf. *supra*, no. 18), gave the impression that the door could be open for a similar recognition of substantial change of circumstances in domestic law.

54. Then came in 2016, as described above, the reform of the French law of contracts. This gave the Belgian Government impetus to rapidly launch a reform of the Belgian law of obligations. A group of experts prepared a draft in a remarkable short time; after having been subject to public consultation, the draft is currently submitted to Parliament. The chances of adoption seem to be high. Nobody can predict when exactly the new law will be enacted, but it could be in the relatively near future.

55. On our subject, the expected decision has been taken. As France since 2016, Belgian law will have a provision in its revised Civil code allowing for adaptation or termination of a contract in case a substantial change of circumstances occurs. The proposed Article 77 introduces the following rules (free translation):

Article 77. Change of circumstances

Each party must perform its obligations even though performance has become more onerous, either because the cost of performing has increased, or because the value of the other party's performance has decreased.

When performance becomes excessively onerous due to an unforeseeable change of circumstances upsetting the equilibrium of the contract, in a way where it could not be reasonable to demand performance from the obligor, the obligor may invite the other party to renegotiate the contract with a view to adapt or terminate it. Parties continue to perform their obligations during the period of renegotiations.

In case of refusal to renegotiate, or failure of renegotiation, the judge may, at the request of either party, adapt the contract with a view to making it conform to what the parties would have reasonably agreed upon when the contract was entered into if they had taken the change of circumstances into account, or terminate the contract, partly or fully, at a date and according to modalities determined by the judge.[49]

As in the recent French reform, the proposed text only deals with the issue of excessive onerosity (*imprévision*). The first paragraph, obviously inspired by Article 6.2.1 of the UNIDROIT Principles (cf. *supra*, no. 20), states the basic principle that the mere fact that performance has become more onerous does not exonerate from having to perform one's obligations. However, if it has become excessively onerous due to circumstances meeting the qualifications stated in the second paragraph, a special regime is applicable.

The aggrieved party may then *"invite"* the other party to renegotiate the contract, with a view to adapt or terminate it. Here again, the first step is to attempt to renegotiate the contract, thus taking into consideration common practice as revealed by hardship clauses. One may notice that while the BGB entitles the aggrieved party to *"demand"* renegotiation, and the French Civil code to *"ask for"* renegotiation, the Belgian draft provides that it may *"invite"* the other party to renegotiate—shades of differences!

In case of refusal to renegotiate, or failure of renegotiation, the Belgian draft allows each party to ask the judge to adapt the contract or to terminate it. Of special interest are the criteria spelled out in the provision to guide the judge endeavouring to adapt the contract: *"...with a view to making it conform to what the parties would have reasonably agreed upon when the contract was entered into if they had taken the change of circumstances into account".* We have seen that a similar, but shorter, formula appear in the UNIDROIT Principles (*"... with a view to restore its equilibrium"*; cf. *supra*, no. 20), and a still different one in PECL (*"... in order to distribute between the parties in a just and equitable manner the losses and gains resulting from the change of circumstances*"; cf. *supra,* no. 24). This is inspired from contractual practice, where it is extremely frequent that criteria are given for readaptation—but in the context of renegotiation by the parties themselves.

56. Unfortunately in our view, the Belgian draft relies on judicial intervention in case renegotiation is refused or has failed. Here we can only recall the strong reluctance of practitioners to let a judge interfere with the existence or the contents of their agreement (cf. *supra*, no. 8). This important point was repeated in several instances, most recently when expressing

reservations in our comments of the French reform; there, however, we found merits in the provision of an ultimate discussion between parties before calling on the judge (cf. *supra*, nos. 51 and 52).

57. This survey of recent regulations of hardship in several European countries demonstrates that the experience of practice, as illustrated in the study of 1976 and many subsequent publications, is now regularly inspiring the drafters of new rules. Earlier legislation, when existing, almost always left it to the judge to adapt or terminate the contract under certain conditions. All the parties could do was to ask the judge to intervene (cf. *supra*, no. 39). Since their inception, the *UNIDROIT Principles* and the *Principles of European Contract Law* initiated a new generation of rules on hardship which take actual practice into consideration; these two sets of Principles have been frequent models for further initiatives that were taken to regulate hardship at the domestic level.

Nowadays, a renegotiation of the contract regularly appears in domestic legislation as the first stage of the procedure when a situation of hardship arises (Russia, Estonia, Germany, France, Belgium; cf. *supra*, nos. 44, 45, 47, 51 and 55).

However, refusal or failure of renegotiation is the crucial problem that has to be met when such renegotiation is provided. On this point, we have seen that practice varies (unilateral or bilateral right to terminate or suspend the contract and/or intervention of a third party or access to court; cf. *supra*, no. 8). No absolute satisfactory solution can be found, and it is understandable that national regulators also hesitate, as the drafters of international instruments have (cf. *supra*, no. 37). But practice is also taken into consideration, to various extents, especially when the right to terminate the contract is given to the aggrieved party or to both parties (Estonia, Germany—cf. *supra*, nos. 45 and 47); this threat could be an incentive for a constructive renegotiation. Less satisfactory, in our view and considering the reservations expressed by many practitioners, is the frequent solution leaving it to the judge to intervene in case of refusal or failure of renegotiation (Russia, Belgium—cf. *supra*, no. 43 and 55); France tries to postpone it by suggesting a last common agreement to terminate the contract or … to appeal to the judge (cf. *supra*, nos. 51-52).

III. THE ICC CLAUSE ON HARDSHIP

59. The International Chamber of Commerce has paid special attention to the treatment of hardship in international contracts by issuing first *Hardship provisions—Drafting suggestions*" in 1985, and then a *Hardship Clause* in 2003. A revised version of that clause is currently under discussion.

Since these ICC initiatives will be especially presented and commented in later contributions to this Conference (together with the proposed new draft of the *ICC Force Majeure Clause*), we shall only briefly refer to them in connection to the different developments evoked in the present contribution.

60. When the Working Group on International Contracts was finalising its chronicle on hardship clauses in 1977, we wondered whether we should conclude our first analysis of a specific type of contractual provision by offering a Model clause. This was the cause of substantial discussions, but

the conclusion was clearly against such an approach (the Working Group never deviated from this position when dealing with a succession of other clauses after the hardship chronicle).

Reasons were given. The analysis of a large number of clauses had shown many different aspects of the hardship clause, each of which may have a real importance. In addition, various insufficiencies had been pointed out to which drafters of hardship clauses should remedy. Consequently, it was felt that an "ideal" clause, which would cumulatively include all the improvements suggested, would be a sort of legal monstrosity on account of its size and complexity. In addition, each sector of the economy, each type of contract, each negotiation has its peculiarities. A hardship clause included in a contract for the supply of crude oil should not be worded in the same way as a hardship clause in a loan agreement on international financial markets. The diversity of the situations where these clauses appear is another reason why the idea to elaborate a model clause was in our view to be abandoned.

We considered then that our analysis of hardship clauses should rather be used as a memorandum, completed by various suggestions and critical observations, in which drafters of hardship clauses should be able to find the elements which they think are adapted to the proposed operation, in view of the general context of the negotiations.

61. In 1985, when ICC issued the first version of its force majeure clause, it also published provisions on hardship, presented as *"drafting propositions"*, explicitly stating that this was *"not a standard clause"*. These provisions suggested a procedure to be followed in case of hardship; the aggrieved party could ask for adaptation of the contract, and parties would then consult with each other *"with a view to revising the contract on an equitable basis, in order to ensure that neither party suffers excessive prejudice."* Then came a choice of four alternative further steps in case parties would not agree on a revision of the contract within 90 days: the contract remains unchanged, each party can ask the ICC Standing Committee for the Regulation of Contractual Relations to designate a third person who would make non-binding recommendations to adjust the contract, each party is entitled to submit the issue to arbitrators or courts, each party can refer the case to the ICC Standing Committee in order to obtain the appointment of a third person who would then decide on the parties' behalf.[50]

62. In 2003, this was replaced by a full-fledged *ICC Hardship Clause*, with the following content:

> 1. A party to a contract is bound to perform its contractual duties even if events rendered performance more onerous than could reasonably have been anticipated at the time of the conclusion of the contract.
> 2. Notwithstanding paragraph 1 of this Clause, where a party to a contract proves that:
>   a. the continued performance of its contractual duties has become excessively onerous due to an event beyond its reasonable control which it could not reasonably have been expected to have taken into account at the time of the conclusion of the contract; and that
>   b. it could not reasonably have avoided or overcome the event or its consequences,

the parties are bound, within a reasonable time of the invocation of this Clause, to negotiate alternative contractual terms which reasonably allow for the consequences of the event.

3. Where paragraph 2 of this Clause applies, but where alternative contractual terms which reasonably allow for the consequences of the event are not agreed by the other party to the contract as provided in this paragraph, the party invoking this Clause is entitled to termination of the contract.

The ICC comment was that the Clause *"now provides one formulation with clear alternative consequences, negotiation or termination, the latter of which would in most cases provide an incentive to the former. The Clause amalgamates elements of Article 1467 of the Italian Civil Code and of Article 6.2.2 of the UNIDROIT Principles of International Commercial Contracts."*

63. The proposed new version of the ICC Hardship clause would introduce a formal modification to paragraph 2 (b)[51], and mainly replace paragraph 3 by two alternative provisions, giving the party invoking the choice the possibility either to terminate the contract (3 A) or to request a judge to adapt or terminate it (3 B).

Since this will be extensively discussed when specific contributions are presented at this Conference, we will not express comments on this Hardship clause and its envisaged modification, except to seize the occasion to congratulate the working group of the ICC Commission on Commercial Law and Practice for the excellent work they have accomplished since many years in preparing model contracts and clauses.

64. Whether, in the case of hardship, it is advisable to draft a model clause or rather to offer negotiators a detailed and critical analysis of the different possible aspects of a certain clause (a solution analogous to the *"legal guide"* formula) can still be debated. A model clause can easily be *"copied and pasted"* in the contract, but perhaps too easily with respect to the specific type on contract. Of course, if a clause is offered as a *"model"*, it also means it can serve as a starting point from which negotiators can do some fine adjustments to better reflect the specific characteristics of their contract—and it should.

CONCLUSION

65. *Pacta sunt servanda*, but only *rebus sic stantibus*? The issue is not new and jurists have argued about it at least since the Middle Ages. The binding force of contracts is a basic principle of contract law, belonging to the essence of what a contract is meant to be: an instrument by which each party can rely on performance of the obligations undertaken by the other party. It is a major tool in the functioning of the economy.

Yet, circumstances may change in such a substantial way that one of the parties may find that continuing to perform its obligations as initially agreed would place it in a situation of serious *"hardship"*, i.e. great difficulties: performing becoming excessively onerous or deprived of economic sense.

The issue is whether, if such a situation arises, the binding force of contracts should not be reconsidered. Some legal systems give precedence to the principle and deny the right to adapt or terminate the contract; others, more numerous, accept to admit exceptions, under various legal approaches, but always, for good reasons, under restrictive conditions.

The issue has been around for centuries, but it was often reactivated by the occurrence of exceptional events affecting contracts. For instance, in the 20th century, the cancellation of the London procession for the coronation of King Edward VII in 1902,[52] the dramatic inflation of 1923 in Germany,[53] the closing of the Suez Canal in 1956[54] or the reunification of Germany in 1990.[55]

66. The recent phenomenon that we have tried to describe and comment (the appearance of several important new legal texts regulating hardship) is partly due to an event of a very different type, by no means catastrophic or of major political importance: the revelation of the richness and inventiveness of contractual practice concerning hardship.

Legal rules or case law on hardship are in principle *not* binding. When negotiators wondered about what would happen to their future contract should circumstances radically change, and checked on the solutions offered by the applicable law, sometimes they found that there was no solution, sometimes that the solution was not very appealing (usually the possibility to ask a court to terminate the contract, or even worse, to adapt it). But since freedom of contract allowed them to substitute their own remedies to the legal ones, they took advantage of it, and started to draft what was going to become widely known as *hardship clauses*. Over the years, such clauses became more and more sophisticated, and many variations appeared on ways to draft the different parts of the provision.

For a long time, this development went largely unnoticed in legal circles, outside the world of practitioners. It all changed with the studies of contractual practice which started to appear in the 1970s.

67. It was not only a revelation for academics, which resulted in renewed presentations of the subject in teaching and in legal treatises on contracts. It also influenced the drafting of specific provisions in the several harmonisation instruments that have been elaborated since the end of the 20th century, starting with the UNIDROIT and the European Principles, which themselves influenced, to various degrees, important domestic reforms in several countries (among which Germany and France). This is what we have mainly tried to describe (being fully aware that other examples could have been found in national systems).

It is obvious that most of the legal provisions on change of circumstances that we have presented belong to a new generation, as compared to the articles previously present in some civil codes (cf. *supra*, no. 39). The example of hardship clauses has influenced contemporary codifiers, mainly with the very common provision of an initial attempt by the parties themselves to renegotiate the contract, also by the concern to regulate the situations when renegotiation is either refused or fails. There, however, most recent regulations still tend to resort to court intervention to adapt and/or terminate the contract, which does not seem to correspond to the general expectations of practitioners as reflected in hardship clauses (cf. *supra*, no. 8).

The new legal rules that have been commented call for improvements, naturally at various degrees. The *DCFR* provision, for instance, seems to be the least satisfactory (cf. *supra*, nos. 27-28), while we have found special merit in Estonian law (cf. *supra*, no. 45). In Belgium, still at the stage of draft legislation, attempts are being made to modify the proposed rule on hardship (cf. *supra*, no. 56).

68. In any case, the main message is to encourage negotiators to verify the contents of the rules on change of circumstances in the applicable law, and depart from them in case they are not satisfied. Hardship clauses still have a future!

NOTES

1. Even though the title of this contribution refers to "the first study on hardship clauses", credit must be given to the regretted Professor Bruno Oppetit, who had published his own analysis a few months before the chronicle of the Group (B. Oppetit, L'adaptation des contrats internationaux au changement des circonstances; la clause de "hardship", *Journ. Dr. Int.*, 1974, pp. 794-814). However, when he and I exchanged views after our respective publications, he told me that when preparing his article, he had been able to obtain three or four hardship clauses—as compared to the more than 50 clauses initially collected by the Working Group. Yet his study was excellent, but our method of gathering a large group of practitioners so motivated to share their concrete experiences was bound to enable us to considerably enlarge the analysis.
2. Les clauses de hardship. Aménagement conventionnel de l'imprévision dans les contrats à long terme, *Dr. Prat. Comm. Int.*, 1976, pp. 7-49; The Hardship Clauses, *Int. Trade Law and Pract.*, 1976, pp. 61-88.
3. M. Fontaine, *Droit des contrats internationaux. Analyse et rédaction de clauses*, 365 pp., Paris, F.E.C., 1989 (Chapter on hardship, pp. 249-285); M. FONTAINE and F. DE LY, *Droit des contrats internationaux. Analyse et rédaction de clauses,* 2nd ed., 715 pp., Brussels, Bruylant, and Paris, F.E.C., 2003 (Chapter on hardship, pp. 487-530).
4. M. Fontaine and F. De Ly, *Drafting International Contracts—An Analysis of Contract Clauses*, 653 pp., New York, Transnational Publishers, 2006 (Chapter on hardship, pp. 453-492).
5. M. Fontaine and F. De Ly, *La redazione dei contratti internazionali—a partire dall'analisi delle clausole* (trad R.M. Morresi), 834 pp., Milan, Giuffrè, 2008 (Chapter on hardship, pp. 479-630).
6. M. Fontaine and F. De Ly, *La redacción de contratos internacionales—Análisis de cláusulas,* 720 pp., Cizur Menor (Navarra), Civitas et Thomson Reuters, 2013 (Chapter on hardship, pp. 491-533).
7. Since the first publication of the chronicle, hardship clauses have been the subject of many further studies, the references of which are given in the successive editions of the book (we have already quoted the pioneer study of B. Oppetit, *supra*, note 1). We will especially mention the book by M. Prado, *Le hardship dans le droit du commerce international*, Brussels and Paris, Bruylant and FEC, 2003, 345 pp.
8. This is the subject of our present contribution. Another major development related to hardship appears in the impressive number of arbitral and court decisions rendered worldwide on the issue in recent years. To take the example of decisions inspired by the corresponding provisions in the UNIDROIT Principles (cf. *infra*, nos. 19-22), the CELEX data base (<http://www.unilex.info>) currently lists 39 cases on article 6.2.1. (including 11 ICC awards), 10 on article 6.2.2 and 25 on article 6.2.3 (including 14 ICC awards).
9. cf. the references above, in footnotes 2 to 6.
10. The Working Group considered that in spite of the reference to the term "arbitrator" in some of the clauses examined, such intervention did not actually have the nature of arbitration, as it was not meant to end a dispute by rendering an award, but to readapt or terminate a contract. This position was later qualified in the English book version (M. Fontaine and F. De Ly, *Drafting International Contracts—An Analysis of Contract Clauses*, *op. cit.*, pp. 490-491).
11. M. Fontaine and F. De Ly, *Drafting International Contracts—An Analysis of Contract Clauses*, *op. cit.*, pp. 467-468.
12. ibid., pp. 458-459.
13. See for instance A. A. Schwartz, A "Standard Clause Analysis" of the Frustration Doctrine and the Material Adverse Change Clause, *57 UCLA L. Rev.*, 789 (2009-2010); D. Philippe, Warranties

and Representations—Material Adverse Change. Faux amis et innovation, in *La rédaction des contrats internationaux. Conseils aux praticiens et approche de droit comparé*, Brussels, 2012, pp. 233-266.

14. cf. K. Zweigert and H. Kötz, *An Introduction to Comparative Law*, II, 1977, p. 189.
15. cf. *supra*, footnote 3.
16. Comp. article 7.1.7 of the UNIDROIT Principles and Art. 1 of the ICC Force Majeure Clause (as well as the much better drafted Art. 1 of the proposed new version). cf. also the chapter on Force majeure clauses in M. Fontaine and F. De Ly, *Drafting International Contracts—An Analysis of Contract Clauses*, *op. cit.*, especially pp. 401-418 and 439-431.
17. On this point of history of Article 79, see for instance C. M. Bianca and M. J. Bonell, *Commentary on the International Sales Law—The 1980 Vienna Convention*, 1987, pp. 572-575.
18. See for instance M. Almeida Prado, *Le hardship dans le droit du commerce international*, 2003, *op. cit.*, p. 107; p. Schlechtriem and C. Witz, *Convention de Vienne sur les contrats de vente internationale de marchandises*, 2008, p. 254.
19. This Opinion is available on www.cisg.law.pace.edu/.
20. Cass., June 19, 2009, *Rechtsk. Weekbl.*, 2009-2010, 744, *Rev. Dr. Comm.*, 2009, 988. An English translation is available on the Pace University CISG site. On this decision, cf. A. Veneziano, UNIDROIT Principles and CISG; Change of Circumstances and Duty to Renegotiate According to the Belgian Supreme Court, *Unif. Law Rev.*, 2010, pp. 137-151; B. Fauvarque-Cosson, Renégociation et révision judiciaire du contrat en cas de changement de circonstances; l'interprétation audacieuse de la CVIM par la Cour de cassation belge, *Rev. contrats*, 2010, pp. 1405-1416; M. Fontaine, Hardship, CISG and the UNIDROIT Principles; an Important Decision of the Belgian Cour de Cassation, in U. Celli, M. Basso et A.do Amaral (coord.), *Arbitragem e Comercio Internacional. Estudios em Homenagem a Luiz Olavo Baptista*, São Paulo, 2013, pp. 123-139.
21. Compare the two studies of force majeure and hardship clauses in M. Fontaine and F. De Ly, *Drafting International Contracts—An Analysis of Contract Clauses*, *op. cit.*, pp. 401-451 and 453-492.
22. The same concern lead the Working Group to refer to the French expression *"Force majeure"*, also commonly used in international contracts, in Article 7.1.7 of the Principles.
23. cf. for instance E. McKendrick, Comments to Arts. 6.2.1-6.2.3. Hardship, in S. Vogenauer (ed.), *Commentary on the UNIDROIT Principles of International Commercial Contracts*, 2nd ed., Oxford University Press, Oxford, 2015, pp. 806-822; F. Bortolotti, *Manuale di diritto commerciale internazionale*, CEDAM, Padova, I, 2001, pp. 138-143.
24. In the UNIDROIT Principles, the notion of *"court"* also includes arbitral tribunals (art. 1.11).
25. cf. F. Bortolotti, *op. cit.*, p. 143.
26. The only outcome was a proposal for a *Regulation on a Common European Sales Law* (COM(2011) 635 final), which was later withdrawn (COM(2014)910 final, annex 2, pt. 60).
27. cf. M. Fontaine, The Draft OHADA Uniform Act on Contracts and the UNIDROIT Principles of International Commercial Contracts, Unif. Law Rev., Rome, 2004, pp. 573-584.
28. cf. M. Fontaine, L'avant-projet d'Acte uniforme OHADA sur le droit des contrats; quelques réflexions dans le contexte actuel, in L'arbitre, l'avocat et les entreprises face au droit des affaires de l'OHADA, JADA—Journal africain de droit des affaires (electronic publication; <http://www.jadaf.fr/>), special issue, 2013, pp. 74-86.
29. Guinea Conakry and Guinea Bissau belong respectively to the Spanish and Portuguese legal traditions. Part of Cameroon is common law territory. The Democratic Republic of Congo legal system has originally been influenced by Belgian law.
30. cf. M. Fontaine, *Le rayonnement international du droit français des contrats. Le cas particulier de l'OHADA*, *Recueil Dalloz*, Paris, 2016, pp. 2008-2017.
31. Available on the site <www.ohadac.com>.
32. cf. M. Fontaine, *Les objectifs de l'harmonisation du droit des contrats. Deux projets OHADA et les Principes OHADAC; objectifs contrastés*, *European Review of Private Law*, 2016, pp. 393-408.
33. These model clauses are also available on the site <www.ohadac.com>.
34. Apart from other important roles some of them have played, such as influencing national and arbitral case law (cf. J. Bonell, An International Restatement of Contract Law, The UNIDROIT Principles of International Commercial Contracts, 3rd ed., Transnational, Ardsley, NY, 2005, pp. 277-300).
35. These texts were quoted in an appendix to the initial publication of the chronicle, *Int. Trade Law and Practice*, 1977, pp. 46-48. Generally, such texts relied on court intervention to remedy the situation (comp., however, the provisions cited concerning Ethiopia and Czechoslovakia).

36. On these famous "Coronation cases", cf. for instance M. Furmston, in Cheshire, Fifoot and Furmston's *Law of Contract*, 14th edition, London, Butterworth, 2001, pp. 632-633, 636-637.

37. For a substantial comparative law study of the issues, cf. D. Philippe, *Changement de circonstances et bouleversement de l'économie contractuelle*, Brussels, Bruylant, 1986, 714 pp.; also see the bibliography appearing in M. Fontaine and F. De Ly, *Drafting International Contracts—An Analysis of Contract Clauses, op. cit.*, pp. 453-454, footnote 1.

38. We refer to the translation by W.E. Butler, *Civil Code of the Russian Federation*, Simmonds & Hil, The Primrose Academy, London, 1997. Article 451 appears on pages 209-210.

39. Translation published on the site <https://www.riigiteataja.ee/en/eli/ee/Riigikogu/act/507022018004/consolide>.

40. *"Demand"* is the term used in the English translation we have used. Subject to further verification, the corresponding term in the original Estonian language seems to have the same strong meaning (comp. *infra*, nos. 49, 51 and 55).

41. On the German approaches to change of circumstances before the 2002 reform, *cf.* for instance p. Schechtriem, *Schuldrecht. Allgemeiner Teil*, 4th ed., Mohr Siebeck, Tübingen, 2000, pp. 163-170, as well as the very thorough study by D. Philippe, *op. cit.*, pp. 215-331. On the new § 313, *cf.* W.-T. Schneider, La codification d'institutions prétoriennes, in *La réforme du droit allemand des obligations*, dir. C. Witz and F. Ranieri, Société de Législation Comparée, Paris, 2004, pp. 44-47.

42. Translation published on the site < http://www.gesetze-im-internet.de/*bgb*/>. Original text;
§ 313 Störung der Geschäftsgrundlage

    1. Haben sich Umstände, die zur Grundlage des Vertrags geworden sind, nach Vertragsschluss schwerwiegend verändert und hätten die Parteien den Vertrag nicht oder mit anderem Inhalt geschlossen, wenn sie diese Veränderung vorausgesehen hätten, so kann Anpassung des Vertrags verlangt werden, soweit einem Teil unter Berücksichtigung aller Umstände des Einzelfalls, insbesondere der vertraglichen oder gesetzlichen Risikoverteilung, das Festhalten am unveränderten Vertrag nicht zugemutet werden kann.
    2. Einer Veränderung der Umstände steht es gleich, wenn wesentliche Vorstellungen, die zur Grundlage des Vertrags geworden sind, sich als falsch herausstellen.
    3. Ist eine Anpassung des Vertrags nicht möglich oder einem Teil nicht zumutbar, so kann der benachteiligte Teil vom Vertrag zurücktreten. An die Stelle des Rücktrittsrechts tritt für Dauerschuldverhältnisse das Recht zur Kündigung".

43. German law distinguishes between "Rücktritt" from and "Kündigung" of a contract, the latter term being applicable in long-term agreements ("Dauerschuldverhältnisse").

44. cf. A. Benabent, *Droit des obligations*, 15th ed., 2016, no. 306.

45. English translation quoted from <https://www.trans-lex.org/601101/_/french-civil-code>. Original text;

    Article 1195

    Si un changement de circonstances imprévisible lors de la conclusion du contrat rend l'exécution excessivement onéreuse pour une partie qui n'avait pas accepté d'en assumer le risque, celle-ci peut demander une renégociation du contrat à son cocontractant. Elle continue à exécuter ses obligations durant la renégociation.

    En cas de refus ou d'échec de la renégociation, les parties peuvent convenir de la résolution du contrat, à la date et aux conditions qu'elles déterminent, ou demander d'un commun accord au juge de procéder à son adaptation. A défaut d'accord dans un délai raisonnable, le juge peut, à la demande d'une partie, réviser le contrat ou y mettre fin, à la date et aux conditions qu'il fixe.

46. It will be remembered that in French, *"demander"* does not mean *"to demand"*, but *"to ask"*.

47. cf. p. Wery, *Droit des obligations*, I, 2nd ed., Larcier, Brussels, 2011, nos. 580-583.

48. ibid., nos. 581, 584-588.

49. Original French text;

    Article 77. Changement de circonstances.

    Chaque partie doit exécuter ses obligations quand bien même l'exécution en serait devenue plus onéreuse, soit que le coût de l'exécution ait augmenté, soit que la valeur de la contre-prestation ait diminué.

    Lorsque l'exécution devient excessivement onéreuse en raison d'un changement imprévisible de circonstances qui bouleverse l'économie du contrat, de telle sorte qu'on ne puisse raisonnablement en exiger l'exécution du débiteur, celui-ci peut inviter le créancier à renégocier le contrat en vue de l'adapter ou d'y mettre fin. Les parties continuent à exécuter leurs obligations pendant la durée des renégociations.

En cas de refus ou d'échec des renégociations dans un délai raisonnable, le juge peut, à la demande de l'une ou l'autre des parties, adapter le contrat afin de le mettre en conformité avec ce que les parties auraient raisonnablement convenu au moment de la conclusion du contrat si elles avaient tenu compte du changement de circonstances, ou mettre fin au contrat en tout ou en partie à une date et selon des modalités fixées par le juge.

50. This ICC Standing Committee existed at the time in the context of ICC Rules on Contract Regulation, which have been abandoned in 1994, due to lack of applications.

51. As proposed, it would be more appropriate to read at the end of para. 2 (b): "...overcome the consequences of the event".

52. We refer to the famous *"Coronation cases"* which followed the litigation between people who had rented balconies along the itinerary to watch the procession and the owners of the balconies.

53. cf. *supra*, no. 46.

54. cf. M. Furmston, in Cheshire, Fifoot and Furmston's *Law of Contract*, *op. cit.*, p. 639.

55. cf. *supra*, no. 46, and W. Schneider, *op. cit.*, p. 45.

Chapter 2

Adaptation of Contracts by Arbitrators

Realities and perspectives

by Pascale Accaoui Lorfing*

INTRODUCTION

The adaptation of contracts by arbitrators is admitted by legal and contractual provisions under certain conditions. Arbitrators are allowed to intervene in contracts when circumstances impact contract performance and alter substantially its equilibrium.

Historically, arbitrator's adaptation of contracts was not admitted because of the *duality of arbitration in some Civil law systems*. According to this approach, the judge settles a legal dispute, while a third-party fixes a contractual element.[1] The criteria that distinguishes between the two categories is that the judge (so the arbitrator) settles legal disputes, which is not the case when he may adapt the contract[2]. Scholars and practitioners have disagreed on the question whether arbitrators have power with respect to the contract, but not for the same reasons. Some authors argue that the power to adapt the contract is not within arbitrators' jurisdictional power.[3] Contract adaptation by arbitrators is also not admitted by the two doctrines of *Common Law* that deal with the change in circumstances theory: *frustration of purpose* and *commercial impracticability*. These doctrines that recognize the judge's power to rescind the contract, lead equally to the refusal of adaptation of contracts by judges.

The reluctance to admit arbitrator's contract adaptation is also reflected in *ICC instruments*. In 1978, the *ICC Rules for the Regulation of Contractual Relations*[4] provided for contract adaptation by a third party, whose binding decision would be of contractual nature and therefore, would be inserted in the contract.[5] These rules however have never been applied.[6] The actual *ICC Hardship Clause* 2003 provides that the parties failure to agree on adaptation will bring a claim to "arbitration or litigation under the general dispute resolution terms in the contract (...)"[7] without any reference to arbitrator's power to adapt the contract. The ICC instruments mentioned above do not provide for arbitrators' intervention in the contract and do not give a solution that will enable its continuation.

Moreover, arbitrators' adaptation of contracts hits the principle of *intangibility of contract* that governs international contract law. This

* Pascale Accaoui Lorfing has a Ph.D. in International Law (Paris II—Assas). Specialized in investment contracts and arbitration. She is an Associate to Lamy International Contracts (Investment Contracts, Contractual provisions on hardship, equilibrium provision and Force Majeure). She is affiliated to the *Groupe de Travail sur les Contrats Internationaux* (G.T.C.I.), La *Société de Législation Comparée* and the *MENA Legal Club*. She is the author of *La renégociation des contrats internationaux*, Editions Bruylant, 2011, and of many publications in the field of International and Investment Contract Law. The author would like to thank Maria Beatriz Burghetto, Arbitration specialist who provided input during the development of this article.

principle requires the necessary agreement of parties for any modification or revision of their contract. Adaptation of contracts by arbitrators is therefore an exception to this principle. It allows parties to pursue the execution of the contract under conditions different from which fundamentally altered the contract equilibrium. In arbitral matters, the *respect of parties' will by arbitrators is a fundamental rule* whether for applicable rules that govern the contract or for the obligations that bind the parties. This principle nevertheless is limited by international mandatory rules and by public policy rules of the law of the seat of arbitration and by the law of the enforcement of the arbitral award, where possible recourse against the arbitral award could be brought.

Adaptation of contracts by arbitrators is of great interest in international commercial contracts. The evolution of contractual practice has led to the creation of contractual clauses that deal with typical situations of long-term contracts and of great complexity. In addition, ensuring contract performance has been recognized as part of contributing to its stability. *International contractual practice* thus reflects the need of maintaining the contract if external circumstances modify contract conditions rendering its execution always possible but at excessively imbalanced conditions. Contractual provisions related to change in circumstances reveal the parties' obligation to renegotiate contract conditions as to adapt it to new circumstances.

The grounds on which arbitrators may intervene in a contract in order to adapt it, in case of change in circumstances, are the following: Arbitrators adaptation of a contract is admitted if (i) the parties expressly provide for such power in the contractual provisions; (ii) the applicable legal provision on hardship expressly provides for courts' intervention to adapt the contract (so do the arbitrators) or (iii) maybe if arbitrators act as *amiables compositeurs* pursuant to the power that the parties have expressly granted to them.

In this paper I will focus on realities and perspectives of contract adaptation by arbitrators. The realities of legal provisions on hardship result from a careful analysis of contractual and legal provisions on hardship and the power given to arbitrators (I). The perspectives of contract adaptation by arbitrators will determine its conditions, scope and limits (II).

I. THE REALITY OF CONTRACT ADAPTATION BY ARBITRATORS

The common denominator of hardship conditions in legal and contractual provisions is that the triggering event renders performance excessively onerous, albeit not impossible, which affects the party in charge of said performance. We will focus on contract adaptation by arbitrators according to legal provisions (I.A.), to contractual provisions (I.B.) and to arbitrators' power when acting as *amiables compositeurs* (I.C.).

I.A. Current status of legal provisions on hardship: lack of uniformity

The main purpose of legal provisions on hardship is to maintain the original equilibrium between the parties' obligations during the performance of the contract, in the face of situations that may lead to the disruption of such balance. This may include the power to adapt the contractual provisions to that end in national legal provisions on hardship (I.A.1.) as much as in international legal provisions (I.A.2.).

I.A.1. National legal provisions on hardship

National legal provisions on hardship do not necessarily provide for judicial adaptation of contracts in case of hardship (a). Furthermore, parties' failure to agree on contract adaptation is not always a prerequisite for judicial intervention when admitted (b).

a. National legal provisions do not necessarily provide for judicial adaptation of contracts in case of hardship

Many national legal provisions on hardship do not foresee judicial intervention to adapt the contract. A quick analysis shows that either judicial intervention with the view to adapting the contractual terms is not provided for at all (i), or it may only lead to contract termination as a sole solution (ii).

i. No judicial intervention at all

The fact that legal provisions contain no reference to the judge's role in hardship situations does not necessarily mean that the contract will be maintained under unbearable or unfair conditions for one of the parties. Legal provisions on hardship usually provide for parties' intervention. The disadvantaged party may request the resolution of the contract unless the other party offers to equitably modify the contract. This is possible in the case of Italian, Portuguese and Brazilian laws.

Article 1467 of the Italian Civil Code allows the prejudiced party, if the conditions for hardship are met, to ask for the resolution of the contract. However, resolution may be avoided if the other party offers to equitably modify the contractual terms:

> (...) the party who is obliged to such performance can demand the resolution of the contract (...) The party against which the resolution is demanded may prevent this by offering to modify equitably the conditions of the contract.

Article 437 of the Portuguese Civil Code also does not provide for the judge's intervention to adapt contracts:

> (...) If the circumstances on which the parties have based their decision to contract change unexpectedly, the burdened party has a right to terminate the contract, or to alter it according to fair judgment, (...).

In the same vein as the *Italian Civil Code, Article 478 of Brazil Civil Code* provides:[8]

> (...) the disadvantaged party may request the termination of the contract.

And *Article 479* states that:

> Termination may be avoided if the defendant agrees to modify equitably the terms of the contract.

On the other hand, national legal provisions on hardship may foresee judge intervention in the contract but not necessarily to adapt the contract.

ii. Judicial intervention to terminate the contract in situations of hardship

Other national legal provisions on hardship allow the intervention of the judge in the contract—not necessarily to adapt it, but rather to terminate it.

Thus *Article 112 of the Slovenian Civil Code* provides, in its § 1, after recalling the conditions for hardship:

> (...) the party whose obligations have been rendered more difficult to perform or the party that owing to the changed circumstances cannot realise the purpose of the contract may request the rescission of the contract...

In § 5, said Code provides for the court's intervention in the following terms:

> If a court rescinds a contract owing to changed circumstances it shall at the request of the other party instruct the party that requested the rescission to reimburse the other party for an appropriate part of the damage incurred for reason of the rescission of the contract.

Under English law, a party is committed to perform its contractual obligation even where it is objectively unable to do so (*Paradine v Jane*).[9] A party is however excused from performing its obligation in the case of the perishment of a person or a thing that the existence of which the performance was dependent on (*Taylor v Caldwell).*[10] The concept of *frustration of purpose* developed by courts, implied that the contract had been frustrated because the parties' contractual assumptions had disappeared (*Coronation cases).*[11]

The doctrine of the *frustration of purpose* was applied to situation of change of circumstances in a case where the court held:

> Frustration occurs when the law recognises that without default of either party a contractual obligation has become incapable of being performed because the circumstances in which the performance is called for would render it a thing radically different from that which was undertaken by the contract.[12]

In other words, according to the doctrine of the *frustration of purpose,* when applied to a change of circumstances, the performance is no longer possible (*"a contactual obligation has become incapable of being performed")* because the conditions have become totally different from what the parties have agreed upon at the time of the conclusion of the contract.

In conclusion, according to English law, one can say that in case of change of circumstances, parties may either continue to perform their contract or terminate it. English courts have no power to adapt the contract to the changed circumstances.[13]

Similarly, the doctrine of *commercial impracticability* (United States) leads to the termination of the contract where its performance becomes impracticable, i.e. performance would only be possible "at an excessive and unreasonable cost".[14] However, the *Uniform Commercial Code (UCC)* that includes this notion in its provision *s 2-615*, provides:

> (...) a delay in delivery or non-delivery in whole or in part by a seller (...) is not a breach of his duty under a contract of sale, if performance as agreed has been made impracticable by the occurrence of a contingency the non-occurrence of which was a basic assumption on which the contract was made (...).

The provision's official comment no. 6 states:

> In situations in which neither sense nor justice is served by either answer when the issue is posed in flat terms of "excuse" or "no excuse", adjustment under the various provisions of this Article is necessary, especially the sections on good faith, on insecurity and assurance and on the reading of all provisions in the light of their purposes, and the general policy of this Act to use equitable principles in furtherance of commercial standards and good faith.

The American legal doctrine of commercial impracticability is about an event that renders the performance of the contract extremely burdensome or difficult for one party, granting power to the court to release such party of its duty to perform. This concept stands between two civil law code concepts: that of "hardship", as the trigger event may substantially impact contract conditions, and that of "force majeure", as by court decision, a party may be excused from performing its obligation.

Parties may accept to revise the terms of the contract, but such revision is not the court's role. In *Aluminium Company of America (ALCOA) v Essex Group Inc (1980)*[15] the judge, however, determined a new mechanism of price calculation. He did not consider the contract's termination as the best solution in a case where the claimant had pointed to an extraordinary increase in the price of the goods and a potentially huge loss for it, according to the contractual period. This approach has not been followed by other judges.

In Common law systems, the change of circumstances that impacts substantially the performance of the contract leads to the court's intervention in order to terminate the contract by excusing parties from performing it, but by no means in order to adapt it. This approach focuses on a judicial relief—partial or total—for parties in case of unexpected circumstances having a detrimental effect on the performance of the contract.

In addition, where legal provisions on hardship provide for judicial intervention in the case of hardship, they do not necessarily subject such intervention to the condition of a prior disagreement between the parties on how to adapt the contract.

b. Parties' failure to agree on contract adaptation is not always a prerequisite for judicial intervention

Under some legal provisions on hardship, parties have no legal obligation to renegotiate contract terms, i.e. they are not obliged to try to adapt the contract when faced with a situation of hardship.

The meeting of the conditions for hardship to be deemed to exist is therefore sufficient to allow the judge to intervene in the contract. This is what most legal provisions in the Middle East & North African (MENA) countries provide for.[16] They allow judicial intervention in hardship situations without considering the role of parties in such situations.

Article 147 (2) *of the Egyptian Civil Code*[17] stipulates:

1. The contract is the law of the contracting parties; it may not be revoked or amended except by the parties' agreement or for the reasons provided for by law.
2. However, if public exceptional circumstances occurred and could not have been expected, and the occurrence of which makes the fulfilment of the contractual obligation, though not impossible, but exhausting to the debtor to the extent that it threatens him with grave loss, the judge may reduce the exhausting obligation to a reasonable margin after balancing the interests of the two parties and taking into consideration the [surrounding] circumstances. Any agreement to the contrary shall be void.

In other legal provisions on hardship, the judge may be asked by the burdened party to intervene in the contract without any consideration of the parties' role in contract adaptation. The parties' role is limited to request the judge's intervention, as provided for in *Article* 6 :258 of the *Dutch Civil Code*:

1. The Court may, upon request of one of the parties (...);

and by *Article 1440 of the Peruvian Civil Code*:

> the aggrieved party may request a court to reduce or increase the consideration, such that the excessive burden will cease.
>
> If this were not possible due to the nature of the performance, the circumstances or if the defendant so requests, the court will order the termination of the contract. The termination shall not extend to the obligations already performed.

The analysis of national legal provisions shows that, far from being uniform, adaptation of the contract by a court (or by an arbitral tribunal) is not necessarily the solution that parties may expect when faced with a situation of hardship and that contract termination is a real option which they should bear in mind.

International legal provisions on hardship are illustrative of contract adaptation by arbitrators.

I.A.2. International legal rules on hardship (UNIDROIT and PECL)

International legal rules on hardship employ practically the same wording regarding the adaptation of the contract by arbitrators, where parties fail to agree.

The 2016 UNIDROIT Principles confirm the parties' obligation to perform the contract in the event of hardship (Article 6.2.1), provide a definition of hardship (Article 6.2.2.) and lay out the effects of hardship in Article 6.2.3, including the following powers of the court:

3. Upon failure to reach agreement within a reasonable time either party may resort to the Court.
4. If the Court finds hardship it may, if reasonable,
   a. Terminate the contract at a date and on terms to be fixed, or,
   b. Adapt the contract with a view to restoring its equilibrium.

Similarly, the Principles of European Contract Law (PECL)[18] provide in Article 6:111 (3) on Change of Circumstances:

3. If the parties fail to reach agreement within a reasonable period, the Court may:

    a. Terminate the contract at a date and on terms to be determined by the Court; or

    b. Adapt the contract in order to distribute between the parties in a just and equitable manner the losses and gains resulting from the change of circumstances.

In either case, the Court may award damages for the loss suffered through a party refusing to negotiate or breaking off negotiations contrary to good faith and fair dealing.

If these Principles apply in a given arbitration, these provisions allow arbitrators to adapt the contract.

Consequently, hardship is admitted if parties foresee the application of UNIDROIT Principles in a choice-of-law clause. Express submission by the parties to the UNIDROIT Principles as governing law of a contract is however rare.[19] Generally, the application of these Principles by arbitrators results from the reference made by the parties in the choice-of-law clause to "general principles of law"[20] or "rules of natural justice" or "fairness"[21]. In the absence of a choice-of-law clause, arbitrators may apply "the rules of law"[22] they consider appropriate. They may choose the UNIDROIT Principles, by reference to transnational principles[23] or to avoid any choice of national law by interpretation of the parties' intention[24].

Arbitrators have stated that the UNIDROIT Principles "rather than [being] vague principles or general guidelines (...), are mostly constituted by clearly enunciated and specific rules coherently organized in a systematic way (...)"[25] and consequently "have enjoyed universal acceptance and, moreover, are at the heart of those most fundamental notions which have consistently been applied in arbitral practice (...)."[26]

Nevertheless, these Principles are only applied "as far as they can be considered to reflect generally accepted principles and rules"[27]. This clearly means that these Principles may not reflect generally accepted principles. They may not be applied, for instance, in the case where there is a "theory of changed circumstances that does not form part of widely recognised and generally accepted legal principles."[28]

One can therefore conclude that the reference to general principles of law or to an equivalent notion does not lead to the application of concepts that are not yet generally accepted (be it by application of the UNIDROIT Principles or not), as it is for the concept of hardship. Furthermore, in the absence of a clear expression of the parties' will, arbitrators are generally reluctant to admit the theory of changed circumstances[29]. Among many others, three examples are picked up and analysed below.

The first, *ICC Case no. 8486* (1996)[30], relied on the application of a national law that provides for the theory of changed circumstances, to be complemented by the Principles. The arbitrator interpreted the concept in a restrictive manner. In the presence of a choice-of-law clause designating Dutch law as the law applicable to an international contract between a Dutch party and Turkish parties, the tribunal referring to Article 6:258 of the Dutch Civil Code on hardship, stressed the exceptional character of this concept of hardship and interpreted the provision not only according to

Dutch law but also by reference to the UNIDROIT Principles which recognise the concept[31] in the international context. The sole arbitrator gave effect to the UNIDROIT Principles and upheld the parties' obligation to perform the contract, stating that the conditions of the Dutch provision on hardship were not met. The sole arbitrator justified his approach by reference to Dutch legal doctrine.[32] This case is particular as it seems that the applicable—national—law, according to the national legal doctrine, relied upon by the arbitrator, must be applied in light of UNIDROIT Principles when applied in an international context.[33] This is to say that this approach may not be widely applicable, given that not all national laws require decision-makers to submit to the UNIDROIT Principles in international cases. For some authors this approach is unwelcome as it may lead to uncertainty for parties.[34]

On the other hand, the sole arbitrator in this case stated that the conditions for hardship had not been met and therefore the parties had to continue performing the contract. The questions that come to mind then are: what would have happened if the sole arbitrator had concluded that hardship conditions had been met and what provisions would have been applied? While the Dutch provision on hardship provides for contract adaptation or termination by the court, the UNIDROIT Principles and the PECL provide that parties should renegotiate the contract as a first step and that the court's intervention should only take place once the parties have failed to agree on new terms. The issue to be determined would have certainly been more complicated in that case, given that the Dutch provision is mandatory,[35] i.e. parties "may not derogate contractually from it".[36]

In the second example, *ICC Case* no. 7110 (April 1998), the arbitral tribunal had to decide if, and to what extent, the theory of changed circumstances in Articles 6.2.1 to 6.2.3 of the UNIDROIT Principles was in accordance with general principles of law or usages over which there is an international consensus. The approach of the arbitral tribunal is interesting as it is different from an earlier interim award rendered in the same case, in June 1995[37].

The former award (1995)[38] was about two parties, an English company and an Iranian government agency, that had entered into nine equipment supply contracts that contained no express choice-of-law provision. Certain provisions in some of these contracts referred to the "rules of law" or to "natural justice" as rules to be applied to settle any issue. The arbitral tribunal's reasoning was based on the interpretation of the parties' apparent intention to exclude the application of domestic law. The majority of the tribunal with a dissenting opinion held that, in the absence of a choice-of-law provision, the contract is submitted to general principles of law by the reference made to the UNIDROIT Principles that are considered as an expression of these general principles of law[39].

The second arbitral award in *ICC Case no. 7110* (April 1998)[40], stated that "the theory of changed circumstances does not form part of the widely recognised and generally accepted legal principles", doing so without any reference to UNIDROIT provisions on hardship. This means that, according to the arbitral tribunal, the theory of changed circumstances does not constitute a general principle of law as it is not accepted by legal principles. This confirms arbitrators' reluctance to modify the contract—or even to admit the existence of a hardship situation—in the absence of express parties' intention. It is interesting to note on the other hand that arbitral awards have not recognised that hardship is an established usage either.

In the third case, the tribunal had to decide whether the theory of changed circumstances as stated in Articles 6.2.1 to 6.2.3 of the UNIDROIT Principles is a trade usage that has to be taken into consideration in all cases.

In *ICC Case no. 8873* (1997) the dispute arose between two companies, a Spanish one and a French one, for the construction of works in a third country that faced unforeseen circumstances which substantially increased the cost of construction. The choice-of-law clause had designated Spanish law to govern the contract "to the exclusion of any other law".[41] The contractor requested the renegotiation of the contract and pleaded for the application of the UNIDROIT Principles, namely Articles 6.2.2. and 6.2.3. as these Principles represent trade usages to be taken into consideration by arbitrators under Article 13 (5) of the ICC Rules of Arbitration and Conciliation and Article VII of the 1961 Geneva Convention on International Arbitration. The tribunal stated first that according to Spanish law, which applied to the merits, trade usages must be taken into consideration in the absence of applicable rules.

The reasoning of the arbitral tribunal had two steps. The tribunal stated first that the UNIDROIT Principles may be applied where parties have accepted that their contract should be submitted to those Principles or where they have stated that their contract shall be governed by the general principles of law, by *lex mercatoria* or an equivalent set of rules. As the parties had made no reference to any general principles of law in their contract, and as they had chosen Spanish law to govern their contract, there was no room left for the application of the UNIDROIT Principles.

The tribunal stated then that the only way to justify the application of the UNIDROIT Principles was to consider them as a "codification" of existing usages and that the UNIDROIT Principles should be applied as "codified usages". To reach this conclusion, the tribunal had to prove that the rules invoked by the claimant, especially related to hardship, equated an internationally and generally established usage.

The tribunal's conclusion was that, even if there was a tendency in favour of the equilibrium of the contract as illustrated by contractual provisions on hardship, "the obligation to equilibrate the contract (...) is however exceptional, only admitted within the framework of contractual provisions that has to determine precisely the case that justifies the hardship and its consequences". It should then "exclude to consider the provisions on hardship contained in the Principles as '*usages du commerce*'". The arbitral tribunal pursued: "It is, on the contrary, rules that do not correspond, at least as is actually, to the usual practice of business in the international commerce and by consequence could not be applied unless the parties made an express reference to them, which is not the case here."[42] This award stated in a precise and unambiguous manner that the notion of change of circumstances is not a trade usage. It has an exceptional character and should be accepted only by virtue of an express contractual provision.

As far as the UNIDROIT Principles and PECL are concerned, and more specifically as to the change of circumstances according to ICC arbitral awards,[43] neither the change of circumstances that impacts the execution of the contract is a "widely and generally accepted legal principle", nor does it represent an international trade usage to be taken into consideration in any case by arbitrators. Consequently, one may conclude that the concept of change of circumstances and more specifically the adaptation of the contract by the court, as stated in the UNIDROIT Principles and PECL will not be applied by arbitrators if the parties do not refer explicitly to it, i.e. by clearly stipulating the arbitrators' power to adapt the contract. On the other hand, the concept of hardship is by no means a trade usage that arbitrators should take into account in "any cases", i.e. even where the parties did not express their will in that sense. Contract adaptation by parties and/or by courts/arbitrators should be provided for expressly in order to be admitted and implemented.

Contractual provisions on hardship may also provide for the contract adaptation by arbitrators.

I.B. The realities of contractual provisions on hardship

Contractual provisions on hardship may reveal the parties' intention to adapt the contract. They may provide for the adaptation of the contract by arbitrators. A careful analysis may, however, inform on the parties' intention not to allow arbitrators to adapt the contract (I.B.1.). Contractual provisions on hardship may also not always specify how arbitrators should adapt the contract (I.B.2.).

I.B.1. The exclusion of contract adaptation by arbitrators

The exclusion of contract adaptation by arbitrators may result from parties' express exclusion of arbitrators to adapt the contract. In that respect, parties may predict that their failure to agree on hardship does not lead to the adaptation of the contract by arbitrator: "the failure of the parties to agree to any such revision shall not be a dispute subject to settlement by arbitration under art. (...)".[44] Parties may be more explicit. They may exclude their failure to agree on adaptation in the wording of the arbitration clause itself: "failure to agree to a proposed modification may under no circumstances give a right to ask for an arbitration pursuant to art. (...)."[45]

The exclusion of arbitrators to adapt the contract may result from the parties' projection of the contract fate if they fail to agree on hardship. The contract may remain in force "while the revision did not take place, price provisions in force will still be applicable...";[46] or may be terminated "if parties fail to agree, neither the buyer nor the seller are therefore bound by the contract." In the latter case, the contract is terminated without indemnity, by an advance notice under specific contractual conditions.[47] Furthermore, arbitrators may come to the same conclusion after interpreting the parties' will not to maintain the contract if they fail to agree on the price.[48]

Arbitrators may not adapt the contract when parties provide for the adaptation of the contract by a third party that is not an arbitrator. Contractual provision on hardship may provide for an expert to determine the meaning of hardship.[49] It may also designate an expert to determine the issue of the contract when parties were unable to adjust the contract. The provision usually specifies a period of time after parties fail to reach an agreement on adjustment before the intervention of an expert, and mentions the conditions of his nomination, his power, and the extent of its decision[50].

Parties should be aware of the difference between an expert and an arbitrator. The expert renders a technical decision on a technical point. The decision once agreed upon is part of the contract. Its non-execution is equivalent to the inexecution of the contract and that may lead to arbitration. The arbitrator exercises a judicial power; parties are bound by the decision he renders that is an award, although this can be challenged for excess of authority.

This has been clearly stated in an arbitral award[51]. An expert was nominated by parties[52] who "reserved their rights to assert their legal views on the definition of this contractual term if an arbitration should become necessary".[53] The tribunal concluded that "the definition submitted to the Expert was not therefore intended to become a legally binding interpretation of the hardship Clause."[54] This approach is focusing on the fact that an expert is different from an arbitrator. On the other hand, what is stated in front of an expert does not equal what is stated in front of an arbitrator, i.e. it has no legal value concerning the interpretation of parties' contractual provisions.

Contractual provisions on hardship that provide contract adaptation by arbitrators do not necessarily clarify how arbitrators should proceed.

I.B.2. A lack of guidelines on how arbitrators should adapt the contract

Parties may provide for contract adaptation by arbitrators in a general way.[55] It is possible that contractual provisions do not determine useful guidelines that would help arbitrators to adapt the contract. For example, when it is stated: "(...) Failing an agreement within 120 days either Party may refer the matter to arbitration in line with the provisions on arbitration of the Contract,"[56] the only requirement is the parties' disagreement on adaptation. Parties may fall short of giving sufficient indications to arbitrators as to how they should proceed practically to adapt the contract.

Parties may however give some tiny indication by stipulating that "(...) Failing to reach agreement on such equitable solution, the matter may be referred by either Party to arbitration pursuant to Article 31."[57] Here, arbitrators adapting the contract should search for an "equitable solution"[58] too.

An example of parties' lack of guidance to arbitrators in a contractual provision on hardship is illustrated in *J. S. C. Techsnabexport v Palmco Corporation (2006),*[59] even if this case provides an example of an absence of legal ground for contract adaptation by arbitrator. The analysis of the contract provisions by the arbitral tribunal establishes a lack of indications and parameters on the price that may have permitted the arbitral tribunal to adapt the contract.[60]

In another case,[61] the parties' dispute concerns an indexation clause and a price review clause in the contract. The reference, in the price review clause, to a parameter[62] is made without any specification. The arbitrators mentioned the "absence of a clear contractual basis for attributing a special meaning on the term (...)."[63]

The analysis of contractual provisions shows that parties may exclude arbitrators' adaptation of the contract or provide for it. In the latter case, however, contractual provisions lack to provide arbitrators with useful guidelines as to their expected role.[64]

The adaptation of the contract by arbitrators also depends on their power to act as *amiables compositeurs*.

I.C. The realities of arbitrators' power to act as *amiables compositeurs*

Arbitrators' power to act as *amiables compositeurs* allows them to temper the harsh effect of legal and contractual provision (I.C.1.). The issue is to determine whether their decision, based on equity could involve the adaptation of the contract (I.C.2.)

I.C.1. Arbitrators' power of *amiable composition*

Under most arbitration laws and rules, the arbitrators' power to act as *amiables compositeurs* should expressly and precisely be granted to them by parties and, consequently, precisely stipulated in the arbitral agreement. The limits to that power are delineated by the parties' will and by international public order. Arbitrators, acting as *amiables compositeurs,* may derogate from the application of rules of law if such application leads to an unequitable solution. They have the same power with regard to contractual provisions. Contractual clauses that grant arbitrators the power to act as *amiables compositeurs* reflect parties' will to avoid a strict application of the contract where it would lead to an unfair situation.

The equitable solution that arbitrators are expected to render is with respect to the parties' will and aims at finding an acceptable solution for them. Consequently, the decision rendered by arbitrators acting as *amiables compositeurs* will be guided by their conception of fairness and justice. The use of this power is left to arbitrators' appreciation, even if some scholars consider this power as an "intense obligation"[65]. This means that arbitrators may render a decision based on the applicable law, but this is not an obligation[66], since their power to act as *amiables compositeurs* allows them to dismiss or remove the rules of law if their application leads to an unfair solution[67]. Arbitrators may therefore, on behalf of fairness, modify the meaning of a strict rule of law or discard the strict application of a contractual provision.

The equitable solution expected from arbitrators acting as *amiables compositeurs* would consist for example in fixing a reasonable time-limit to perform contractual obligations[68] in the absence of such an indication in the contract. It is also within their specific power to grant additional time for performance, based for example on certain difficulties in the international context.[69] Thus, *amiables compositeurs* have the power to interpret the contract according to its surrounding circumstances. In one case, where the parties had failed to agree on a definitive price, the *amiables compositeurs* interpreted the sense and the scope of a revision clause,[70] just like arbitrators ruling in law would have done. They analysed the parties' respective positions according to the circumstances—the existence of several contractual provisions on the price, a letter of engagement that fixed an upper limit price, and granted the buyer a price reduction comparing to other prices fixed between the buyer and other clients and decided to choose a price that had been mentioned by one of the parties. The *amiables compositeurs* created no new obligation in that case, but rather ensured the efficiency of the existing one.

The analysis of some arbitral awards mentioned above gives an indication of how arbitrators exercise their power of *amiable composition*. It would appear that the exercise by arbitrators of their power of *amiable composition* has been within the respect of the contractual balance, in accordance with the respect of parties' will[71].

Does arbitrators' power of *amiable composition* allow them to adapt the contract in the absence of express parties' authorisation, for example in a situation of hardship?

I.C.2. Effects of arbitrators' power to act as amiables compositeurs

Arbitrators who have the power to act as *amiables compositeurs* may temper the consequences of rules of law or of contractual provisions based on equitable considerations, such as those cases where their implementation would lead to an unfair situation for one of the parties.[72] Nevertheless, this power, given to arbitrators acting as *amiables compositeurs* in order to temper the harsh effect of legal or contractual provisions, has limits. It does not comprise the power to revise the contract or modify the general economic foundation of the contract.

In fact, it is by no means the objective of arbitrators, when acting as *amiables compositeurs* to adapt the contract in the absence of a clear intention of parties granting them such power.[73] But it may well be that, in a given situation such an adaptation may nevertheless be the effect of the power granted to them. Indeed, some authors consider that the power of *amiable compositeur* given to arbitrators does authorise them to adapt the contract,[74] in view of the harsh conditions imposed on a party who is victim of a hardship situation. Thus, the inequitable effects of unforeseen circumstances on the performance of contractual obligations may sometimes lead to their adaptation.[75]

However, this is not the position adopted by arbitral tribunals in general. The double limits that are imposed on arbitrators acting as *amiables compositeurs* lie in their lack of power to revise the contract and to modify the general economic foundation of the contract.

The first limit, i.e. *amiables compositeurs'* lack of power to revise the contract,[76] has been expressly stated by arbitral awards.[77] In the absence of a specific power to do so given by the parties, arbitrators are not allowed to substitute themselves to parties in order to reinstate the balance of the contract, even in situations where the parties fail to agree when they themselves try to do so.[78] In addition, it has been stated that the power of *amiable compositeur* is not an authorisation given to arbitrators to exceed the framework of the dispute, nor to revise the contract by replacing the parties' renegotiation of the contractual terms.[79] An arbitral tribunal stated explicitly that the power of *amiables compositeurs* does not allow them to revise the contract or to modify its terms even in a situation where the original circumstances surrounding the contract have changed, thus impacting the performance of the contract.[80]

Arbitrators' power to act as *amiables compositeurs* does not allow them to modify the general economic foundation of the contract in the sense that the modification of such economic foundation is the substitution of the existing obligations for new ones that do not or may not reflect the parties' intention.[81]

French courts have held this position[82] at a time where there was no legal provision on hardship. In the well-known case *EDF v Shell*[83], the court, who had the power to act as *amiable compositeur* found that, if the parties failed to reach an agreement, the court will determine

> according to the solutions that parties would have proposed, if the formula that would be suitable from the financial point of view, modify the contractual conditions and therefore will forbid the judge to impose it.[84]

Arbitrators when granted the power to act as *amiables compositeurs* may take into account equitable considerations when rendering their award if the solution under the applicable law may lead to an unfair situation. The equitable character of their decision could sometimes lead, according to the parties' express will, to an adjustment of the contract, if the performance of the contract according to the conditions that resulted from the change in circumstances proved to be too onerous or unfair for one of the parties.

However, *amiables compositeurs* may not impose obligations on parties, nor create new obligations that the parties had not envisaged. They may only temper the effects of the existing ones.

The reality of contract adaptation by arbitrators enlighten the perspectives that may be drawn in that respect.

II. THE PERSPECTIVES OF CONTRACT ADAPTATION BY ARBITRATORS

Once admitted, contract adaptation by arbitrators request the verification of the existence of hardship and its effects (II.A.), before the examination of the scope (II.B.) and the limits of the power of arbitrators to adapt the contract (II.C.).

II.A. Verification of the existence of hardship and its effects

One of the tasks of arbitrators is to determine the existence of hardship and its effects. They must assess first, whether the conditions for the existence of hardship are met (II.A.1.). They further have to verify whether the parties have renegotiated the contract and, if that is the case, they must evaluate the way they did it (II.A.2.).

II.A.1. Meeting of hardship conditions

Prior to adapting the contract, arbitrators must assess whether a hardship situation exists in the particular contractual relationship. Arbitrators identify the conditions and the effects of events on the contractual terms by applying legal or contractual provisions, in search of the parties' intention. This assessment is within their judicial power. First, arbitrators determine the ground on which their analysis will be based (contractual term/legal provision). They enumerate the hardship conditions and analyse the circumstances and their consequences on the equilibrium of the contract.

Arbitrators apply the legal interpretation rules of the applicable law and set out "the legal principles (they) consider relevant to the dispute issues of contractual interpretation."[85] Their analysis takes into consideration the contract—its significant terms, the relevant circumstances—and the parties' intention. If the contractual terms are clear, the tribunal will not search for extrinsic evidence.

An example of clear contractual terms that identify hardship conditions can be found in Article 6.2.1. of UNIDROIT Principles. A hardship situation has an exceptional character, and it takes place after the conclusion of the contract. The event giving rise to the hardship situation must not have been reasonably taken into consideration by the disadvantaged party at the conclusion of the contract and the risk of the occurrence of such event must not have been undertaken by the disadvantaged party. With regard to the *impact* of said event, Article 6.2.1. states: "There is hardship where the occurrence of events fundamentally alters the equilibrium of the contract either because the cost of a party's performance has increased or because the value of the performance a party receives has diminished". Hardship is an "exceptional situation",[86] illustrated "[w]hen supervening circumstances are such that they lead to a fundamental alteration of the equilibrium of the contract".[87]

In the presence of a contractual provision on hardship, arbitrators will focus on the foreseen requirements related to the change of circumstances that is beyond the parties' control, its impact on the contract and the criteria to take into consideration when assessing the disequilibrium. The change of circumstances may be in a specific field, on the energy market for instance. The change of circumstances may have occurred in comparison to what parties have reasonably expected when entering into the contract or related to the price formula included in the contract that "does not reflect the development of the said marginal market".[88] The change of circumstances should be beyond parties' control, which is not difficult to determine when the criteria are objectively outside parties' will.

Concrete examples are given by arbitral awards on how hardship provisions are implemented. A change of circumstances may be illustrated by the change of the index that is required to the determination of the price, according to some specific criteria contractually mentioned that are obviously outside the control of the parties.[89]

ICC case no. *15051 (2010)*[90] is related to a dispute concerning gas price and supplies between a producer and a buyer and specifically addresses the existence of an extraordinary price review due to hardship, which was contested by respondent. The arbitrators' approach was first to verify whether there was a contractual provision on hardship in order to establish the parties' intention. In that particular case, Article VIII and Article 8.3 (b) of (contract 1 and contract 2) required the following cumulative conditions namely

> A change of the circumstances upon which the Parties relied for establishing the general provisions of the Contracts and which is
>
> a. Significant
>
> b. Beyond the control of the Parties (extraneous event);
>
> c. Not of temporary nature
>
> d. Unforeseeable; and
>
> e. Causing significant hardship to a Party"[91].

The arbitral tribunal analysed an extraordinary price review that was drafted with the same wording as that of the UNIDROIT Principles. The conditions of such contractual provision were the following: an unforeseeable and significant change of the circumstances upon which the parties had relied for establishing the general economic provisions of the contracts, beyond the control of the parties (extraneous event) and not of temporary nature, that caused significant hardship to a party.[92] The arbitrators then determined *the meanings of the hardship* conditions, according to the nature of the agreement and its environment. Thus, the tribunal held that the "wording 'general economic provisions of the Contracts' refers to the price formula of the (Contracts) and both parties are in fact in broad agreement within this interpretation".[93] The tribunal established then that "the relevant market" was the "international energy market" as the parties' intention was to include "pivot points referring to Brent prices".[94] Accordingly, the tribunal concluded that the "evolution of the Brent price was part of the parties' shared assumptions (...and ...) that a disruption of this predicate could possibly destroy the equilibrium upon which the contracts were concluded".[95]

A *significant change of circumstances* was the second hardship condition. The arbitrators analysed it in accordance with the parties' intent[96]: "will depend upon the magnitude of the increase of the Brent price during the reference period"[97] and "will call for some kind of extreme and drastic change of the system, an exceptionally high yardstick"[98] before assessing that the "requirement of a significant clause is satisfied".[99]

In addition, the rise of the Brent price was obviously an extraneous event given its general character.[100] The *extraneous event* requirement is determined according to the environment of the contract as stated by arbitrators in this case: "Regarding the extraneousness of the rise of Brent price, it goes without saying that this development was not caused by or linked to a Party, given the general character of this event. This condition is therefore satisfied".[101]

The *non-temporary nature of the hardship* led the tribunal to assess the duration of the rise, i.e. it had to choose a span of time according to the specific contractual circumstances and it concluded that this condition was also satisfied.[102]

As for the *unforeseeable character*, the tribunal's analysis was to determine "i) what development may or may not have been foreseeable, ii) what is the period of reference to apply the test of unforeseeable character... [and] iii) whether such test should be applied *in concreto* or *in abstracto*"[103]. It was clear for the tribunal that what was at stake was the foreseeability of the intensity of the fluctuation[104] during a period of reference.

The *significance of hardship* is of a great importance as it may or may not "consist in a reduced profit (*lucrum cessans*) and would not be limited to actual losses (*damnen emergens*)".[105] In this case, the tribunal assessed such significance by analysing the parties' intention expressed in the letters they had exchanged.

The *importance of the prejudice* would determine to what extent extraordinary conditions impact the contract. In the case under analysis, the tribunal stressed that the change of circumstances must cause a "certain imbalance that would require immediate relief, namely adjustment of the prices before the expiration of the ordinary price revision period. (...) there is a need for a deep imbalance before an 'extraordinary' (the word implies an exceptional event) review takes place".[106] This was not the case according to the tribunal who found that an average price differential of 24% was not sufficient to constitute a significant hardship.[107]

ICC Case 11265 (2009)[108] was related to the extreme difficulties that claimant had to face in order to perform its contractual obligation. The arbitral tribunal rejected the allegation of hardship asserting that a legal provision on hardship should not be the occasion for a party to escape its commercial miscalculation.[109] The tribunal applied UNIDROIT Principles with no opposition from the parties. According to the tribunal, the increase in the cost of the delivery of the goods by the claimant did not lead to the fundamental alteration of the contractual equilibrium as stated in Article 6.2.2 of the UNIDROIT Principles.[110] The other requirements of the provision had not been met: the contractual risk of change of circumstances had been undertaken by the defendant (the delivery of 30 trucks). As for the unforeseeable character, the tribunal held that, the affected party had significant experience in the field. It was reasonable to conclude that such party should have taken into consideration the situation. As to the requirement of the event to be beyond parties' control, the tribunal stressed that the defendant should have exercised its influence on decisions taken during the meetings, and that the defendant did not do his best to obtain the trucks.[111]

Another example of price revision clause is present in *ICC case* no. *13989,*[112] where the underlining contract provided in Article 11.6:

> (1) if at any time either Party shows that circumstances on the energy market, beyond the control of the Parties, have changed as compared to what Parties reasonably expected when entering into this Contract and/or if the Price resulting from the price formulae hereof does not reflect the development of the said marginal market, then such Party may request other Party, in writing, substantiating the grounds for the Price revision (...).

This clause provides for a change of circumstances in the energy market, beyond the parties' control. Such change must be analysed in comparison with what the parties expected at the time of the conclusion of the contract ("what parties reasonably expected when entering into this Contract"), and/or the change of the price formulae—that is no more than a reflection of the "development of the said marginal market".

The meaning of the conjunction "and/or" was at issue in that case. To claimant, it meant that both criteria may be "used either jointly or alternatively" as "the first part or limb focussed on the origin or the cause of the change; the other part or limb focussed on its effect".[113] The respondent's approach focused on the interpretation of the provision keeping in mind "that the key second limb must have been satisfied, whether individually or collectively, with the first limb". The tribunal concluded that "either party may invoke the price revision procedure (...) demonstrating that it complies with either or both of the criteria in the parts or limbs of paragraph 1 of that Article".[114]

The tribunal's reasoning is interesting. In its interpretation of the meaning of the provision it states that "Neither criterion permits a price revision to be sought unless there have been either significant changes in circumstances on the energy market, as described in the first criterion, or significant disparity or disparities between the price established under the price formulae and the development of "the said marginal market". Satisfying the latter criterion may also mean that the former will also have been met but it does not follow that the reverse is not possible".[115]

The tribunal decision was that "construing the phrase 'and/or' to allow a party to invoke price revision under the contract, by showing that either or both criteria have been met gives effect to both the word 'and' and the word 'or', which according to the general principles on which the parties have agreed, is the right meaning of this paragraph of Article 11.6 (...)".[116]

However, contractual provisions on hardship may be unclear and lead to a dispute between the parties on the scope of the hardship and its meaning. Arbitrators should then establish the meaning of the provisions according to the applicable law. We can find an example of this in *ICC Case no. 15610,*[117] on an underlying contract that contained the following contractual hardship clause:

> 18.2 (1) in the event that, during the term of this Contract and due to circumstances, which could not have been reasonably foreseen as of the date in which the Contract was entered into,
>
> (2) either Party suffers severe and unforeseeable hardship for a periodic of time not shorter that 6 (six) months (...),
>
> (3) The Party which is suffering the above mentioned severe and unforeseeable hardship shall give, to the other Party written notice thereof,
>
> (4) which will specify (i) the date and nature of the event or events which caused the change alleged by it; (ii) an evaluation of the hardship that has been suffered; and (iii) the proposal made by that Party to remedy that hardship.

This contractual provision inserted in an LPG[118] contract shows that the conditions for the existence of hardship are related to the unforeseen circumstances that begin to exist after the conclusion of the contract and that cause suffering to either party during at least 6 months. Such lack of any other requirement led the arbitral tribunal to hold that "it will, of course, be necessary to consider much more of the Parties' contractual wording than this brief extract. It will be noted, however, that the phrase 'severe and unforeseeable hardship' is not expressly defined in the LPG Contract".[119].

According to the claimant, the hardship clause that was inserted in the contract—drafted in an ambiguous manner—"requires the restoration of the 'equitable character' of the contract when the 'gateway' of severe and unforeseeable hardship occurs" on the ground that "references to 'equity' appear stated in the hardship clause".[120] The claimant's reasoning is of interest as that party considered that the contract was "a fair and equitable agreement" at the time of its conclusion and that in case of hardship, parties must "restore the equitable character of the contract" as a remedy.[121] Nothing in the provision, as it is reproduced, indicates, however, any reference to the fair and equitable standard. The respondent's position was that the clause requires to determine the existence of "severe and unforeseeable hardship", and the contract does not provide any lesser "equitable" standard. The respondent seems not to reject any role for the equitable solution.[122] The arbitral tribunal interpreted the contract according to New York law as commonly accepted by the parties as the applicable law. It "well established principles (...) that common sense and good faith (...) of contractual interpretation (...) to arrive at the objective meaning jointly intended by the parties".[123] In the presence of a contractual disposition on hardship as a *lex specialis*, the arbitral tribunal found inappropriate "to have regard to Section 2-615 of the New York Uniform Commercial Code of the common law doctrine of commercial impracticability".[124] The arbitral tribunal found that the parties' intention was clear enough to exclude extrinsic evidence to establish their "common or objective understanding of the basis for pricing under the LPG Contract (...)". In doing so, the tribunal took into consideration the "(...) Project and the Natural Gas Agreement as part of the factual material relevant to the interpretation of the LPG Contract's Hardship Clause".[125]

As a next step, once the arbitral tribunal has verified the meeting of the hardship conditions, it will evaluate the contractual renegotiation by the parties where this requirement is provided for in legal or contractual provisions on hardship.

II.A.2. The contractual renegotiation by parties

As mentioned above, the requirement for contractual renegotiation may not be included in legal or contractual provisions on hardship. Nevertheless, when it is provided for, parties are under the obligation to renegotiate the contract.[126] It may not lead to an obligation to reach an agreement unless otherwise mentioned. The role of the arbitrators is therefore to verify that the parties renegotiate contract conditions (a) and that they renegotiate them in good faith (b).

a. The assessment of the parties' renegotiation of the contract

Parties are under the obligation to renegotiate contractual conditions when such renegotiation is required in contractual or legal provisions. Such renegotiation, however, should not be the occasion for a party to escape its commercial miscalculation,[127] or to escape from the contract.[128] Even if it is of an exceptional character, it has been held that "the fundamental change of circumstances entitled each of the Parties to *unilaterally* request, if not the termination of the Contracts, then at least an adaptation of its terms, in particular the *postponement* of the contractual dates by a reasonable period of time".[129]

As stated by Article 6.2.1. of UNIDROIT Principles and by legal provisions on hardship, parties are bound to perform their obligations when performance becomes more onerous for one of the parties. Meanwhile, they have to renegotiate their contract in order to try to perform it under conditions that will reduce the impact of events that were at the origin of the hardship situation.

An example of a contractual provision that provides for the parties' renegotiation is analysed by the arbitral award in *ICC Case no. 13898 (2014).*[130] In that case, a contractual provision on price revision (Article 11.6) provided in its § 4 that "the Parties shall make their best endeavour to reach a reasonable revision in pricing formulae (...)". While parties have an obligation to renegotiate their contract, there is, however no obligation to reach an agreement on adaptation as parties should make "their best endeavour".

To sum up, parties should meet after the occurrence of the hardship triggering event that impacts contractual conditions substantially. Usually, the prejudiced party informs the co-contracting party of the excessive situation, asking for a meeting to discuss the issue. Such notification marks the starting point of the renegotiation. The other party should therefore reply by accepting the meeting and exchange propositions to try to find a mutually-accepted solution. This would not mean that the latter party has accepted the adaptation of the contractual terms, but that it agrees on the process to achieve it. The parties' behaviour during this process may be subject to arbitrators' assessment. Such assessment is within their jurisdictional power.

The parties' renegotiation may lead or may not lead to an agreement on the issue to be determined, i.e. the adaptation of the contract. If they agree on new contractual terms, the parties resume the performance of the contract and arbitrators will not have to intervene in order to adapt the contract.

Parties may not agree on the existence of hardship or on hardship's negative effects on one of the parties to the contract. In that case, arbitrators will have to determine the reasons for the parties' failure to agree.

b. The assessment of the parties' renegotiation according to good faith requirements

Arbitrators assess parties' behaviour during the contract renegotiation process in order to establish its conformity with good faith requirements.

The parties' failure to agree on the existence of hardship and of its impact on their contractual obligations may result from their behaviour during the renegotiation process that was contrary to good faith[131]. For instance, the co-contracting party may avoid the renegotiation process by not responding to the party who is suffering the impact of hardship[132], or by making unreasonable offers.[133] The party may try to unduly improve its contractual position,[134] or refuse a reasonable offer.[135] Arbitrators have then to determine which party is responsible for the disagreement and may invite the parties to resume their negotiation.

The failure of parties to agree on the adaptation of their contract allows arbitrators to adapt the contract, provided this is stipulated in the contract or required in applicable legal provisions on hardship. The scope of contract adaptation by arbitrators needs therefore to be specified.

II.B. Scope of contract adaptation by arbitrators

Contract adaptation by arbitrators, when provided for in legal provisions on hardship, is an option and not an obligation (II.B.1.). Consequently, where contract adaptation in the face of a change of circumstances is not favoured by arbitrators, other solutions may apply (II.B.2.).

II.B.1. Contract adaptation by arbitrators is an option, not an obligation

Arbitrators' intervention in order to adapt the contract may result from legal provisions on hardship. These provisions usually designate the judge and determine the scope of the latter's intervention. Arbitrators' intervention in order to adapt the contract may result also from contractual provisions on hardship. Usually, a specific authorisation for arbitrators to adapt the contract is given within the contractual provision on hardship. Such clauses state that if parties fail to agree on whether the contract should be adapted or how it should be adapted, either party may refer such matter to arbitration[136]. In some cases, parties allow for a certain period of time to attempt to reach an agreement.[137]

Arbitrators' intervention may result from the parties' implicit intention. The parties' disagreement may lead to the implementation of the arbitration clause in the absence of any specific power given to arbitrators by parties. In that case, the applicable law will determine arbitrators' powers and their scope.[138]

Legal provisions on hardship give an option to arbitrators to adapt the contract. This is reinforced by the term "may" that is used in the legal provision when it is stated that the "judge" or the "court" may adapt the contract. This option is especially important where those legal provisions are of a mandatory nature. Therefore, phrases such as "*According to the circumstances*",[139] or "*After weighing up the interests of the parties*",[140] or "*Taking into consideration the interests of both parties*"[141] and "*If justice so requires*"[142] reinforce the choice given to arbitrators. This wording should help arbitrators to decide whether or not to adapt the contract. When taking their decision to adapt the contract or not to adapt it, arbitrators must give particular care to the contract's environment, the interests of both parties, and the continuation of the contract under the best conditions.

Is the same option left to the discretion of arbitrators by non-mandatory legal provisions? Non-mandatory legal provisions on hardship take the same approach to the adaptation of contracts by arbitrators. Arbitrators have the faculty to choose between the adaptation of the contract or its termination. The adaptation of the contract by arbitrators is hence a solution among others. Legal provisions on hardship act as guidelines that help arbitrators when adapting a contract. Their general wording gives arbitrators latitude to decide, depending upon what arbitrators consider essential for their decision to be taken. Such guidelines are nevertheless not without limits, as arbitrators are usually careful to render an award that is acceptable by both parties, i.e. not challengeable on the ground of excess of authority.

Given that contract adaptation by arbitrators, where provided for by legal provisions on hardship, is an option and not an obligation, other solutions may be possible as Article 6.2.3 of UNIDROIT Principles indicates. Art. 6.2.3. UNIDROIT Principles deals with *Effects of hardship* and provides:

> (4) If the court finds hardship, it may, if reasonable,
>
> (a) terminate the contract at a date and on terms to be fixed, or,
>
> (b) adapt the contract with a view to restoring its equilibrium.

Commentaries on the UNIDROIT Principles state that contract adaptation or termination of the contract by the court may not be appropriate and "in consequence the only reasonable solution will be for the Court either to direct the parties to resume negotiations with a view to reaching agreement on the adaptation of the contract, or to confirm the terms of the contract as they stand."[143]

The option given to arbitrators whether to adapt the contract or not is the one chosen by Lithuania in Article 6.204 of its Civil Code[144] which states:

> (...) The court may
>
> 1. dissolve the contract and establish the date and terms of its dissolution;
> 2. modify the conditions of the contract with a view to restoring the balance of contractual obligation of the parties.

The same option is left to the judge by Article 1091 of the Civil and Commercial Code of the Argentine Republic[145] while the former Civil Code provided for the contract termination by the prejudiced party unless the other party offers to adapt the contract equitably.[146]

The choice given to arbitrators between contract adaptation and termination of the contract -in part or in its entirety- is the solution adopted by The Netherlands in Article 6 :258 of the Dutch Civil Code and in Greece by Article 388 of the Greek Civil Code.[147] The same solution has been adopted by Peru in Article 1440 of its Civil Code and France in Article 1195 of its Civil Code.[148]

Do MENA countries' legal systems give the same option to arbitration on hardship? Generally speaking, they provide for judicial intervention in the contract to reduce to reasonable limits the obligation that has become excessive. Arbitrators have the power to analyse the circumstances surrounding the contract by taking into consideration the interests of both parties. Arbitrators have a choice, not an obligation, as they "may" reduce to "reasonable limits" the obligation that has become excessively onerous. What if in a particular case, contract adaptation is not possible? May arbitrators terminate the contract if circumstances and parties' interests point to that solution? Or is their choice limited to maintaining the *status quo* or adapting the contract to the changed circumstances? The wording used by legal provisions gives arbitrators large leeway to choose the solution they deem the best, i.e "if justice so requires".[149]

To invite the parties to resume their negotiations is also within arbitrators' power and it may appear more appropriate in particular cases, even in the absence of such an option in the legal or contractual provisions on hardship. Arbitrators may invite the parties to find a solution, such as price indexation or price revision provisions. This does not mean that arbitrators have no power at all.

The arbitral tribunal's approach in *ICC Case no.* 10351 (2001)[150] is of interest in this regard. The parties disagreed on the application of an indexation price formula for the purchase of a liquefied natural gas under a long-term sales contract. The parties had frequently modified the pricing clause in many of their contracts. The latest revision concerned a price formula that included a correction factor. The calculation resulted from a complex formula, the implementation of which resulted in higher prices. In a partial award, the arbitral tribunal ordered the parties to negotiate the revision of the correction factor[151] within a period of time (3 months). The tribunal's final award would then confirm their agreement on a particular formula. If the parties disagreed, the tribunal would determine the formula and the amounts according to the parties' respective arguments and submissions.

Arbitrators may provide for the adaptation of the contract. As a consequence, the extent of their power should be specified.

II.B.2. The extent of contract adaptation by arbitrators

The extent of contract adaptation by arbitrators is clarified according to the meaning given to their power (a) and to the methodology applied by arbitrators (b).

a. Meaning of contract adaptation by arbitrators

Where admitted by legal provisions, contract adaptation by arbitrators is often set out in such a way that it narrows the scope of their intervention. Mandatory legal provisions fix in practically the same terms the limits of arbitrators' intervention to adapt the contract.

According to legal provisions on hardship, the meaning of contract adaptation by arbitrators is close to an adjustment of contract conditions to a reasonable level that allows parties to perform the contract. Such adjustment is made according to what parties would have agreed upon at the conclusion of the contract.

Therefore, contract adaptation by arbitrators means, according to legal provisions on hardship "[to] reduce to reasonable limits the obligation that has become excessive"[152] or "to reduce the debtor's performance to the appropriate extent".[153] Other legal provisions on hardship provide more indications to arbitrators such as: "[to] reduce to reasonable limits by lessening its extent or increasing its consideration, the obligation that has become excessive".[154] Interestingly, some legal provisions define arbitrators' contract adaptation thus: "to reduce the oppressive obligation to a reasonable degree either by narrowing its extent or by awarding a balancing interest"[155] or "to return such onerous obligation to a reasonable level".[156]

Other legal provisions on hardship give no detail or specification on the extent of arbitrators' power to adapt the contract or even on how they would proceed. These provisions usually provide for a revision of the contract without any further elaboration. This is the case, for example, of Article 1195 of the French Civil Code, that provides for the judge to revise the contract, while Article 6 :258 of the Dutch Civil Code provides that "the Court may (...) modify the effects of an agreement", and section 388 of Greek Civil Code provides that the "Court may (...) reduce the debtor's performance to the appropriate extent (...)". Section 2411 of the Hungarian Civil Code states briefly that "the court may amend a contract when (...)".

Art. 6.2.3. (4) (b) of the UNIDROIT Principles states that arbitrators "may (...) adapt the contract with a view to restoring its equilibrium". This is to say, and the commentary sheds light on it: "the court will seek to make a fair distribution of the losses between the parties".[157]

Legal provisions on hardship grant arbitrators' powers within certain limits. Their role is often limited to reducing the excessive effects of hardship on contract conditions to a reasonable level by a proper balancing of interests. Contract adaptation by arbitrators is therefore far from a revision of contract conditions. Contractual provisions on hardship may provide for contract adaptation by arbitrators in the arbitration clause and/or in the contractual provisions that deal with changes of circumstances or price indexation. Arbitrators' power to adapt the contract is not so much the re-establishment of the original contractual equilibrium, i.e. the one that existed at the time of the conclusion of the contract. It consists rather to eliminate the excess of increased onerosity in the contractual obligation by reducing it to a reasonable level—within the normal risk of the contract.

Once the existence of hardship is determined, arbitrators undertake the adaptation of the contract.

b. **Methodology of contract adaptation by arbitrators**

Arbitrators may choose not to adapt a contract, not necessarily because it is an option left to their discretion,[158] but they may conclude that hardship conditions are not met. On the other hand, when adapting a contract, arbitrators may depart from contractual provisions based on parties' intention.

Accordingly, arbitrators may choose to invite the parties to resume a revision of the contract. Following the solution adopted by the parties, the arbitrators will render an award that reflects the parties' intention, if they agree on a formula, or if they submit their indications on a proposed one.[159]

Arbitrators, when adapting a contract are bound by contractual and legal provisions on hardship. The guidance provided thereby helps or should help arbitrators in settling the issue.

Arbitrators adapting a contract may face a lack of clarity of the particular contractual provisions. Even though, "in the absence of clear meaning of a contractual term, arbitrators interpret the contract",[160] arbitrators shall rely *"on the general principles* of (the contract law of the State whose law is applicable) (...) in accordance with the plain and ordinary meaning of the words thereof as read in the particular context in which the relevant terms are used by the Parties".[161] When such common intention cannot be established by arbitrators, the contract should be interpreted in such a way to give a meaning to all the provisions and according to the reasonable meaning given by parties in the same circumstances.[162] On the other hand, contractual provisions that are "clear and unambiguous (...) must be enforced by a court or tribunal according the plain meaning of (their) terms, without reference to extrinsic materials outside the four corners of the instruments."[163]

This is a methodology to be applied by arbitrators when adapting a contract.

Thus, *the legal provisions give indications* that help arbitrators in adapting contracts. Arbtirators may render an award *"according to the circumstances"*[164] and *"after weighing up the interests of the parties"*.[165] When *"taking into consideration the interests of both parties"*,[166] arbitrators have the same latitude as a court in their appreciation[167] to render an award *"if justice so requires"*.[168] The UNIDROIT Principles are more specific as the adaptation "will not necessarily reflect in full the loss entailed by the change in circumstances, since the court will, for instance, have to consider the extent to which one of the parties has taken a risk and the extent to which the party entitled to receive a performance may still benefit from that performance."[169]

Arbitral awards provide examples of the methodology applied by arbitrators.[170] Careful attention is given on *parties' intention to interpret the contractual provision according to the way it was drafted.*

When adapting the contract, arbitrators have "*to comply with the intention of the parties*"[171] to determine if their intention was the contract adaptation and not its termination. The adjustment will be in accordance with the existing indices or substitution of one of them, in order "to be nearly comparable to the effects sought from the original indices as any reliable data then available will allow."[172]

Arbitrators who adapt a contract should also focus on the "*interpretation of the contractual price formula currently in force*" as mentioned in *ICC Case no.10351* (2009).[173] In that case, the dispute arose after a change in the Platts formula that was the link for determining the gas price in the contract. The contractual provision on price revision had been applied without success. The arbitrators note:

> If we consider the circumstances in which Rider No. 7 was made, this tells us a lot about the interpretation of the contractual price formula currently in force. It highlights the tensions between the gas producer, concerned about changes in oil prices, and the gas purchaser, anxious to sell within its gas market the quantities it undertook to buy in the very long term (take-or-pay)... More specifically, it shows that, when they negotiated Rider No. 7, the parties were aware that the indexation of the price of LNG to Platts' FOB breakeven prices did not mean that they were being indexed to a basket of products in competition with natural gas. This is attested by the following facts.[174]

Arbitrators adapting a contract interpret the parties' intention in such a way as to reach a *"fair and equitable revision"*[175] as stated by the parties in the contractual provision on hardship. Arbitrators should then follow the same model that should have been applied by parties. In *Gas Natural Aprovisionamientos SDG, SA v Atlantic LNG Co. of Trinidad and Tobago,*[176] the Court's reasoning was as follows: "It is undisputed that the Tribunal was specifically charged with the duty to revise the pricing scheme once it determined that the contractual preconditions were met. The Tribunal having made that determination, Article 8.5(a) required it to reach 'a fair and equitable revision' of the contract price".

Arbitrators also give importance to *parties practice during the* life of a contract.

Arbitrators interpreting the parties' intention will focus on the parties' behaviour during the performance of the contract and shed the light on their intention on contract adaptation. The following *ICC Case no. 10351* (2001)[177] gives a good example of arbitrators' approach: the parties were in a disagreement over changes in the indexation of gas prices in a long-term contract for the purchase by the claimant of liquid natural gas from respondent. Article VIII of the contract on the fixation of the price had been, by parties' agreement (Amendment 7), replaced by another reference for the price formula that resulted in higher prices. Claimant argued that the previous formula was to be applied and claimed reimbursement of the amounts it had paid in excess. Article IX of the contract, on the price revision, determined the procedural conditions in detail stating for the parties agreement to proceed to the adjustment of the contractual price and provided certain conditions mentioned in that clause. The parties' performance of the contract revealed that they modified the reference for the fixed price (Art. VIII).[178] This helped arbitrators to determine their agreement on the price reference and its articulation with the revision provision. The parties' disagreement on the meaning and the scope of the contractual indexation formula (Art. VIII (3))[179] was thus analysed in the light of all the elements mentioned above.

In *ICC Case no. 12936*[180] shows the importance of the parties' practice during the implementation of the contract that is different from what was foreseen in the contract. A significant change in the practice impacts the nature of the supply agreement.[181] In that case, the arbitral tribunal pointed out the oral and tacit amendments by parties to their contract, that showed an "intention of the parties to make an amendment subsequent to the conclusion of the contract".[182] The parties' practice could thus lead to change the contract without following the contractual procedure. According to the arbitrators, this also had *a consequence on the nature of the contract and its consequences*. The "(master supply agreement) had clearly become a framework agreement, fixing certain terms and conditions for sale contracts yet to be made".[183]

In some cases, arbitrators apply the existing contractual formula showing the limitation of the scope of their intervention.[184] Arbitrators may also adapt the contract by respecting the contractual provisions already existing.[185] The question is then to what extent arbitrators should adapt the contract, i.e. should they offset the whole of the economic hardship or only remove the substantial element of hardship? An answer is given by *Superior Overseas Developement Corp.*[186] The court members were divided between those who were in favour of removing the whole economic hardship and those who considered they should focus on the substantial part of the hardship. The decision taken favoured the removal of the substantial element of the hardship.[187]

Once arbitrators have established the methodology they will use, the question is then to what extent arbitrators should adapt a given contract.

An analysis of arbitrators' adaptation of contracts shows that they pay a careful attention to the provisions on hardship, the way contractual provisions are drafted, the environment of the contract and the usages in the parties' field of activity, as explained below.

The adaptation of the contract by arbitrators is, however, not without limits.

II.C. Limits of contract adaptation by arbitrator

The limits to contract adaptation by arbitrators are those specified by parties in the contractual provisions (II.C.1.). Such limits also result from challenges against arbitral awards (II.C.2.).

II.C.1. Limits fixed by legal or contractual provisions

Contractual or legal provisions on change of circumstances outline arbitrators' power. They provide for the scope of the arbitrators' jurisdiction if parties fail to agree on the existence or the effects of hardship.[188] Arbitrators interpret the scope of the existing contractual provisions; they do not create new legal obligations.[189] As a consequence, arbitrators' adaptation of the contract is within their jurisdictional power.[190]

Contractual provisions may provide the criteria for the adaptation of a contract by arbitrators, or at least give indications that might help them achieve that goal. Contractual provisions, however, may not be as clear as expected or sufficient to enlighten arbitrators' decision-making process. Even though, arbitrators follow their methodology in searching the parties' intentions.

Once the power to revise the contract is given to arbitrators, they will adapt it according to the limits set out by the legal rules applicable to the contract and by contractual provisions. The limits fixed by legal rules on hardship when adaptation of the contract is envisaged are those to render a decision "according to the circumstances (...) if justice requires (by) taking into consideration the interests of both parties". The limits also are those according to the power of *amiable compositeur*. On the other hand, when arbitrators are to revise the contract, they will first look at the contractual provisions. Normally, arbitrators should first determine if contractual preconditions are met; secondly, they should adapt the contract in a way which fits what parties stated in the provisions. Parties should be aware of this when drafting contractual provisions. The more precise the provisions are, the clearer the limits for arbitrators will be.

An example of the above is the *EDF v Shell*[191] case. The power of *amiables compositeurs* had been given to the court by the parties. An adaptation clause was included in the contract, but the parties could not reach an agreement on the terms of such adaptation. The court invited them to resume their negotiations and decided that if the parties failed to reach an agreement again, it would choose the financial equation to be applied in order to modify the contractual terms among those to be proposed by the parties. In fact, the court chose not to impose any particular equation on the parties, but only one chosen among those advanced by the parties.

The more indications are given in the contractual provisions, the more restrictive the arbitrator's power of contract adaptation will be. In *ICC Case no. 13898 (2014),*[192] a price revision provision may be an example of this. In its § 4, the provision stated:

> The Parties shall make their best endeavor to reach a reasonable revision in pricing formulae with due regard to the location of Gas reserves, reservoir productivity, average Gas daily delivery and Gas quality as well as terms and conditions thereof. Likewise, gathering, compressing, transportation and all elements affecting pricing formulae including but not limited to being and acting as an efficient and prudent operator on the part of Seller shall be considered.

The § 5 states:

> Moreover, such elements shall include relevant conditions at Buyer's market, the cost of distribution and transmission as well as all relevant factors and circumstances being pertinent to the said market and the Gas industry as a whole.

And § 9 specifies that

> In any case, the Contract Price provisions shall allow Natural Gas supplied hereunder to be sold in the competition with marginal substitutable forms of energy in the Buyer's market.

However, in practice, contractual provisions on hardship may contain less details on the way the parties may or should adapt the contract. This would be the case, for instance, when the price review provision requires the parties to reach "a fair and equitable revision"[193] of the contract price. When parties fail to reach an agreement, the arbitrators' adaptation of the contract will have to be fair and equitable too. That is to say that a broad discretionary power is recognised to arbitrators on the ground of the wording of the contractual provisions.

The limit of contract adaptation by arbitrators is the parties' lack of satisfaction with the award rendered. Indeed, arbitrators may impose an undesirable contractual adjustment. This would raise the question of the suitability of arbitration as a forum for resolving disputes especially in long-term contracts in specific field sectors such a gas. An arbitrator's award on adaptation of the contract may be challenged by an unsatisfactory party.

II.C.2. Challenges against the arbitral award

Once rendered, an arbitral award is final and binding for the parties. Arbitral awards may be challenged for annulment before the national courts of the seat of arbitration according to the rules set by its applicable arbitration law. Their enforcement may also be challenged, as stated by the *Convention on the Recognition and Enforcement of Foreign Arbitral Awards* (New York 1958)[194] on seven exclusive grounds upon which courts may refuse to recognise or enforce an award.

The legal grounds upon which courts may refuse to recognise an award are very restrictive. The excess of arbitral power is among them, as provided in Art. V (1) (c) of the *Convention on the Recognition and Enforcement of Foreign Arbitral Awards* (New York 1958) which states that a court may refuse to enforce an arbitration award if it

> deals with a difference not contemplated by or not falling within the terms of the submission to arbitration, or it contains decisions on matters beyond the scope of the submission to arbitration.

Similarly, the *UNICITRAL Model Law on International Commercial Arbitration* of 1985 (with amendments in 2006) (UNCITRAL Model Law) sets out the same grounds as the 1958 New York Convention for refusing recognition or enforcement of an arbitral award.[195]

An illustration of this is given by *Gas Natural Aprovisionamientos, SDG, SA v Atlantic LNG Company of Trinidad and Tobago.*[196] In that case, the parties failed to agree on the application of a price review clause that was inserted in the contract. The seller referred the matter to arbitration in order to settle the issue. The tribunal rendered an award introducing a new two-part pricing mechanism with retroactive effect. This new formula impacted the seller who had to reimburse the buyer. The seller challenged the award for excess of authority before the competent court, arguing that the arbitrators had actually rewritten the contract between the parties.

In the *Gas Natural* case, the challenging party invoked Article V(1) (c) of the 1958 New York Convention, as implemented by 9 U.S.C. § 207, which similarly provides that a court may refuse to enforce an arbitration award for excess of authority.

The Court pointed out that the *vacatur* of an arbitration award is infrequent, and the provision referred to above is interpreted narrowly. The excess of authority that may give rise to a challenge of the arbitral award is to be understood as

> whether the arbitrator *had the power*, based on the parties' submissions or the arbitration agreement to reach a certain issue, *not whether the arbitrator correctly decided that issue*.[197]

Moreover,

> As long as the arbitrator is even arguably construing or applying the contract and acting *within the scope of his authority* that a court is convinced he committed serious error does not suffice to overturn his decision.

In its interpretation of contractual provisions,

> arbitrator may not ignore the plain language of the contract (...) a court should *not reject an award on the ground that the arbitrator misread the contract.*

The court made sure that the arbitral tribunal established the meeting of contractual preconditions. The arbitral tribunal analysed the impact of the event on the contract conditions[198] and confirmed the unexpected impact of U.S. prices on the Spanish market price of LNG, that satisfied the hardship requirement.[199] As to the power to revise the contract, the court's approach was that it had to make sure that the Tribunal had the power to decide whether the requirements for a price re-opener had been met, and that the arbitrators had the power to revise the contract.[200] The court then went on to analyse the wording of the contractual provisions that provides the parties to reach "a fair and equitable revision" of the contract price.[201] Another contractual provision establishing a pricing scheme was analysed by the seller to argue the excess of arbitrators' powers by imposing another price scheme.[202] The Court dismissed the assertion by holding that the parties had omitted to fix limitations to the arbitrators when adapting the contract:

> Indeed, Atlantic's submissions to the Tribunal acknowledged the Tribunal's broad authority in this regard. In them Atlantic opined that the relevant contractual terms "do not appear to expressly limit this Tribunal's award to the imposition of a single pricing formula." Atlantic's argument concerning the dual pricing formula is better understood as a challenge to the merits of the Tribunal's decision. Such a challenge is unavailing since the Court does not review arbitration awards for legal or factual errors.

Moreover, the court pointed out that the contractual provisions applicable in that case failed to impose limits to the tribunal authority to impose a price:

> Atlantic has not shown that the parties reached any agreement that limited the Tribunal's authority to impose a dual price structure. It is true that when the Tribunal requested post-hearing briefing from the parties as to "[w] hether it is possible to have two different prices based on two different markets," both parties argued against such a scheme. GNA argued in favour of a single Spanish price for all deliveries; Atlantic contended that a single price based on the New England market should apply to all deliveries. These arguments over the wisdom of a dual pricing scheme, however, cannot be reasonably construed as an agreement to restrict the Tribunal's authority to adopt that scheme.

On the other hand, the court pointed to the parties' admission in principle of two different prices fixed by the Tribunal.

> Indeed, in opposing the Tribunal's suggestion of a two-price system, Atlantic limited its analysis to "the present facts," while accepting that under certain circumstances "it might, in theory, be possible to 'have two different prices based on two different markets.'" Thus, Atlantic foresaw that a dual scheme would be permissible, and it points to no stipulation by the parties depriving the Tribunal of the power to fashion such a price.

The court concluded that the arbitral tribunal did not exceed its power in adapting the contract:

> These arguments over the wisdom of a dual pricing scheme, however, cannot be reasonably construed as an agreement to restrict the Tribunal's authority to adopt that scheme.

The *Gas Natural* case shows a concrete application of a hardship provision in a manner that parties did not intend. The arbitrators' imposition of the dual pricing scheme was possible because of lack of "structural limitation on permissible prices revisions" in the contract's provisions and the ability left to arbitrators to reach a "fair and equitable revision of the contract price", as stated in the hardship provision. The arbitral tribunal's solution resulted from a careful analysis of the parties' intention, notably the acceptance by one party (claimant) of the admission of two different prices fixed by the tribunal. The *Gas Natural* case shows the importance of drafting contractual provisions on change of circumstances and more specifically concerning the scope of the arbitrators' power to adapt the contract.

The same approach was adopted in *Quintette Coal* arbitration (award of 28 May 1990)[203]. In 1981, Quintette Coal Ltd and a group of ten Japanese companies entered into a long-term coal sale contract that entailed the opening of a new mine in an isolated region. Contractual provisions were inserted on indexation, price review[204], hardship[205] and inequity review[206], providing for parties' review of the contract conditions in a spirit of cooperation and best efforts, beside an arbitration clause[207].

The arbitral tribunal adapted the contract by fixing, based on Articles 7 (Review Price) and 9 (Iniquity Review), many prices for the next five years as requested by the parties. The tribunal considered the intention of the parties, the general decrease of coal price and the evolution of circumstances as expected by the tribunal. The arbitral award was challenged on the ground of arbitral tribunal's excess of authority. In fact, *Quintette* held that the arbitrators lacked the power to proceed with a variation of the price. According to the claimant, the arbitrator's adaptation of the contract was outside the parameters set out by the parties. Indeed, the arbitrators had actually modified the contract, as opposed to adapting it. The court rejected the challenge against the award as Article 9 of the contract granted jurisdiction to the arbitrators to interpret the parties' will. The decision of the tribunal has been however criticised by many scholars[208] for excess of power on the part of the arbitrators.

CONCLUSION

The adaptation of contracts by arbitrators is now recognized. It may result from the specific power given by parties to arbitrators in a contractual provision on hardship. Applicable law to the contract may also provide for the same option. This assertion has nevertheless its limits.

A careful analysis of legal provisions on hardship shows a lack of uniformity as to the judge power to adapt the contract. Some legal provisions on hardship do not foresee the adaptation of contracts by judges (so by arbitrators). Arbitrator will not adapt the contract if the contract is also governed by a Common Law system. Furthermore, in the absence of clear intention of parties as to contract adaptation by arbitrator, article 6.2.1.to 6.2.3 of UNIDROIT Principles on hardship will not be applied. In the same vein, hardship concept is not yet considered as an international trade usage. Therefore, the arbitrators will not take it into account "in any case" according to national and international legislation on arbitration.

A careful analysis of contractual provisions on hardship reveal that adaptation of contracts by arbitrators is not necessarily the option chosen by parties. Finally, the power of *amiable compositeurs* given by parties to arbitrators will allow the arbitrators to reduce the inequitable effects of applicable legal rules and of contractual provisions. The reduction of inequitable effect by arbitrators may not have an effect of the adjustment of contract.

Nevertheless, the perspectives of contract adaptation by arbitrators reveal that arbitrators may adapt the contract according to scope and limits given by parties and by legal provisions on hardship with a view of possible challenges against the arbitral award.

Contract adaptation by arbitrators implies henceforth the choice of legal provision on hardship that recognizes contract adaptation by arbitrators. It may also result from the insertion of a contractual clause on hardship that does not exclude it or that foresees it. In this latter case parties would be well advised to determine the criteria that will guide arbitrators in their approach. Parties should be also aware to determine the scope of adaptation of contracts by arbitrators.

An ICC Model Clause on hardship would be the reflection of international contractual practice. The ICC Model Clause will determine the powers of arbitrators, the scope and the limits of their mission. The ICC Model Clause should be drafted as follows: In the context of contractual provision on change in circumstances that impacts the contract equilibrium, arbitrators may intervene when parties try to renegotiate and fail to agree on contract adaptation. Arbitrators then invite parties to resume their negotiations and try to reach an agreement. If parties reach an agreement on contract adaptation, arbitrators will include it in their arbitral award that will bind the parties. If Parties fail to reach an agreement after having tried to renegotiate the contract, arbitrators will ask them to bring propositions that they will take into account in their arbitral award.[209] Another suggestion would be to consider whether parties' failure to agree paves the way to adaptation of contract by arbitrators.

NOTES

1. See former art. 1592 French Civil Code (mandataire); See Italian civil law (arbitrator). This is the case in Italian civil law where a distinction is made between arbitrato ritual or arbitraggio and arbitrato libero or irrituale. The same distinction is made in German law between schiedsgerichten and schiedegutachten.
2. See Henry Motulsky, Ecrits, Tome II, Notes et Etudes sur l'arbitrage, Dalloz, 1974 ; See Bruno Oppetit, "L'arbitrage et les contrats commerciaux à long terme", Revue de l'arbitrage 1976, no. 2, p. 91 ss., spec. 97 s.
3. See Bernardini, Piero, "The Renegotiation of the Investment Contract", *Foreign Investment Law Journal*, vol. 13, no. 2, fall 1998, p. 411 s., spec. p. 421: "Even if such a power is expressly conferred, it may be doubted that it has an adjudicatory nature"; Oppetit Bruno, "L'adaptation des contrats internationaux aux changements de circonstances : la clause de "hardship", *Journal de Droit International* 1974.755, spéc. p. 808-809.
4. See Rules for the Regulation of Contractual Relations, ICC Publication no. 326 (1978).
5. See Adaptation of Contracts, Rules—Standard Clauses—Application to Standing Committee (ICC Publication no. 326), 1978; In the same vein, see Bruno Oppetit See Bruno Oppetit, "L'arbitrage et les contrats commerciaux à long terme", *Revue de l'arbitrage* 1976, no. 2, p. 91 ss., espec. p. 104.
6. These rules have been abrogated in 1994. See Derains Yves, "A Report on the ICC Rules on the Regulation of Contractual Relations (ICC Publication no. 326)", *ICC Bulletin*, vol. 5, no. 2, 1994, p. 3; See Accaoui Lorfing Pascale, *La renégociation des contrats internationaux*, Editions Bruylant, 2011, spec. no. 405, p. 286 s.
7. See *ICC Force majeure Clause 2003—ICC Hardship Clause 2003*, ICC Publication no. 650, p. 17
8. See ICC case 12794 (2004) (final award), *ICC International Court of Arbitration Bulletin* vol. 23, no. 1, (2012), p. 57 s.
9. See *Paradine v Jane (1647) Aleyn* 26; 82 ER 897.
10. See *Taylor v Caldwell* 3 B & S 826; 122 ER 309.
11. The *Coronation cases* concern the illness of the king that led to the cancellation of the ceremony that was the purpose of the renting contract of flat balconies to watch the procession.
12. See *Davis Contractors Ltd v Fareham Urban District Council* (1956) AC 696.
13. See *British Movietonews Ltd v London and District Cinemas Ltd* [1952] AC 166. ; See also *Maritime National Fish Ltd. v Ocean Trawlers Ltd* [1935] AC 524 ; Philippe Denis, *Changement de circonstances et bouleversement de l'économie contractuelle*, Bruylant, Bruxelles, 1986, p. 389; Puelinckx A.H., "Frustration, hardship, force majeure, imprévision, Wegfall der Geschäftsgrundlage, Unmöglichkeit, changed circumstances" (1986) 3(2) *Journal of International Arbitration*, 47–66
14. See *Mineral Park Land Company v PA Howard*, 172 Cal 289 (1916), "(...) a thing is impossible in legal contemplation when it is not practicable, and a thing is impracticable when it can only be done at an excessive and unreasonable cost", esp. p. 293.
15. See *Aluminium Company of America (ALCOA) v Essex Group Inc,* 499 F Supp 53 (WD Pa 1980).
16. The same wording is present the most legal system of MENA countries.
17. The author expresses her gratitude to Dr. Mohamed S. Abdel Wahab, Zulficar & Partners, for his precious help in providing useful information on Egyptian Law and Egyptian Case laws.

    According to an unofficial translation.

    1. « العقد شريعة المتعاقدين، فلا يجوز نقضه ولا تعديله إلا باتفاق الطرفين، أو للأسباب التي يقررها القانون.
    2. ومع ذلك إذا طرأت حوادث استثنائية عامة لم يكن في الوسع توقعها وترتب على حدوثها أن تنفيذ الالتزام التعاقدي، وإن لم يصبح مستحيلاً، صار مرهقاً للمدين بحيث يهدده بخسارة فادحة، جاز للقاضي تبعاً للظروف وبعد الموازنة بين مصلحة الطرفين أن يردّ الالتزام المرهق إلى الحد المعقول، ويقع باطلاً كل اتفاق على خلاف ذلك».
18. See. Lando O. & Beale H. *Principles of European Contract Law. Full text of Parts I and II combined.* The Hague: Kluwer Law International, 2000.
19. See Mayer Pierre, "The Role of the UNIDROIT Principles in ICC Arbitration Practice 2002", in Special Supplement 2002: UNIDROIT Principles of International Commercial Contracts: Reflections on their Use in international Arbitration, p. 105 s.
20. See ICC Case no. 7110, partial award dated July 13, 1995; See De LY, F., "National Report—The Netherlands: An Interim Report Regarding The Application of the UNIDROIT Principles in International Commercial Contracts in the Netherlands", in M.J. Bonell, ed., *A New Approach to International Commercial Contracts: the UNIDROIT Principles of International Commercial Contracts*, (London, Kluwer 1999), p. 203-231, and his analysis. See Mayer, Pierre, "The Role of the UNIDROIT Principles in ICC Arbitration Practice 2002", *op. cit.*

21. See ICC 9474
22. The UNCITRAL Model Law states that in the absence of a choice of applicable law by the parties, the arbitral tribunal shall apply the law determined by the conflict rules which it considers applicable. This restrictive approach excludes the recourse to the UNIDROIT Principles as governing law.
23. See ICC Case no. 7110, partial award dated July 13, 1995, with a dissenting opinion
24. See ICC Case no. 7375
25. See ICC Case no. 7110, partial award dated July 13, 1995, with a dissenting opinion.
26. See ICC Case no. 7375 (g).
27. ibid.
28. See ICC Case no. 7110, of May 4, 1998, Partial Award no. 2 as cited by F. De Ly, *op. cit.*
29. See Nassar Najla, *Sanctity of Contracts Revisited*, Dordrecht, Nijhoff, 1995.
30. See ICC Case no. 8486 (1996) (originally in German), 'Collection of ICC Arbitral Awards 1996-2000', p. 321;

    J.D.I. 1998. 1047–1049; Translated in English in *Yearbook of Commercial Arbitration* 1999, 162–173; see Berger Klaus Peter, *The Creeping Codification of the New Lex Mercatoria*, Second Edition Wolters Kluwer 2010, esp. p. 230; Brunner Christoph, *Force Majeure and Hardship Under General Contract Principles. Exemption for Non-Performance in International Arbitration*, Wolters Kluwer, 2009, esp. p. 40; MAYER Pierre, "The Role of the UNIDROIT Principles in ICC Arbitration Practice", 2002, *op. cit.*
31. Probably also because the national provision was inspired by the international legal instrument.
32. See ICC Case no. 8486 (1996), esp. §[7] "In Dutch national legal practice, the general provision [of Art. 6:248 BW] is applied with the utmost restraint (...). According to Art. 3:12 BW, 'Dutch common opinion of law' is the determining factor in the first place; it is replaced by the common opinion in international contract law when the provision is applied in an international context. Both are influenced in a decisive manner by the principle of contractual good faith (*pacta sunt servanda*) expressed in Art. 1.3 of the UNIDROIT Principles for International Commercial Contracts. (...)

    This common opinion of law must also be taken into consideration for the application of national law to international relationships (...)

    The necessity and admissibility of the interpretation of national law in the light of the UNIDROIT Principles is also asserted especially for Dutch law (...)".
33. See the analysis of De Ly, F., "National Report—The Netherlands : An Interim Report Regarding The Application of the UNIDROIT Principles in International Commercial Contracts in the Netherlands", in M.J. Bonell, ed., *A New Approach to International Commercial Contracts : the UNIDROIT Principles of International Commercial Contracts*, (London, Kluwer 1999), p. 203-231, no. 4.
34. See Mayer, P., *op. cit.* "Yet if the international nature of contracts is systematically invoked in order to exclude the provisions of the chosen law in favour of the principles applicable to international contracts, the parties' forecasts will be undermined without any real justification.".
35. Other legal provisions on hardship are mandatory as for instance those of MENA countries.
36. See ICC Case no. 8486 (1996) spec. § 5 : "Art. 6:258 applies here even if the parties agreed on specific ‹grounds for discharge› in Clause 25 of the General Conditions, as, according to Art. 6:250 BW, the parties may not derogate contractually from [Art. 6:258], which must be applied mandatorily (see Nieuwenhuis/Stolker/Valk, Burgerlijk wetboek, 2nd ed. (1994), Books 3, 5 and 6, Art. 258, note 1)".
37. See ICC Case no. 7110 (June 1995), original in English, *ICC International Court of Arbitration Bulletin*, Vol. 10, No. 2, Fall 1999, 39-54
38. See ICC Case no. 7110 (July 13, 1995); See De LY, F., "National Report—The Netherlands: An Interim Report Regarding The Application of the UNIDROIT Principles in International Commercial Contracts in the Netherlands", in M.J. Bonell, ed., *A New Approach to International Commercial Contracts : the UNIDROIT Principles of International Commercial Contracts*, (London, Kluwer 1999), p. 203-231.
39. See De Ly F., *op. cit.* esp. p. 27.
40. See ICC Case no. 7110 (April 1998), (second arbitral award), Excerpts of the award published in *ICC International Court of Arbitration Bulletin,* Vol. 10, No. 2, Fall 1999, 54-57.
41. See ICC 8873 (1997) (in French), Art. 26 states "This contract will be governed in its entirety by Spanish law, to the exclusion of any other law". ("Ce contrat sera entièrement régi par le droit espagnol, à l'exclusion de tout autre droit").

42. See ICC Case no. 8873 *op. cit.* as freely translated by the author from the following arbitral developments "Or, si l'on peut admettre l'existence d'une tendance, dans certaines branches, à stipuler avec une certaine continuité des clauses de hardship, il est certain que dans la pratique des affaires l'obligation de rééquilibrer le contrat (par la négociation et, le cas échéant, par l'intervention d'un tiers, comme prévu dans l'article 6.2.3, paragraphe 4 des Principes UNIDROIT), qui caractérise la hardship, constitue un principe tout-à-fait exceptionnel, qui n'est accepté que dans le cadre de clauses contractuelles, qui devront déterminer en détail les situations justifiant la hardship ainsi que les conséquences de celle-ci. Il est donc exclu que l'on puisse considérer les dispositions en matière de hardship contenues dans les 'Principes UNIDROIT' comme des usages du commerce. Il s'agit, au contraire, de règles qui ne correspondent pas, au moins à l'état actuel, à la pratique courante des affaires dans le commerce international et qui ne seront par conséquent applicables que lorsque les parties y ont fait une référence expresse, ce qui n'est pas le cas ici."
43. See ICC Case no. 7110 (second award) op. cit.; ICC Case no. 8873 op. cit.
44. See Indonesian Mining Agreement of 1981 between *Batubara & UTAH / ARCO*, in De Cuyper, J.-Q. & Peter, W., "Renegotiation of Long Term International Agreements and Flexibility: Consideration on the Ground of the *Ghana / Valco Case*", *International Business Law Journal* 1995.775.
45. See *"Andriamena" Chronium Agreement of 1966 between Madagascar a Société d'Electrométallurgie et des Aciéries Electriques d'Ugine*, as cited by Wolfgang Peter, *Arbitration and Renegotiation of International Investment Agreements*, Kluwer Second Edition, 1995, p. 249.
46. See ICC Case no. 10351 (2001) (partial award), *ICC International Court of Arbitration Bulletin*, vol. 20, no. 2, 2009, p. 86 s., as freely translated: "Tant qu'une révision n'est pas intervenue, les dispositions de prix en vigueur demeureront applicables (...)".
47. See Fontaine, M., (ed), *Droit des contrats internationaux. Analyse et rédaction des clauses*, FEDUCI Paris 1989, spec. p. 272.
48. See ICC Case no. 3938, as cited by Peter, W., & De Cuyper, J.-Q. *op. cit.*
49. See ICC Case no. 15610, final award, London, *ICC International Court of Arbitration Bulletin* vol. 25/1, p. 70: "as they submitted their dispute to the Expert (...)", § 144.
50. The provision states the following:
    b. If the parties shall not within ninety (90) days after any such request have reached agreement on the adjustments (if any) in the said prices or price revision mechanism which are to be made then the matter may forthwith be referred by either party for determination by experts to be appointed in the manner set out in Article xviii hereof ...
    c. The experts shall determine what (if any) adjustments in the said prices or in the said price revision mechanism shall be made for the purposes aforesaid and any reviewed prices or any change in the price revision mechanism so determined by such experts shall take effect six (6) months after the date on which the request for the review was first made".
51. See ICC Case no. 15610, *Bulletin e-chapter, Extracts from ICC Arbitration in Oil and Gas Disputes*, vol. 25, no. 1, 2014
52. See ICC Case no. 15610 *op. cit.* § 144. Parties who "jointly defined 'hardship' to the Expert (...)". The excerpts of the award did not mention neither the conditions nor the extent of expert intervention.
53. ibid.
54. ibid.
55. See Block, G., "Arbitration and Changes in Energy Prices: A Review of ICC Awards with respect to Force Majeure, Indexation, Adaptation, Hardship and Take-or-Pay Clauses", *ICC International Court of Arbitration Bulletin*, vol. 20/2, 2009, p. 51s., esp. p. 55: "In the absence of an agreement, the Parties may refer their dispute to arbitration (as set out in article (...)".
56. See Polkinghorne M., "Predicting the Unpredictable: Gas Price Re-Openers", *The Paris Energy Series no. 2*, June 2011, citing the *ECT Paper*, 'Putting A Price on Energy, International Pricing Mechanisms for Oil and Gas', ECT 2007, that provides for "Stylized Provisions of a Price Review Clause" p. 155, esp. p. 155.
57. See Bernardini, P., "The Renegotiation of Investment Contracts" (1998) 13 *ICSID Review—FILJ* 411, 416.
58. See *Gas Natural Aprovisionamientos, SDG, S.A. v Atlantic LNG Company of Trinidad and Tobago,* United States District Court for the Southern District of New York (2008 WL 4344525 (S.D.N.Y.)).

59. See *J. S. C. Techsnabexport v Palmco Corporation* SCC Arbitration 010/2006; *Arbitral tribunal:* Bernard Hanotiau (chairman), Hans Danelius & Robert Briner (arbitrators); *Place of arbitration:* Stockholm, Sweden, that authorizes the arbitrator to interpret the will of the parties and to fill the gaps; Applicable Law: Swedish law.
60. ibid. "...indication of the level at which a higher price should be determined and contains no such parameter to be found in Addendum no. 4"; therefore, "(...) the Tribunal cannot find (...) a basis for determining a higher price than the provisional price agreed for 2005 in the Addendum".
61. See ICC Case no. 13504, (Extract), *ICC International Court of Arbitration Bulletin*, 2009, vol. 20, no. 2, p. 93 s. see Block Guy, "Arbitration and Changes in Energy Prices: A Review of ICC Awards with respect to Force Majeure, Indexation, adaptation, Hardship and Take-or-Pay Clauses", *ICC International Court of Arbitration Bulletin*, vol. 20/2, 2009, p. 51s., esp. p. 61.
62. "the value of Natural Gas".
63. See ICC Case no. 13504, *op. cit.* § 114.
64. See Block Guy, "Arbitration and Changes in Energy Prices: A Review of ICC Awards with respect to Force Majeure, Indexation, adaptation, Hardship and Take-or-Pay Clauses", *ICC International Court of Arbitration Bulletin*, vol. 20/2, 2009, p. 51s., esp. p. 59.
65. See Loquin Eric, *Amiable composition en droit comparé et international. Contribution à l'étude du non-droit dans l'arbitrage commercial*. LITEC 1980. E. Loquin says "ardente obligation".
66. Loquin Eric, "Les pouvoirs des arbitres internationaux à la lumière de l'évolution récente du droit de l'arbitrage international", *Journal de Droit International* 1983.293.
67. For a distinction between equity and the power of *amiable composition* see CCI 2093/3100, Clunet 1980. 955-959, obs. Yves Derains "cependant, cet usage de l'équité (as provided for in domestic substantive law) reste enfermé dans un cadre limité défini par la loi elle-même, alors que l'amiable compositeur peut, et parfois, doit recourir à l'équité pour écarter certaines dispositions de la loi". Free translation: "However this usage of fairness (as provided for in domestic substantive law) is within a limited framework defined by law, while the *amiable compositeur* may and sometimes should have recourse to the fairness to disregard some legal provisions".
68. See ICC Case no. 6503 (1990), *ICC Arbitral Awards 1991-1995*, p. 613.
69. See ICC Case no. 3327 (1981), *ICC Arb. Awards 1974-1985*, p. 433.
70. See ICC Case no. 3344 (1981), *ICC Arbitral Awards 1974-1985*, p. 440; *Clunet* 1982.978 s., obs. E. Gaillard.
71. See ICC Case no. 10049 (2003) *UNILEX*; ICC 9704 (2000) *UNILEX*; ICC 7986 (1988), *Journal de Droit International* 2002.1071, comm. Y. Derains.
72. See Gaillard Emmanuel et Savage J., (ed), *Fouchard, Gaillard, Goldman, On International Commercial Arbitration*, Kluwer, 1999, no. 31 s., p. 23 s.
73. See ICC Case no. 3938 (1982), Craig W. L, Park W. W. & Paulsson J, *International Chamber of Commerce Arbitration*, Third Edition, Oceana Publications, p. 52 s.
74. See Loquin Eric, *L'amiable composition en droit comparé*, *op. cit.* esp. no. 600, p. 350.
75. See David. René, *L'arbitrage dans le commerce international*, Economica 1981, no. 376, p. 464.; Mezger. E., 'L'arbitrage commercial et l'ordre public', *Revue Trimestrielle de Droit* Commercial 1948.617.
76. See Peter Wolfgang, & de Cuyper J.-Q., 'Renegotiation of Long term International Agreements and Flexibility: Consideration on the ground of Ghana / Valco Case', *Internatinal Business Law Journal* 1995.775;
77. See ICC Case no. 3267 (1979), *Journal de Droit International* 1980.961, obs. Y. Derains, VII Y.B.Com. Arb. 1982.96;
78. See ICC Case no. 2694 (1977), *ICC Arbitral Awards 1974-1985* p. 320.
79. See ICC Case no. 3327 (1981), *ICC Arbitral Awards 1974-1985*, p. 433; *Journal de Droit International* 1982.971, obs. Y. Derains.
80. See ICC Case no. 4972 (1989), *ICC Arbitral Awards 1986-1990*, p. 380.
81. See CA Paris, (1ère Ch. Suppl), 19 avril 1991, Société Parfums Stern France c. CFFD et autre, *Revue de l'arbitrage* 1991.673, obs. E. Loquin.
82. See C.A. Paris (1ère Ch. Suppl.) 6 mai 1988, Société Unijet, *Revue de l'arbitrage* 1989.83, note E. Loquin
83. See Paris, 1ère Ch., 28 septembre 1976, *JCP* 1978.II.18810, note J. Robert.

84. See Paris, 1ère Ch., 28 septembre 1976, *JCP* 1978.II.18810, note J. Robert, "(...) que c'est seulement en cas d'échec de cette négociation, et en connaissance des solutions proposées, que la Cour dira si la formule qui pourrait éventuellement convenir sur le plan financier modifie les données des contrats en cours et interdit par conséquent au juge de l'imposer."
85. In ICC Case no. 15610, the arbitral tribunal interpreted the LPG Contract, including its hardship Clause according to the law of New York, *Bulletin e-chapter, Extracts from ICC Arbitration in Oil and Gas Disputes*, vol. 25, no. 1, 2014, spec. § 132: "The necessary starting point to the hardship Clause is the interpretation and effect of the LPG's contractual wording under the relevant legal principles of New York law relating to the interpretation of commercial agreements, such as the LPG Contract."
86. See ICC Case no. 8486 (1996), final award (original in German), Journal de Droit *International 1998, no. 4, p. 1047-1052; Yearbook Commercial Arbitration 1999, vol. XXIV a, p.p*. 162-173.
87. See commentary no. 2 under art. 6.2.1. of UNIDROIT Principles on hardship.
88. All these examples are given by ICC Case no. 13898 (2014) § 7, related to art. 11.6 (1) on Price Revision, extract from partial award available in the *ICC Dispute Resolution Library,* www.iccdrl.com.; Martin Timothy A, "ICC Oil and gas Cases in the MENA Region", *ICC International Court of Arbitration Bulletin*, vol. 25 no. 2, 2014 p. 21 s., spec. p. 27.
89. See ICC Case no. 3344 (1981), *Collection of ICC Arbitral Awards, 1974-1985*, p. 440, concerning the substitution and adjustment of indices.
90. See ICC Case no. 15051 (August 2010), Bulletin e-chapter, *Extracts from ICC Arbitration in Oil and Gas Disputes*, vol. 25, no. 2, 2014, p. 40 s.
91. ibid. (§ 362)
92. See § 362 of the award.
93. See ICC Case no. 15051 (august 2010), § 364.
94. See ICC Case no. 15051 (august 2010), § 364.
95. See ICC Case no. 15051 (august 2010), § 366.
96. ibid. § 370 "Thus, the "*bouleversement*" will call for some kind of extreme and drastic change of the system, an exceptionally high yardstick ".
97. See ICC Case no. 15051 (august 2010), § 368.
98. See ICC Case no. 15051 (august 2010), § 370.
99. See ICC Case no. 15051 (august 2010), § 371.
100. See ICC Case no. 15051 (august 2010), § 372.
101. See ICC Case no. 15051 (august 2010), § 372.
102. See ICC Case no. 15051 (august 2010), § 373-375.
103. See ICC Case no. 15051 (august 2010), § 376.
104. See ICC Case no. 15051 (august 2010), § 377.
105. See ICC Case no. 15051 (august 2010), § 391.
106. ibid. § 402.
107. See ICC Case no. 15051 (august 2010), § 409.
108. See ICC Case no. 11265 (2009), *ICC International Court of Arbitration Bulletin*, vol. 20, no. 2.
109. See ICC Case no. 7177 (2004), (extract), *ICC International Court of Arbitration Bulletin* vol. 15, no. 2.
110. ibid. § 138.
111. ibid. § 131.
112. See ICC Case no. 13898 (2014) (extracts), ICC digital library.
113. ibid. § 52.
114. ibid. § 58
115. ibid. § 60.
116. ibid. § 62.
117. See ICC Case no. 15610, Bulletin e-chapter, *Extracts from ICC Arbitration in Oil and Gas Disputes*, vol. 25, no. 1, 2014.
118. Liquified Petroleum Gas.
119. See ICC Case no. 15610, § 62.
120. ibid. § 134.
121. ibid. § 135.

122. ibid. as it stated that "References to the equitable character (of the contract in hardship provision) become relevant as to contractual adjustments after a party has proven severe and unforeseeable hardship".
123. See ICC Case 15610, § 171.
124. ibid. § 170
125. ibid. § 174.
126. See Accaoui Lorfing Pascale, *La renégociation des contrats internationaux*, Bruylant, Collection FEDUCI, 2011, esp. p. 245 s., no. 361 s.
127. See ICC Case no. 7177 (2004), (extract), *ICC International Court of Arbitration Bulletin* vol. 15, no. 2.
128. See ICC Case no. 10021 (2000), *UNILEX*
129. See ICC Case no. 7365 (2004) (final award), (extract), spec. § 8.18, *ICC International Court of Arbitration Bulletin* vol. 15, no. 2, p. 108.
130. See ICC Case no. 13898 (2014) (extracts), *icc digital library*
131. See ICC Case no. 2103 (1972), *Collection of ICC Arbitral Awards 1975-1885,* p. 23; ICC Case no. 5910 (1988), *Collection of ICC Arbitral Awards* 1986 -1990, p. 371.
132. See ICC Case no. 3344 (1981), *Collection of ICC Arbitral Awards 1974-1985*, p. 440 s. esp. p. 443.
133. See ICC Case no. 2291 (1975), *Collection of ICC Arbitral Awards 1974-1985*, p. 274 s. esp. p. 275.
134. See ICC Case no. 2508 (1976), *Collection of ICC Arbitral Awards, 1974-1985*, p. 292 s. esp. p. 294.
135. See ICC Case no. 2478 (1974), *Collection of ICC Arbitral Awards 1974-1985*, p. 233, esp. p. 234.
136. See ICC Case no. 9812 (1999), final award, (extract), *ICC International Court of Arbitration Bulletin*, vol. 20, no. 2, p. 69 s.: "either Party may refer such matter to arbitration under the provisions of Article 15 hereof for decision in accordance with the criteria contains in lit. (a) above".

    See Block Guy, "Arbitration and Changes in Energy Prices: A Review of ICC Awards with respect to Force majeure, Indexation, adaptation, Hardship and Take-or-Pay Clauses", *ICC International Court of Arbitration Bulletin*, vol. 20, no. 2, 2009, p. 51 s., espec. p. 60 s.
137. See ICC Case no. 13898 (2014), final award (extract): "In case the Parties are unable to agree on an equitable revision from the date of serving the said notice within a period of six months the dispute shall be referred to arbitration under Article 22 hereof". *ICC digital* Library; see also ICC Case no. 9812 (1999), final award, *op. cit.*; and ICC Case no. 3344 (1981), *Collection of ICC Arbitral Awards 1974–1985,* Kluwer 1990, p. 440.
138. See Bernardini Piero, "The Renegotiation of the Investment Contract", *ICSID Review—Foreign Investment Law Journal*, vol. 13, no. 2 (1998), pp. 420-421, at p. 422.; Gotanda Yves "*Renegotiation and Adaptation Clauses in Investment Contracts, Revisited*", *Vand. International Journal of Transnational Law*, vol. 36 (2003), p. 1471.
139. See art. 147 of the Libyan Civil Code.
140. *See* art. 171 of the Qatar Civil Code; art. 198 of the Kuwait Civil Code.
141. See art. 147 of the Libyan Civil Code.
142. See art. 249 of the UAE Civil Code; art. 205 of the Jordan Civil Code.
143. See commentary no. 7 "Court measures in case of hardship" under Art. 6.2.3. UNIDROIT Principles.
144. See Girsberger D., and Zapolskis P., "Fundamental Alteration of the Contractual Equilibrium Under Hardship Exemption" *Jurisprudence* 2012, 19 (1), p. 121 -141 ; http://www.mruni.eu/lt/mokslo_darbai/jurisprudencija/ ; Lietuvos respublikos civilinis kodeksas. *Valstybės žinios.* 2000, Nr. 74-2262, su vėlesniais pakeitimais ir papildymais. [*The Civil Code of the Republic of Lithuania. Official Gazette. 2000, No. 74-2262, with further amendments and supplements*]. Baranaukas, E., Zapolskis, P., "The Effect of Change in Circumstances on the Performance of Contract" http://www.mruni.eu/en/mokslo_darbai/jurisprudencija/
145. The actual Article 1091 of the Civil and Commercial Code of Argentina on hardship provides : "Imprevisión. Si en un contrato conmutativo de ejecución diferida o permanente, la prestación a cargo de una de las partes se torna excesivamente onerosa, por una alteración extraordinaria de las circunstancias existentes al tiempo de su celebración, sobrevenida por causas ajenas a las partes y al riesgo asumido por la que es afectada, ésta tiene derecho a plantear extrajudicialmente, o pedir ante un juez, por acción o como excepción, la resolución total o parcial del contrato, o su adecuación. Igual regla se aplica al tercero a quien le han sido conferidos derechos,

o asignadas obligaciones, resultantes del contrato; y al contrato aleatorio si la prestación se torna excesivamente onerosa por causas extrañas a su álea propia" available at http://servicios.infoleg.gob.ar/infolegInternet/anexos/235000-239999/235975/texact.htm

146. Article 1198 of the now repealed Civil Code of Argentina on hardship, available at http://servicios.infoleg.gob.ar/infolegInternet/anexos/105000-109999/109481/texact.htm

147. See ICC Case no. 7177 (2004) (extract), *ICC International Court of Arbitration Bulletin*, vol. 15 no. 2, p. 107.

148. See. Ph. Stoffel-Munck, "La révision du contrat par l'arbitre à la lumière de l'article 1195 du *Code civil*", *Revue de l'arbitrage*, 2017, no. 1, p. 51 s.; J. Heinich, "Acclimater la révision pour imprévision dans les contrats et droit français", *Numéro Spécial, Gazette du palais, Colloque annuel de l'Association Droit et Commerce 2017*, p. 66 s.; see also O. Deshayes, T. Génicon et Y.-M. Laithier, *Réforme du droit des contrats, du régime général et de la preuve des obligations. Commentaire article par article*, 2016, Lexis Nexis, V° art. 1195 ; T. Revet, "Le juge et la révision du contrat", *R.D.C.* 2016.273, no. 16.

149. See art. 249 of the United Arab Emirates Civil Code; Article 205 of the Jordanian Civil Code.

150. See ICC Case no. 10351 (2001), extract from partial award, *ICC International Court of Arbitration Bulletin*, vol. 20, no. 2, 2009, p. 86; also available in the *ICC Dispute Resolution Library*, library.iccwbo.org

151. See ICC Case no. 10351 (2001), § 201 "(...) non sans relever que les parties lui ont expressément reconnu ce pouvoir (...) le Tribunal arbitral ordonne aux parties de négocier la révision du facteur L/C, de sorte que celui-ci continue à remplir son rôle de correction conformément à l'avenant no. 7, nonobstant l'introduction de la nouvelle formule Platt's".

See ICC Case no. 10351 (2001), § 202, freely translated. See also Martin Timothey, "ICC Oil & Gas Cases in the MENA", *ICC Court of Arbitration Bulletin*, Extract vol. 25/2, 2014, p. 21 s. spec. p 27

152. See Article 205 of the Jordanian the Civil Code; Art. 107 (3) of the Algerian Civil Code; Art. 147 (2) of the Egyptian Civil Code; Art. 148 of the Syrian Civil Code; Art. 146 of the Iraqi Civil Code; Art. 117 of the Sudan Law of Civil Transactions; Art. 249 of the United Arab Emirates Civil Code; Art. 147 of the Libyan Civil Code.

153. See Section 388 of the Greek Civil Code.

154. See Bahraini Art. 130 of the Legislative Decree 19/2001 promulgating the Civil Code.

155. See Art.198 of the Kuwaiti Civil Code.

156. See Art. 171 of the Qatari Civil Code.

157. See commentary 7 § 2 on Art. 6.2.3. of UNIDROIT Principles.

158. For example, when legal provisions on hardship provide for the termination of the contract for example.

159. See Timothy Martin, "ICC Oil & Gas Cases in the MENA", *ICC Court of Arbitration Bulletin*, Extract vol. 25/2, 2014, p. 21 s. spec. p. 27).

160. See ICC Case no. 13504 (2007), § 88, in Timothy Martin, "ICC Oil & Gas Cases in the MENA", *ICC Court of Arbitration Bulletin*, Extract vol. 25/2, 2014, p. 21 s.; see Block Guy, *op. cit.* esp. p. 61.

161. See ICC Case no. 13504, § 88, in Martin, Timothy, *op. cit.* p. 21 s ; see Block Guy, *op. cit.* esp. p. 61: "(...) Accordingly, in the absence of a particular provision in the [Contract] as to the meaning of 'the value of Natural Gas', the Arbitral Tribunal considers that this expression should be interpreted as referring to the ordinary market value of gas, and that the market value of gas is to be determined on the basis of prices obtained or obtainable in actual transactions in the various market segments constituting the end user market of the Buyer".

162. See ICC Case no. 13898 (2014), extract from partial award available in the *ICC Dispute Resolution Library*, *www.iccdrl.com.*; see also Martin,Timothy, *op. cit*. esp. p. 27.

163. See ICC Case no. 15610 (2014), Final award, ICC International Court of Arbitration Bulletin vol. 25, no. 1, p. 70s.

164. See Art. 147 of the Libyan Civil Code.

165. See Art. 171 of the Qatar Civil Code; art. 198 of the Kuwait Civil Code.

166. See Art. 147 of the Libyan Civil Code.

167. See Section 388 of the Greek Civil Code *"According to the appreciation of the court"*.

168. See Art. 249 of the United Arab Emirates Civil code; art. 205 of the Jordanian Civil Code.

169. See commentary 7 § 2 on Art. 6.2.3. of UNIDROIT Principles.

170. See ICC Case no. 9812 (1999) in Block Guy, *op. cit.* spec. p. 59, and others arbitral awards examples given by the author.

171. See ICC Case 3344 (1981), *Collection of ICC Arbitral Awards 1974-1985* espec. p. 440. The dispute concerned an indexation clause and the substitution and adjustment of price indices.

172. See ICC Case no. 9812 (1999), *op. cit.* "(...) If within (2) months from the date of the said notice no such agreement has been reached, then (at the request of either Party) the matter shall be referred to an arbitrator/ expert for determination in accordance with the provision (x) ...
In any determination to be made by an arbitrator/expert hereof, such determination shall comply with the intention of the Parties that this Agreement shall not be terminated because of any of the events mentioned in Article . . . hereof, but that it is intended that such adjustments to the existing indices be made or that such substitute indices be used as are necessary so that the adjusted indices or the substitute indices will in effect be as nearly comparable to the effects sought from the original indices as any reliable data then available will allow".

173. See ICC Case no. 10351 (2009), partial award, in MartinTimothy, *op. cit.* espec. p. 27; See also Block Guy, *op. cit.* esp. p. 58.

174. See ICC Case no. 10351 (2009), *op. cit.* § 156-157.

175. See. *Gas Natural Aprovisionamientos SDG, SA v Atlantic LNG Co. of Trinidad and Tobago* 2008, U.S. Dist. LEXIS 69632 WL 4344525 (S.D.N.Y. Sept. 16, 2008)

176. *Op. cit.*

177. See ICC Case no. (2001) (partial award), *ICC International Court of Arbitration Bulletin*, vol. 20, no. 2, 2009, p. 86 s.

178. See ICC Case no. 10351 (2001), § 143.

179. ibid. § 166 s.

180. See ICC Case no. 12936, in Block Guy, *op. cit.* spec. p. 63.

181. ibid. "Whatever the real basis for the determination of the Contract Price may have been, the evidence presented in the course of the proceedings shows that a differential had regularly been included into the price determination. This practice had been adopted right from the beginning and been followed constantly."
"In any event, however, and much more important for the outcome of these arbitration proceedings, the Parties followed from the outset a practice that significantly departed from the contracts they had made in writing. The existence of such practice and the modification of the nature of the [master supply agreement] that resulted therefrom will be analysed below."

182. ibid. "By agreeing to an oral or tacit amendment to their contract, parties are therefore deemed to have simultaneously waived the requirement of form that had been stipulated in their contract (...) For an amendment to a contract to be effective, it is therefore sufficient that evidence regarding the intention of the parties to make an amendment exists. As pointed out above, such intention may be derived from the conduct of the parties subsequent to the conclusion of the contract, and, as regards the present case, there is no doubt that Claimant is prevented by its conduct from relying on such 'modification in writing' clause."

183. ibid. "As a result, the [master supply agreement] had clearly become a framework agreement, fixing certain terms and conditions for sale contracts yet to be made. Without entering into complete sale contracts, there was no obligation for [Respondent] to take off certain quantities of crude oil under the [master supply agreement], failing which it would have to pay a penalty. Accordingly, the termination of this framework agreement (...) could not result in an obligation for [Respondent] to pay penalties."

184. See Crivellaro Antonio, "La révision du contrat dans la pratique de l'arbitrage international", *Revue de l'arbitrage*, 2017 no. 1, p. 69 s., spec. p. 82.

185. See *State of Kuwait v The American Independent Co. (Aminoil)*, (1982), *International Legal Materials*, 1982, p. 1002; see also *Wintershall AC ans Other v Governement of Qatar* (1989), *International Legal Materials* 1989, p. 814; see also *Mobil Oil Iran v Gcvernement of the Islamic Republic of Iran, Iran-US Claims Tribunal*, Collection of Awards, Rep. 3, 1990.

186. See *Superior Overseas Developement Coproration v British Gas Corporation* (1982) 1 Lloyd's Rep 262, 264-265, Court of Appeal before Lord Justice Waller, Lord Justice Donaldson & Lord Justice Ackner.

187. See Roberts Peter, *Gas Sales & Gas Transportation Agreements: Principles & Practice*, Third Edition, Sweet & Maxwell, Thomson Reuters, 2011, p. 191, "the majority opinion of the Court of Appeal was that the adjustment of a price under a price review proposition which was intended to relieve substantial economic hardship should be applied to offset the whole of the economic hardship and not merely the substantial part; at first instance, however, (and in the dissenting judgment in the Court of Appeal) the view was taken that the price adjustment should be such as to remove the substantial element of the hardship but should not remove the hardship altogether."

188. Arbitration clause will state, at least for arbitrator's competence if "any failure ...".

189. See Prujiner Alain, "L'adaptation forcée du contrat par arbitrage" *McGill Law Journal* 1992.428, espec.p. 438.

190. See David Robert, *L'arbitrage dans le commerce international*, Paris, Economica, 1982; de Boisséson, Matthieu, *Le droit français de l'arbitrage : interne et international*, Paris, GLN—éditions, Joly, 1990, p. 185 s. ; Sanders Peter, "L'arbitrage dans les transactions commerciales à long terme", *Rev. Arb.* 1975.83 ; Georges Bernini and H.M. Holtzman, "Les techniques permettant de résoudre les problèmes qui surgissent lors de la formation et de l'exécution des contrats à long terme", *Rev. Arb.* 1975.18.

191. See Paris, 1ère Ch., 28 Septembre 1976, *JCP* 1978.II.18810, note by J. Robert.

192. See ICC Case no. 13898 (2014) (extracts), *op. cit. ICC digital library*

193. See *Gas Natural Aprovisionamientos, SDG, SA v Atlantic LNG Company of Trinidad and Tobago* (2008) WL 4344525 (S.D.N.Y.).

194. See http://newyorkconvention1958.org This site deal with issues related the New York Convention (Guide, Convention, provisions, jurisdictions, case law, *travaux préparatoires)*.

195. Its Article 36 (1) (a) (iii) provides that "(1) Recognition or enforcement of an arbitral award, irrespective of the country in which it was made, may be refused only: *(a)* at the request of the party against whom it is invoked, if that party furnishes to the competent court where recognition or enforcement is sought proof that: (...) (iii) the award deals with a dispute not contemplated by or not falling within the terms of the submission to arbitration, or it contains decisions on matters beyond the scope of the submission to arbitration, provided that, if the decisions on matters submitted to arbitration can be separated from those not so submitted, that part of the award which contains decisions on matters submitted to arbitration may be recognized and enforced (...)".

196. See *Gas Natural Aprovisionamientos, SDG, SA v Atlantic LNG Company of Trinidad and Tobago* (2008) WL 4344525 (S.D.N.Y.).

197. The bold italic is from the author.

198. See *Gas Natural Aprovisionamientos, SDG, SA v Atlantic LNG Company of Trinidad and Tobago* (2008) WL 4344525 (S.D.N.Y.): "Although the liberalized market was foreseen by both sides the real test is whether those developments significantly disrupted the expected relationship between the Contract Price and the value of natural gas".

199. ibid. "Even if deregulation was foreseen, other changes in the market for LNG could be unexpected ones. Indeed, Atlantic itself had argued to the Tribunal that *the impact* of U.S. prices on the Spanish market price of LNG *was unexpected* and satisfied the first precondition of Article 8.5(a)".

200. "To the contrary, the Final Award explicitly describes the requirements of Article 8.5(a), and it then applies them in a separate section labeled "Application of Contract Provisions to the Issues Raised in this Proceeding."

201. ibid. "The Tribunal having made that determination, Article 8.5(a) required it to reach "a fair and equitable revision" of the contract price".

202. *i*bid. "the Tribunal exceeded its powers by imposing a pricing scheme that (...) skewed the original bargain between the parties and effectively rewrote their contract".

203. See Neilson W.A.W., "Adjusments in Long-Term Supply Contracts : the Saga of the Quintette Coal Arbitration", *Canadian Business Law Journal,* 1991.76; Gautier Pierre-Yves, "L'arbitrage Quintette devant les juges de Colombie-Britannique : la clause de hardship: invitation à l'*ultra petita*", *Revue de l'arbitrage*, 1991.611; Prujiner Alain, "L'adaptation forcée du contrat par arbitrage" *McGill Law Journal* 1992.428.

204. Clause 7 was related to *Review Price* and read as follows: "The review shall be made taking into consideration the then prevailing market price for metallurgical coal being supplied and sold to Buyer from major Canadian suppliers under long term contracts and also the quality differential, if any, in comparison with those coals".

205. Clause 8 related to *"Mutual cooperation* : "Both Buyer and Seller recognize that circumstances may arise that could not have been foreseen at the time this contract was entered into. Both parties agree to use their best effort to solve any hardships or difficulties arising from such unforeseeable circumstances in the spirit of mutual good will and cooperation".

206. Clause 9 related to *Inequity Review*: "If any significant change in the metallurgical coal market takes place at any time during the term of the contract either party shall have the right to request a price review. The parties shall discuss the matter in good faith to reach a fair and reasonable adjustment".

207. Arbitration Clause: "All unresolved disputes, controversies or differences between the parties arising out of or in connection with or resulting from this Agreement, or the breach hereof, any failure of the parties to reach agreement with respect to matters provided for herein and all matters of dispute relating to the sale of Coal by Seller to Buyer shall be finally determined by arbitration (...)".

208. Gautier, Pierre-Yves, "L'arbitrage Quintette devant les juges de Colombie-Britannique : la clause de hardship : invitation à l'*ultra petita*", *Revue de l'arbitrage*, 1991.611

209. See Polkinghorne M., "Predicting the Unpredictable: Gas Price Re-Openers", The Paris Energy Series no. 2, June 2011, citing the ECT Paper, Putting A Price on Energy, International Pricing Mechanisms for Oil and gas, ECT 2007, that provides for "Stylized Provisions of a Price Review Clause" p. 155.

Chapter 3

Rules on Force Majeure as Illustrated in Recent Case Law

by Christoph Brunner*

I. INTRODUCTION

In today's highly complex and fragile world, declarations of force majeure have almost become commonplace. Depending on their impact they are even publicly reported. For example, in November 2017, the German chemical company BASF declared force majeure for vitamin A and E products after a fire occurred during the startup of one of its plants in Germany. In July 2018, BASF announced that it partially lifts force majeure.[1]

In March 2018, the Norwegian company Hydro declared force majeure at its Alunorte alumina refinery in Brazil's northern state of Pará following an order by the country's authorities to cut output by 50%.[2] The Brazilian Government ordered Alunorte to operate at half of its capacity because of concerns that severe rainfall in Brazil's northern state of Pará had caused water contamination from the refinery, allegations that Hydro denied.[3]

In April 2018, it was reported that Swiss-based trading and mining giant Glencore will declare force majeure on some aluminum supply, days after the United States sanctioned major supplier Rusal and its major shareholder.[4]

By making the force majeure declarations, the companies claim that their contractual performance obligations are suspended and they are thus not liable for damages, or even that they may be allowed to walk out of the relevant contracts. Yet may BASF, Hydro and Glencore be excused from non-performance due to fire in its own plant (BASF) or acts of public authority (Hydro and Glencore)? The answer primarily depends on the relevant contract including, as the case may be, a force majeure clause, the interpretation of the force majeure clause in conjunction with other relevant clauses and, in addition, the applicable law. In today's commercial practice, most contracts include a force majeure clause. The prevalence of force majeure clauses means that there is only limited scope of application for the relevant domestic law doctrines such as frustration (English law), impossibility of performance (civil law systems) or impracticability (American law). Particularly in international commercial transactions, the result is that in the vast majority of cases it is the force majeure clause, and not the applicable law, which will regulate the legal consequences of events beyond the risk and control of the parties on their contractual obligations.[5]

* Partner, Peter & Partners International Ltd, Switzerland; Titular Professor for Commercial Law and Arbitration, University of Bern.

If well drafted and adjusted to the specific risks and needs of the contracting parties, a force majeure clause may offer greater certainty than that afforded by the relevant doctrines of the applicable law.[6]

However, parties frequently adopt more or less standardised 'boilerplate' language as a force majeure or 'Act of God' clause instead of tailoring force majeure provisions to their actual risks.[7] Considering the often broad and unspecific language of force majeure clauses (including catch-all phrases such as 'any other impediment beyond a party's control'), certainty may again be achieved by interpreting such clauses in a manner consistent with the groups of cases and principles that apply under the force majeure excuse according to general contract principles as reflected in Article 79 CISG[8] and Article 7.1.7 UNIDROIT Principles[9] and which have been established by case law under various legal systems.

Many contractual force majeure clauses, including for example the ICC Force Majeure Clause 1985, the ICC Force Majeure Clause 2003 or the 1999 FIDIC Conditions of Contract, widely correspond with the essential features of the force majeure excuse under general contract principles.[10] Frequently, the groups of cases and principles that have been developed by case law under domestic legal systems are similarly relevant for the force majeure excuse under general principles or essentially congruent contractual force majeure clauses. In comparative law it has been acknowledged for many years that "[t]he test adopted [by Article 79 CISG, Article 7.1.7 UNIDROIT Principles] is one which all legal systems treat as crucial, whether they say so or not, and this explains why the results of decided cases are so often alike".[11]

Against the above background it can be seen that established or persuasive case law, whether rendered under Article 79 CISG, in applying similar doctrines under domestic laws or in interpreting a contractual force majeure clause, is generally of great practical relevance.[12] Whenever appropriate in the light of the terms of a force majeure clause and the applicable law, the clause should be interpreted in a manner consistent with established groups of cases and principles.[13]

Of course, parties may include in their force majeure clause an event which would not, under the applicable law or the general force majeure excuse, afford exemption, or provide for diverging legal consequences. For example, it has been pointed out that the traditional prerequisite of unforeseeability (implicit risk assumption regarding events that are specifically foreseeable at the time of contract conclusion)[14] is no longer a constant in force majeure clauses.[15] With regard to certain defined force majeure events the parties may expressly say that a force majeure event under the contract may be foreseeable. It appears that courts in some states in the United States decline to read an unforeseeability requirement into a force majeure provision that is silent on the question.[16] However, if the force majeure clause is silent about the requirement of unforeseeability, the latter should be implied in accordance with the force majeure excuse under general contract principles, unless other elements or rules of contract interpretation clearly suggest otherwise.[17]

II. THE FORCE MAJEURE EXCUSE AS A GENERAL PRINCIPLE OF LAW

II.A. Short overview of the various approaches under domestic law: impossibility of performance, frustration of contract, impracticability

II.A.1. Impossibility of performance

Under the traditional doctrine of impossibility of performance, the obligor is released from its contractual duty to perform if the impossibility occurred after formation of the contract and cannot be attributed to any kind of fault of the obligor, i.e. wilful or negligent action or omission causing impossibility.[18] Not only objective impossibility (neither the obligor nor anybody else is able to perform), but also subjective impossibility (the obligor is unable to perform, but others could perform) release the non-performing obligor, provided, however, that the obligor is not at fault, or even without fault, that no extension of liability applies, either to impediments caused by fortuitous events when the obligor was in default (*mora debitoris*) or to impediments for which the obligor has contractually assumed the risk. The concept of impossibility includes situations of physical (absolute) impossibility, e.g. where specific goods identified to a sales contract are destroyed as a result of an intervention of third parties or a natural disaster. It also covers cases of so-called "legal impossibility", e.g. where the object of performance is subjected to confiscation, expropriation, embargos, export or import restrictions or where performance is otherwise rendered impossible by an act of public authority, as well as economic impossibility (impracticability), i.e. cases of (extreme) economic hardship rendering performance "excessively or unreasonably onerous".[19]

II.A.2. Frustration of contract

Contrary to civil law, in English common law the obligor's liability does not depend on fault. The doctrine of frustration was established in 1863 in *Taylor v Caldwell*[20] to mitigate the rigour of the common law's insistence on literal performance of absolute promises. Frustration of contract has been defined as follows: "The doctrine of frustration operates to discharge a contract where, after the formation of the contract, something occurs which renders performance of the contract impossible, illegal, or something radically different from that which was in the contemplation of the parties at the time of entry into the contract."[21] It is emphasised that the scope of the doctrine is narrow: frustration is not to be invoked lightly to relieve contracting parties of the normal consequences of imprudent commercial bargains.

Under English law a main advantage of a force majeure clause is said to consist in the degree of remedial flexibility which it affords, which is in stark contrast with the rigid and drastic consequences of the finding that a contract has been frustrated, where the contract is immediately and automatically brought to an end, irrespective of the wishes of the parties.[22]

II.A.3. Impracticability

As regards the standard adopted in the US, *Restatement (Second) of Contracts—§ 261. Discharge by Supervening Impracticability states* the general principle under which a party's obligation may be discharged due to impracticability: "Where, after a contract is made, a party's performance is made impracticable without his fault by the occurrence of an event the non-occurrence of which was a basic assumption on which the contract was made, his duty to render that performance is discharged, unless the language or the circumstances indicate the contrary." The doctrine of impracticability is based on the central inquiry whether the non-occurrence of the circumstance (i.e. the impediment to performance) was a "basic assumption on which the contract was made". Insofar, the decisive question is to determine which party assumed the relevant risk. Moreover, the term 'impracticability' has deliberately been preferred to the term 'impossibility' on the grounds that the latter may be understood to be limited to situations of absolute impossibility or may not be appropriate as an all-embracing term to describe the required extent of the impediment to performance. Generally there is a significant convergence of the requirements of the exemptions under American law and the force majeure (and hardship exemption) under general contract principles, making the consideration of American case law also meaningful for determining their content.[23]

II.B. The force majeure excuse under the CISG, the UNIDROIT Principles and contractual force majeure clauses

A comparative law analysis shows that under all major contract laws an obligor may be excused in one way or another if non-performance is brought about by a force majeure event. While the relevant requirements vary from one system to another, in substance the differences appear to be only nominal in nature. The force majeure exemption (excuse due to an impediment beyond the obligor's risk and control) under Article 79 CISG and Article 7.1.7 UNIDROIT Principles has overcome these differences and reflects a good digest of the decisive requirements.

The force majeure excuse under general contract principles contains the following requirements:[24]

1. The obligor did not assume the risk of the occurrence of the impediment, in particular, it could not reasonably be expected to have taken the impediment into account at the time of conclusion of the contract (no explicit or implicit risk assumption); and
2. The impediment was beyond the obligor's (typical) sphere of control; and
3. The non-performance was caused by the impediment; and
4. The impediment or its consequences could not reasonably have been avoided or overcome.

The force majeure excuse was explicitly recognised as a general principle of law by the Iran-United States Claims Tribunal.[25]

It may be presumed that the force majeure excuse as reflected in Article 79 CISG was also influenced by contractual force majeure clauses existing at the time.[26] Typical force majeure clauses which are regularly inserted as boilerplate clauses in international commercial contracts are essentially in line with Article 79 CISG/Article 7.1.7 UNIDROIT Principles. In particular, the ICC Force Majeure Clause 1985 is based on the general force majeure formula corresponding to Article 79(1) CISG.[27] It also includes an illustrative list of force majeure events and provides for the effects of grounds of relief in a somewhat more detailed manner.[28] The ICC Force Majeure Clause 2003 similarly includes a general force majeure formula and a list of events, the occurrence of which alters the evidential balance in favour of the party invoking the clause.[29] The general formula triggering the consequences of force majeure set out in paragraph 1 of the Clause includes within it elements of the previous ICC Force Majeure Clause 1985, Article 79 CISG, Article 8:108 PECL and Article 7.1.7 PECL.[30]

III. SALIENT FEATURES OF THE FORCE MAJEURE EXCUSE AS ILLUSTRATED BY RECENT CASE LAW

The cases discussed below have been selected to address a few particular issues of interest; they are not intended to be an exhaustive summary of all recent cases on force majeure.

III.A. Typical sphere of control of the obligor—responsibility for its own organization and the measures to be taken to perform the contract

III.A.1. Introduction

A primary aspect of the obligor's typical sphere of control is the proper and careful organisation of its business and the necessary measures for the proper performance of the contract. In general, only 'external' impediments over which the obligor has no influence can excuse the obligor. Thus, 'internal' impediments to performance which are caused by 'intra-firm' or 'production process-related' events relating to an ordinary preparation, organisation and implementation of the measures that are necessary for effecting performance belong to the sphere of control of the obligor.[31] The obligor must organise its business in an orderly manner. In commercial dealings it may generally be expected that each party organises its firm so as to avoid or overcome events which may disrupt the ordinary function of the firm, regardless of whether such events are specifically unforeseeable or whether the event occurs without the fault of the obligor or its personnel. This principle is illustrated by *Great Elephant Corp v Trafigura Beheer BV (The Crudesky)* (III.A.2. below). However, extraordinary tortious or criminal acts (so-called excess acts) such as acts of sabotage (but not occasional thefts), which lead to impediments to performance, will normally be considered beyond the obligor's sphere of control.[32]

The above principles are also relevant to evaluate whether *new* risks such as *cyber-attacks* may exempt a party based on force majeure.[33] In particular, a party who has suffered from a cyber security incident is unlikely to be protected if the incident was brought about by its own failings, such as not adhering to its own IT security policies or industry standards or its non-compliance with agreed IT security in the contract itself. The required measure of control with regard to IT issues may also depend on the nature of the parties' businesses and the purpose of the contract. The more crucial technology is to the relevant party's business, the less likely it is that an attack or accident on such infrastructure may be considered beyond its reasonable control.[34]

III.A.2. *Great Elephant Corp. v Trafigura Beheer BV (The Crudesky)*[35]

The dispute involved a chain of sale contracts of Nigerian crude oil. In breach of local regulations, Total, the operator of the Akpo oil terminal in Nigeria, commenced the loading of the vessel *Crudesky* without the presence of a representative of the Nigerian Oil Ministry because its employees thought that the irregular loading had been authorised. This led to the vessel being detained by the Nigerian authorities for a month and a half, only being released upon payment by Total of a fine of USD 12 million. The buyers at the top of the chain incurred considerable demurrage as a result of the delay and sought to pass their losses down the chain. The Court of Appeal decided, reversing the Commercial Court's judgment, that force majeure clauses in the sale contracts did not protect the sellers of the cargo because the events leading to the breaches of contract were not beyond the control of Total, to whom the sellers in the chain had delegated the performance of their obligation under the sale contracts to load the cargo.[36]

The Court found that Total had failed to comply with the applicable Terminal Procedure Guide, which provided for the DPR (Nigerian Department of Petroleum Resources) to sign the inwards clearance certificate of the vessel on arrival and before loading commenced. In practice, this had become a requirement for the DPR in Lagos to grant clearance through the official channel of communication with Total in Lagos, which Total at Lagos did not seek until 1 September, after loading had already commenced. Under these circumstances, Total had opted to take a riskier route via their Terminal representative instead of going through the official channel in Lagos. This was an action which was within Total's control.[37] The Court stated in particular:[38]

> It goes without saying that a force majeure clause must be construed in accordance with its own terms; it also need hardly be emphasised (a) that it is an exceptions clause and any ambiguity must be resolved against the party seeking to rely on it and (b) that the concept of being "beyond [a corporate person's] control" sets a comparatively high hurdle since corporations usually do have a significant measure of control over their own business, see (...). All that said, it is necessary to look at the individual clauses.

III.B. Impediment beyond the typical sphere of risk and control of the obligor: procurement of generic goods

III.B.1. Introduction

The seller of generic goods bears the procurement risk. Any subsequent "impediments" to performance will not affect the seller's obligation to procure generic goods inasmuch as the seller still has the possibility to select other goods of the relevant category, i.e. as long as the goods of the relevant type are available on the market or from the sources identified in the contract. The extent of the procurement risk depends on whether the seller has an unlimited obligation to procure under the contract or only a restricted one; that is, it depends on how the sources of performance by which the seller is to perform have been determined in the contract (e.g., global market, locally restricted market, particular manufacturer or supplier, particular stock, etc.) Unless indicated otherwise in the contract, the seller of generic goods must procure the goods on the (worldwide) market. The seller remains obligated to procure the goods at least as long as goods of that type of goods exist. By contrast, the procurement risk is restricted if the contract limits the seller's delivery obligation to one or several source(s) of supply.[39] The question as to whether or to what extent the procurement risk is contractually limited is a typical area of dispute. A case in point is the Award in ICC Case 19566 of 2014 (III.B.2. below).

III.B.2. *Global Tungsten & Powders Corp. v Largo Resources, Ltd*, Award in ICC Case 19566 of 2014[40]

The Parties' claims arose out of a Supply Agreement (Agreement) and a Letter of Intent. As set out in the Preamble to the Agreement, "Seller [Largo] agrees to sell, and Buyer [GTP] agrees to purchase" tungsten[41] concentrate meeting certain specifications and derived from certain sources, "on the (...) terms and conditions set out in the Agreement". According to Section 1 of the Agreement, the "Initial Term" of the Agreement was from 1 July 2011 to 30 October 2015, with the possibility of a two-year extension. The Agreement was governed by the law of Pennsylvania and, because the Agreement is a sales contract, the Uniform Commercial Code (UCC), as adopted in Pennsylvania.

It was undisputed that Largo did not deliver the Monthly Minimum quantities of tungsten concentrate provided for under the Agreement. Largo sought to limit its obligations to GTP in this respect by arguing that the Agreement should be interpreted as requiring supply only from Currais Novos. In addition, Largo relied among others on force majeure. GTP contended that the plain language of the Agreement did not limit Largo's supply obligation to "Material" sourced from Currais Novos. The following contract clauses were considered:[42]

> [Second] "WHEREAS" clause of the Preamble (...): "[Largo] agrees to sell, and [GTP] agrees to purchase the Material (as defined below) derived from the mine site, the tailings described on (sic) Exh. A attached hereto *or from such other sources* as may be approved in writing by [GTP], all on the following terms and conditions..." (emphasis added) (...)
>
> [F]irst paragraph of Section 3 of the Agreement (...): "[Largo] commits to ship Material to [GTP] a minimum per month of metric ton units of WO3 contained ('mtu's') equal to the Monthly Minimum (defined below) in accordance with purchase orders issued by [GTP] (sic)." (...)
>
> Section 2 defines Material as "Wolframite, Ferberite, Huebnerite or Scheelite tungsten ore concentrate of Brazilian Processing Facility origin or equivalent non-U.S. Defense Department Logistic Agency (DLA) origin material, as may be mutually agreed in writing in advance, in accordance with [GTP's] specification MT02000-04A attached as Exh. B hereto ('WO3' or the 'Material').

The Arbitral Tribunal found in particular:

> 86. We agree with Largo. We find that its obligations to supply tungsten concentrate to GTP under the Agreement were inextricably tied to production at Currais Novos.
>
> 87. In particular, we fail to see how GTP could reasonably claim that Largo was under an obligation to supply Material from any source other than the mine site at Currais Novos when GTP itself never "approved" (as set out in the Preamble) or "agreed" (as per Section 2 and Section 3, 3rd paragraph) or "consent[ed]" (Section 3, 5th paragraph) to the supply of alternatively-sourced Material, as required by the Agreement. (...)
>
> 88. There is no evidence that GTP ever demanded that Largo supply Material from any other source than Currais Novos, or that it indicated to Largo that it (Largo) was required to do so to satisfy its obligations under the Agreement. This was acknowledged by Dr. Laursen. (Tr. 446, 448, 451). It was also acknowledged by GTP's Counsel. (Tr. 24-25, 37-38). To the contrary, the Parties' course of

performance indicates clearly that they both intended that the Material to be supplied under the Agreement was to be sourced from Currais Novos. (...)

91. But there is more here than mere course of performance, which could be said to provide ex post facto confirmation of the Parties' intentions under the Agreement. Support for the understanding of the Parties' intentions, as indicated by their conduct, is found as well in the text of the Agreement itself. (...)

94. (...) Taking "[t]he whole instrument ... together" (Hart v Arnold, 884 A.2d at 332], that is, interpreting the Agreement "as a whole, giving effect to all of its provisions" (In re Spring Ford Indus., Inc., 338 B.R. 255, 262 (E.D. Pa. 2006)), we are of the view that Largo's argument as to the proper interpretation concerning the source of Material to be supplied to GTP (...) is the more compelling. (...)

95. We also agree with Largo that the terms of Section 3, 5th paragraph, provide a further helpful means of understanding Section 2 and of interpreting the Agreement "as a whole". If, as GTP claims, Largo's supply obligations were to supply GTP tungsten concentrate of any origin whatsoever, then the option offered to Largo in Section 3 to source material from elsewhere, and the requirement that GTP expressly consent to this beforehand, would be meaningless.

96. Finally, even if GTP were correct regarding the Parties' intentions as reflected in the particular terms of the Agreement on which GTP relies -- primarily the Preamble and Sections 2 and 3 -- the fact remains that the Agreement also requires that certain defined steps be taken before Largo's supply obligations could be expanded either to permit or to require Largo to supply GTP tungsten concentrate from sources other than Currais Novos. As previously discussed, no such steps were ever taken by either Party and Largo was, accordingly, under no such obligation.

97. In sum, we find that the text of the Agreement supports Largo's interpretation of its obligations as concerns the source of Material to be supplied to GTP. We consider that the Parties' intent in this regard is further borne out by their course of actual performance, which, far from contradicting the terms of the Agreement, helps to explain those terms and provides a compelling indication of what the Parties intended the Agreement to mean.

Largo's force majeure excuse was based on Section 15 of the Agreement (the force majeure clause). Largo argued that, since the end of October 2012, its water supplies at Currais Novos had been depleted because of an unprecedented drought in the Currais Novos area, as a result of which the operation of the plant and the production of tungsten concentrate had been suspended. Largo contended that, since that date, it was excused from its delivery obligations under the Agreement because the drought was an 'act of God' that had prevented or hindered it from delivering any tungsten concentrate under that Agreement.

GTP accepted that the northeastern area of Brazil (including Currais Novos) had been affected by a severe drought, but contended that Section 15 did not relieve Largo from its performance obligations because of a number of reasons, including in particular (i) the alleged non-restriction of Largo's supply obligations to Currais Novos, so that the drought in northeastern Brazil would have been irrelevant (as seen above, that argument was rejected by the Tribunal); (ii) Largo had never overcome the unrelated production issues arising out of the failure of the concentrators to perform as expected or intended, so that even if there had been no drought, Largo would have been unable to meet its supply obligations under the Agreement (this is a causation issue which will be discussed below at III.G.2.); (iii) Largo had failed to demonstrate that it had insufficient water available to it to enable it to produce the agreed monthly quantities of tungsten concentrate (this issue relates to the non-performing party's duty to overcome the impediment, discussed below at III.E.3.)

III.C. Impediment beyond the typical sphere of risk and control of the obligor: performance becomes more burdensome versus hardship

III.C.1. Introduction

The risk that performance may become more burdensome, even if not foreseeable at the time of contract conclusion, in principle falls into the obligor's sphere of risk and control. Under Article 79 CISG, the risk that the market price for the goods sold drops after conclusion of the contract or that the goods otherwise lose their value is borne by the buyer; the risk of a price increase or an increase in the costs of procurement or manufacture is borne by the seller.[43] Generally, a party is liable for its own financial ability to perform; it guarantees its financial ability and cannot be excused because of lack of money. In particular, the *seller* is not exempted if it cannot acquire the goods or materials to manufacture them because a business loan has been terminated, even if without its fault. An exemption is only possible if, because of unforeseeable circumstances, a very extraordinary depreciation of money occurs, or the seller's delivery, acquisition or production costs increase to such an extent that a case of economic impossibility has occurred.[44] The *buyer's* sphere of control also includes its having money to pay the purchase price. Liquidity issues are no ground for exemption. It further falls into the buyer's sphere of control to ensure that it has the necessary foreign currencies to pay the purchase price. The buyer can be exempted only if payment in the foreign currency is forbidden due to an act of state and payment is not possible by any other means, or would be unreasonable according to good faith.[45] Both *Tandrin Aviation Holdings Ltd v Aero Toy Store LLC and another* and ICC Case 18769 of 2014 (*Cessna v Gulf Jet*) illustrate the principle that an economic downturn may not constitute a force majeure event (III.C.2. and III.C.3. below.)

However, under Article 79 CISG (and the force majeure excuse under general principles), it should be assumed along with the prevailing view expressed by legal commentators that not only factual, but also economic impediments to the obligation to perform may have an exemptive effect for the obligor, provided that said impediments are exceptionally serious.[46] Where the line between such situations and situations of hardship or economic impossibility (limit of sacrifice) is to be drawn must be decided on a case-by-case basis taking into account all relevant circumstances including any risk assumption by the obligor (e.g. as a result of a speculative transaction).[47] Applying an abstract guideline for the limits of reasonability (hardship threshold) likely represents a practical need, but must not prevent an assessment taking all relevant circumstances of the individual case into consideration.[48] A case in point where the Arbitral Tribunal granted relief under Article 79 CISG, interpreted or supplemented in light of the hardship rules of Articles 6.2.1 to 6.2.3 UNIDROIT Principles, is the Award in ICC Case 16369 of 2011, *Swiss buyer v Kosovo seller* (III.C.4 below).

III.C.2. *Tandrin Aviation Holdings Ltd v Aero Toy Store LLC* and another[49]

The case involved the sale by Tandrin to ATS of an executive jet aircraft for USD 31.75 million. ATS paid a USD 3 million deposit but failed to take delivery of the aircraft or pay the residual purchase price. Due to a severe deterioration in the global economic situation, the buyer was unable to obtain financing to enable it to proceed with the purchase. The buyer argued that the "unanticipated, unforeseeable and cataclysmic downward spiral of the world's financial markets" fell within the force majeure clause;[50] therefore it did not have to honour the sale agreement. The Court rejected the argument:

> It is well established under English law that a change in economic/market circumstances, affecting the profitability of a contract or the ease with which the parties' obligations can be performed, is not regarded as being a force majeure event. Thus a failure of performance due to the provision of insufficient financial resources has been held not to amount to force majeure—see The Concadoro [1916] 2 AC 19; and likewise a rise in cost or expense—see *Brauer & Co (GB) Ltd v James Clark (Brush Materials) Ltd* [1952] 2 All ER 497, [1952] 2 Lloyd's Rep 147, [1952] 2 TLR 349.

The buyer further pointed to the contract wording of the force majeure clause and argued that the change in economic situation was "any other cause beyond the seller's reasonable control", and that this should also apply to causes beyond the buyer's control. In rejecting this argument, the court considered *inter alia* that there was not even a remote connection in any of the specific examples of force majeure to economic downturn, market circumstances or the financing of the deal. It is likely that the court's decision would have been the same if the clause had been construed to be "mutual" and had referred to "any other cause beyond either party's reasonable control".[51]

III.C.3. *Cessna Finance Corporation v Gulf Jet LLC* (Final Award), ICC Case 18769 of 2014[52]

The arbitration was brought by the Cessna Finance Corporation, an American corporation, for amounts due and owing and for damages in respect of the breach of two aircraft lease agreements (the Leases) between Cessna and Gulf Jet LLC, a Dubai-based company incorporated under the laws of the United Arab Emirates. Cessna alleged that Gulf Jet defaulted on its payment obligations under the Leases which eventually led to the repossession and resale of the aircraft by Cessna in accordance with the terms of the Leases. Following the sale of the two aircrafts, Cessna claimed a total of USD 8.33 million in respect of both Leases plus additional interest and costs. Cessna also claimed against two UAE citizens as guarantors.

Gulf Jet had ceased making payments under each of the two Leases and argued that circumstances of economic hardship at that time gave rise to a different defence negating the consequence of non-payment as a breach. Gulf Jet asserted that the payment obligations under the Lease became impossible to perform by reason of the severe economic crisis which occurred in Dubai following the economic downturn commencing in September 2008. It submitted that for reasons beyond its control, it became impossible for Gulf Jet to operate and exploit the use of the leased Cessna jets solely by reason of the economic crisis in the Emirate of Dubai. Gulf Jet asserted that under the Laws of the Emirate of Dubai, a judge "will have the option to endorse the discontinuity of the lease or reduce the burden to a reasonable extent". Gulf Jet also characterised this defence as the "occurrence of a force majeure being the economic crisis".

The Sole Arbitrator rejected Gulf Jet's submissions. He held in particular:

> 133. First, despite the significant reliance by Gulf Jet on a law of the United Arab Emirates or a law of the Emirate of Dubai, none was identified for appropriate review and consideration to establish the applicability of such a broad concept of force majeure to the Leases in this case. (...)
>
> 134. Second, and more importantly, the laws of the Emirate of Dubai or the United Arab Emirates simply do not apply to this dispute. The Leases are governed by the laws of the State of Kansas in the United States of America. (...)
>
> 135. Third, as submitted by the Claimant, the Leases and the Guarantees expressly provide that force majeure is no excuse for non-performance. Paragraph 15 of each Lease provides in part as follows:
>
> > " ... Lessee acknowledges and agrees that its obligation to pay any sums due to OWNER hereunder shall not be discharged, diminished or otherwise affected by any force majeure, and shall not be deemed paid unless and until such sums are actually and fully received by OWNER in United States dollars in the United States." (emphasis added)
>
> Therefore, by its own agreement, Gulf Jet is precluded from raising and relying on a force majeure event.
>
> 136. Fourth, even if there was a form of force majeure clause in the Leases, the application of Kansas law would likely preclude the extension of any standard force majeure clause to include risks of changing economic or market conditions of the type described and relied upon by Gulf Jet. (...)
>
> 137. (...) Indeed, Cessna assumed no risks associated with a force majeure clause as no such clause was included in the Leases. No such clause can be implied as a matter of Kansas law as force majeure was expressly excluded. (...)

III.C.4. *Buyer (Switzerland) v Seller (Kosovo)*, Final Award, ICC Case 16369 of 2011[53]

The Kosovo Seller (which was a socially-owned enterprise, at the time put under the administration of a UN agency) entered into a contract for the supply of a commodity with the Swiss Buyer. The contract provided for several deliveries and a purchase price based on a price formula with fixed parameters and variables. It was governed by "the substantive law of Switzerland". The CISG applied as part of Swiss law.

Twenty-one days after the contract was signed, Buyer communicated the date on which the first shipment was to be loaded; also on that day, the price of the commodity collapsed. As a consequence of the collapse, which continued over a period of time, the formula agreed in the contract led to a purchase price that was minimal and even negative in respect of certain deliveries. Seller failed to deliver any of the agreed quantities, and Buyer could not perform under the onward sale contract with Second Buyer.[54]

The Sole Arbitrator rejected the view that the contractual force majeure clause could provide exemptive relief to the Seller, especially on the ground that the force majeure clause's catch-all phrase "or any other cause whatsoever beyond the control of Seller or Buyer whether of the foregoing nature or not" should be limited to events *ejusdem generis* with those previously enumerated.[55]

However, the Sole Arbitrator then went on and essentially considered that by means of interpretation or gap-filling, Article 79 CISG should be interpreted in light of the hardship rules of Articles 6.2.1 to 6.2.3 UNIDROIT Principles.[56] In finding that the prerequisites of hardship are met, he stated:[57]

> [114] The agreed purchase price according to Clause 6 of the Contract was determined by reference to the [Exchange]. Of the basis price certain deductions (Treatment Charge and Penalties) were to be made (...). On the basis of the agreed formula (price parameters minus deductions) the average contract price to be paid by the Claimant would have been (...). During the month preceding the Contract (when the Parties presumably negotiated and the Contract was drafted), specialized trade media reported (i) that stored reserves were decreasing; (ii) that numerous sources of supply were no longer available; (iii) that the outlook for the following years targeted [a higher sum]. And indeed the average price for the month before the Contract was higher than the August price.
>
> [115] When the Contract was signed this was the general outlook. The price was comparatively low, yet applying the contractual purchase price formula the contractual quantity would still have yielded [a certain amount].
>
> [116] From that moment on, the market almost collapsed. And when the Claimant three weeks after the conclusion of the Contract instructed the Respondent to prepare for the loading of the first shipment this was against the background of a historic low in the commodity's price. Applying the contractual purchase price formula, the result was negative. To say that the performance the Respondent was to receive had diminished would be putting it exceedingly mildly.
>
> [117] Moreover, the short-term outlook continued to be bleak: based on the Claimant's submissions, the price continued to be negative in the following two months and would have been again negative four months later.
>
> [118] The remaining requirements of Art. 6.2.2 are also met. The market breakdown occurred after the conclusion of the contract (a). It could, in view of the situation and the expectations as described supra, not reasonably have been taken into account by the Respondent (b). It was beyond the control of the Respondent (c).
>
> [119] At this point the question arises as to whether the risk of the market breakdown was not assumed by the Respondent (Art. 6.2.2(d)). Indeed, where parties to a contract of sale for delivery over a period of time agree on the market price at any point in time the seller may well be deemed to have assumed even the risk of not receiving any consideration in return for the goods sold. Exchange rates may collapse without that collapse qualifying as hardship. Yet the case at hand is different. The price formula agreed in Clause 6 with certain fixed parameters and a number of variables, including increases and decreases of the treatment charge in function of above-average and below-average settlement prices in the Tribunal's view reflects the Parties' understanding that market shocks were not to be assumed by either one of them but rather constituted a shared risk.

The Sole Arbitrator concluded "that adaptation (rather than termination) is both reasonable" and "fair" and determined, in accordance with a proposal made by the Buyer responding to the Tribunal's additional queries, that "X per metric ton was the relevant minimum basis for the purposes of the contractual price formula according to Clause 6 of the Contract."[58]

III.D. Unforeseeable impediment

III.D.1. Introduction

In general, the obligor can only be exempted if the impediment to performance was not foreseeable at the time of contract conclusion and it, or its consequences, could not be avoided or overcome.[59] The requirement of "foreseeability" is to be seen in the context of risk allocation. If the impediment was specifically foreseeable at the time of contracting, it is presumed that the obligor has assumed the risk of its occurrence. This presumption may be rebutted if the circumstances clearly suggest that the obligor has not assumed the relevant risk. In particular, it must be assessed whether the extent and time of the impediment to performance was specifically foreseeable.[60] The issue is illustrated by the 2006 award in a case administered by the Centro de Arbitraje de México (CAM) (III.D.2. below).

III.D.2. CAM Award of 2006 *(El Niño)*[61]

A Mexican grower (respondent) and a US distributor (claimant) concluded in September 2004 a one-year exclusive agreement according to which respondent undertook to produce specific quantities of squash and cucumbers and to provide them to claimant on an exclusive basis, while claimant had to distribute the goods on the Californian market against a commission. The contract included a choice of law in favour of the UNIDROIT Principles as the applicable substantive law. The US distributor claimed damages as a result of the Mexican grower's failure to provide the goods. The latter objected that its failure to deliver the goods was due to the destruction of the crops by a series of extraordinarily heavy rainstorms and flooding caused by the meteorological phenomenon known as *El Niño*. According to respondent, these events amounted to a case of force majeure and/or hardship and therefore any liability on its part was excluded.

On the Mexican grower's defence that the rainstorms and flooding which destroyed the crops amounted to a case of force majeure, the arbitral tribunal held that the meteorological events in question did not meet the requirement set out in Article 7.1.7(1) UNIDROIT Principles defining force majeure, i.e. that the non-performing party could not reasonably be expected to have taken the impediment into account at the time of the conclusion of the contract. While the rainstorms and flooding were undoubtedly beyond respondent's control, according to the tribunal, their occurrence could not be considered unforeseeable by respondent which in the course of its long-standing activity in the agricultural sector had already several times experienced similar events.

This award may be criticized on the basis that it does not seem to discuss whether the grower had to provide the products *only out of its own production*. The limitation of the grower's procurement obligation to deliver crop only from its own production may imply that it did not assume the risk of exceptional weather conditions affecting its own crop, irrespective of the question of foreseeability. In contrast to wholesalers or large dealers (as sellers), growers/producers are generally not in a better position than buyers to assume the risk of extreme weather conditions.[62] Moreover, the interest of growers/manufacturers to sell out of their own production, without assuming the risk of adverse weather conditions (even if generally foreseeable), at least to the extent that their effects cannot be reasonably avoided or overcome, and to limit their procurement risk accordingly, may be self-evident from the circumstances.

III.E. Insurmountable impediments (could not have been overcome)

III.E.1. Introduction

The obligor must take measures reasonable and appropriate under the circumstances to avoid or overcome the impediment or its consequences as far as possible. For example, if the transportation route is closed in a manner that was not foreseeable (e.g. because of early pack ice), the obligor must divert the goods if at all possible and bear the additional costs as long as the performance of his obligations does not become excessively onerous.[63]

Of particular interest are the Suez Canal cases: as a result of the closing of the Suez Canal due to hostilities in the Middle East in 1956 and again in 1967, ocean carriers and sellers (on CIF terms) were forced to use the longer and more costly route around the Cape of Good Hope. Both American and English courts rejected the carriers' and sellers' argument that they were excused, on the grounds that carriage through the Suez Canal was not intended to be an exclusive method of performance, and that carriage around the Cape of Good Hope was an alternative way of performing. In the Suez Canal cases, the increase in cost by taking the route around the Cape of Good Hope did not amount to hardship, and was not held to frustrate the contract.[64]

An impediment can be overcome if the obligor is capable of employing a commercially reasonable substitute for the performance (e.g. generic goods which are only marginally different) or the performance modality (e.g. other packaging, other transport route, other place of delivery, etc.) the obligor owes.[65] The problem is illustrated by the Paris Chamber of Arbitration Case 3150 of 2011 (III.E.3. below) and also by the Award in ICC Case 19566, *Global Tungsten & Powders Corp. v Largo Resources, Ltd* (III.E.3. below).

If it is at issue whether the non-performing party may rely on an act of public authority as an excuse for non-performance, the relevant act should principally be considered as a factual element under the contract in dispute and the applicable doctrine of excuse. This means that a legal impediment may have to be overcome.[66] The Arbitral Award of the Permanent Court of Arbitration of 2009 in *Granuco S.A.L. v The Food and Agricultural Organization of the United Nations* is an illustration (III.E.4. below).

III.E.2. Award in CAP Case No. 3150 of 2011[67]

The French Seller entered into two sale and purchase contracts with the German Buyer for the sale of "French rapeseed conventional 00". The contracts were governed by French law. They required that the rapeseed meet the requirements of German law on the production of sustainable biofuels (*Biokraftstoff-Nachhaltigkeitsverordnung*) and bioliquids (*Biomassestrom-Nachhaltigkeitsverordnung*). The German legislation referred to in the contracts constituted the transposition of the 2009 European Directive on the promotion of the use of energy from renewable sources (ENR Directive) in Germany. The Seller was thus contractually obliged to provide a sustainability certificate in accordance with the German legislation transposing the ENR Directive. The Seller did not provide such certificate, claiming force majeure because at the relevant time the ENR Directive had not been transposed in France and there was no French body authorised to issue sustainability certificates. The Tribunal found no force majeure, considering that it was established that two other French operators had obtained certificates complying with German legislation and valid in Germany from a German body in the relevant period. However, the Tribunal considered that the probative value of the certificates in respect of French goods obtained by others was "questionable" and concluded that according to French law, the Seller breached (only) an accessory, rather than essential contractual obligation.[68]

III.E.3. *Global Tungsten & Powders Corp. v Largo Resources, Ltd*, Award in ICC Case 19566 of 2014[69]

As seen above (III.B.2.), GTP asserted that Largo had failed to demonstrate that as a result of the unprecedented drought in the Currais Novos area it had insufficient water available to enable it to produce the agreed monthly quantities of tungsten concentrate. The issue as to whether Largo would have been in a position to reasonably overcome the impediment (drought) was addressed by the Arbitral Tribunal as follows:[70]

The availability of water at Currais Novos

153. In addressing this issue, the Tribunal begins with an observation as to the ambit of Section 15 [the force majeure clause[71]]. While the language of that section, is in our judgment, broad enough to cover partial as well as total prevention of performance, it is for the affected party (which seeks to avail itself of the plea of force majeure as an excuse for non-performance) to establish on the evidence either that it was totally prevented from performing, or that it was partially prevented from performing, by the force majeure event on which it relies. Thus, if it Claims only to have been partially prevented from performing, it is for the affected party to establish the extent to which it was affected. However, in this case, Largo has not asserted that at any time it was partially prevented from performing. It has maintained simply that, by reason of the drought, it is excused from performance since October 2012. In other words, its claim is that the drought has totally prevented it from performing its supply obligations under the Agreement since that date. There is, therefore, no room in this case for a finding of partial prevention.

154. One of the ways in which Largo thought that it might be able to address the problem caused by the drought was by installing a new water reticulation System. (...)

165. The brand new water reticulation system that was contemplated was, in any event, not installed. We understand the commercial reasoning that lay behind Largo's decision not to install the new System, although we suspect that it may also have been prompted, at least in part, by Largo's recognition of the fact that it had not yet overcome the concentrator problems that had so beset operations at the plant from the very beginning. However, we are here concerned only with the applicability of Section 15 of the Agreement, which requires that the affected party use its "commercially reasonable best efforts" to overcome the force majeure event. The evidence was that the new water reticulation system would have cost approximately US$120,000-$165,000 (or 150,000 Brazilian Reals). (Exhs. C-115 and C-116; Tr. 784-785 (Brennan)). While these figures are not precise,

we are satisfied that the obligation on Largo to use its "commercially reasonable best efforts" to overcome the problem presented by the drought warranted expenditure of that order. In January 2013, Largo had just drilled 13 new wells, and refurbished one other well; as a result of which the amount of makeup water then available was sufficient for the production of 2,847 tons of tungsten concentrate in that month. While there was a high level of uncertainty as to how much makeup water would be available in the future, the making of that "comparatively minor expense" (Largo P-H Mem., ¶172) would, in our judgment, have satisfied Largo's best efforts obligation under Section 15; and, in the event, would have allowed some production under the contract to continue for several months thereafter.

166. GTP also suggested that Largo could also have solved the problem caused by the drought by trucking water to the plant. That suggestion we unhesitatingly reject. The drought affected the whole of northeastern Brazil, so the only available source of water would have been from the coast, which was over 230 kilometers away. In order to truck in sufficient water to maintain the targeted production rate of 150 tons per hour, it would be necessary to employ thirty tracks an hour—in other words, one every two minutes, on a continuous basis—over a period of at least 1 1/2 to two days per month. Even if physically possible, the suggestion is, in our view, both economically unviable—as Mr. Brennan and Menchen both stated—and utterly unrealistic. (Tr. 839-41 (Brennan); Tr. 948-50 (Menchen)).

167. GTP submitted that that was not good enough, since Section 15 expressly provides that "business impracticability" does not amount to force majeure. However, in our judgment the two paragraphs of Section 15 have to be read together. In the second paragraph of the same section it is provided that: 'The Parties shall use their commercially reasonable best efforts to avoid the occurrence and remove the causes of an event of Force Majeure and to continue performance of their respective obligations hereunder promptly following the removal of such causes.'

In our view, in contrast to the comparatively inexpensive construction of a more efficient water reticulation system, the shipment of sufficient quantities of water in by truck from the coast, at a rate of 720 trucks per day (even if only for two days a month), would call for efforts on the part of Largo well beyond the "commercially reasonable best efforts" that it was required to make in an attempt to address the problem. A "business impracticability" that does not give rise to force majeure means, in our judgment, a situation that can be addressed by the affected party using its commercially reasonable best efforts; not one that can only be addressed by going to unrealistic, impractical and uneconomic extremes.

168. Finally, we have previously noted that, as Largo submitted, once the drought took effect continuous production was no longer possible—and would not have been possible even had the new water reticulation System been in place. We recognize that to run the plant for a short period each month is not a commercially attractive proposition. However, it is clearly possible to do so. Largo has given evidence that over the period in which production has been suspended, various tests have been carried out, and that the plant has been run for a few days at a time, using the limited water that was available, for that purpose. (Tr. 889-90, 917-18 (Menchen)). There was therefore no impediment (other than the fact that Largo had not yet resolved the concentrator problem) to Largo's running

the plant each month for a sufficient period of time to produce as much tungsten concentrate as the available makeup water would permit. (...)

170. As we have noted above, Largo has not advanced a case of partial prevention in respect of the early months of the drought. On the contrary, Largo's personnel were commenting at that time—both internally and to GTP—that they had sufficient water available to run the plant for several months. On the basis of that evidence, and in the absence of any more precise information as to the amount of makeup water that was available from other sources, such as the lake; or as to the date by which the new water reticulation system could have been installed; or the like (on all of which Largo bears the burden of proof), we conclude that Largo has failed to make out its force majeure excuse prior to June 2013.

III.E.4. *Granuco S.A.L. v The Food and Agricultural Organization of the United Nations*, Permanent Court of Arbitration, Award of 2009[72]

Claimant, a Lebanese company with a plant in Spain, concluded a contract with respondent, the Food and Agricultural Organization of the United Nations (FAO), for the delivery of animal feed with particular specifications indicated in the contract. When claimant failed to comply with the delivery terms despite reiterated requests by respondent to perform, respondent terminated the contract. Claimant objected to the termination, arguing, among others, that its non-performance was caused by an "EU Decision" coming into force after contract conclusion which prohibited the export of the types of feed ordered by respondent from European Union member states to third countries—in the case at hand to Iraq. The Arbitral Tribunal decided in favour of respondent. The contract provided for the application of "general principles of law to the exclusion of any national legal system", and the Tribunal, in accordance with the Parties' pleadings, subsequently applied the UNIDROIT Principles. As to claimant´s argument that the EU Decision amounted to a case of force majeure, the Tribunal held that the EU Decision did not represent an absolute impediment to perform because claimant was able to transfer its plant from Spain to Brazil and could have performed the contract from that new location.

III.F. Temporary impediment—when a force majeure event can be considered as having come to an end and legal effects

III.F.1. Introduction

Generally, impediments to performance only exempt the obligor as long as they exist.[73] After the temporary impediment has fallen away, the obligor must again perform; the effect of the exemption is then to give the obligor extra time for performance. Depending on the effect of the interruption on the progress of the contract, the extra time may be greater than the length of the interruption caused by the temporary impediment.[74] This principle was applied in *Carboex SA v Louis Dreyfus Commodities Suisse SA* (III.F.2. below) and in the Award in ICC Case 18982 (III.F.3. below). In that Award one of the key questions was when the temporary force majeure event must be considered as having come to an end (III.F.3. below).

Furthermore, a comparative law analysis suggests that under certain circumstances an equation of a temporary with a permanent impediment to performance—and correspondingly a permanent exemption—may be assumed.[75] Such an equation may be considered where it appears reasonable that the impediment will persist for the whole or such a large part of the period allowed by the contract for performance as to substantially interfere with the contractual purpose. The analysis involves an estimation of the probable length of time during which the impediment is likely to persist, as well as a balancing of the parties' mutual interests in order to assess whether the impediment substantially interferes with the contractual purpose.[76]

III.F.2. *Carboex SA v Louis Dreyfus Commodities Suisse SA* (English Court of Appeal)[77]

The claimant owner, Louis Dreyfus Commodities Suisse S.A. entered into a contract of affreightment (COA) with the respondent charterer, Carboex S.A., a subsidiary of Endesa, the largest electric utility company in Spain, for the carriage of ten cargoes of coal from Indonesia to Spain for use in Endesa's power stations. Carboex chartered four vessels and an issue arose as to whether a delay in discharge at the Spanish port, by reason of an official nationwide haulage strike in Spain and a subsequent unofficial stoppage by truck drivers, was excluded from the computation of time for the charter. The charterer relied on a force majeure clause (Clause 9 COA) which explicitly included "strikes"[78] and asserted that the time lost by each of the vessels did not count against laytime. Some of the vessels arrived at the port after the strikes had finished. One of the questions was whether this clause included delays caused by congestion at the port following strikes, as strikes were already over when the vessel arrived at port. The dispute had been submitted to arbitration, and the arbitrators answered the question in the negative. In reversing the decision, the Commercial Court held that it should be answered in the affirmative, and especially considered that Clause 9 COA also applies in the case of a vessel which is delayed by the after-effects of a strike (congestion at the port) which has ended.

In dismissing the appeal and confirming the Commercial Court decision, the Court of Appeal took the view that the general language of Clause 9 COA supported the view that it was the parties' intention that the charterer should not only be protected from strikes that directly interfered with cargo handling operations, but also from the *effects* of strikes that prevented or delayed the vessel entering berth in order to discharge.

This decision thus confirms the principle that the effects of a force majeure event may extend beyond the time at which the event itself ends. It will depend on the circumstances of the individual case to determine the extra time after the force majeure event has ended during which the exemption is still operative.

III.F.3. Final Award in ICC Case 18982 of 2014[79]

The case involved a natural gas transportation contract between a carrier and a shipper for a three-year period. For the purposes of this transportation, the carrier used a pipeline owned by a third party. After a natural disaster affected the operation of the pipeline, the owner of the pipeline closed it for several months, pending performance of important repair works and safety measures. The parties were in disagreement as to when the force majeure situation was lifted and when transportation should resume as provided for under the contract. The contract contained a typical force majeure clause and was subject to Swiss law.

While the carrier asserted that the transportation of gas would have resumed on date X when it informed all shippers that the gas transportation would be available with full capacity the following day, the shipper maintained that the resumption on date X had only been declared to be "on a temporary basis" and might have to be interrupted on a notice that might be as short as just "a few hours". The shipper's position was that the monthly transportation charge was suspended until a significantly later date Y as a consequence of the force majeure events, when the transportation of gas could again be carried out without any restriction through the pipeline on a partially re-routed section which was constructed in the meantime.

The Tribunal considered that a force majeure event can be regarded as having come to an end when the performance of the obligations affected by the event is again fully possible and unrestricted, i.e. is not subject to other or more extensive restrictions than those which might have affected the performance before the occurrence of the force majeure event, provided that minor discrepancies should not be taken into account.[80] On a particular date (date Z, after date X but prior to date Y), it was established and communicated to the shipper that the probability of a preventive interruption of at least once per month was only about 0.3%. The Tribunal found that a probability of 0.3% was objectively an insignificant risk, and therefore a minor restriction or limitation to the performance of the contract as compared to the situation which prevailed before the occurrence of the force majeure events. Thus it found that force majeure was lifted as from that date. It was uncontested that the shipper would need another two to three business days to get the business back up again after the lifting of the force majeure. As a result, the suspension of the shipper's payment obligations was suspended for additional three business days and thereafter the shipper could have reasonably resumed its nominations and shipping activities and was thus again liable under the ship-or-pay scheme of the contract.

III.G. Causation

III.G.1. Introduction

Under the general force majeure exemption it is required that the unforeseeable impediment which could not be avoided or overcome was the cause of the non-performance.[81] If the goods are lost during an unforeseeable natural disaster due to defective packaging (contributing cause), the obligor cannot exempt itself if the loss of the goods would not have occurred without the contributing cause, i.e. the defective packaging. By contrast, the obligor is excused had the loss occurred even if the goods had been properly packed.[82] In the latter scenario, the force majeure event is a supervening stand-alone cause, and the fact that the negligent packaging would also on its own have caused the loss does not prevent the obligor from relying on the exemption. This principle has also been confirmed in *Global Tungsten* (Award in ICC Case 19566; III.G.2. below).

Moreover, there is generally no causal link between the impediment and the non-performance if the impediment did not yet exist at the time when the performance was due and should have been effected (cases of default).[83] However, if the parties have agreed on a force majeure clause, the language of that clause may of course provide that an exemption is even possible if the obligor is in default. The point is illustrated by the Award in ICC Case 19222 of 2016, *General Dynamics United Kingdom Ltd. v State of Libya* (III.G.3. below).

III.G.2. *Global Tungsten & Powders Corp. v Largo Resources, Ltd*, Award in ICC Case 19566 of 2014[84]

It has been seen above (III.B.2) that GTP argued that Largo's force majeure defence should also fail on the grounds that there would have been another concurrent (stand-alone) cause for Largo's non-performance, i.e. its production problems with the concentrators that were unrelated to the drought and non-availability of sufficient water at Currais Novos. In rejecting the argument, the Arbitral Tribunal stated as follows:[85]

> 150. GTP next argued that Largo had not proved that the drought—as opposed to the unrelated production problems with the concentrators—was the cause of its non- performance after October 2012. We shall return to the factual element of this argument shortly, but it also has a legal element, raising the question whether, as a matter of law, a supplier will be excused from performance where it is hindered or prevented from meeting its supply obligations by two separate causes, for one of which the supplier is responsible and the other of which it is not. This issue has been considered by courts in New York and elsewhere, and in our judgment the answer is clear. The existence of the force majeure event trumps the supplier's inability to perform for other reasons. In other words, if—because of the force majeure event—the supplier could not have supplied the product even if there had been no other impediment to its doing so, then it is entitled to rely on the force majeure event to excuse its non-performance; it does not have to prove that it would have been able to perform had the force majeure event not occurred. (See *Commonwealth Edison Co. v Allied-General Nuclear Serv.*, 731 F. Supp. 850, 860 (N.D. Ill. 1990); *New York Trust Co. v Island Oil & Transp. Corp.*, 34 F.2d 653, 654 (2nd. Cir. 1929); *Fratelli Pantanella S.A. v International Comm. Corp.*, 89 N.Y.S. 2d 736, 739-40 (N.Y. Sup. Ct. 1949)). Therefore, for the purposes of the force majeure defense, we put to the side the fact that, throughout the period of the drought, Largo has faced continuing production problems at the plant.

III.G.3. *General Dynamics United Kingdom Ltd. v State of Libya*, Award in ICC Case 19222 of 2016[86]

On 5 May 2008, the State of Libya (Libyan Procurement Department) (seller, respondent) and General Dynamics United Kingdom Limited (seller, claimant) entered into a contract whereby respondent purchased the Libyan Tactical Communication and Information System (LTCIS) from claimant. The LTCIS is a digitized communications and information system aimed at providing secure voice and data communications in the tactical domain, integrated into vehicles. The LTCIS contract provides for the supply of the LTCIS, the installation of LTCIS into the former 32nd Brigade Libyan Army vehicles and related services such as training. The LTCIS contract was subject to Swiss law (excluding the CISG) and included a force majeure clause.

Between March 2009 and August 2010, Milestones 1 to 4 as set out in Annex I to the LTCIS contract were performed by claimant and paid for by respondent in accordance with the LTCIS contract. Half of the payment for each Milestone was set off against the advance down payment, and the other half was paid from the Confirmed Letter of Credit in favour of claimant.

On 26 July 2010, claimant invoiced respondent for the amount of GBP 8,249,816 for Milestone 5. On 9 November 2010, claimant invoiced respondent for GBP 821,134 corresponding to Milestone 6. Respondent did not at that time provide claimant with the acceptance certificates necessary under the LTCIS contract in order for claimant to receive payment under the Confirmed Letter of Credit. The matter of non-payment for Milestones 5 and 6 was the subject of negotiations between the parties in January and February 2011.

In February 2011, events in Libya led to civil unrest and ultimately civil war, international sanctions, international military intervention, and the fall of the Libyan Government led by Muammar Gaddafi. On 22 February 2011, claimant issued respondent with written notice of a force majeure event pursuant to Condition 22 of the LTCIS contract.

The Arbitral Tribunal considered that the military situation in Libya was an impediment excusing respondent's performance under the force majeure clause and especially considered that this was the case even though respondent was in default prior to the force majeure events arose:[87]

> 250. With reference to Condition 22.1 of the LTCIS Contract, the Tribunal is of the view that the military situation in Libya from 17 February until 23 October 2011 falls squarely with the events contemplated as potential force majeure impediments, i.e. "civil commotion, riot, terrorism or the threat of terrorism, insurrection or hostilities whether or not declared, war, conditions which may adversely affect the safety of their employees and/or equipment...". Indeed, this was the very basis for Claimant's own notice of force majeure on 22 February 2011.
>
> 251. Further, the Tribunal is persuaded that Respondent was actually impeded from performing its obligations regarding payment for Milestones 5 and 6 while those force majeure conditions prevailed. (...)
>
> 263. Claimant argues that Respondent may not rely on force majeure because it was already in default before the alleged force majeure events arose, breaking the causal link to the force majeure impediment, consistent with Article 103 of the Swiss Code of Obligations.[88]
>
> 265. The Tribunal recalls that the wording of Condition 22.1 of the LTCIS Contract is unequivocal in stating that "[t]he Parties shall not be in default and will assume no liability or responsibility for the consequences arising out of the interruption of their performance of this Contract by any [force majeure events]". The effect of the operation of Clause 22.1 is to "suspend performance up to a period equal to the delay". This strong and unambiguous wording of the agreement between the Parties must, in the Tribunal's opinion, operate so as to suspend Respondent's obligations and excuse it from any default, liability or responsibility arising there from. The clear language of the Parties' agreement prevails over the non-mandatory provision of Article 103 of the Swiss Code of Obligations. Therefore, even though Respondent was in default prior to the force majeure event, Condition 22.1 of the LTCIS Contract excludes Respondent from bearing the burden of any liability or responsibility arising out of the interruption, and prevails over Article 103 in this respect. (...)

III.H. Notice requirement (and relevance of actual notice)

III.H.1. Introduction

Article 79(4) CISG and Article 7.1.7(3) UNIDROIT Principles provide that the non-performing party must ensure that notice of the impediment and of its effect on its ability to perform is received by the other party within a reasonable time after the non-performing party knew or ought to have known of the impediment. The obligor's duty to warn the obligee of the occurrence of the obstacle and of its consequences for the performance under the contract is an application of the general obligation of good faith.[89]

In case of a failure to notify the other party within a reasonable period of time, the other party is entitled to damages for any loss resulting from the non-receipt or late receipt of such notice. This is explicitly provided for in Article 79(4) sentence 2 CISG and Article 7.1.7(3) UNIDROIT Principles. The obligee is financially to be put in a situation as if the notice had been given in time and in sufficiently complete form. It follows that the obligor's exoneration from its performance obligation does not depend on the compliance with the duty to notify. Contractual force majeure clauses may take a different approach, and provide that the notice requirement is a condition precedent to invoking force majeure. However, as convincingly pointed out by the Tribunal in *Global Tungsten* (Award in ICC Case 19566; below b.), "clear language is required in order for a force majeure notice obligation to be construed as a condition precedent", and "that whether or not the party complaining of lack of notice had actual knowledge of the circumstances giving rise to the force majeure event is a relevant consideration." The Tribunal concluded that under the circumstances the language of the force majeure clause "provided always that prompt written notice shall be given" was not enough to construe it as condition precedent, especially as the party complaining of the lack of notice had been given actual notice.

The question as to whether the non-performing party is precluded from relying on the force majeure clause by its failure to give formal notice was also answered in the negative in the Award in ICC Case 19222 of 2016, *General Dynamics United Kingdom Ltd. v State of Libya* (III.H.3. below).

III.H.2. Global Tungsten & Powders Corp. v Largo Resources, Ltd, Award in ICC Case 19566 of 2014[90]

In *Global Tungsten*, the Arbitral Tribunal had to deal with the often litigated question whether the requirement of the force majeure clause calling for a written notice of force majeure by the affected party had been met, and if not, whether it is to be considered as a condition precedent to the right to invoke force majeure.[91]

> 174. It is clear, in our judgment, that Section 15 of the Agreement calls for a written notice of force majeure to be given by the affected party:
>
> > "In the event of any ... act of God ... preventing or hindering Seller ... from giving ... delivery of Material under this Agreement, deliveries may be suspended during such time of Force Majeure declared by the affected Party, providing always that prompt written notice shall be given by the affected party to the other Party"(emphasis added).
>
> 175. GTP argues that, in order to comply with this provision, the notice had specifically to claim force majeure—which the e-mail of October

29, 2012 did not—and it relies in this connection on the evidence of Mr. Brennan, who confirmed in cross-examination that he deliberately did not claim force majeure at that time, because with all the other problems that were then affecting the plant, he did not want to antagonize GTP. (Tr. 793). GTP points out that the commercial purpose of the notice requirement in Section 15 is not simply to tell the other party that a problem has arisen, but to alert it to the fact that, as a consequence, the affected party is claiming certain contractual consequences; namely, that its obligation to make deliveries under the contract is suspended *pro tem*; that a problem has arisen which they are required to work together to try to resolve; and, that—absent possible termination if the event continues long enough—the contract term will be extended by a period equal to the period of suspension. Thus, GTP submits that, while Largo provided it with the necessary information to support a claim of force majeure on October 29, 2012, it plainly did not advance a claim that it was excused from performance under the contract on account of the drought at that time; and therefore cannot now rely on force majeure as a defense.

176. Largo argues that the information that mattered—the drought, its impact on the plant, and the fact that operations were being suspended—were all conveyed in that communication, and that it is irrelevant that the talismanic words "force majeure" were not used. It contends that, as a matter of law, actual notice of a force majeure event, and of its impact on the performance of the affected party, is sufficient notice. (...)

182. What we take from these cases is, first, that the intention of the parties, as reflected in the language they have chosen, will be determinative; secondly, that clear language is required in order for a force majeure notice obligation to be construed as a condition precedent; thirdly, that whether or not the party complaining of lack of notice had actual knowledge of the circumstances giving rise to the force majeure event is a relevant consideration; and, fourthly, that, if it is not a condition precedent, the obligation will be construed as a duty, failure to comply with which will not deprive the breaching party of the right to invoke force majeure unless the breach is a material breach.

183. In our judgment, bearing these considerations in mind, Largo has the better of this argument for two reasons.

184. First, while Section 15 requires that written notice be given, it does not require that the affected party must declare force majeure by using that term in order for the clause to be triggered. We conclude that if written notice is given both of the force majeure event that is relied upon and of the fact that deliveries may be suspended during the period in which that event is operative—both of which conditions were satisfied in this case—then the notice is a good notice under the clause, even though the words "force majeure" are not used. We accept Largo's submission that Mr. Brennan's e-mail of October 29, 2012 (coupled with the press release that was attached to that e-mail) advised Dr. Laursen of the drought, of the impact that the drought was having on the plant, and of the imminent suspension of operations at the plant as a result; and that that was sufficient to give GTP actual notice of the circumstances giving rise to the claim of force majeure that was later made. The words "force majeure" are, in our judgment, a convenient shorthand or label by which to describe the relevant event and its consequences. Their use is not a *sine qua*

non to the applicability of the clause under Pennsylvania law, however, unless the Parties clearly provided to the contrary (which they have not).

185. Secondly, if we are wrong about that, we would accept Largo's submission that the requirement in Section 15 that the affected party expressly declare force majeure is to be considered not as a condition precedent to the right to invoke force majeure, but as giving rise to a contractual duty, breach of which will only deprive the affected party of that right if the breach is a material breach—namely, one that causes harm or prejudice to the other party. There being no evidence of any harm to, or prejudicial effect on, GTP by virtue of Largo's not having been declared force majeure in so many words before September 13, 2013 (when it served its Answer and Counterclaim), the Tribunal concludes that Largo's failure to do so cannot be characterized as a material breach. Accordingly, Largo is not deprived of its right to invoke force majeure as a result.

186. We have given close consideration to the fact that Mr. Brennan deliberately decided not to declare force majeure in October 2012, but it does not affect our conclusion. In our judgment, his decision not to call a spade a spade at that point in time did not turn a good notice into a bad notice, or a minor breach into a material breach. It is, accordingly, irrelevant.

Force Majeure Conclusion

187. In summary, we are satisfied on the evidence that the drought has prevented Largo from meeting its delivery obligations under the Agreement since June 30, 2013; and we conclude that Largo is entitled to rely on the drought as a force majeure event excusing it from performance since that date.

III.H.3. General Dynamics United Kingdom Ltd. v State of Libya, Award in ICC Case 19222 of 2016[92]

The Arbitral Tribunal in *General Dynamics* similarly considered whether the affected party's failure to give notice of the force majeure impediment precluded it from relying upon that impediment to excuse its non-performance:[93]

269. The Tribunal recalls the language in Condition 22.1 of the LTCIS contract, which states in relevant part:

> The Parties shall not be in default and will assume no liability or responsibility for consequences arising out of the interruption of their performance of this Contract by any external, absolute, invincible and/or unforeseen events such as any labour disputes which delay work, epidemics, fires, floods, unusually severe weather or any other natural disturbances or natural physical disasters; civil commotion, riot, terrorism or the threat of terrorism, insurrection or hostilities whether or not declared, war, conditions which may adversely affect the safety of their employees and/or equipment, restrictions due to quarantines, blockades, embargoes, severe market shortages, inability to obtain raw materials or components; and all similar causes beyond the reasonable control of the Parties that arise without the fault or negligence of the Parties or their subcontractors and that result in the delay or failure to execute the work provided in the Contract. Such circumstances shall result in an excusable delay, and the affected Party shall notify the other Party in writing, by electronic means, or registered letter within five (5) working days of the date the concerned Party first becomes

aware of said events, and provide an estimate of the consequences. A delay resulting from any of the stated events, or significant events of a similar uncontrollable nature, shall suspend performance up to a period equal to the delay or otherwise to be mutually agreed upon by both Parties.

270. The provision first, and in no uncertain terms ("shall not be in default", "will assume no liability", "shall result in an excusable delay"), excuses a delay or default arising out of a force majeure interruption, before mentioning the requirement to give notice. Based on the structure and language of Condition 22.1, the Parties did not intend notice to be a prerequisite, or condition precedent, to the operation of this provision. The requirement to give notice is an additional one.

271. The Tribunal therefore disagrees with Claimant's assessment that only delays which have been the subject of a notice may be excused. (178) "A delay resulting from any of the stated events... ", does not, as argued by Claimant, (179) refer to "stated events" in a notice, but the potential force majeure events outlined in Condition 22.1. So much is clear when the words are read in context: "the stated events, or significant events of a similar uncontrollable nature". Similar references are made throughout the provision to the "said events", being shorthand for all possible force majeure events listed in Condition 22.1.

272. The Tribunal finds further confirmation in the statement that a delay resulting from force majeure events "shall suspend performance up to a period equal to the delay", i.e., the length of the suspension is determined by reference to the objective fact of the delay, rather than by reference to any notice, unless the Parties mutually agree otherwise. (...)

277. The Tribunal accepts Respondent's submission in this respect that failure to give notice, as a breach of the duty to act in good faith, creates liability in damages for any loss suffered by Claimant as a result of not being informed (see ¶196 above).

278. According to Claimant, notice would have put it in a position to "evaluate and, if necessary, deny that the claimed force majeure event actually interrupts the concerned obligation, or propose possible solutions ... to overcome any perceived obstacles to performance". (183) It also objects that Respondent did not claim force majeure until its Statement of Defence in these proceedings. (184) However, Claimant was aware of the military situation in Libya and its impact upon the performance of the LTCIS Contract, having issued its own force majeure notice in relation to the same events. Claimant cannot, in the Tribunal's view, claim to be unaware of the implications of the force majeure events for Respondent's performance of the LTCIS Contract as well as its own. (...)

282. On the basis of the foregoing, the Tribunal is not persuaded that Claimant missed an opportunity to evaluate and oppose Respondent's force majeure impediment (or to consider granting Respondent any further extensions of the grace period to remedy its default, or otherwise waiting, before issuing an Article 107(2) Notice), or that it suffered harm for which Respondent is liable as a result of its failure to give notice of force majeure. For the same reason, the Tribunal does not consider it decisive that Respondent made no claim of force majeure prior to its Statement of Defence in these proceedings. (...)

284. The Tribunal therefore finds that notwithstanding the lateness of Respondent's upon force majeure, it is not precluded from relying

upon that provision by its failure to give formal notice to Claimant, which was well aware of the circumstances prevailing in Libya at the time.

IV. CONCLUSION

The above presentation of recent case law by arbitral tribunals and state courts provides instructive insights into commonly litigated issues on force majeure. Although the presented case law is a selection and does not claim to be comprehensive, two important conclusions may be drawn from the decisions.

First, they confirm that in international commercial contracts, the impact of force majeure events is mostly regulated by the terms of a force majeure clause rather than by the relevant doctrine of the applicable law. In all but one or two out of the eleven decisions the contract included a force majeure clause. However, this does not mean that the applicable law would have been meaningless; in fact, most decisions also make reference to the applicable law, often for the purpose of contract interpretation and to seek guidance from established case law on the relevant issue, either rendered in the context of force majeure clauses or the rule on force majeure of the applicable law.

Second, while the eleven decisions above were rendered under English law, Pennsylvania law (including the UCC as adopted in Pennsylvania), Kansas law, the CISG (being part of Swiss law), French law, the UNIDROIT Principles, and Swiss law (excluding the CISG), the substantive discussion of the respective issue of force majeure is mostly consistent with the groups of cases and principles that apply under the force majeure excuse according to general contract principles as reflected in Article 79 CISG and Article 7.1.7 UNIDROIT Principles and which have been established by case law under various legal systems. This goes to show that especially in international arbitrations, the uncertainty associated with the (to some extent necessarily) broad or unclear language of many contractual force majeure clauses may be overcome by interpreting them in a manner consistent with the groups of cases and principles that apply under general contract principles and are evidenced by persuasive case law.

NOTES

1. See <https://www.basf.com/en/company/news-and-media/news-releases/2018/07/p-18-245.html> (Trade News, 2 July 2018).
2. See <https://www.metalbulletin.com/Article/3791423/Hydro-declares-force-majeure-at-Alunorte-alumina-refinery.html> (published on 2 March 2018).
3. See <https://www.metalbulletin.com/Article/3822580/Alunorte-full-restart-date-still-uncertain-Hydro-Q2-earnings-drop-vs-last-year.html> (published on 24 July 2018).
4. See <https://uk.reuters.com/article/uk-glencore-aluminium/glencore-to-declare-force-majeure-on-some-aluminium-supply-source-idUKKBN1HI2O9> (Business News, 11 April 2018). It was further reported: 'The inclusion of Rusal marks the first time a major international company has been targeted by Washington in its moves to punish Russia for alleged meddling in the 2016 U.S. election. International financial groups have been quickly distancing themselves from Rusal shares, bonds and metal. The company has been dropped from global equity and debt indexes while its metal will not be allowed on the London Metal Exchange (LME) and the CME Group.'
5. Ewan McKendrick, "Preparing for the Unexpected: Force Majeure and Hardship Clauses in Practice", a paper presented to the Centre of Construction Law 25th Anniversary Conference held at King's College London on 28th June 2012, January 2013, p. 3. This finding is also confirmed by the review of recent case law presented below; see *infra* IV.

6. For English law see McKendrick, *supra* note 5, p. 4, with reference to *RDC Concrete Pte Ltd v Sato Kogyo (S) Pte Ltd* [2007] SGCA 39 (Singapore Court of Appeal), (2008) 115 Con LR 154, para. 56.

7. Karl-Heinz Böckstiegel, "Vertragsklauseln über nicht zu vertretende Risiken im internationalen Wirtschaftsverkehr", *Recht der internationalen Wirtschaft*, 1984, pp. 1-2; id., "Hardship, Force Majeure and Special Risks Clauses in International Contracts", *Adaptation and Renegotiation of Contracts in International Trade and Finance* (Norbert Horn, ed.), Kluwer Law and Taxation Publishers, 1985, pp. 159, 160-61.

8. United Nations Convention on Contracts for the International Sale of Goods (Vienna, 1980).

9. UNIDROIT Principles of International Commercial Contracts (latest edition 2016). Article 7.1.7 UNIDROIT Principles on force majeure has already been included in the first 1994 edition of the UNIDROIT Principles.

10. Christoph Brunner, *Force Majeure and Hardship under General Contract Principles, Exemption for Non-Performance in International Arbitration*, Kluwer Law International, 2009, pp. 107-08, 385.

11. Konrad Zweigert & Hein Kötz, *Introduction to Comparative Law*, 3rd ed., Oxford University Press, 1998, p. 514.

12. See generally Brunner, *supra* note 10, pp. 110-390.

13. id., especially at pp. 388-390. See, e.g., Award in ICC Case 11265, *ICC International Court of Arbitration Bulletin*, Vol. 20/2, 2009, pp. 53-54, 90 at para. 128 (interpretation of a force majeure clause in light of Article 7.1.7 UNIDROIT Principles).

14. On the unforeseeability requirement see Brunner, *supra* note 10, pp. 156-167.

15. Alan Howard & Luke van Houwelingen, "Crafting Robust Force Majeure Clauses", Law360, 26 March 2018, available at <www.crowell.com>; see also G. Brian Wells, "It's Not My Fault: Recent Force Majeure Decisions", <www.wyattfirm.com/theme/wyatt/pdf/Wells_ForceMajeure.pdf> (last visited 10 August 2018); Helen Morton, "Common Issues with Force Majeure Clauses", <https://essexcourt.com/publication/common-issues-with-force-majeure-clauses/>, published on 26 April 2018, para. 27 "Although this may seem counter-intuitive, a force majeure clause may simply be the parties' method of dealing with possible (and foreseeable) future events. Indeed in a shipping context a bout of 'abnormal' weather on the high seas is unlikely to be unforeseeable; this is often precisely what a force majeure clause is designed to cover."

16. Howard & van Houwelinge, ibid. On this issue see especially the article of Klaus Peter Berger in this Dossier, *infra*. p.page 137

17. cf. *Borregaard Indus., Ltd. v AMRI Rensselaer, Inc.* (Final Award), ICDR Case No. 50 122 T 00481 09, 12 October 2010, *Arbitrator Intelligence Materials*, Kluwer Arbitration Online (unforeseeable language of the first sentence in the contractual hardship clause applies also to the rest of the hardship clause as a whole). As under most rules of contract interpretation, contracts are to be construed as a whole, courts and arbitral tribunals generally have to read force majeure clauses or individual terms or phrases not in isolation but as an integral part of their general context, and to give effect to all the terms rather than to deprive some of them of effect. See Articles 4.4, 4.5 UNIDROIT Principles; Brunner, *supra* note 10, p. 384.

18. Many civil law systems recognise this contract excuse in a more or less distinct form; see Brunner, *supra* note 10, pp. 77-88.

19. ibid., pp. 78-80. Situations of 'economic unaffordability' may have to be dealt with under the doctrine of change of circumstances (*clausula rebus sic stantibus*) or a similar doctrine. ibid., p. 79.

20. 3 B & S 826 (1863), 2 New Rep. 198.

21. Ewan McKendrick, *Contract Law*, 8th ed., Oxford University Press, 2016, p. 690; see also id., in *Chitty on Contracts, The Law of contracts*, Vol. 1, General Principles, Chapter 24, "Discharge by Frustration", Sweet & Maxwell, 1999, para. 24-001; Guenter Treitel, *Frustration and Force Majeure*, 3rd ed., Sweet & Maxwell, 2014.

22. McKendrick, *supra* note 5, p. 4.

23. See Brunner, *supra* note 10, pp. 94-100.

24. Brunner, *supra* note 10, pp. 111-112; see *also* TransLex-Principle No. VI.3—Force majeure, with Commentary, References and Contract Clauses, available at <https://www.trans-lex.org/944000/_/force-majeure/>.

25. *Anaconda-Iran, Inc. v The Government of the Islamic Republic of Iran, et al.*, award No. ITL 65-167-3 of 10.12.1986 at 41-43, 13 Iran-U.S. C.T.R. 199, 211-12, *Y.B. Com. Arb. 1988*, p. 319. The Tribunal stated: "Under a variety of names most, if not all, legal systems recognize force majeure as an excuse for contractual non-performance. Force majeure therefore can be considered a

general principle of law. It follows that the right to invoke force majeure does not depend on, or arise out of, an express contractual provision." See *also* Brunner, *supra* note 10, pp. 108-110, with further references.

26. Brunner, *supra* note 10, pp. 107-108.
27. See Comment No. 1 on the 1985 ICC Force Majeure Clause (ICC Publ. No. 421; TransLex DocID 700650). Paragraph 1 states: "1. A party is not liable for a failure to perform any of his obligations in so far as he proves—that the failure was due to an impediment beyond his control; and—that he could not reasonably be expected to have taken the impediment and its effects upon his ability to perform into account at the time of the conclusion of the contract; and—that he could not reasonably have avoided or overcome it or at least its effects."
28. See TransLex DocID 700650. See *also* TransLex-Principle VI.3 (Force majeure).
29. See ICC Force Majeure Clause 2003 (ICC Publ. No. 650; TransLex DocID 700700). Paragraph 1 states: "Unless otherwise agreed in the contract between the parties expressly or impliedly, where a party to a contract fails to perform one or more of its contractual duties, the consequences set out in paragraphs 4 to 9 of this Clause will follow if and to the extent that that party proves: [a] that its failure to perform was caused by an impediment beyond its reasonable control; and [b] that it could not reasonably have been expected to have taken the occurrence of the impediment into account at the time of the conclusion of the contract; and [c] that it could not reasonably have avoided or overcome the effects of the impediment."
30. (Unpublished) paper by Charles Debattista (draftsman-in-chief) on the ICC Force majeure and Hardship Clauses 2003, ICC Seminar of 8 April 2003, at para. 7.
31. See Brunner, *supra* note 10, pp. 167-171; id., in *CISG Commentary* (Christoph Brunner & Benjamin Gottlieb, eds.), Kluwer Law International, forthcoming 2018, Art. 79 CISG paras. 8-11, with further references.
32. id., *supra* note 31, Art. 79 CISG para. 9.
33. See Craig Rogers et al., "Is a cyber-attack 'Force Majeure'? Je ne crois pas!", <www.eversheds-sutherland.com/global/en/what/articles/index.page?ArticleID=en/Commercial/Is-a-cyber-attack-force-majeure>, published on 12 December 2017.
34. ibid.
35. [2013] EWCA Civ 905 (Court of Appeal), 25 July 2013.
36. Case notes by Charles Kimmins & Socrates Papadopoulos at <www.20essexst.com/case/great-elephant-corp-v-trafigura-beheer-bv>.
37. Case note by David Martin-Clark at <www.onlinedmc.co.uk/index.php/Great_Elephant_Corp_v_Trafigura_Beheer_-_The_Crudesky>.
38. [2013] EWCA Civ 905 at para. 25.
39. See Brunner, *supra* note 10, pp. 171-185.
40. Final Award in ICC Case No. 19566/AGF/RD, 24 November 2014, *Arbitrator Intelligence Materials*, Kluwer Arbitration Online.
41. Tungsten, or wolfram, is a rare metal found naturally on Earth almost exclusively combined with other elements. As a free element (not combined with other elements) it is remarkable for its robustness, especially the fact that it has the highest melting point of all the elements discovered. Tungsten's many alloys have numerous applications, including incandescent light bulb filaments. Source: Wikipedia.
42. id., paras. 78-81.
43. cf. Cour de cassation (France), 17 February 2015, CLOUT case No. 1501 "An increase in price of raw materials needed for the production of heating appliances was deemed to be in the seller's sphere of risk"; Tribunale Civile di Monza, 29 March 1993, CISG-online 102 "Price increase of 30% does not entitle the seller to modify or avoid the contract"; Award of the Bulgarian Chamber of Commerce and Industry, 12 February 1998, <www.unilex.info> "The buyer could not exempt himself from his obligations to pay the price and accept the goods on the basis that the market situation for the goods had developed negatively or the trade volume had lessened, there were problems with the storage of the goods and the currency of payment had appreciated; all these circumstances belonged to the buyer's commercial risk." cf. also Guy Block, 'Arbitration and Changes in Energy Prices: A Review of ICC Awards with respect to Force Majeure, Indexation, Adaptation, Hardship and Take-or-Pay Clauses', *ICC International Court of Arbitration Bulletin*, Vol. 20/2, 2009, p. 53 "ICC arbitral tribunals have ruled that neither increases nor decreases in oil prices, no matter how large or unexpected, can be considered to constitute force majeure"; citing ICC cases 2216, 2478, 2508); Award in ICC Case 11265, ibid. at p. 54; Brunner, *supra* note 10, pp. 218–221, 420–483.
44. See Brunner, *supra* note 31, Art. 79 CISG paras. 11, 26.

45. 1978 Secretariat Commentary, available at CISG-online, Art. 65 para. 10; Tribunal of International Commercial Arbitration at the Russian Federation Chamber of Commerce and Industry, 1 October 1995, CISG-online 207 "No exemption if the buyer and his bank do not have freely-convertible currency in which to make payment"; Award in ICC Case No. 7197 of 1992, *Journal du droit international* 1993, p. 1028, summarised at <www.unilex. info> (The Bulgarian buyer who did not order the agreed letter of credit because of a Bulgarian payment moratorium for foreign debts was not exempted because it did not prove that the failure to order the letter of credit was impossible as a result of the moratorium and could also not be overcome; additionally, the moratorium was already in force at the time of contract conclusion and was therefore foreseeable for the buyer). For the (necessarily flexible) legal effects see Brunner, *supra* note 31, Art. 79 CISG para. 33 and references there.

46. For cases in which hardship was recognised as grounds for exemption according to Article 79: Hof van Cassatie [Belgian Supreme Court], 19 June 2009, para. 1, CISG-online 1963 'Scafom International' case; cf. below; CISG AC-Opinion No. 7, Opinion 3.1–3.2, Comments 26–40; Brunner, *supra* note 10, pp. 213–227, 391–426; id., *supra* note 75, Art. 79 CISG para. 26 with further references; Peter Schlechtriem & Ingeborg Schwenzer, *Commentary on the UN Convention on the International Sale of Goods*, 4th ed., Oxford University Press, 2016 (cited: Schlechtriem/Schwenzer/Schwenzer), Art. 79 para. 31. In the Scafom International case, the Belgian Supreme Court held that because the steel prices for steel pipes for scaffolding had increased by 70% in an unforeseeable manner, the buyer was under an obligation to renegotiate the price. In finding for an obligation to renegotiate, the Court took account of Art. 6.2.3 UNIDROIT Principles. However, the decision's reasoning is not detailed and does not elaborate on the applicability, particularly as regards the applicable threshold and legal consequences of Art. 79; the 70% threshold is therefore subject to criticism or caution (Brunner, *supra* note 31, Art. 79 CISG paras. 29–33).

47. Brunner, *supra* note 10, pp. 220, 424-426, 431-432, 438-441.

48. See ibid., pp. 431-432: "Since both common law systems, including in particular English and major civil law systems recognize an exemption due to frustration of purpose, an alteration in the region of a *80-100% decrease in the value received*, or a *corresponding increase in the cost of performance* of the same order of magnitude (excluding any profit margin) or of about *100-125%* (including a typical profit margin, see below) may therefore be seen as a general point of reference for the hardship test under general contract principles." But see Ingeborg Schwenzer, "Force Majeure and Hardship in International Sales Contracts", *Victoria University of Wellington Law Review*, Vol. 39, 2008, pp. 709, 717, (threshold of 150–200% required); see also Schlechtriem/Schwenzer/Schwenzer, *supra* note 46, Art. 79 para. 31 (price changes of over 100% are not, as a rule, grounds for exemption).

49. [2010] EWHC 40 (Comm).

50. The force majeure clause stated: "Force Majeure. Neither party shall be liable to the other as a result of any failure of, or delay in the performance of, its obligations hereunder, for the period that such failure or delay is due to: Acts of God or the public enemy; war, insurrection or riots; fires; governmental actions; strikes or labor disputes; inability to obtain aircraft materials, accessories, equipment or parts from vendors; or any other cause beyond Seller's reasonable control. Upon the occurrence of any such event, the time required for performance by such party of its obligations arising under this Agreement, shall be extended by a period equal to the duration of such event."

51. Alistair Campbell, *Economic downturn isn't force majeure*, <www.brodies.com/binformed/legal-updates/economic-downturn-isnt-force-majeure>. The fact that the clause was restricted to causes beyond the seller's control just gave the court additional grounds on which to reject the buyer's arguments (ibid.). On the question whether the 'buyer' or other recipient is denied any excuse due to irresistible supervening events if the force majeure clause applies by its terms only to the 'seller' or other supplier, see Brunner, *supra* note 10, p. 388.

52. Final Award in ICC Case 18769/VRO/AGF, 17 January 2014, *Arbitrator Intelligence Materials*, Kluwer Arbitration Online.

53. Published in *Yearbook Commercial Arbitration* 2014, pp. 169-215.

54. id., p. 172.

55. id., p. 201, paras. 103-104. However, this finding is not uncontestable. The words of a catch-all provision that follows the enumeration of a list of specific events (e.g., 'or any other causes beyond a Party's control') are, as a general rule, to be construed as having their natural and larger meaning and are not limited to events *ejusdem generis* with those previously enumerated in the list (see Brunner, *supra* note 10, p. 387 and references there).

56. id., pp. 202-203, paras. 107 *et seq.*

57. id., pp. 203-206.

58. id. p. 206, para. 126; but cf. also *supra* I. at notes 15-17.

59. Article 79(1) CISG; Article 7.1.7(1) UNIDROIT Principles.

60. Brunner, *supra* note 10, pp. 156-167.
61. Centro de Arbitraje de México (CAM), arbitral award of 30 November 2006, abstract on <www.unilex.info/case.cfm?id=1149>.
62. Brunner, *supra* note 10, pp. 161-162, 183.
63. Brunner, *supra* note 10, pp. 320-340.
64. In the Suez Canal cases, cost increases of 30% have been held to be clearly insufficient to constitute impracticability (*American Trading & Prod. Corp. v Shell Intl. Marine*, 453 F.2d 939 [2d Cir. 1972]). See Brunner, *supra* note 10, pp. 325–326, 329, 428–430 and references there.
65. Brunner, *supra* note 31, Art. 79 CISG para. 40 with references.
66. See Brunner, *supra* note 10, pp. 281-284, 321, 323-329.
67. The Paris Chamber of Arbitration Award No. 3150 is published in *Yearbook Commercial Arbitration*, Vol. 39, 2014, pp. 65-76.
68. From the published Award, the practical relevance and consequence of this finding is unclear.
69. See *supra* note 40.
70. ibid. at paras. 153 *et seq.*
71. ibid. at para. 134: 'In the event of any strike, act of God, lockout, combination of workmen, interference by trade unions, suspension of labor, fire, accident, lack of railway or seaborne freight facilities preventing or hindering Seller or Buyer from giving or receiving delivery of Material under this Agreement, deliveries may be suspended during such time of Force Majeure declared by the affected Party, providing always that prompt written notice shall be given by the affected party to the other Party. It is expressly provided that in no event shall business impracticability, failure of equipment, failure of subcontractor or supplier, or any cause not specifically enumerated in this Section constitute a cause of Force Majeure.
The occurrence of an event of Force Majeure shall not terminate this Agreement, absent the written consent of Buyer and Seller to the contrary; provided, however, that either Party may, at its option, terminate the Agreement if an event of Force Majeure prevents, or such Party reasonably anticipates that it will prevent, the other Party from meeting its obligations in whole or in substantial part under this Agreement for more than (a) ninety (90) consecutive calendar days during the Term hereof or (b) a cumulative amount of one hundred eighty (180) calendar days during any one year period during the Term hereof. Provided this Agreement is not terminated following an event of Force Majeure, the Term of this Agreement shall be extended for a period equal to the period during which the event of Force Majeure prevents Buyer or Seller from meeting its or their respective obligations, as the case may require, in whole or in substantial part. The Parties shall use their commercially reasonable best efforts to avoid the occurrence and remove the causes of an event of Force Majeure and to continue performance of their respective obligations hereunder promptly following the removal of such causes. If an event of Force Majeure prevents Buyer or Seller from meeting its or their respective obligations hereunder in part, but not in whole, Buyer and Seller shall use their commercially reasonable best efforts to equitably adjust their respective obligations hereunder consistent with and in furtherance of the purposes hereof.'
72. Summary published at <http://www.unilex.info/case.cfm?id=1881>.
73. See, e.g., Article 79(3) CISG; Article 7.1.7(3) UNIDROIT Principles.
74. See Article 7.1.7(2) UPICC, Comment 2 and Illustration 2: "A contracts to lay a natural gas pipeline across country X. Climatic conditions are such that it is normally impossible to work between 1 November and 31 March. The contract is timed to finish on 31 October but the start of work is delayed for a month by a civil war in a neighbouring country which makes it impossible to bring in all the piping on time. If the consequence is reasonably to prevent the completion of the work until its resumption in the following spring, A may be entitled to an extension of five months even though the delay was itself of one month only."
75. Brunner, *supra* note 10, pp. 249–260; id., *supra* note 31, Art. 79 para. 36; see also Christoph Brunner & Angelina Sgier, in *UN-Kaufrecht—CISG* [Christoph Brunner, ed.], 2nd ed., Stämpfli, 2014, Art. 79 para. 36; but see Schlechtriem/Schwenzer/Schwenzer, *supra* note 46, Art. 79 para. 43 "permanent exemption only if the obligor would be pushed 'beyond the limit of sacrifice'".
76. Brunner, ibid.
77. *Carboex S.A. v Louis Dreyfus Commodities Suisse S.A.* [2012] EWCA Civ 838 (Court of Appeal); see also the decision of the Commercial Court in *Carboex SA v Louis Dreyfus Commodities Suisse SA* [2011] EWHC 1165 (Comm).
78. Clause 9 COA, which concerned laytime at the discharging port, stated: "In Case of strikes, lockouts, civil commotions or any other causes included but not limited to breakdown of shore

equipment or accidents beyond the control of the Charterers consignee which prevent or delay the discharging, such time is not to count unless the vessel is already on demurrage." (emphasis omitted).

79. Unpublished. The present author was a member of the Arbitral Tribunal in ICC Case 18982.

80. Award (unpublished) in ICC Case 18982 at para. 71.

81. cf. Award in ICC Case 7197 of 1992, <www.unilex.info> "Exemption of a Bulgarian buyer rejected, among other reasons, because it did not prove that the failure to open a letter of credit was caused by an order of the Bulgarian government regarding a payment stop on foreign debts."

82. cf. Brunner, *supra* note 10, pp. 340-342; Yesim M. Atamer, in *UN Convention on Contracts for the International Sale of Goods (CISG)* (Stefan Kröll, Loukas Mistelis & Pilar Perales Viscasillas, eds.), 2nd ed., C.H. Beck, Hart, Nomos, 2018 (cited: Kröll/Mistelis/Perales Viscasillas/Atamer), Art. 79 para. 59; Ulrich Magnus, in *J. von Staudingers Kommentar zum Bürgerlichen Gesetzbuch mit Einführungsgesetz und Nebengesetzen. Wiener UN-Kaufrecht (CISG)*, Sellier—de Gruyter, 2018 (cited: Staudinger/Magnus), Art. 79 para. 31; Schlechtriem/Schwenzer/Schwenzer, Art. 79 para. 16 fn. 51 (however, the use of the term 'concurrent cause' in para. 16 appears to be misleading).

83. See Brunner, *supra* note 10, p. 341.

84. See *supra* note 40.

85. ibid. at para. 150.

86. Final Award in ICC Case 19222/EMT, 5 January 2016, *Arbitrator Intelligence Materials*, Kluwer Arbitration Online.

87. ibid. at paras. 246-267.

88. It states (ibid. at para. 239): 'Article 103 states: (1) An obligor in default is liable in damages for late performance and even for accidental loss or damage. (2) He may discharge himself from such liability by proving that his default occurred through no fault of his own or that the object of performance would have suffered the accidental loss or damage to the detriment of the oblige even if performance had taken place promptly.'

89. Brunner, *supra* note 10, pp. 342–345.

90. See *supra* note 40.

91. ibid. at paras. 173-187.

92. See *supra* note 86.

93. ibid. at paras. 268-284.

Chapter 4

Analysing the ICC Force Majeure Clause 2003

by Prof Filip De Ly*

I. INTRODUCTION

Contract performance may under certain strict conditions be excused if the debtor is not capable of performance due to certain events which in civil law countries is encompassed within the broad notion of "force majeure" or in common law jurisdictions is covered by the doctrine of frustration of contracts. The civil and common law approaches to exemption from performance are quite different particularly regarding their objectives and requirements and are discussed in other contributions. By way of summary, the common law approach starts from strict liability and—to mitigate the insistence on literal performance of absolute promises—only if the initially envisaged purpose of the contract cannot be achieved by certain events external to the debtor including a significant change of circumstances, may the contract be terminated by virtue of the doctrine of frustration.[1] By contrast, the civil law by and large is based on fault liability where non-performance in itself does not establish liability but where first the nature of the non-performed obligation must be determined. If the obligation is a warranty, there will be strict liability; if the obligation relates to a promise to obtain a result, the creditor will have to prove that the promised result was not achieved while, if the obligation is of a best efforts basis, the creditor has a higher burden of proof to the effect that the debtor did not use its best efforts in the performance of the obligation. The doctrine of force majeure that has a statutory basis in most civil law jurisdictions comes particularly into play with regard to obligations to obtain a certain result as the debtor is liable if the result has not been achieved unless it is successful in arguing that the result was not achieved due to the creditor's fault or due to an event of force majeure. Civil law jurisdictions among themselves also show differences as to the requirements for force majeure: the external nature of the event, the foreseeability of the event and the impossibility to avoid the event with some jurisdictions taking a strict approach of these requirements and other jurisdictions adding an element of reasonableness as to any such events beyond the control of the debtor. Finally, force majeure in the civil law does not terminate the contract but only excuses the debtor from performance.

The theories of frustration of contracts and exemption from performance based on force majeure, apply equally to domestic and international contracts. In an international setting, the differences between various jurisdictions mentioned above emphasise the relevance of the law

* Professor of Law, Erasmus School of Law, Erasmus University Rotterdam; Council Member, ICC Institute of World Business Law.

applicable to the contract. Moreover, the events that might qualify as a frustrating or force majeure event arise frequently in practice and debtors often have to declare force majeure to suspend or terminate contractual performances. On an international plane, any such events may arise particularly in relation to doing business in countries with a higher risk profile related to climatological or political factors. Moreover, international contracts are more prone to opportunistic behaviour by a debtor to attempt to terminate a contract or to avoid its performance by invoking frustration or force majeure. The applicable law and appropriate dispute resolution methods often raise issues as to interpretation, application and enforcement of contracts. The question, thus, arises whether risks are not also to be avoided by creating more certainty, predictability and a level playing field between the contracting parties as to the definition of frustrating or force majeure events, the requirements for applying frustration of contracts and force majeure doctrines and the consequences of these doctrines by means of drafting appropriate clauses in contracts. Frequently, international contracts contain express clauses dealing with these issues.[2] The follow-up question is then whether international contract practice may not be assisted by a model clause which can be used in low value contracts to reduce transaction costs, in contracts with less sophisticated users that can rely inexpensively and quickly on a trusted model or as guidance for tailor-made contracts. Any such approach, furthermore, may also contribute to a better level playing field for users.

This contribution, in this respect, will discuss and analyse the 2003 ICC Force Majeure Clause[3] in the next section.

II. THE ICC FORCE MAJEURE CLAUSE 2003

For the reasons outlined in the Introduction, the ICC Commission on Commercial Law and Practice (CLP) in 2001 formed a task force to work on a revised edition of the ICC Force Majeure and Hardship publication of which the present writer was a member.[4] The mandate of the task force was to revise the ICC Force Majeure Clause 1985.

The task force met on a number of occasions between August 2001 and November 2002, subsequently submitted a proposal for an ICC Force Majeure and Hardship Clause to the CLP which adopted the proposal. The model clauses were published in February 2003 by ICC Publishing as the ICC Force Majeure Clause 2003 (Clause) and the ICC Hardship Clause 2003.[5] This contribution is limited to the ICC Force Majeure Clause 2003 and does not address the ICC Hardship Clause 2003. For reasons of convenience, reference will be made hereafter to force majeure events and force majeure clauses but these are intended also to cover frustration of contracts or similar clauses in contracts governed by the law of a common law country. It may, in this respect, be noted that also in such contracts, these clauses are also referred to as force majeure clauses. There is no empirical evidence as to the use of the Clause in practice.[6]

At present, a task force of the CLP is working on revised ICC clauses regarding force majeure and hardship. It is premature to compare the 2003 clauses with the draft revision clauses. It is hoped that this contribution may assist the task force in its endeavours to finalise the revised clauses.

As a preliminary and important observation, it is to be emphasised that—notwithstanding the advantages of a model clause—it is subject to party autonomy in a number of respects. First, the parties are free to adopt it and incorporate it in their contract. By virtue of party autonomy, the parties may adopt a model clause in full or in part or adjust it to their concerns and needs as they wish. The ICC Force Majeure Clause 2003 reflects this in part in paragraphs 1 and 3 where the consequences of force majeure enumerated in paragraphs 4 to 9 of the Clause are subject to express or implied agreement to the contrary (paragraph 1) or where the list of events which constitute force majeure are also subject to express or implied agreements to the contrary (paragraph 3).

Second, there may be myriad reasons for the parties to draft a tailor-made clause reflecting the particular features of a transaction, of the sector in which they operate or any other considerations. An example may be a unilateral force majeure clause as one may envisage in construction contracts where the main obligation of the employer is to pay for the works performed and where no frustrating or force majeure excusing events may be needed while the performance of the works by the contractor may well be affected by force majeure.

Third, the ICC Force Majeure Clause 2003 has been drafted in a balanced way in order to ensure the equality of debtors and creditors. Thus, it is particularly relevant for situations where time and costs matter and where there is hardly time or budget to draft tailor-made clauses or where parties are in relatively equal negotiation positions that they prefer to choose an internationally recognised platform ensuring their level playing fields. On the contrary, where parties are in unequal bargaining positions, the party in the stronger position may prefer its own template and impose it upon the other party.

II.A. Application

The ICC Force Majeure Clause 2003 applies if it is adopted by the parties expressly or impliedly or by reference. It does not constitute international custom, trade usage or by and large will not apply as a course of dealing between the parties. Parties are, thus, advised to opt for clear language incorporating the Clause into their contract. Any such incorporation may create hurdles if it is incomplete or ambiguous. The Introductory Note in this respect states that any reference in a contract to the "ICC Force Majeure Clause" shall, in the absence of evidence to the contrary, be deemed to be a reference to the ICC Force Majeure Clause 2003. This statement is aspirational but does not bind judges or arbitrators and, in the end, is a matter of construction under the applicable law or rules of law, also considering that there was a previous edition of an ICC Force Majeure Clause being the 1985 version. The statement, however, may constitute some persuasive authority and, in the context of the revision, it is relevant to pay some attention to this problem particularly regarding the relationship between the 2003 Clause and the revised Clause. Finally, the Clause may also have some persuasive authority even if not adopted by the parties as evidencing international best practice for force majeure clauses and shedding some light as to how force majeure events are to be interpreted and applied.

II.B. General Approach of the Clause

When preparing the 2003 Clause, the task force discussed various approaches in international practice regarding force majeure clauses. Traditionally, contracts under common law worked with lists of events often labelled "Acts of God". Contracts under civil law—often aligning with the statutory rules in a Civil Code—frequently copied the statutory requirements into a force majeure clause but (because of the repetition of the statutory rules without added value) amended or supplemented black letter statutory law with enumerating events that might qualify as force majeure to avoid the uncertainties attached to the lack of definition of such events in the Codes or statutes.

The task force was thus faced with some options: a common law list approach, a civil law open-ended approach or a combination of both. The list approach has the advantages of being clear, certain and of easy application but the drawbacks are the difficulties of defining the list of events (without each time adding language such as "any other event of a similar nature", the *eiusdem* rule) and of the closed nature of any list. An open-ended approach has the advantage of being capable of capturing events of an unexpected or new nature but the big disadvantage of providing scant assistance to business and their counsel who have to work with it as was already the experience in contracts in civil law jurisdictions which added lists to a general standard. The mixed approach combines the best of both worlds: a defined list of events with a fall back under a general standard. This was the reason for the task force to adopt this approach.

The general standard, however, does not only work as a fall back but also operates as a filter regarding listed events as a listed event as such does not trigger the clause and its effects but subjects it to the requirements of the general standard that a debtor needs to act reasonably to avoid or overcome the event or its effects.

II.C. The General Standard

As indicated, the general standard has two functions: it may be invoked in the absence of a listed event and a listed event must be tested against the requirements of the general standard. In addition, the general standard is combined with a rule regarding the burden of proof. The debtor invoking the general standard must prove that the requirements formulated by the general standard are met. This evidentiary rule seldom will raise problems under the applicable law as it is an expression of the general rule applicable in most jurisdictions that a party asserting that it is excused from performance by an event or that the contract is frustrated by certain events bears the burden of proof regarding the existence of such an event and of the requirements such event must meet.

The general standard is to be found in paragraph 1 of the Clause and reads as follows:

> Unless otherwise agreed in the contract between the parties expressly or impliedly, where a party to a contract fails to perform one or more of its contractual duties, the consequences set out in paragraphs 4 to 9 of this Clause will follow if and to the extent that that party proves:
>
> [a] that its failure to perform was caused by an impediment beyond its reasonable control; and

> [b] that it could not reasonably have been expected to have taken the occurrence of the impediment into account at the time of the conclusion of the contract; and
>
> [c] that it could not reasonably have avoided or overcome the effects of the impediment.

The drafting of the general standard was based on Article 79 (1) of the Convention on the International Sale of Goods (CISG)[7] with two differences: (1) the Clause provides that an impediment is to be beyond the reasonable control of the debtor while the word "reasonable" is lacking in Article 79 (1) CISG; and (2) the Clause as to avoidance or overcoming the effects of the impediment—unlike CISG—does not cover avoidance or overcoming the impediment itself. One may understand why the first difference was incorporated into the Clause. The task force revising the Clause, however, may contemplate aligning with Article 79 (1) CISG as to the second difference if consensus can be reached that a debtor not only needs to avoid or overcome the effects of the impediment but also needs to deal with the event itself.

Subject to these two differences, in interpreting and applying the general standard, inspiration and guidance may be found in Article 79 (1) CISG and the extensive case law and scholarly writings on the subject. The alignment of the Clause with Article 79 (1) CISG reflects a broader development in comparative law, particularly in civil law jurisdictions[8] but also in Article 2 of the Uniform Commercial Code in the United States, to replace strict sub-standards regarding the external cause of the event, the absolute unforeseeability of the event and the absolute impossibility to perform caused by the event by more flexible and lenient sub-standards such as an event beyond the control of the debtor (rather than external to the debtor), an event not contemplated at the time of the conclusion of the contract (rather than unforeseeability) and an event that could not reasonably have been avoided or overcome (rather than absolute impossibility to perform).

Paragraph 1 (as well as paragraph 3) of the Clause apply equally to force majeure events existing at the time of the conclusion of the contract and those arising thereafter. While most situations will arise after the contract has been concluded, there may be rare circumstances where such events exist at the time of contracting while the parties are not aware of such events. The Clause applies to both situations as the task force considered that also regarding existing events (as opposed to subsequent events) the parties may benefit from the provisions of the Clause.

Paragraph 2 of the Clause is interesting as it is not often found in force majeure clauses and deals with a neglected but important issue in contractual relationships as to contractual liability and exemption from liability regarding the use of third parties such as subcontractors in the performance of the contract. It provides as follows:

> Where a contracting party fails to perform one or more of its contractual duties because of default by a third party whom it has engaged to perform the whole or part of the contract, the consequences set out in paragraphs 4 to 9 of this Clause will only apply to the contracting party:
>
> [a] if and to the extent that the contracting party establishes the requirements set out in paragraph 1 of this Clause; and

[b] if and to the extent that the contracting party proves that the same requirements apply to the third party.

This provision is again modelled after the CISG, more specifically Article 79 (2) CISG which, however, is drafted differently in relation to the second condition, i.e. the requirement that the third party would also be exempt if Article 79 (1) were applied to him. It is submitted that the Clause did not intend to deviate from Article 79 (2) CISG and that, under the Clause, application of the general standard to a third party engaged, fully or in part, in the performance of the contract will lead to exemption of the debtor as if the third party were the debtor. Thus, the third party is identified with the debtor and force majeure on the part of the third party meeting the requirements of the general standard qualifies as force majeure of the debtor. As there is a specific regulation regarding the position of third parties engaged in the performance of the contract under the general standard, force majeure on the part of the third party has not been listed under the listed events of paragraph 3 of the Clause. On the other hand, force majeure on account of the third party will not automatically imply that the debtor is exempted under paragraph 1 of the Clause; the requirements of the general standard will also have to be tested in relation to the debtor. Thus, a debtor engaging a third party in the performance of its contractual obligations will be exempted if the criteria of paragraph 1 of the Clause are met both as to the debtor and as to the third party.

Finally, the general standard does not expressly provide a provision to deal with self-induced force majeure,[9] i.e. a force majeure event caused by the debtor (or for which he contributed), for example where a state-owned exporter causes a government agency to refuse an export licence under circumstances where the exporter would gain from non-performance by reselling at a higher price. As self-induced force majeure is not beyond the reasonable control of the party causing the force majeure event or such event might have been avoided or overcome, there was no need to specifically address this issue.

II.D. Listed Events

From the discussion above, it has become clear that the listed events are not exclusive and do not constitute a closed list and still enable a debtor to proof exemption from performance with regard to non-listed events under the general standard. This section discusses the listed events and their nature. It may be noted that the Clause as to listed events deviates from CISG, from most Civil Codes and from the Sale of Goods Act in combining a general standard with a list of events. It is submitted that this is a major benefit of the Clause as compared to uniform and domestic law.

The listed events to a certain extent trigger the application of the force majeure clause in that they put the creditor in a better evidentiary position as it does only have to prove the existence of the event which then automatically, by operation of its listing, qualifies as a force majeure event. However, any such force majeure event does not then trigger the Clause, as the force majeure event must still be tested against the general standard's requirement; the debtor still needs to prove that it could not reasonably have avoided or overcome the effects of the listed event. On the other hand, evidence of an event which qualifies as a listed event does not need to be tested against the other two requirements of the general standard. As paragraph 3 of the Clause refers only to paragraphs 1[a] and 1[b], a listed event is presumed to have established that the event is beyond the reasonable control of the debtor and that it was not contemplated at the time of the conclusion of the contract. The absence of a reference to paragraph 1 [c] of the Clause implies that also in the case of a listed event, evidence is required by the debtor that he could not reasonably have avoided or overcome the event. Under a listed event, the debtor, thus, has the burden of proof of the event and that it could not reasonably have avoided or overcome the impediment but not that it was beyond his reasonable control or was not contemplated at the time of contract formation. Conversely, as the evidentiary presumption does not finally dispose of the requirements of reasonable control and within the contemplation of the parties at the time of contracting, the presumption shifts the burden of proof to the creditor that still can prove that the event was within the reasonable control of the debtor or that the event was within the contemplation of the parties when concluding the contract.

For information purposes, the 2003 ICC Clause listed events may be quoted in full:

> In the absence of proof to the contrary and unless otherwise agreed in the contract between the parties expressly or impliedly, a party invoking this Clause shall be presumed to have established the conditions described in paragraph 1[a] and [b] of this Clause in case of the occurrence of one or more of the following impediments:
>
> [a] war (whether declared or not), armed conflict or the serious threat of same (including but not limited to hostile attack, blockade, military embargo), hostilities, invasion, act of a foreign enemy, extensive military mobilisation;
>
> [b] civil war, riot rebellion and revolution, military or usurped power, insurrection, civil commotion or disorder, mob violence, act of civil disobedience;
>
> [c] act of terrorism, sabotage or piracy;
>
> [d] act of authority whether lawful or unlawful, compliance with any law or governmental order, rule, regulation or direction, curfew restriction, expropriation, compulsory acquisition, seizure of works, requisition, nationalisation;
>
> [e] act of God, plague, epidemic, natural disaster such as but not limited to violent storm, cyclone, typhoon, hurricane, tornado, blizzard, earthquake, volcanic activity, landslide, tidal wave, tsunami, flood, damage or destruction by lightning, drought;
>
> [f] explosion, fire, destruction of machines, equipment, factories and of any kind of installation, prolonged break-down of transport, telecommunication or electric current;
>
> [g] general labour disturbance such as but not limited to boycott, strike and lock-out, go-slow, occupation of factories and premises.

This list of events, largely copied from the earlier ICC Force Majeure Clause, does not need further discussion as they correspond to similar lists often found in force majeure clauses. The fall back of the general standard may solve gaps in the list or in situations where the listed event leads to interpretation or application problems. In those cases, the difference between the exemption regime for listed events and the general standard is to be found in the different evidentiary treatment. A gap in the list or a problem regarding the interpretation of an event may require relying on the general standard and the debtor may also have to prove that the impediment was beyond its reasonable control and was not contemplated at the time of the conclusion of the contract.

II.E. Effects of a Force Majeure Event

Triggering force majeure under the Clause requires the debtor—under paragraph 4—to give notice without delay as of the time when the impediment causes the failure to perform. If notice is not given without delay, any time from which the debtor is relieved from non-performance only runs as of the time notice reaches the creditor.

If force majeure is successfully triggered, it exempts the debtor from its duty to perform its obligations under contract as of the time notice is given. Under paragraph 5 of the Clause, the debtor is also exempted from any liability in damages or any other contractual remedy for breach of contract as of the same moment. Paragraph 7 obliges the debtor to take all reasonable means to limit the effect of the impediment or event invoked upon performance of its contractual obligations. These provisions all follow the civil law approach under which force majeure does not terminate the contract but is only an excuse for non-performance. As the excuse is legitimised by law or under the Clause, there also is no room for other remedies for breach of contract as the breach is excused.[10] On the other hand, the debtor has an obligation to mitigate the effects of its excuse.

Under paragraph 6, an important distinction is made between events which only temporarily prevent the debtor to perform and events which make it indefinitely impossible to perform. This is an essential provision to clarify the uncertainties under the law of civil law jurisdictions as to whether force majeure, although it is only an excuse for non-performance, leads to a freezing of the contractual relationship and its coming to a standstill and eventually to a no-fault *de facto* termination. Contract practice has dealt with this problem for a long time with provisions providing for a suspension of the contract pending the force majeure situation in cases where the force majeure situation is considered to be temporary and with procedural and substantive provisions as to the rights and obligations of the parties, often with a right for the creditor to terminate the contract if the force majeure situation exceeds a certain period of time.[11] It is fortunate that paragraph 6 of the Clause also adopted this approach in providing that the debtor is not relieved permanently from performing his obligations but that a temporary force majeure situation only exempts from performance to the extent and as long as force majeure impedes performance by the debtor.[12] The debtor is then under an obligation to notify the creditor as soon as the force majeure situation ceases to impede the performance of its contractual obligations. The task force did not add a provision entitling the creditor to terminate the contract if the force majeure situation exceeds a certain period as it is difficult to determine any such period as it is context specific. Parties adopting the Clause may consider reflecting on this issue and amend the Clause if so desired.

The effects for a creditor being bound by a contract suspended on account of a temporary force majeure situation which does, however, not exclude the debtor, may be mitigated by paragraph 8 of the Clause which entitles either party to terminate the contract by notification within a reasonable period to the other party provided the duration of the force majeure situation has the effect of substantially depriving either or both contracting parties of what they were reasonably entitled to expect under the contract. Paragraph 9 complements paragraph 8 with a provision under which a party deriving a benefit before the termination of the contract by reason of anything done by another party in the performance of the contract, shall pay to the other party a sum of money equivalent to the value of such benefit. Paragraph 8 is an escape clause addressing the duration of the force majeure situation which, however, may lead to opportunistic behaviour and to interpretation problems as to whether a termination is warranted in view of the open-ended criterion of substantial loss of reasonable expectations under the contract. Parties may be advised to consider whether under the circumstances the maximum duration of the force majeure situation is not to be determined in advance.

III. CONCLUSION

The ICC Force Majeure Clause 2003 may be considered as state of the art when it was published reflecting international best practice as well as the most recent developments in uniform law and comparative law. Evidently, parties to international commercial contracts may consider not adopting this model or adopt it only in part or with some modifications. In other respects, the Clause may be useful for certain users, sectors or situations or as persuasive authority from various perspectives. The revision work of the task force is to be encouraged to take a fresh look at the Clause and, based on its analyses, to come forward with a new clause which may serve the interests of the international business community.

NOTES

1. For the English position, see *National Carriers Ltd v Panalpina (Northern) Ltd* [1981] AC 675 (HL), *J. Lauritzen A/S v Wijsmuller B.V.* (The Super Servant Two) [1990] 1 Lloyd's Rep 1 (CA).
2. Fontaine, Marcel and De Ly, Filip, 'Drafting international contracts, An analysis of contract clauses', Ardsley, New York, Transnational, 2006, 401-451 (reprint Martinus Nijhoff, Leyden, 2009). For the French edition, see Fontaine, Marcel and De Ly, Filip, 'Analyse et rédaction de clauses', second edition, Brussels/Paris, Bruylant/Forum européen de la communication, 2003, 715 pp.; for the Italian edition, see Fontaine, Marcel and De Ly, Filip, 'La redazione dei contratti internazionali, A partire dall'analisi delle clausole', edited by Renzo Maria Morresi, Milan, Giuffré, 2008, 834 pp.; and for the Spanish edition, see Fontaine, Marcel and De Ly, Filip, 'La redacción de contratos internacionales, Análisis de cláusulas', Madrid, Civitas Thomson Reuters, 2013, 720 pp.
3. See also Bortolotti, F., 'Le clausole di forza maggiore nei contratti internazionali, con particolare riferimento alla *ICC Force Majeure Clause 2003*', Diritto del commercio internazionale, 2004, 3-24.
4. The task force was chaired by Professor Jan Ramberg, its draftsman-in-chief was Professor Charles Debattista and other members were Alexis Mourre, René von Samson-Himmelsterna, Fabian von Schlabrendorff and Peter Delargy.
5. ICC Publication No. 650, Paris, ICC Publishing, February 2003, 23 pp.
6. In one case to be decided by a sole arbitrator under the Stockholm Chamber of Commerce (SCC) Arbitration Rules (Case V 068/2011), Russian and German parties were involved in a dispute where there also a challenge to the jurisdiction of the arbitrator which was rejected. In the jurisdictional challenge, reference was made to the following choice of law provision: "The Parties agree hereby that International Law shall apply in case of settlement of any disputes arising out or in connection with this Contract. This Contract shall be governed by the regulations of the International Chamber of Commerce, Paris (France) with regard to Force Majeure circumstances." The SCC Board decided that this clause did not amount to a situation where the SCC did not manifestly lack jurisdiction over the dispute; the sole arbitrator endorsed that decision and ruled that the reference to the ICC Rules on Force Majeure were substantive provisions irrelevant for the determination of his jurisdiction under the SCC Arbitration Rules. The informa-

tion referred to above is to be found in Mutis Tellez, Felipe, *Prima Facie* Decisions on Jurisdiction of the Arbitration Institute of the Stockholm Chamber of Commerce: Towards Consolidation of a "Pro Arbitration" Approach, available at https://sccinstitute.com/media/29996/felipe-mutis-tellez_paper-on-scc-challenges-on-jurisdiction.pdf.

7. Paragraph 1 of the Clause was also inspired by the provision of the UNIDROIT Principles of International Commercial Contracts now in its fourth edition of 2016 (Article 7.1.7 (Force majeure)), available at www.unidroit.org.

8. A most recent example is France which replaced strict force majeure conditions with the new Article 1218 of its Civil Code which provides as follows: "*Il y a force majeure en matière contractuelle lorsqu'un événement échappant au contrôle du débiteur, qui ne pouvait être raisonnablement prévu lors de la conclusion du contrat et dont les effets ne peuvent être évités par des mesures appropriées, empêche l'exécution de son obligation par le débiteur.*
Si l'empêchement est temporaire, l'exécution de l'obligation est suspendue à moins que le retard qui en résulterait ne justifie la résolution du contrat. Si l'empêchement est définitif, le contrat est résolu de plein droit et les parties sont libérées de leurs obligations dans les conditions prévues aux articles 1351 et 1351-1."

9. The expression and the problems created by self-induced force majeure go back to an English case *Czarnikow Ltd v Centrala Handlu Zagranicznego Rolimpex* [1979] AC 351.

10. Article 79 (5) CISG provides in this respect that nothing in its force majeure Article 79 prevents either party from exercising any right other than to claim damages under CISG. Article 7.1.7 of the UNIDROIT Principles is even more generous as it states that nothing in its force majeure article prevents a party from exercising a right to terminate the contract or to withhold performance or request interest on money due.

11. Fontaine, Marcel and De Ly, F., *op. cit.*, 429-437.

12. Likewise, Article 79 (3) CISG provides for excuse from non-performance for the period during which the impediment exists but does not deal with permanent effects of force majeure situations or with duration limits. Article 7.1.7 (2) of the 2016 UNIDROIT Principles in this respect provides that if the impediment is temporary, the excuse shall have effect for such period as is reasonable having regard to the effect of the impediment on the performance of the contract.

Chapter 5

Revision of the ICC Force Majeure and Hardship Clause

by Prof Dr H. Ercüment Erdem*

I. INTRODUCTION

It has been on the agenda of the International Chamber of Commerce ("ICC") Commission on Commercial Law and Practice (the "CLP Commission") since 2016 to draft a short and simplified version of the ICC Force Majeure Clause 2003 (the "2003 FM Clause") for easier use, especially, by small and medium-sized enterprises (the "SME"s).

The reason that led to such drafting is the fact that the 2003 FM Clause is currently preferred to be included in contracts by way of reference, instead of full incorporation, due to its rather long and complex nature. This issue becomes more important when shorter contracts of less sophisticated companies are taken into consideration. The CLP Commission considered that the 2003 FM Clause is not user-friendly for such companies, since reference to a clause outside of a contract is complicated. The CLP Commission, accordingly, formed a working group (the "Working Group"), which created the short form of the 2003 FM Clause (the "Short Form") for such situations, to be directly incorporated into contracts. During this process, the Working Group had to find the right length, as a too short or general clause would not be helpful to judges or arbitrators. In any event, any perceived gaps in the Short Form are to be interpreted by reference to the long form.

After the first draft of the Short Form was prepared, the CLP Commission agreed to a proposal suggesting that the 2003 FM Clause should be revised, as well as the ICC Hardship Clause 2003 (the "2003 Hardship Clause") (the 2003 FM Clause and the 2003 Hardship Clause, collectively, the "Clauses"), to accompany the Short Form. In the revised 2003 FM Clause (the "New FM Clause") and the revised 2003 Hardship Clause (the "New Hardship Clause") (the New FM Clause and the New Hardship Clause, collectively, the "New Clauses"), the language and mechanism of the Clauses are to be simplified.

II. NEW FM CLAUSE

II.A. In General

In principle, the New FM Clause follows the structure of the 2003 FM Clause, but aims to simplify and render it more user-friendly. This being said, the New FM Clause also comes with some novelties in terms of its structure, as it now includes definitions of "Force Majeure" and "Affected Party," as well as paragraph headings.

* Founder and Senior Partner of Erdem & Erdem Law Office

The 2003 FM Clause does not define 'force majeure,' but describes it in its first paragraph. The Working Group of the New FM Clause adopts a different approach, and defines 'force majeure.' In accordance with the first paragraph of the New FM Clause,

> "Force Majeure" means the occurrence of an event or circumstance ("Force Majeure Event") that prevents or impedes a party from performing one or more of its contractual obligations under the contract, if and to the extent that the party affected by the impediment ("the Affected Party") proves:
>
> a. That such impediment is beyond its reasonable control; and
>
> b. That it could not reasonably have been foreseen at the time of the conclusion of the contract; and
>
> c. That the effects of the impediment could not reasonably have been avoided or overcome by the Affected Party."

Feedback from some of the National Committees was that the Notes of the 2003 FM Clause render the Clause less comprehensible and difficult to use since the SMEs are confusing to distinguish the main text of the 2003 FM Clause from the Notes. The Working Group of the New FM Clause took into consideration this feedback and deleted the Notes, although they are very useful to better understand the provisions of the Clause. Instead of the Notes that are intended to comment on the provisions, the Working Group has elected to insert explanation boxes, if needed, after certain paragraphs to highlight various important points of that paragraph.

All of these structural changes are aimed to create a user-friendly and easy-to-understand text, not only for lawyers, but for the parties, as well.

II.B. Main Conditions

The 2003 FM Clause has not gone through fundamental changes. The New FM Clause retains the following conditions for the occurrence of a force majeure event, the same as in the 2003 FM Clause, while bringing some changes to the wording, as follows:

a. The impediment is beyond the affected party's reasonable control;

b. It could not reasonably have been foreseen at the time of the conclusion of the contract; and

c. The effects of the impediment could not reasonably have been avoided, nor overcome, by the affected party.

In order for an event to be considered as a force majeure under the New FM Clause, all of these three conditions must be established, together. There is no difference between the 2003 FM Clause and the New FM Clause in establishing these conditions. In fact, this system was already established in the 1985 ICC Force Majeure Clause (the "1985 FM Clause"). The 2003 FM Clause amalgamated the 1985 FM Clause with the well-established and accepted elements introduced by international documents, such as Article 79 of the United Nations Convention on Contracts for the International Sale of Goods ("CISG"), Section 8:108 of the Principles of European Contract Law ("PECL"), and Article 7.1.7 of the UNIDROIT Principles of International Commercial Contracts 1994.

The New FM Clause maintains the system introduced through the 2003 FM Clause for the non-performance by third parties. It is generally understood that these third parties are the sub-contractors. This provision establishes its basis in Article 79(2) of the CISG. The party invoking the Force Majeure must prove that the conditions set forth in the first paragraph of the FM Clause are established with respect to itself, and with respect to the third party.

II.C. Presumption

The 2003 FM Clause contains a list of events that are presumed to fulfil the conditions of being beyond the relevant party's reasonable control, and reasonably unforeseeable. If any event listed is realized, the affected party is released from the obligation to prove that this event is beyond its reasonable control, and could not be reasonably foreseen at the time of conclusion of the contract. Therefore, the affected party must prove only that the effects of this event could not have been reasonably avoided, nor overcome. If an event is not listed, the party invoking this event as a Force Majeure must establish all three conditions set forth in the first paragraph of the New FM Clause.

The Working Group carefully considered whether to retain this presumption and the events listed. Some members of the Working Group argued that the list of events should be illustrative only, and should not create a presumption, as was the case in the 1985 FM Clause. The others maintained to retain the existing structure of presumption, but proposed to simplify the list. As the purpose of the New FM Clause is to be more user-friendly and less complicated for SMEs, the Working Group decided to keep the presumption as it is in the 2003 FM Clause. In doing so, the Working Group believed to provide predictability for users who are not customizing the drafting of this type of clause into their contracts.

While adding to or removing from the list of such presumptions, the Working Group has consulted with those who have overseen the development of various ICC model contracts, including other working groups of ICC and National Committees, and obtained their sector-specific opinions. Dozens of court decisions and arbitral awards have been reviewed in order to determine the most common force majeure events that have led to disputes between contracting parties in the past.

In the New FM Clause, the following events are not listed, contrary to the 2003 FM Clause: armed conflict or serious threat of the same (including but not limited to hostile attack, blockade, military embargo), civil commotion or disorder, mob violence, act of civil disobedience, curfew restriction, and compulsory acquisition.

On the other hand, taking the recent global developments into account, currency and trade restrictions, as well as embargos and sanctions, are now included in the list. Certain other changes have also been made, such as the rewording of "act of God, plague, epidemic, natural disaster, such as, but not limited to, violent storm, cyclone, typhoon, hurricane, tornado, blizzard, earthquake, volcanic activity, landslide, tidal wave, tsunami, flood, damage or destruction by lightning, drought" as "plague, epidemic, natural disaster or extreme natural event" for simplification purposes.

For the sake of the principles of party autonomy and freedom of contract, the parties are, again, allowed to add or delete events to and from the list, taking into account particular situations, e.g. by excluding acts of authority or export restrictions, or by including labour disturbances affecting only their own enterprise, provided that adding new events to the list does not relieve them from proving that the effects of the impediment could not reasonably have been avoided, nor overcome.

II.D. Notification

Another novelty of the New FM Clause is the inclusion of an explicit paragraph regarding the notification requirement. According to the newly added paragraph 4, the party affected by the impediment shall give notice of the event without delay to the other party. In the 2003 FM Clause, the notice requirement is not structured independently, but is found within paragraphs 4, 5, 6 and 8 of the 2003 FM Clause. The Working Group considered that a separate paragraph for the notice requirement would be more appropriate in light of the very important consequences attached to the notice.

II.E. Consequences of Force Majeure

The consequences of force majeure remain essentially the same as the 2003 FM Clause; however, there are few modifications:

II.E.1. Suspension of the Performance of the Obligations by Non-Affected Party

Under the New FM Clause, it is clearly provided that the non-invoking party is entitled to suspend the performance of its obligations, if applicable, from the date of the notice. The Working Group considered that the suspension of the obligations by the non-affected party is a legal and logical consequence when the affected party is prevented from performing its obligations due to force majeure. It is also an application of the well-established principle of *exceptio non adimpleti contractus* that finds its place in several national laws (see, for example, Article 97 of Turkish Code of Obligations No. 6098 ("TCO"); Article 82 of the Swiss Code of Obligations ("SCO"); for the sale contracts, Article 1612 of the French Civil Code ("FCC"); and Section 320 of the German Civil Code ("BGB")). The principle of *exceptio non adimpleti contractus* is also regulated in Article 7.1.3 of the UNIDROIT Principles of International Commercial Contracts 2016 (the "UNIDROIT Principles").

II.E.2. Termination of the Contract

During the drafting of the 2003 FM Clause, according to the note accompanying paragraph 8 that deals with contract termination, the previous working group faced two options regarding the moment at which temporary suspension of the contract through force majeure would last long enough to lead to termination: The first was to establish a fixed period; the second was to provide a formula to calculate that period. The working group adopted the latter approach because it was felt that it would be difficult to establish a single period that would be appropriate for all sectors of industry, and in all circumstances.

The New FM Clause derogates from such approach: In order to increase certainty and foreseeability, a maximum duration of 120 (one hundred and twenty) days has been provided, which can be changed by agreement of the parties at any time according to their needs. Accordingly, in addition to the general rule to determine each particular case as to when the duration of the impediment is unsustainable, and entitles the parties to terminate the contract, the New FM Clause suggests that unless otherwise agreed, the contract may be terminated by either party if the duration of the impediment exceeds 120 (one hundred and twenty) days. By fixing a maximum duration, the Working Group added a new option to the formula exercised by Article 25 of the CISG, Section 8:103 of the PECL, and Article 7.3.1 of the UNIDROIT Principles.

II.F. Short Form

The Short Form comprises the main elements of the long form, but attempted to do so in only three paragraphs. In order to prevent any discrepancies between the long form and Short Form, both texts employ the exact wording; however, the Short Form, as its name suggests, is shorter. Therefore, the Short Form does not have paragraph titles and explanatory boxes. Some paragraphs are unified; this is the case for the consequences of force majeure (save for the last sentence that deals with suspension by the non-affected party), temporary impediment and contract termination. Some paragraphs are not addressed in the Short Form, such as non-performance by third parties, notification, duty to mitigate, and unjust enrichment.

Although the Working Group has not yet decided how to present the Clause in general, the Short Form will be in such form and shape so that the parties may copy and paste it directly into their contracts.

III. NEW HARDSHIP CLAUSE

III.A. In General

The main revisions to the Clauses relates to hardship. Several national laws deal with hardship situations and suggest solutions that may substantially differ from country to country. In order to more clearly define hardship situations, the parties may wish to regulate this in their agreement, independent from the governing law of the contract. While the CLP Commission and the Working Group intend to satisfy this need through a standard clause, which can be included in individual contracts, discussions have ensued as to whether or not to include a judge's or an arbitrator's authority to adapt a contract in the event of the parties' failure to agree on alternative contractual terms in a hardship situation.

During the drafting of the 2003 Hardship Clause, the tendency leaned away from a judge's or arbitrator's intervention and, therefore, only a termination option was available. Fear that the judge or arbitrator would adapt the contract in such a way that neither party would prefer played a role in shaping this drafting.

The Working Group kept the first and second paragraphs of the 2003 Hardship Clause as is, but provided new options, such as consequences of the hardship.

III.B. New Options

Taking into consideration the global trend towards attempting to maintain the contract where possible ("*favor contractus*"), i.e. termination being the last resort, the Working Group decided to include three alternatives in the New Hardship Clause: Provided that the parties are unable to agree upon alternative contractual terms: (i) the party invoking this Clause may terminate the contract (Option 3A); (ii) either party may request the judge or arbitrator to adapt or terminate the contract, as appropriate (Option 3B); and (iii) either party may request the judge or arbitrator to declare its termination (Option 3C).

In fact, two remedies are available: Termination or adaptation. According to the Working Group, including an option for adaptation by a judge or arbitrator may act as an incentive for the parties to agree to alternative terms by themselves in order to avoid third party intervention.

Option 3A is the same as the existing solution of the 2003 Hardship Clause, which provides that the party invoking this Clause is entitled to terminate the contract. The only difference brought to the existing solution is to emphasize that the party who is invoking this Clause and terminating the contract is not entitled to request adaptation without the agreement of the other party. The reason for this emphasis is to make clear that if the the applicable law provides for adaption of the contract, the party invoking the Hardship cannot request adaptation on its own without the agreement of the other party.

Option 3B provides for the party invoking the hardship clause to request the judge or arbitrator to adapt the contract or declare its termination, as appropriate, as allowed for under various national laws, as well as the UNIDROIT Principles. It is important that the Clauses point in the same direction as the UNIDROIT Principles, as many model contracts drafted by the ICC CLP Commission, including, but not limited to, the ICC Model NCND (Non-Circumvention and Non-Disclosure) Agreement, the ICC Model International Consulting Services Contract, and the ICC Model Commercial Agency Contract, regulate that the contract shall be governed by, among others, the UNIDROIT Principles. An approach, similar to that of the UNIDROIT Principles, will prevent any possible discrepancies within the contract in terms of hardship situations.

Pursuant to Article 6.2.3 of the UNIDROIT Principles on the effects of hardship, upon failure to reach agreement within a reasonable time, either party may resort to the court, upon which the court may, if reasonable, (a) terminate the contract on a date, and on such terms to be fixed, or (b) adapt the contract with a view to restoring its equilibrium. The New Hardship Clause does not differ from the UNIDROIT Principles.

The below-examined national laws also provide for adaptation of the contract in the event of hardship:

> Under Turkish law, Article 138 of the TCO regulates that the party invoking the hardship clause is entitled to ask the judge to adapt the contract and, where this is not possible, to terminate it.

> German law, under Section 313 of the BGB, allows for adaptation of the contract, and if adaptation of the contract is not possible, or one party cannot reasonably be expected to accept it, the disadvantaged party may terminate the contract.

> Swiss law does not include a general hardship clause, while the adaptation option is accepted by the courts. This being said, Article 19 of the draft general section of the SCO that is expected in 2020, regulates that the court may adapt or void the contract, if, according to the principle of good faith, the performance of an obligation becomes unreasonable due to an unforeseeable change in circumstances.

> Despite adaptation was a legal resort, which has been refused by the French courts for many years, Article 1195 of the FCC, introduced by the Law of Obligations Reform of 2016, provides that in the event of refusal, or upon the failure to renegotiate, the parties may agree to terminate the contract from the date, and on the conditions that they so determine, or through common agreement, and request that the court order its adaptation. In the absence of an agreement within a reasonable time, the court may, at the request of a party, adapt the contract or put an end to it, on a date, and subject to such conditions it so determines.

Option 3C is a modified version of the existing solution of the 2003 Hardship Clause and the new Option 3A. The Working Group discussed this solution at length, and decided that termination by the invoking party may be arbitrary and could be misused. Therefore, the Working Group preferred to involve the judge or the arbitrator in the termination. While revising the solution brought by the 2003 Hardship Clause, the Working Group was aware of the potential difficulties that the involvement of a judge or an arbitrator may cause, such as lengthy and costly procedures in some jurisdictions. However, the Working Group prefers that the judge or the arbitrator assess burdensome conditions that may lead to termination of the contract, since termination should be the last resort.

IV. CONCLUSION AND NEXT STEPS

The process that started with the idea of creating the Short Form 2003 FM Clause progressed with updates to the Clauses, as well. The 2003 FM Clause remains largely unchanged, in substance, but the New FM Clause includes certain structural changes to make it more simple and user-friendly. The most significant changes may be summarized, as follows:

> Simplification of the list of presumed force majeure events;

> Separate paragraph for the notice requirement;

> Suspension of the performance by the non-affected party when the affected party invokes force majeure;

> Fixing a time period of 120 days for the duration of the force majeure after which the contract may be terminated, together with the general formula of depriving the parties of what they were reasonably entitled to expect from the contract.

The 2003 Hardship Clause has gone through a fundamental change through the introduction of the adaptation option, aside from termination. The Working Group took into consideration the UNIDROIT Principles, as well as the recent developments in national laws, and agreed that including an option for adaptation or termination by a judge or arbitrator could be an incentive for the parties to agree to alternative terms by themselves.

The New Clauses have not yet taken their final shapes, awaiting comments and approvals from the National Committees. The Working Group discussed the draft attached to this paper in its meeting of 24 October 2018, the day prior to the CLP Commission meeting. The conference planned to be organized by ICC Italy in May of 2019, to be held in Rome, will also focus on the New Clauses, perhaps with the participation of UNIDROIT. The Working Group will take into account the views to be brought forward at such events to produce the final versions of the New Clauses, with the aim to benefit the business world in the most efficient manner possible.

Once approved by the National Committees and the CLP Commission, the New FM Clause will enter into force. However, it will not abrogate the 2003 FM Clause. The parties may continue to use the 2003 FM Clause, and will be able to do so by making clear reference to that Clause.

Attachment
DRAFT ICC FORCE MAJEURE CLAUSE ("Clause") (Long Form)

The concept of force majeure is known by most national laws but a force majeure clause nevertheless generally forms part of the contracts. Force majeure may be construed differently depending on the jurisdiction and the bargaining powers of the parties. That is why the ICC has created two balanced Force Majeure Clauses, the "Long Form" and the "Short Form".

The ICC Force Majeure Clause (Long Form) can be included in the contract or incorporated by reference by stating "The ICC Force Majeure Clause (Long Form) is incorporated in the present contract". Parties may also use the Clause as the basis for drafting a "tailor-made" clause, which takes into account their specific needs.

Should the parties prefer a shorter clause, they can include in their contract the "Short Form" of the ICC Force Majeure Clause. The Long Form nevertheless gives guidance on issues in which the Short Form is silent.

As regards the question of what constitutes force majeure, the ICC Force Majeure Clause intends to achieve a compromise between the general requirements of force majeure, which need to be met in all cases and the indication of events presumed to be beyond the control of the parties and not foreseeable at the time of the conclusion of the contract. For that purpose, the ICC Force Majeure Clause provides a general definition (paragraph 1) and a list of force majeure events (paragraph 3) which are presumed to qualify for force majeure (Paragraph 3). Parties are invited to check the list and verify if some events should be deleted from or added to it, in accordance with their specific needs.

The main consequence of successfully invoking force majeure is that the Affected Party is relieved from its duty to perform and from responsibility or damages from the date of occurrence of the event (provided that the other party has been notified timely) and, in case of a temporary impediment, until the impediment ceases to prevent the performance.

1. DEFINITION

"Force Majeure" means the occurrence of an event or circumstance ("Force Majeure Event") that prevents or impedes a party from performing one or more of its contractual obligations under the contract, if and to the extent that the party affected by the impediment ("the Affected Party") proves:

a. that such impediment is beyond its reasonable control; and

b. that it could not reasonably have been foreseen at the time of the conclusion of the contract; and

c. that the effects of the impediment could not reasonably have been avoided or overcome by the Affected Party.

The definition of Force Majeure provides a lower threshold for invoking the clause than impossibility of performance. This is expressed by the reference to reasonableness in conditions (a) to (c) of the clause.

2. NON-PERFORMANCE BY THIRD PARTIES

Where a contracting party fails to perform one or more of its contractual obligations because of default by a third party whom it has engaged to perform the whole or part of the contract, the contracting party may invoke Force Majeure only to the extent that the requirements under paragraph 1 of this Clause are established both for the contracting party and for the third party.

This paragraph intends to exclude that non-performance by a third party or sub-contractor can be considered as such as Force Majeure. The Affected Party must prove that the Force Majeure conditions are as well met for the non-performance of the third party, to which also the presumption of paragraph 3 of this Clause will apply.

3. PRESUMED FORCE MAJEURE EVENTS

In the absence of proof to the contrary, the following events affecting a party shall be presumed to fulfil conditions (a) and (b) under paragraph 1 of this Clause, and the Affected Party only needs to prove that condition (c) of paragraph 1 is satisfied:

The Presumed Force Majeure Events commonly qualify as Force Majeure [if preventing the performance of the contract]. It is therefore presumed that in the presence of one or more of these events the conditions of Force Majeure are fulfilled, and the Affected Party need not prove the conditions (a) and (b) of paragraph 1 of this Clause (i.e. that the event was out of its control and unforeseeable), leaving to the other party the burden of proving the contrary. The party invoking Force Majeure must in any case prove the existence of condition (c), i.e. that the effects of the impediment could not reasonably have been avoided or overcome.

a. war (whether declared or not), hostilities, invasion, act of foreign enemies, extensive military mobilisation;

b. civil war, riot, rebellion and revolution, military or usurped power, insurrection, act of terrorism, sabotage or piracy;

c. currency and trade restriction, embargo, sanction;

d. act of authority whether lawful or unlawful, compliance with any law or governmental order, expropriation, seizure of works, requisition, nationalisation;

e. plague, epidemic, natural disaster or extreme natural event;

f. explosion, fire, destruction of equipment, prolonged break-down of transport, telecommunication, information system or energy;

g. general labour disturbance such as boycott, strike and lock-out, go-slow, occupation of factories and premises.

Parties may add or delete events from the list, according to particular situations, e.g. by excluding acts of authority or export restrictions, or by including labour disturbances affecting only their own enterprise. Parties are reminded that adding new events to the list does not relieve them from proving that condition (c) of paragraph 1 is satisfied.

4. NOTIFICATION

The Affected Party shall give notice of the event without delay to the other party.

5. CONSEQUENCES OF FORCE MAJEURE

A party successfully invoking this Clause is relieved from its duty to perform its obligations under the Contract and from any liability in damages or from any other contractual remedy for breach of contract, from the time at which the impediment causes inability to perform, provided that the notice thereof is given without delay. If notice thereof is not given without delay, the relief is effective from the time at which notice thereof reaches the other party. The other party may suspend the performance of its obligations, if applicable, from the date of the notice.

The main purpose of this paragraph is to clarify that the Affected Party is relieved from the performance of the obligations subject to Force Majeure from the occurrence of the impediment, provided that a timely notice is given. In order to avoid the Affected Party invoking Force Majeure only at a later stage (e.g. when the other party claims non-performance) where a timely notice is not given, the effects of the Force Majeure are delayed until the receipt of the notice.

The other party may suspend the performance of its obligations upon the receipt of the notice to the extent these obligations result from the obligations impeded by Force Majeure and they are suspendable.

6. TEMPORARY IMPEDIMENT

Where the effect of the impediment or event invoked is temporary, the consequences set out under paragraph 5 above shall apply only as long as the impediment invoked prevents performance by the Affected Party of its contractual obligations. The Affected Party must notify the other party as soon as the impediment ceases to impede performance of its contractual obligations.

7. DUTY TO MITIGATE

The Affected Party is under an obligation to take all reasonable means to limit the effect of the event invoked upon performance of the contract.

8. CONTRACT TERMINATION

Where the duration of the impediment invoked has the effect of substantially depriving the contracting parties of what they were reasonably entitled to expect under the contract, either party has the right to terminate the contract by notification within a reasonable period to the other party. Unless otherwise agreed, the parties expressly agree that the contract may be terminated by either party if the duration of the impediment exceeds 120 days.

This paragraph 8 establishes a general rule for determining in each particular case when the duration of the impediment in unsustainable and entitles the parties to terminate the contract. In order to increase certainty and foreseeability, a maximum duration of 120 days has been provided, which can of course be changed by agreement of the parties at any time according to their needs.

9. UNJUST ENRICHMENT

Where paragraph 8 above applies and where either contracting party has, by reason of anything done by another contracting party in the performance of the contract, derived a benefit before the termination of the contract, the party deriving such a benefit shall pay to the other party a sum of money equivalent to the value of such benefit.

DRAFT ICC FORCE MAJEURE CLAUSE ("Clause") (Short Form)

This Short Form is a reduced version of the Long Form, which is limited to some essential provision. It is intended to users who wish to incorporate in their contract a balanced and well-drafted standard clause covering the most important issues, which can arise in this context.

Users must be aware that this Short Form, by its very nature, has a limited scope and does not necessarily cover all issues, which may relevant in the specific business context. When this is the case, parties should draft a specific clause on the basis ot the ICC Long Form.

1. "Force Majeure" means the occurrence of an event or circumstance that prevents or impedes a party from performing one or more of its contractual obligations under the contract, if and to the extent that that party proves: [a] that such impediment is beyond its reasonable control; and [b] that it could not reasonably have been foreseen at the time of the conclusion of the contract; and [c] that the effects of the impediment could not reasonably have been avoided or overcome by the affected party.
2. In the absence of proof to the contrary, the following events affecting a party shall be presumed to fulfil conditions (a) and (b) under paragraph 1 of this Clause: (i) war (whether declared or not), hostilities, invasion, act of foreign enemies, extensive military mobilisation; (ii) civil war, riot, rebellion and revolution, military or usurped power, insurrection, act of terrorism, sabotage or piracy; (iii) currency and trade restriction, embargo, sanction; (iv) act of authority whether lawful or unlawful, compliance with any law or governmental order, expropriation, seizure of works, requisition, nationalisation; (v) plague, epidemic, natural disaster or extreme natural event; (vi) explosion, fire, destruction of equipment, prolonged break-down

of transport, telecommunication, information system or energy; (vii) general labour disturbance such as boycott, strike and lock-out, go-slow, occupation of factories and premises.

3. A party successfully invoking this Clause is relieved from its duty to perform its obligations under the contract and from any liability in damages or from any other contractual remedy for breach of contract, from the time at which the impediment causes inability to perform, provided that the notice thereof is given without delay. If notice thereof is not given without delay, the relief is effective from the time at which notice thereof reaches the other party. Where the effect of the impediment or event invoked is temporary, the above consequences shall apply only as long as the impediment invoked impedes performance by the affected party. Where the duration of the impediment invoked has the effect of substantially depriving the contracting parties of what they were reasonably entitled to expect under the contract, either party has the right to terminate the contract by notification within a reasonable period to the other party. Unless otherwise agreed, the parties expressly agree that the contract may be terminated by either party if the duration of the impediment exceeds 120 days.

DRAFT ICC HARDSHIP CLAUSE ("Clause")

Several domestic laws deal with hardship situations, through rules intended to protect the disadvantaged party in case events have rendered performance more onerous than could reasonably have been anticipated at the time of the conclusion of the contract. However the solutions adopted by national laws may be substantially different from country to country. When the national laws request the parties to renegotiate the contract, and the renegotiation fails, the consequences of such failure may vary: under some laws the disadvantaged party will only be entitled to terminate the contract, while under others the disadvantaged party will have the right to request adaptation of the contract to the changed circumstances by the judge or arbitrator.

In order to increase certainty, parties may wish to regulate this situation in their agreement, independently from the law governing the contract. The ICC Hardship Clause intends to satisfy this need through a standard clause which can be included in an individual contract.

1. A party to a contract is bound to perform its contractual duties even if events have rendered performance more onerous than could reasonably have been anticipated at the time of the conclusion of the contract.
2. Notwithstanding paragraph 1 of this Clause, where a party to a contract proves that:
   a. the continued performance of its contractual duties has become excessively onerous due to an event beyond its reasonable control which it could not reasonably have been expected to have taken into account at the time of the conclusion of the contract; and that
   b. it could not reasonably have avoided or overcome the event or its consequences,

the parties are bound, within a reasonable time of the invocation of this Clause, to negotiate alternative contractual terms which reasonably allow to overcome the consequences of the event.

3A: Party to terminate	3B: Judge adapt or terminate
Where paragraph 2 of this Clause applies, but where the parties have been unable to agree alternative contractual terms as provided in that paragraph, the party invoking this Clause is entitled to terminate the contract, but cannot request adaptation without the agreement of the other party.	Where paragraph 2 of this Clause applies, but where the parties have been unable to agree alternative contractual terms as provided for in that paragraph, either party is entitled to request the judge or arbitrator to adapt or terminate the contract, as appropriate.

3C: Judge to terminate
Where paragraph 2 of this Clause applies, but where the parties have been unable to agree alternative contractual terms as provided in that paragraph, either party is entitled to request the judge or arbitrator to declare the termination of the contract

Paragraph 3 deals with the situation where the parties are unable to agree alternative contract terms. In this case, there are mainly two options: contract termination by one of the parties, or adaptation or termination by the judge or arbitrator having jurisdiction under the contract. Under option A, the party invoking hardship will be entitled to terminate the contract on its initiative. Under option B, (which is admitted under a number of national laws as well as under the UNIDROIT Principles, the parties are entitled to request a judge or arbitrator to adapt or terminate the contract. If option B is considered inappropriate by the contractual parties, who fear the adaptation of the contractual balance by a third party (judge or arbitrator), parties can choose option A or C, which do not involve adaptation of the contract. Under option A, the party invoking hardship will be entitled to terminate the contract on its initiative—and the other party may thereafter claim the unlawfulness of such decision—, whereas under option C, either party may request the judge or arbitrator to declare the termination.

Chapter 6

Force Majeure Clauses and their Relationship with the Applicable Law, General Principles of Law and Trade Usages

by Klaus Peter Berger*

I. INTRODUCTION

Almost every major international business contract contains a force majeure clause. This drafting practice is so widespread and has persisted over such a long period of time that the exoneration of a party due to a force majeure event ("Acts of God", "*vis major*") is the most prominent example of a transnational legal principle of the New Lex Mercatoria.[1] In the past, force majeure clauses were often boilerplate clauses, included in the contract without negotiation or amendment.[2] In recent times, these clauses have become increasingly sophisticated and detailed.[3] However, their great popularity and increasing sophistication has not saved force majeure clauses from sharing the fate of other contractual clauses: more often than not, they are drafted in a manner that does not clearly reflect the will of the contracting parties. This includes the unequivocal definition of their scope, the clear formulation of the legal requirements of the force majeure defence and, above all, their relationship with comparable defences under the law applicable to the contract.[4] The core question in this context is whether the clause is meant to be self-sufficient in the sense that the clause is to replace the force majeure provisions of the applicable law or whether the clause is merely intended to supplement these provisions of the applicable law.[5] While in the first scenario, a court or arbitral tribunal would feel more inclined to detach the interpretation of the clause from the applicable domestic law, the latter scenario would provide an incentive to interpret the clause solely in the context of that domestic law.[6]

The fact that these clauses usually remain silent about their relationship with the applicable law has been identified as a characteristic feature of traditional clauses dealing with changed circumstances.[7] That finding is surprising at best, given that a) exemption clauses are among the most important clauses to shape the risk-profile of international business contracts[8] and b) the very reason why parties insert a force majeure clause into their contract is to create a greater degree of certainty as to their obligations and potential liabilities when faced with such events during the

* Klaus Peter Berger is a professor of law at the University of Cologne, Germany. He is an arbitrator specialising in Construction and Engineering, Finance and Banking, Joint Ventures, Mergers and Acquisitions, and Oil and Gas. He is a Board Member of the German Arbitration Institute (DIS); and the author of numerous publications on domestic and international arbitration (for a full list see www.klauspeterberger.de).

lifetime of the contract.[9] In light of the fact that force majeure clauses are so widely used, the relationship of these clauses with trade usages[10] or general principles of law[11] provides an additional challenge for international arbitrators.

The present contribution examines three ICC Awards in which the arbitral tribunals, beyond the resolution of the dispute before them, have endeavoured to shed some light on the correct approach in determining the relationship between the force majeure clauses on the one hand and domestic law, general principles of law, and trade usages on the other.

II. ICC AWARD NO. 4462 *(National Oil Corporation v Libyan Sun Oil Company)*

II.A. Summary of the Case

ICC Award No. 4462 of 31 May 1985[12] provides a perfect example of the difficulties that a tribunal is faced with when the parties have not clarified the relationship between the force majeure provision inserted into their contract and the force majeure rules of the applicable domestic law.

On 20 November 1980, Claimant, National Oil Corporation (NOC), a Libyan State enterprise and Respondent, Libyan Sun Oil Company (*Sun Oil*), a company incorporated in the USA concluded an Exploration and Production Sharing Agreement (EPSA). The EPSA obliged *Sun Oil* to undertake, finance and carry out an oil exploration programme in Libya. The EPSA was to be governed by and interpreted according to Libyan law and contained an ICC arbitration clause. The agreement was concluded for a term of 20 years and contained the following force majeure provisions:

> **Article 22—Force Majeure**
>
> 22.1. Excuse of Obligations
>
> Any failure or delay on the part of a Party in the performance of its obligations or duties hereunder shall be excused to the extent attributable to force majeure. Force majeure shall include, without limitation: Acts of God, insurrection, riots, war, and any unforeseen circumstances and acts beyond the control of such Party.
>
> 22.2. Extension of Term; Termination
>
> If operations are delayed, curtailed or prevented by force majeure, and the time for carrying out obligations under this Agreement is thereby affected, the term of this Agreement and all rights and obligations hereunder shall be extended for a period equal to the period thus involved...

On 9 December 1981, the US Government issued a Passport Order declaring US passports no longer valid for travelling to Libya. With reference to this Passport Order, *Sun Oil* suspended performance and invoked the force majeure provision of the EPSA. It claimed that in light of the fact that all of its personnel consisted of US citizens, who were now unable to enter Libya, further performance of the EPSA had become impossible.

On 12 March 1982, the US Government issued an Export Regulation, which limited exports to Libya. The Regulation required *Sun Oil* to obtain a license in order to continue its operations in Libya but the company's application for such a license was denied. *Sun Oil* then invoked Art. 22 of the EPSA again, stating that the Export Regulation constituted a further event of force majeure.

NOC, however, refused to accept any of these events as constituting force majeure and initiated arbitration proceedings before the ICC on 19 July 1982. On 31 May 1985, the ICC arbitral tribunal rendered a first award on the issue of force majeure in favour of NOC, which was followed by a final award on 23 February 1987 also in favour of NOC.[13] Interestingly, the tribunal in the ICC Arbitration No. 5864 dealt with a similar scenario in which the President of the United States had issued an order enjoining US companies from working in Libya but reached the opposite conclusion.[14]

II.B. The Problem

The main difficulty for the arbitral tribunal in the ICC Case No. 4462 resulted from the fact that Art. 22, the force majeure provision of the EPSA, differed from Art. 360 of the Libyan Civil Code, a non-mandatory[15] provision of the applicable law of the contract. Art. 360 of the Libyan Civil Code contains the following broad and general definition of force majeure:

> An obligation is extinguished if the debtor establishes that his performance has become impossible by reason of causes beyond his control.[16]

The tribunal noted that pursuant to that provision as interpreted by the Supreme Court of Libya, force majeure is established only if an event has occurred that, a) is beyond the control of the parties, b) is unforeseeable at the time the agreement, out of which the parties' duties to perform arise, is entered into, and c) renders the performance of the obligation of the non-performing party absolutely impossible. These requirements are in fact very similar to the general elements of force majeure clauses in international business contracts. Apart from a definition of eligible force majeure events in a specific or generic way or by way of a combination of both, such clauses typically contain the following requirements for any event that qualifies as force majeure under the definition contained in the clause:

- unforeseeability,
- unavoidability,
- uncontrollability and
- the effect of rendering a party's obligation impossible.[17]

These requirements are now also reflected in Art. 1218 (1) of the French Civil Code.[18] They are in line with international arbitral practice.[19] Art. 22.1 EPSA, however, adopts only the first of the three constituting elements of the Libyan law on force majeure unaltered,[20] namely that the event must be beyond the control of the parties. Apart from that, the term "unforeseen" instead of "unforeseeable" is employed and instead of referring to the impossibility requirement of Libyan law, it merely provides that any default in performance shall be excused "to the extent attributable" to force majeure. Additionally, rather than referring to the absolute impossibility of performance, Art. 22.2 provides for an extension of term or termination of the contract if the original time schedule is "affected" by force majeure. Due to this wording of the provision it was unclear whether and, if so, to what extent the parties had intended to exclude the requirements of unforeseeability and impossibility of the applicable Libyan law.

II.C. The Views of the Parties

The parties agreed that the tribunal would need to look at the wording of the force majeure clause in Art. 22 of the EPSA to determine the intentions of the parties as to the relationship between the contractual force majeure framework and its conceptualization under Libyan law. They also agreed with the tribunal that the insertion of the force majeure clause in the contract demonstrated their intention to modify Art. 360 of the Libyan Civil Code. In this context, the tribunal observed "a certain trend, which is displayed to a greater or lesser extent in long term international contracts, to define force majeure less strictly than under most domestic contracts".[21] The fact remained, however, that in the absence of express stipulation the extent of the intended modification or detachment from the applicable domestic law remained unclear.

The parties had diametrically opposing views as to how the tribunal should approach the determination of the relationship between the contractual clause and the statutory law in a case such as the one before the tribunal in which the parties have remained silent on that question. The parties' difference of opinion related specifically to the meaning that should be attached to such silence.

Respondent *Sun Oil* argued that Art. 22 differed in a number of important respects from the "rigid legal doctrine" of the applicable Libyan law. In light of the parties' silence as to the relationship between the Libyan law and the contract, Art. 22 should be qualified as "self-sufficient", *i.e.* as setting up "a specific force majeure regime, much more flexible and liberal than the one provided for under Art. 360 of the Libyan Civil Code".[22]

Claimant *NOC*, on the other hand, took the opposite view. It argued that the parties are, in theory, capable of modifying the force majeure rules of the Libyan Civil Code. In the case before the tribunal, however, the parties' silence must be taken to mean that they "did not expressly exclude any of the conditions required under Libyan law to establish force majeure". Consequently, Claimant maintained that "the parties are deemed to give [force majeure] the usual meaning", *i.e.* the one contained in the applicable Libyan law as construed by the Libyan Supreme Court. In other words, the conditions for force majeure established under the applicable Libyan law should be read into the contractual force majeure regime established in Art. 22 EPSA.[23]

II.D. The Scope of Force Majeure Events

Using the wording of the clause as a starting point for its analysis, the tribunal noted that the clause does not specifically define the individual elements of the force majeure defence. The clause merely provides a generic description of what constitutes force majeure: "any failure or delay on the part of a party in the performance of its obligations or duties ...", and a non-exhaustive list of events which shall fall within the scope of the force majeure clause: "*Force majeure shall include, without limitation: ... any unforeseen circumstances and acts beyond the control of such Party.*" In the eyes of the arbitrators, the "extensive" definition "*... any ... circumstances*" demonstrated "without any doubt" the parties' intention to extend the scope of force majeure events beyond the cases traditionally deemed to constitute an irresistible obstacle to performance. In international contract practice, these events include the ones specifically listed in the clause (*"Acts* *of God, insurrection, riots")*, as well as terrorist attacks, sabotage or piracy, strikes or boycotts, acts of governments, blockades, sieges or sanctions, accidents, fires, explosions, plagues, natural disasters and similar external events beyond the control of the parties.[24]

II.E. The Tests of "Unforseeability" and "Impossibility"

While the tribunal's linguistic analysis served to clarify the scope of force majeure events covered by Art. 22 EPSA and their legal consequences, it did not answer the vital question as to "how far ... the parties intend[ed] to go in making this approach [used in the clause] more flexible" than the force majeure concept enshrined in Art. 360 Libyan Civil Code. This question relates in particular to the two remaining requirements under Art. 360 of the Libyan Civil Code, pursuant to which the force majeure event must be unforeseeable at the time the agreement out of which the parties' duties to perform arise is entered into and must render the performance of the obligation of the non-performing party absolutely impossible.

II.E.1. Unforseeability test

Rather than adopting the Libyan Supreme Court's interpretation of Art. 360 of the Libyan Civil Code, the parties did not require an "unforeseeable" event, but characterized the force majeure event under Art. 22.1 EPSA as "any *unforeseen* circumstances and acts beyond the control of such Party". In light of the parties' use of the adjective "unforeseen" instead of "unforeseeable", the tribunal "did not exclude the possibility" that this choice may be taken to reflect their common intention to waive the unforeseeability requirement or at least, to apply the requirement less strictly than under Libyan domestic law. On this understanding, the fact that the defaulting party did not actually foresee a certain event at the time of the conclusion of the EPSA which it later invoked as a force majeure event would have justified the exemption from performance under Art. 22, even if that party could have foreseen the event in question.[25] Ultimately, the tribunal acknowledged that such an approach "would be difficult to admit, because it would result in allowing the enforceability of contractual obligations to be challenged upon the occurrence of the slightest difficulty".[26]

II.E.2. Impossibility test

Following that careful approach, the arbitral tribunal stressed that the use of the adjective "unforeseen" in Art. 22.1. EPSA—especially read in conjunction with the remaining part of the provision—does not imply that *any* circumstance beyond the control of the parties would, if unforeseen, excuse non-performance regardless of what effect it has on the performance of the obligation. The tribunal once again examined the wording of the clause to determine the limits of the force majeure regime established by the parties in their contract. It held that the use of the word "attributable" ("... failure or delay ... shall be excused *to the extent attributable* to force majeure") does not provide any indication as to the requisite effect of the force majeure event on the ability of performance of the relevant obligation. Rather, in the eyes of the tribunal, the parties, by using the term "attributable", merely wanted to underline the essential requirement of a "direct causal link" between the event invoked as a force majeure event and the non-performance or the delay in performing the obligation.[27]

The tribunal then went on to contrast the clause at hand with force majeure clauses in other international long-term agreements.[28] It reasoned that such clauses increasingly expressly qualify force majeure events as "rendering the performance of the agreement very difficult and/or more expensive than anticipated" or as events "which cannot be overcome by the use of reasonable means at reasonable costs". While such wording leaves no doubt as to the intent of the parties to sidestep the impossibility of performance as the "*sine qua non* requirement of force majeure",[29] the clause at hand did not contain such or similar language.

The mere use of the word "affected" in the clause ("If operations are delayed, curtailed or prevented by force majeure, and the time for carrying out obligations under this Agreement is thereby *affected,* ...") does not provide a clear indication as to whether the parties' intended to waive the impossibility requirement of Art. 360 of the Libyan Civil Code. Under that provision, the fact that the event invoked merely resulted in rendering the performance of the obligation more difficult or more expensive, would not suffice to establish a force majeure defence. Rather, force majeure is only established when the event invoked by the defaulting party results in an "objective", "absolute" impossibility to perform, whether on a temporary or permanent basis, for a party similarly contractually liable and facing a similar situation as the defaulting party.[30] The tribunal held that in the absence of an express exception, however, Art. 22 EPSA could not be construed to exclude the essential requirement of Libyan private law, according to which the force majeure event must have rendered the performance of the obligation impossible.[31] The tribunal justified that conclusion with the principle that "such exceptions to the common law of force majeure must be expressly provided for; they should not be presumed or implied".[32] In ICC case No. 5864, the tribunal had reached the opposite conclusion. In that case, however, the very elaborate force majeure clause contained in the contract itself spelled out the impossibility requirement which is also part of Art. 360 of the Libyan Civil Code.[33]

II.F. The Tribunal's Final Conclusion

On the basis of this analysis, the tribunal reasoned that the force majeure concept in Art. 22 EPSA must be understood as "an unforeseen circumstance, beyond the control of the parties ... which constitutes an obstacle such that an obligor, normally diligent, having the same obligations and placed in the same situation, could not have overcome it".[34] Under this definition, both the Passport Order and the Export Regulation of the US Government were insufficient to qualify as force majeure events.[35] Despite undeniably rendering the performance of *Sun Oil*'s contractual obligations more *difficult*, neither of them led to the *impossibility* of performance of its contractual duties. With respect to the Passport Order, the tribunal held that *Sun Oil* would have been able, and was entitled under the EPSA, to work with non-US personnel from within or outside its group and to organize management meetings outside Libya which could be attended by its own managerial personnel. With respect to the Export Regulation, the Tribunal concluded that rather than having to resort to, as is usually the case in such situations, a "theoretical reasonable person" to determine whether performance had become impossible, it could refer to other companies placed in the same circumstances as *Sun Oil*. The tribunal noted that two other US companies that were engaged at the same time as *Sun*

Oil in similar explorations, under similar EPSAs, had not discontinued their activities on the basis of force majeure.[36] On the contrary, they had found ways to continue their exploration activities despite the Export Regulation although that Regulation was binding on them as it was binding on *Sun Oil*. The tribunal therefore held that *Sun Oil* could not successfully invoke the force majeure clause in Art. 22 of the EPSA and was thus not excused from its contractual obligations.

III. ICC AWARD NO. 19299 (*Gujarat State Petroleum Corp. et al v Republic of Yemen et al*)

III.A. Summary of the Case

In the dispute that was the subject of ICC Award No. 19299 of 10 July 2015,[37] Claimants—three petroleum exploration and production companies—had concluded three almost identical Production Sharing Agreements (PSAs) with the Ministry of Oil and Minerals of the Republic of Yemen on 13 April 2008. The PSAs concerned hydrocarbon exploration and production activities in Yemen and entered into force on 17 March 2009, the date when the first exploration period under the contracts commenced. The PSAs were governed by Yemeni law pursuant to the choice-of-law clause contained in Art. 24. In addition, a Yemeni law of 2009 provides that, due to their hybrid, public/private law nature,[38] these contracts also constitute Yemeni law and are therefore part of the legal system of Yemen.[39] The PSAs also provided in the relevant parts that:

> **Art. 22.2**
>
> 'Force Majeure', within the meaning of this Agreement, shall be any order, regulation or direction of the GOVERNMENT, or (with respect to the CONTRACTOR) of the government of the country in which any of the entities comprising the CONTRACTOR is incorporated, whether promulgated in the form of law or otherwise, or any acts of God, insurrection, riot, war, strike (or other labour disturbances), fires, floods or any cause not due to the fault or the negligence of the Party invoking Force Majeure, whether or not similar to the foregoing, provided that any such cause is beyond the reasonable control of the party invoking Force Majeure.
>
> **Art. 22.4**
>
> If the Force Majeure event occurs during the First Exploration Period or the Second Exploration Period or any extension(s) thereof and continues in effect for a period of six (6) Months, thereafter the CONTRACTOR shall have the option upon ninety (90) Days' prior written notice to the MINISTRY to terminate its obligations hereunder without further liability of any kind except for those payments accrued under this Agreement.

From January 2011 onwards, the security situation in Yemen deteriorated, with tribal clashes, attacks and kidnappings occurring on a regular basis. The Government declared a State of Emergency on 18 March 2011 and a number of governments issued travel advisories. On 23 March 2011, the Yemeni House of Representatives approved a finding of a State of Emergency which lasted for 41 days. The Claimants contended that these events fell within the definition of force majeure in Art. 22.2 of the PSAs. On 10 April 2011, they sent a force majeure notice to Respondents pursuant to Art. 22.4 of the PSAs. That notice was rejected by Respondents. After several unsuccessful meetings, Claimants terminated the PSAs pursuant to

Art. 22.4. On 25 February 2013, Claimants initiated arbitration under the ICC arbitration clause contained in the PSAs and requested the tribunal, *inter alia*, to declare that an event of force majeure continuing for a period of six months had existed in Yemen and to declare that the PSAs had been validly terminated by Claimants.

III..B. The Problem

The tribunal was faced with problems relating to the interpretation of the force majeure clause in Art. 22.2 of the PSAs and its relation to the applicable Yemeni law that were very similar to the issues that the tribunal in the *Sun Oil* arbitration had to address. It is therefore not surprising that both Respondents and the tribunal made reference to the reasoning of the tribunal in the *Sun Oil* Award.

III.C. Force Majeure Events

The parties and the tribunal agreed that Art. 22.2 of the PSAs itself listed certain requirements that must be met for an event to be qualified as force majeure under the contract. In order to excuse non-performance under the force majeure defence in Art. 22.2, the relevant event must

- fall under the specific force majeure scenarios listed in the clause *"any order, regulation of direction of the Government ... or any acts of God, insurrection, riot, war, strike ..., fires, floods ..."* or the catch-all clause *"...any cause... whether or not similar to the foregoing ..."*,
- meet the two additional requirements specified in the clause that any such event must not be "*due to the fault or the negligence of the Party invoking Force Majeure*" and is "*beyond the reasonable control*" of that party, and
- must have caused the non-performance of the party invoking force majeure, i.e. Claimants.

The tribunal concluded that force majeure events within the meaning of the catch-all clause "*any cause*" under Art. 22.2 of the PSAs had occurred on numerous occasions and in multiple places, including in the relevant places in the Republic of Yemen between March 2011 and February 2013. Due to these events, Claimants were prevented from sending their personnel to Yemen and were thus unable to perform their obligations under the PSAs.[40]

The tribunal came to this conclusion with particular reference to the official declaration of a State of Emergency by the Yemeni Government as of 18 March 2011 for 41 days which was based, *inter alia*, on riots in some cities, the advice issued by several states to their citizens to leave Yemen due to the "dangerous" situation there, two UN Security Council Resolutions expressing concerns about the "worsening security situation" and the fact that numerous other companies had declared "Force Majeure" on the basis of the deteriorating security situation in the country. The tribunal also emphasised that none of these events were caused by the fault or negligence of Claimants, nor were they within their reasonable control and that they prevented Claimants' performance of their obligations under the PSAs.

Although the tribunal held that it would be sufficient for it to find that *one* of the events listed in Art. 22.2, such as those falling under the catch-all clause, had occurred in the parts of Yemen relevant for Claimants' performance in the relevant period,[41] the tribunal "for the sake of completeness" also determined whether the events would also qualify as "riots" or "insurrections", which are listed as specific force majeure events in Art. 22.2 of the PSAs.[42]

It was in this context that the tribunal was first confronted with the question as to the influence of Yemeni law on the interpretation of the contractual force majeure clause. Respondents argued that, in light of the choice-of-law clause in the contracts, both terms should be interpreted in a way that is consistent with Yemeni law. The term "riots" should therefore be understood in the technical sense of "protests which are illegal [and have therefore been dispersed by the police following a declaration of open fire], not protests which fall within the legitimate right to protest or demonstrate enshrined in the Yemeni constitution".[43] Likewise, the term "insurrection" should be interpreted through the lens of Yemeni law. Consequently, it could only constitute a force majeure event under Art. 22.2 if it fell within one of the criminal acts of insurrection listed in the Yemeni Penal Code.[44]

Claimants disagreed with Respondents' formalistic view. They argued that both terms should be interpreted according to their plain meaning, i.e. by applying the linguistic understanding of that term in both English and Arabic, given that Art. 32 of the PSAs provided that "in any arbitration proceedings under [the PSAs], the Arabic and English versions shall be referred to in interpreting [the PSAs]". The term "riot" should therefore be interpreted as "an unlawful disturbance of the peace by a number of people" (English meaning) or as "any civil disturbance or civil unrest, regardless of reason or cause" (Arabic meaning). Likewise, the term "insurrection" should be given its plain meaning by the tribunal as "a situation in which someone refuses the obedience of an order, regularly paired with the aim to weaken the position of an established authority regardless of the means" (English meaning) or as a "disobedience against the established authority or government, whether or not arms are used" (Arabic meaning).[45]

The tribunal held that the primary purpose of its interpretation of Art. 22.2 of the PSAs is to give full effect to the meaning of the terms used by the parties in Art. 22.2. While the tribunal acknowledged that the PSAs were part of the Yemeni legal system,[46] it also assumed that the parties most likely did not refer to a dictionary or considered the specific technical meaning of such terms under Yemeni law at the time of drafting and concluding the contracts. Therefore, the "common (ordinary/plain) meaning of terms" should be applied.[47] This is in line with international arbitration practice, where arbitral tribunals seek to determine the meaning that reasonable parties of the same kind as the parties would give to a contractual term in the same circumstances, taking into account, in particular, the meaning commonly given to contract terms and expressions in the trade concerned.[48] Adopting this approach, the tribunal applied the common and rather generic meaning of the term "riot" as "a disturbance of peace and order by several people acting together". It concluded that such riots had in fact taken place in those parts of Yemen that were relevant for Claimants' performance of their obligations under the PSAs between March 2011 and February 2013.[49] The tribunal further noted that even adopting Respondents' position that the meaning under Yemeni law should be applied, the result would not be different because a) there is no legal definition of the term "riot" under Yemeni law and b) Respondents had not cogently explained why the incidents in question would not constitute riots if the Yemeni legal meaning of the term is applied. The tribunal reached the same conclusions with respect to the meaning of the term "insurrection" which the tribunal understood to commonly mean "a violent revolt against authority or government".[50]

III..D. Additional Requirements: Unforeseeability and Impossibility?

As in the *Sun Oil* arbitration, the parties disagreed as to whether the additional requirements of the applicable Yemeni law had to be read into the contractual force majeure clause. Respondents made reference to the *Sun Oil* Award and argued that force majeure clauses in production sharing agreements cannot be interpreted independently of the applicable law. As the PSAs are "Yemeni law contract[s],[51] ... the whole of Art. 22 must be read with Yemeni eyes, and with the Yemeni law concepts in mind".[52] The Yemeni law concept of force majeure, however, requires proof that the relevant events were unforeseeable and that performance has become impossible. Respondents argued that the same conclusion would follow from the principles of good faith and good will which, they argued, apply to both the interpretation and performance of the contracts pursuant to Art. 23.10 of the PSAs.

Claimants rejected that view. They argued that all they needed to show is that the requirements of Art. 22.2 are met, whereas other requirements of general Yemeni law are irrelevant. In support of that view they referred to the clear and exhaustive language of Art. 22.2 and maintained that this language "clearly proves the parties' intent to design a bespoke force majeure clause" for which they chose to retain certain elements of the Yemeni force majeure concept ("beyond the control"), but not others such as unforeseeability and impossibility. According to Claimants, the fact that the parties had the intention to insulate the contractual force majeure concept from the applicable Yemeni law also followed from the fact that, unlike other clauses of the PSAs, the parties did not make reference to Yemeni law in Art. 22 and that other provisions dealing with the contractor's right to invoke force majeure made it clear that this is a right solely governed by the PSAs.[53]

The tribunal rejected Respondents' argument that additional legal requirements, (such as unforeseeability or impossibility) should be read into Art. 22.2 of the PSAs and concurred with Claimants that there is neither scope, nor need to imply Yemeni law requirements into Art. 22.2.[54] For the tribunal, the language used in the clause was clear because the parties had used specific and precise wording to describe those force majeure events that would fall within the ambit of the clause. That language included some requirements of Yemeni law on force majeure ("*beyond reasonable control*"), while leaving out others, such as unforeseeability. In light of this clear language used by the parties, the tribunal had no doubts that the parties had agreed in Art. 22.2 on their own "custom-made" and self-contained definition of force majeure.[55] Implying additional requirements of Yemeni law into the clause would impose an additional burden on Claimants which was not envisaged by the parties when they concluded the contract.[56] That reasoning might seem surprising given that the tribunal had acknowledged that the PSAs were part of the Yemeni legal system.[57]

However, the tribunal found further support for its conclusion in the rule that the PSAs are meant to be the exclusive source of the parties' respective rights and obligations in Art. 18.2 of the PSAs. This provision states that the interests, rights and obligations of the parties "shall be solely governed by the provisions of this Agreement".[58] In line with that rule, whenever the parties nonetheless wanted to introduce Yemeni law, they had used specific language to that effect in various provisions of the PSAs. Because of that drafting technique and the fact that the contract was drafted by Respondents themselves,[59] the tribunal rejected Respondents' argument that general Yemeni law should guide the interpretation of its clauses unless the parties have contracted out of that law.[60]

The clear and conclusive language of Art. 22.2 of the PSAs was also the decisive element on which the tribunal distinguished the present case from the factual setting in the *Sun Oil* case, so that the *Sun Oil* Award had only limited persuasive value for the tribunal. While in *Sun Oil*, the tribunal found the force majeure clause to be non-exhaustive and vague ("Force Majeure shall include, without limitation…"),[61] the tribunal in this case found that the force majeure provision of Art. 22.2 was clear and conclusive ("Force majeure shall be…"). While this linguistic aspect alone would have sufficed to distinguish the present case from the *Sun Oil* Award, the tribunal hinted at an additional aspect that, unlike the parties in the *Sun Oil* case,[62] the parties in the present proceedings agreed that Art. 22.2 of the PSAs required that the force majeure event in question must have caused the Claimants' non-performance.[63]

The tribunal also emphasised that a different result could not be reached by reference to the general notions of good faith and good will which were referred to in Art. 23.10 of the PSAs as the basis "of [the parties'] … relationship under this Agreement". The tribunal argued that these principles are not meant to enable arbitrators "to second-guess what the Parties could have added to their common understanding, including, if that should be the case, by reference to provisions of Yemeni law to which the Parties did not refer, not even impliedly".[64] This is in line with international arbitral case law which considers good faith and fair dealing as a flexible behavioural standard, rather than an abstract guideline for the interpretation of a contract.[65] Just as an ultimate precautionary measure, the tribunal concluded that even if the additional requirements proposed by Respondents were introduced into Art. 22.2 of the PSAs, those requirements would have been satisfied.[66]

IV. ICC AWARD NO. 8873 (*French claimant v Spanish respondent*)

IV.A. Summary of the Case

ICC Award No. 8873 of 1997[67] concerned a dispute between a Spanish company and a French company. The parties had concluded a contract for the construction of a road in Algeria by the French contractor. The contract provided for the application of Spanish law and contained a force majeure clause in Art. [x]. During construction, the parties amended the initial contract adjusting the schedule and milestones for the completion of the construction project. Also during construction, the contractor was faced with a number of unforeseen difficulties which occurred, or their effects only became apparent, after the date of the amendment contract. Some of these problems were caused by political, others by economical and natural, events in Algeria. The contractor argued that irrespective of their cause, these events, which led to delays in the finalisation of the construction project, must be qualified as force majeure pursuant to Art. [x] of the construction contract. Nonetheless, the Spanish employer imposed penalty payments on the contractor provided for in the construction contract in case of delay of the works, by deducting these amounts from the contract price it had to pay to the French contractor. At the same time, the French contractor incurred extra costs to overcome the difficulties caused by the unforeseen events. The French contractor initiated the ICC arbitration seeking an order for both a reduction of the penalty payments and reimbursement of the extra costs from the Spanish employer.

IV.B. The Problem

Claimant based its claim on a number of legal grounds which included the applicable Spanish law, the force majeure clause in the contract, standard forms typically used in the construction business, international restatements of contract law as well as customs and general principles of transnational business law. The case therefore addressed basic questions as to the relationship between these various legal sources in a single case, as well as the interpretation of the force majeure clause in the contract. The tribunal noted that in international arbitration, the task to determine this relationship presents itself in a particular fashion, which is reflected in Art. 21 (2) ICC Arbitration Rules[68] as well as Art. VII of the European Convention on International Commercial Arbitration.[69] Both of these provisions call upon arbitral tribunals to consider the stipulations of the contract concluded between the parties and the relevant trade usages. With respect to the latter provision, the tribunal noted:

> ...the Geneva Convention has established, in its Article VII, an internationally uniform principle which applies in lieu of domestic law provisions on the same subject and which grants arbitrators a larger margin of appreciation when it comes to the determination of the role of usages. That rule allows arbitrators to attribute a more important role to trade usages and consequently to rules that have been customarily established at the international level, by companies engaged in international commerce, the only limit being set by the mandatory provisions of the applicable law.[70]

While acknowledging this transnational principle of international arbitration practice, the tribunal emphasised the significance of another important guideline: in the absence of specific contractual clauses, the determination of applicable trade usages that apply in the absence of corresponding contractual stipulations by the parties, must be conducted diligently by the tribunal to avoid "surprise" situations in which the parties find themselves bound by rules, the application of which they could not reasonably have been aware of when they concluded their contract.[71] That balanced approach is reflected, *inter alia*, in Art. 9 (2) CISG which provides that

> ...the parties are considered, unless otherwise agreed, to have impliedly made applicable to their contract or its formation a usage of *which the parties knew or ought to have known* and which in international trade *is widely known to, and regularly observed by*, parties to contracts of the type involved in the particular trade concerned (emphasis added).

Comparable rules are contained in other UN conventions on international trade law such as Art. 11 (3) UN Convention on the Assignment of Receivables in International Trade and in Art. 1.9 (2) of the UNIDROIT Principles of International Commercial Contracts (UPICC).[72]

The tribunal had to determine the proper relationship between the contractual force majeure clause, the force majeure provisions of the applicable Spanish law and the rules on force majeure prevailing in international contract practice. Its analysis was guided by its endeavour to protect the parties' legitimate expectations as to the applicable force majeure regime. The tribunal was particularly sensitive to the parties' expectations in relation to the application of rules and practices which were not laid down in the force majeure clause in Art. [x] of the construction contract.[73] In fact, protection of these party expectations with respect to the applicable rules is a fundamental guideline of arbitral decision-making in general.[74] It is for this reason that in the absence of a contrary indication within the force majeure clause, an interpretation which is in line with general standards of international contracts is to be preferred to an interpretation that blindly follows the requirements of the applicable law.[75]

IV.C. The Penalty

The Claimant argued that the penalty payments claimed by respondent were not justified or had to be reduced by the tribunal on a *pro rata* basis, because the delays were caused by circumstances which qualified as force majeure events under Art. [x] of the contract. The argument that a party is not liable under a penalty clause if it is faced with a force majeure event is in line with international arbitration practice.[76] It is also in accordance with international contract doctrine, according to which force majeure provisions of the applicable law or contractual force majeure clauses should also be applied to agreed payments for non-performance such as those claimed under a penalty clause, because, in the absence of indications to the contrary, it may be presumed that the obligor does not want to assume the relevant risk of such events.[77] That position is also enshrined in some domestic laws, such as Art. 163 (2) Swiss Code of Obligations which provides that a "penalty may not be claimed ... where performance has been prevented by circumstances beyond the debtor's control".[78]

IV.C.1. The Force Majeure Clause and its relationship with the applicable domestic law

The tribunal acknowledged that the primary basis of Claimant's defence against Respondent's penalty payment claims is the force majeure clause in Art. [x] of the construction contract. The tribunal noted that the clause, while providing for specific force majeure events, does not stipulate an exhaustive definition of force majeure. Rather, the clause lists further legal requirements which a force majeure event must meet, namely that a) the relevant event must lead to a situation in which "performance [by the party invoking force majeure] is prevented, delayed or rendered impossible" and b) that the event must be "beyond the reasonable control of such Party".

As to the relationship with the applicable Spanish law, the tribunal held that the requirement of unforeseeability, which according to the tribunal "constitutes an essential element of force majeure in many jurisdictions" including under Art. 1105 of the Spanish Civil Code, did not apply in the present case because it was not expressly mentioned in the force majeure clause. As a result, situations that were foreseeable at the time the contract was concluded, could be qualified as force majeure events under the clause, provided the other express requirements of the clause are met.[79]

The tribunal also dealt with the questions of whether the principle of *perpetuatio obligationis*, contained in Art. 1096 (3) of the Spanish Civil Code,[80] excludes Claimant's force majeure defence. According to that provision, a debtor who delays his performance carries the risk of fortuitous events happening during that delay and is not entitled to rely on force majeure as an excuse for this delayed performance. The tribunal considered it doubtful whether that provision of Spanish law applies to construction contracts (*contrato de obras*) such as the one before it. Irrespective of that doctrinal issue, the tribunal found the provision to be inapplicable in this case based on the fact that

> by providing for a detailed force majeure clause like the one in Art. [x] of the contract, inspired by the current international contract practice, the parties have shown their desire to submit to a force majeure regime that is relatively autonomous, which implies their tacit intention to exclude the application of the dispositive provisions of the applicable domestic law that do not correspond to the usual [international contract] practice like Art. 1096 (3) of the Spanish Civil Code.[81]

IV.C.2. Force majeure events

The tribunal provided a detailed analysis of the various events on which Claimant based its force majeure argument and rejected most of them, albeit for different reasons.

The first force majeure event which, according to Claimant, justified the delays in the performance of the works and a reduction of the penalty imposed by Respondent, was the "climate of insecurity" in Algeria during the construction of the road. Claimant argued that this climate was created by terrorist attacks against foreigners in Algeria, especially against French citizens, and that this lead to a substantial delay of the works to be performed by Claimant. The tribunal rejected that argument for a number of reasons:

a. Like all other companies working in Algeria at that time, Claimant had been aware of the situation when it concluded the contract and had accepted the related risks as of that date.

b. Claimant was unable to prove that these events posed an insurmountable obstacle to the performance of their obligations.

c. Measures taken by the Algerian Government to improve the security situation in the region, in particular through the creation of exclusive zones and stricter controls by the Algerian military, provided "a climate of relative security" at the construction site since the conclusion of the contract, and

d. Claimant did not, as required by the force majeure clause in the contract, notify Respondent of the specific circumstances which it qualified as force majeure, but had merely complained in a general fashion about the alleged "climate of insecurity".[82]

With respect to the notification requirement, the tribunal reasoned that, while it must be applied with flexibility[83], the contractual notification requirement nonetheless means that events that have not been communicated by the party invoking force majeure to the other side when they occurred or are described only in general terms, cannot be taken into account by the tribunal.[84]

The tribunal held, however, that Claimant had complied with this notification requirement with respect to the degradation and temporary closure of a national road used for the transport of materials to the construction site. The tribunal qualified these events as force majeure and estimated that a period of 15 days of the delay was not attributable to Claimant for these reasons. The difficulties encountered by Claimant in the procurement of asphalt caused by the interruption of production at their suppliers' factories in Algeria, which it also invoked as a force majeure event, were likewise accepted by the tribunal. The tribunal estimated that a further period of 20 days of the delay was not attributable to Claimant due to this force majeure event.

Other events invoked by Claimant, such as "other difficulties related to the general context in Algeria" (e.g. difficulties in recruitment of personnel, supply of material, etc.), natural events like sand storms and heavy rain, and the alleged incorrect use of the road by the employer and its sub-contractors (in violation of the instructions for use given by Claimant) were rejected by the tribunal for lack of sufficient proof of the events as such, of their insurmountable character and/or of their causal nexus with the delays.[85]

IV.D. Reimbursement of Extra Costs

The contractor based its claim for the reimbursement of extra costs allegedly caused by the force majeure events on

> the principle that the contractor, when faced with force majeure events, is not only exonerated from his obligation to perform to the extent that this impossibility is caused by the force majeure events but may also claim reimbursement of the extra costs incurred by him to overcome the consequences of that situation.[86]

The tribunal noted that neither the contractual force majeure clause, nor the applicable Spanish law on force majeure contained such a principle. In fact, contractual force majeure clauses are often silent on this point. Some clauses even expressly exclude the parties' right to claim compensation from the other side for extra costs incurred in force majeure situations.[87] The Iran-US Claims Tribunal has developed a rule according to which "[a]bsent a contractual provision to the contrary, costs incurred as a result of force majeure normally are the responsibility of the party on whom they fall..."[88] Claimant, however, argued that such a principle for the reimbursement of costs in force majeure situations follows from the provisions in the FIDIC Conditions of Contract for Works of Civil Engineering Construction[89] and ENAA Model Form International Contract for Process Plant Construction[90] standard form contracts. Due to their frequent use in international contract practice, the principle contained in these standard form contracts should apply to the contract in dispute even though the parties had not agreed on their application.

The tribunal rejected this argument. Given that the parties had not agreed on the application of these standard forms in their contract, the principle could only apply insofar as it constitutes a trade usage. The tribunal qualified 'trade usage' with two cumulative conditions:

- the relevant rule must be qualified as a solution established in trade practice with a sufficient degree of uniformity to justify their direct application without the necessity of prior agreement or negotiation of other elements; and
- it must be proven that the principle is applied by companies in the relevant branch of trade even in the absence of an express stipulation in the contract.[91]

The tribunal thereby made it clear that it understood the notion of trade usages in a narrow, fact-driven sense to mean a practice in a particular branch of trade which is considered binding by all participants in that particular industry.[92] In fact, a number of ICC awards have understood the notion of trade usages in that narrow and traditional sense and have reverted to trade usages as a means to fill contractual gaps and clarify any ambiguities.[93]

The tribunal, however, held that neither of these conditions was fulfilled in respect to a reimbursement claim and it therefore does not constitute a trade usage. As to the first requirement, the tribunal noted that under the two sets of standard form contracts to which the Claimant made reference, the contractor only has a reimbursement claim in very special situations. These situations also differed from one set of standard terms to the other. In the view of the tribunal, this diversity clearly shows that the contended cost-reimbursement rule still lacks the necessary "maturity" to be accepted as a trade usage that would apply irrespective of an agreement by the parties. It would also be "absurd" to apply these provisions in isolation in cases in which the application of the standard forms has not been agreed upon by the parties. According to the tribunal, the reimbursement rules in the FIDIC and ENAA standard form contracts constitute an integral element of a well-balanced system of rights and duties of the parties set out in these standard form contracts. That system intends to establish an "equilibrium of interests" between the parties. According to the tribunal, such an equilibrium could not be established through the isolated application of the reimbursement principle enshrined in certain provisions of these standard form contracts without, at the same time, negotiating a series of supplementary contractual provisions necessary to create that equilibrium.[94] Therefore, the relevant provisions in the standard form contracts must be qualified,

> at least for the moment, as purely contractual solutions which cannot be used outside the context of the standard form contracts into which they are so closely integrated.[95]

This approach of the tribunal is in line with other ICC awards which have held that uniform instruments, including standard form contracts, may serve as proof of a widely accepted practice in a certain industry only if the generality of the alleged trade usage is clearly reflected in those instruments.[96] Put differently, while standard conditions as a whole may be characterised as forming an integral part of an *existing* trade usage,[97] a standard form contract *alone* is not necessarily full-fledged proof of the existence of a specific usage. The tribunal followed that view with respect to the very specific, narrow and isolated remedy of reimbursement of costs in force majeure scenarios, which, in both sets of standard form contracts, forms an integral part of a larger scheme of rights and duties of the parties in force majeure situations.

As to the second requirement, the test of the acceptance of the rule by the relevant business community,[98] the tribunal noted that Claimant was unable to prove that parties in the construction business would consider themselves bound by a rule requiring the employer to reimburse the contractor for extra costs incurred, in the absence of a contractual provision stipulating such a claim.

As an alternative basis for its reimbursement claim, Claimant invoked Art. 6.2.3 (4) (b) of the UPICC which allows a court or arbitral tribunal to adapt the contract to restore equilibrium in hardship situations. Art. 6.2.2. UPICC defines hardship as the "occurrence of events [that] fundamentally alters the equilibrium of the contract either because the cost of a party's performance has increased or because the value of the performance a party receives has diminished".[99] To determine whether the UPICC could be applied in the present case, the tribunal looked at the various options listed in their Preamble. Given that the parties had not expressly agreed on their application and that their choice of Spanish law clearly showed their intent not to have their contract governed by "general principle of law, the *lex mercatoria* or the like", the tribunal considered that the only option of applying the UPICC was if they qualified them as a "codification of existing usages".[100] While the tribunal had used a narrow notion of trade usage to reject the application of the reimbursement rule contained in the FIDIC and ENAA standard form contracts,[101] it obviously resorted to a much wider notion which includes general principles of law in the present context.[102] Unsurprisingly, the tribunal rejected the application of the hardship provisions in the UPICC with arguments similar to those with which it had rejected the application of the reimbursement provisions contained in certain international standard forms:

> [the hardship principle] constitutes a totally exceptional principle which finds acceptance only in the context of contractual clauses which determine in great detail the situations of hardship as well as the consequences thereof. It is therefore impossible to consider the provisions on hardship contained in the UPICC as trade usages. To the contrary, these rules do not correspond, at least at the present moment, to the current practice of international commerce and can only be applied when the parties have expressly referred to them in their contract which they did not in the present case.[103]

The same conclusion was reached by the tribunal in ICC Award No. 13284.[104] Other ICC tribunals have held that the UPICC should be applied only to the extent that "they can be considered to reflect generally accepted principles and rules".[105] In the present case, the tribunal's refusal to apply the hardship provisions of the UPICC was mostly driven by the tribunal's general endeavour to protect the legitimate expectations of the parties with respect to the application of rules and practices which were not laid down in the contract[106] and to the parties' choice of Spanish law as the law governing the contract. In fact, while hardship is an "innovative" and—at least from the perspective of common lawyers—"new" international concept,[107] it is also, to an increasing extent, accepted as a general principle of commercial law,[108] albeit as a strict and narrow exception to the fundamental notion of sanctity of contracts.[109] However, arbitral tribunals should not readily supplant the applicable domestic law with general principles of law such as those incorporated in the UPICC under the guise of trade usages.[110]

Consistent with this view favouring domestic rather than transnational law, the tribunal then went on to examine the provisions and case law on the re-establishment of the contractual equilibrium in exceptional cases pursuant to the principle of *clausula rebus sic stantibus* contained in the applicable Spanish law. It concluded that the events invoked by Claimant did not justify the application of that principle in the present case.

V. CONCLUSION

The three ICC Awards discussed in this contribution reveal that international arbitral tribunals are mindful of the significance of force majeure clauses in international business contracts. All three tribunals acknowledge that the wording of the clause must be the starting point for any determination of the meaning, scope and legal consequences of a force majeure clause. The tribunal in ICC Award No. 19299 made it clear that the purpose of such interpretation must always be to give full effect to the meaning of the terms used by the parties. In doing so, the tribunal held that arbitral tribunals should refrain from introducing concepts of the applicable law through the backdoor of contract interpretation or by application of such vague concepts as good faith or good will. Instead, they should always seek to establish the common, i.e. ordinary/plain meaning of the terminology used by the parties in the force majeure clause. It is in this context that general international contract principles relating to force majeure may have an impact on the tribunal's interpretive task.[111] The awards also confirm the trend identified by the tribunal in ICC Award No. 4462, that such clauses usually seek to establish a force majeure regime that is less strict than that of the law applicable to the contract.

Uncertainties will remain, however, if the parties have not clarified the relationship between the contractual force majeure framework and the relevant provisions of the law governing the contract in the clause itself. That silence was interpreted by the tribunal in ICC Award No. 4462 to mean that exceptions to the impossibility requirement under the applicable law must be expressly provided for in the clause; they should not be presumed or implied. Other tribunals, however, have taken the opposite approach. The tribunal in ICC Award No. 19299 held that implying additional requirements of the law applicable to the contract into the clause when the parties have remained silent on that question would impose an additional burden on the parties which was not contemplated by them when they concluded the contract. In that case, the tribunal found support for its conclusion not only in the clear language of the clause, but also in the exclusive remedy-clause in the contract. The tribunal in ICC Award No. 8873 went a step further and employed a general guideline that has been utilised by other ICC tribunals to determine the degree of acceptable interference of external rules (of whatever nature) in the system of contractual rights and duties established by the contract: international arbitral tribunals, whose jurisdiction is based on the will of the parties, must protect the legitimate expectations of those parties, especially with respect to the application of rules contained in the applicable law, derived from trade usages or general principles of law which are not laid down in the force majeure clause. Parties may have the confidence that arbitral tribunals in future cases will adopt that same cautious approach when it comes to the determination of the relationship of the contractual force majeure regime and the applicable law. However, parties that seek to insulate their contractual force majeure regime from the uncertain influences of the applicable law are well advised to take the necessary precautions at the drafting stage. They should clearly stipulate the specific relationship of that clause with the corresponding concept in the law applicable to the contract.[112]

Supplementing a contractual force majeure clause with such a clarification is highly recommended, particularly in light of the potential creativeness of some parties—as exemplified in ICC Award No. 8873—in trying to establish a basis (in the applicable law, trade usages, general principles of law and international restatements) for the interference with a contractual force majeure regime that was meant to be self-sufficient and conclusive at the time the contract was concluded.

NOTES

1. Osman, *Les Principes Généraux de la Lex Mercatoria*, 1992, p. 19 *et seq.* = https://www.trans-lex.org/106300; Fontaine/de Ly, *Drafting International Contracts*, 2006, p. 442 ("one of the best demonstrations" for the New Lex Mercatoria); Fontaine, *Les Clauses de Force Majeure dans les Contrats Internationaux*, DPCI 1979, at 469, 494 = https://www.trans-lex.org/122600; Derains, *Note to ICC Award No. 7539*, Clunet 1996, at 1034 = https://www.trans-lex.org/196753; Rivkin, *Lex Mercatoria and Force majeure*, in: Gaillard (ed.), Transnational Rules in International Commercial Arbitration (ICC Pub. Nr. 480,4) 1993, at 161, 208 = https://www.trans-lex.org/116100 ("...there is a significant overlapping consensus which provides grounding for an emerging *lex mercatoria* in this area..."); ICC Award No. 3540, Clunet 1981, 915; see also Berger, *The Creeping Codification of the New Lex Mercatoria*, 2nd ed. 2010, 279 *et seq.;* see for the case law of the Iran-US Claims Tribunal Westberg, *Contract Excuse in International Business Transactions: Awards of the Iran-United States Claims Tribunal*, ICSID Rev.-FILR 1989, p. 215, 238 *et seq.* = https://www.trans-lex.org/129600; *Anaconda Iran Ltd. v Iran*, 13 Iran-U.S. C.T.R. 1986, at 199 *et seq. para 43* = https://www.trans-lex.org/231800*:* "Under a variety of names most, if not all, legal systems recognize *force majeure* as an excuse for contractual non-performance. *Force majeure* therefore can be considered a general principle of law. It follows that the right to invoke *force majeure* does not depend on, or arise out of, an express contractual provision"; *Questech Inc. v Iran*, 9 Iran-U.S. C.T.R. 9, at 107 *et seq.* = https://www.trans-lex.org/231400: "This concept of changed circumstances, also referred to as *clausula rebus sic stantibus*, has in its basic form been incorporated into so many legal systems that it may be regarded as a general principle of law", see also TransLex-Principle VI.3., https://www.trans-lex.org/944000 and the comparative law references, arbitral awards and contract clauses reprinted there; see *also* Domingo/Ortega/Rodriguez-Antolin/Zambrana, *Principios de Derecho Global*, 2006, p. 51 https://www.trans-lex.org/101550 ("*Actus Dei nemini facit iniuriam*"); Cheng, *General Principles of Law as Applied by International Courts and Tribunals*, Reprint 1987, p. 227 = https://www.trans-lex.org/101100; Kersley/Broom, *A Selection of Legal Maxims*, 10th ed. 1939, p. 151 *et seq.* = https://www.trans-lex.org/110650 ("*Actus Dei nemini injuriam*—The law holds no man responsible for the act of god").
2. See Brunner, Force Majeure and Hardship under General Contract Principles, 2009, p. 383.
3. Fontaine/de Ly, *supra* note 1, p. 401 *et seq.*, stating that one force majeure clause in a complex contract covered 27 pages; see also ICC Force Majeure Clause 2003, ICC Publication No. 650 = https://www.trans-lex.org/700700.
4. Brunner, *supra* note 2, pp. 384, 386; Plate, *Force Majeure und Hardship in grenzüberschreitenden Langzeitverträgen*, 2005, 4; see also Fontaine, *supra* note 1, 480.
5. See Derains, *Note to ICC Award No. 5864*, Clunet 1997, p. 1077 = https://www.trans-lex.org/196586.
6. See Plate, *supra* note 4, p. 148.
7. See Farnsworth, *On Contracts*, 3rd ed. 2018, § 9.9a.
8. Brödermann, *UNIDROIT Principles of International Commercial Contracts*, An Article-by-Article Commentary, 2018, Art. 7.1.6, No. 2.
9. See Brunner, *supra* note 2, p. 385.
10. See for the significance of usages in international arbitration Jolivet/Marchisio/Gélinas, in: Gélinas (ed.) *Trade Usages and Implied Terms in the Age of Arbitration*, 2016, p. 211 *et seq.*; Derains, Rev d'Arb. 1973, 122 *et seq.*; Loquin, Revue Internationale de Droit Économique 1989, 163 *et seq.*

11. See for the application of general principles of law in international arbitration Kahn, Journal du Droit International 1989, 305 *et seq.*; Berger, World Arbitration & Mediation Review 2011, 97 *et seq.*
12. ICC Award No. 4462 of 1985 (First Award on Force Majeure), *National Oil Corporation v Libyan Sun Oil Company*, International Legal Materials 1990, 565 *et seq.* (excerpts of the First and Final Award in: Yearbook Commercial Arbitration (YCA) XVI (1991), p. 54 *et seq.* = http://https://www.trans-lex.org/204462); see Berger/Erdely, *Force Majeure in International Contract Law, A Critical Analysis of ICC Award No. 4462 (National Oil Corporation v Sun Oil)*, in: The Practice of Arbitration, Essays in Honour of Hans van Houtte, Oxford 2012, p. 61 *et seq.*
13. For more details see the ICC Award No. 4462, *supra* note 12, p. 568 *et seq.*
14. ICC Award No. 5864, Clunet 1997, at 1073 *et seq.* = https://www.trans-lex.org/205864.
15. The provisions on force majeure and related concepts contained in Arab civil codes are usually of a non-mandatory nature, see Amkahn, *Force Majeure and Impossibility of Performance in Arab Contract Law*, Arab Law Quarterly 1991, 297, 307; however, the provisions on contract modification by the court in cases of changed circumstances (economic hardship) in the same civil codes (except for Tunisia) usually specify that they are to be considered mandatory rules of public policy, see Amkahn, *The Effect of Change in Circumstances in Arab Contract Law*, Arab Law Quarterly 1994, 258, 274 *et seq.*
16. An English translation of the Libyan Civil Code of 1954 prepared by Meredith O. Ansell and Ibrahim Massaud al-Arif is available at https://archive.org/stream/LibyanCivilCode1954/Libyan-CivilCode_djvu.txt.
17. See Polkinghorne/Rosenberg, *Expecting the Unexpected: the Force Majeure Clause*, Business Law Int'l. 2015, 49, 57 = https://www.trans-lex.org/138300; Brunner, *supra* note 2, p. 111 *et seq.*, 385, n. 1936; Fontaine/de Ly, *supra* note 1, p. 402 *et seq.*; Plate, *supra* note 4, p. 150 *et seq.*; see also TransLex-Principle VI.3, https://www.trans-lex.org/944000 and the collection of force majeure contract clauses reprinted there.
18. Art. 1218 was included in the French Civil Code through the reform bill of February 2016 and reads: "In contractual matters, there is force majeure where an event beyond the control of the debtor, which could not reasonably have been foreseen at the time of the conclusion of the contract and whose effects could not be avoided by appropriate measures, prevents performance of his obligation by the debtor"; English text available at https://www.trans-lex.org/601101.
19. See *RSM Production Corporation v Central African Republic* (ICSID Case No. ARB/07/2), Interim Award on Jurisdiction and Liability of 7 December 2010, text available at https://icsid.worldbank.org/en/Pages/cases/casedetail.aspx?CaseNo=ARB/07/2, p. 43, para 179: "The force majeure requirements are defined in Art. 28.2 of the Contract, namely unforeseeability, unavoidability and uncontrollability. In the present case, the two parties are bound by that force majeure definition in the Contract. That definition corresponds to the one developed in arbitral case law" (translation by the author).
20. cf. 22.1. EPSA: "... Force majeure shall include, without limitation: ... any unforeseen circumstances and acts *beyond the control* of such Party" (emphasis added).
21. ICC Award No. 4462, *supra* note 12, p. 587.
22. ICC Award No. 4462, *supra* note 12, p. 585.
23. ICC Award No. 4462, *supra* note 12, p. 586.
24. See TransLex-Principle VI.3 (c), https://www.trans-lex.org/944000.
25. See for a critical view of this drafting approach, allowing a negligent party to invoke the force majeure defence even though the relevant event was so obvious that it was foreseeable for any party using ordinary diligence Plate, *supra* note 4, p. 154.
26. ICC Award No. 4462, *supra* note 12, p. 587; see also Nassar, *Sanctity of Contracts Revisited*, 1995, p. 222.
27. See for the nexus requirement as a "safety mechanism" used by international arbitral tribunals to avoid "floodgate" defences and to keep the application of force majeure and hardship defences within their proper ambit Nassar, *supra* note 26, p. 225; see also Brunner, *supra* note 2, p. 340 *et seq.*
28. See for a collection of force majeure clauses from international commercial contracts https://www.trans-lex.org/944000/_/force-majeure/#clauses.
29. ICC Award No. 4462, *supra* note 12, p. 588.
30. The Tribunal referred in that context to the leading "*Latsis*" judgement of the Libyan Supreme Court of June 20, 1971, No. 4-17, published in: Supreme Court Journal, 8th year, No. 1, p. 52 *et seq.*
31. ICC Award No. 4462, *supra* note 12, p. 587.

32. ICC Award No. 4462, *supra* note 12, p. 588.
33. ICC Award No. No. 5864, Clunet 1997, p. 1073, 1076 = https://www.trans-lex.org/205864 with Note *Derains*, *supra* note 5, p. 1077 = https://www.trans-lex.org/196586.
34. ICC Award No. 4462, *supra* note 12, p. 589.
35. But see ICC Award No. 5864, *supra* note 12, p. 1076 *et seq.*, in which the tribunal reached the opposite conclusion, emphasizing that due to the effects of the ordinance issued by the President of the United States enjoining US companies from working in Libya, the American company had a valid force majeure defence because it was forced to close down its operations in Libya and would have violated the US sanctions had it continued its work in Libya, either through its Dutch subsidiary or through an independent enterprise; see also the ICSID Award *RSM Production Corporation v Central African Republic* , *supra* note 19, p. 43, para 152 *et seq.*) in which the Tribunal granted the force majeure defence because the sub-contractors, of which only a limited number existed due to the highly specialized seismic work to be performed, refused to enter the Central African Republic in light of the political emergency situation in that country during the relevant period of time.
36. See for a similar approach (reference to two other parties who had been able to perform in the period for which force majeure was invoked) ICC Award No. 3150, Yearbook Commercial Arbitration 2014, p. 65, 67, para. 33 = https://www.trans-lex.org/203150.
37. ICC Award No. 19299 of 10 July 2015, 1. Gujarat State Petroleum Corp. Ltd., 2. Alkor Petroo Ltd., 3. Western Drilling Contractors Private Ltd. v 1. Republic of Yemen, 2. The Yemeni Ministry of Oil and Minerals, text available at https://www.italaw.com/cases/4209.
38. The hybrid nature of PSAs follows from the fact that the contracts concern development and/or production rights with respect to the host state's natural resources; it must be noted, though, that it is the legal system of the host state that determines whether and to what extent a PSA must be qualified as a public, private or hybrid agreement, see for the Russian Federation: Fet, "The Problem of Investment Protection under Russian Production Sharing Agreements", *Currents: Intl Trade Law Journal* 2007, p. 93, 100 *et seq.* ("mixed character"); Rath, *Das Recht der Production-Sharing Agreements in der Russischen Föderation*, 2006, p. 52 *et seq.* ("contract *sui generis*...subject to private law... with public law elements"); for Indonesia: Umar Purba, "Production Sharing Contract: Is it Within Private or Public Domain", *Indonesian Journal of Intl Law* 2009, 21, 40 ("private contract...[that] belongs to the private domain"); for Uzbekistan: Bayzakova, *Current challenges, future prospects: legal governance of the petroleum industry in Uzbekistan*, Intl Energy Law Rev. 2011, 238, 240 ("a private contract with a foreign element"); for Azerbaijan: Bati, "The Legal Status of Production Sharing Agreements in Azerbaijan", *Journal of Energy & Nat. Resources Law* 2003, 153, 166 ("the Implementing Laws themselves refer to the PSAs as laws").
39. ICC Award No. 19299, *supra* note 37, para. 76.
40. ICC Award No. 19299, *supra* note 37, paras. 115 *et seq.*
41. ICC Award No. 19299, *supra* note 37, p 110: "What is important is the prevention of performance of obligations. Whether this is because of 'riot', 'insurrection' or any other defined Force Majeure event would not matter. Thus, the analysis of one event in and of itself would suffice."
42. ICC Award No. 19299, *supra* note 37, paras. 123 *et seq.*
43. ICC Award No. 19299, *supra* note 37, para. 126.
44. ICC Award No. 19299, *supra* note 37, para. 132.
45. ICC Award No. 19299, *supra* note 37, para. 131.
46. See *supra* note 39.
47. ICC Award No. 19299, *supra* note 37, para. 127.
48. See TransLex-Principle IV.5.1, https://www.trans-lex.org/924000.
49. ICC Award No. 19299, *supra* note 37, para. 128.
50. ICC Award No. 19299, *supra* note 37, para. 133.
51. As production sharing contracts, the agreements were qualified as laws of Yemen pursuant to the Yemeni Laws Nos. 6, 7 and 9 of 2009, para 76; see generally for the legal nature of production sharing agreements *supra* note 38.
52. ICC Award No. 19299, *supra* note 37, para. 139.
53. ICC Award No. 19299, *supra* note 37, paras. 136 *et seq.*
54. ICC Award No. 19299, *supra* note 37, paras. 142 *et seq.*
55. ICC Award No. 19299, *supra* note 37, para. 144; see for a similar approach ICC Award No. 5864, Clunet 1997, at 1073 *et seq.* = https://www.trans-lex.org/205864: "De plus, le tribunal estime que les problèmes de force majeure dans le présent litige sont entièrement réglés par les dispositions du contrat entre les parties").

56. ICC Award No. 19299, *supra* note 37, para. 147.
57. See *supra* note 39.
58. ICC Award No. 19299, *supra* note 37, paras. 76, 149.
59. The tribunal noted that the party-appointed legal experts ultimately agreed that the *contra proferentem* principle of contractual interpretation exists in Yemeni law, paras. 77, 150; see for this rule as a principle of transnational commercial law TransLex-Principle IV.5.4, https://www.trans-lex.org/926000; according to that principle, the party which drafted an ambiguous contract term may not later rely on a meaning of that term which is to the disadvantage of the other side, unless this ambiguity was discussed between the parties when the contract was concluded.
60. ICC Award No. 19299, *supra* note 37, paras. 154.
61. See *supra* II.A.
62. See *supra* note 12.
63. ICC Award No. 19299, *supra* note 37, para. 152.
64. ICC Award No. 19299, *supra* note 37, para. 156.
65. See Berger, *supra* note 1, p. 117; ICC Award No. 3131, Revue de L'Arbitrage 1983, at 525 = https://www.trans-lex.org/203131 (translation from French original): "The notion of good faith not only expresses a psychological state of mind, the knowledge or ignorance of a fact. *It also expresses a 'reference to usages, to a moral rule of behaviour' ... it therefore carries with it a certain standard of behaviour which comes close to a general principle of responsibility"*; see *also* ICC Award No. 2291 of 1975, Clunet 1976, 989, 990 = https://www.trans-lex.org/*202291* (translation from French original): "The [parties'] conventions have to be interpreted in good faith. This means that each party has the obligation to display a behaviour towards the other party which cannot harm the latter, and which takes into account that reasonable renegotiations are usual in international economic contracts [in case of changed economic conditions]...".
66. ICC Award No. 19299, *supra* note 37, paras. 159 *et seq.*
67. ICC Award No. 8873 of 1997, extracts published in Journal du Droit International (Clunet) 1998, p. 1017 *et seq.* with Note Hascher, p. 1024 *et seq.*; ICC International Court of Arbitration Bulletin 1999, p. 78 *et seq.*
68. Art. 21 (2) ICC Arbitration Rules (2017) provides: "The arbitral tribunal shall take account of the provisions of the contract, if any, between the parties and of any relevant trade usages." the provision has remained largely unchanged in the versions of the Rules since 1989.
69. Art. VII of the European Convention on International Commercial Arbitration of 1961 provides that irrespective as to how the tribunal determines the applicable law, "the arbitrators shall take account of the terms of the contract and trade usages."
70. ICC Award No. 8873, Clunet 1998, p. 1017, 1018 (all translations from French by the author); see for the significance of the European Convention in this context Gélinas, in: Gélinas (ed.) *Trade Usages and Implied Terms in the Age of Arbitration*, 2016, p. 253, 258 *et seq.*
71. See Hascher, *supra* note 67, p. 1025, rightly emphasizing that a tribunal may raise the application of a usage *ex officio*, but only under the condition that the parties are granted their right to be heard, the violation of which (unlike the tribunal's application of the law) may be sanctioned by domestic courts in setting aside proceedings.
72. Art 1.9 (2) UPICC provides: "The parties are bound by a usage that is widely known to and regularly observed in international trade by parties in the particular trade concerned except where the application of such a usage would be unreasonable."
73. See Webster/Bühler, *Handbook of ICC Arbitration*, 3rd ed. 2014, No. 21-75.
74. See Riad, in Bortolotti/Meyer (eds.) *The Application of Substantive Law by International Arbitrators, Dossiers of the ICC Institute of World Business Law*, 2014, p. 143, 144: "...we frequently encounter reference to the parties' mutual legitimate expectations in arbitral case law, as the appropriate method ... to achieve justice and fairness in the adjudication of pending cases, whether they are purely commercial or touching long-term developmental transactions"; see also Perret, id., p. 109, 110: "...constraints resulting from a specific rule of the applicable law do not necessarily prevent the arbitrator from seeking the most appropriate solution consistent with the parties' legitimate expectations"; *Jolivet/Marchisio/Gélinas*, *supra* note 10, p. 231: "Certainly, party autonomy is the cornerstone of international arbitration, and it requires a solution to the dispute that is compatible with the expectations of the parties to an international commercial contract."
75. Brunner, *supra* note 2, pp. 30, 386.
76. See Nassar, *supra* note 26, p. 228.
77. Berger, *Private Dispute Resolution in International Business*, Vol.II (Handbook), 3rd ed. 2015, No. 25-17.

78. English text available at www.admin.ch/opc/en/classified-compilation/19110009/201704010000/220.pdf.
79. ICC Award No. 8873, *supra* note 67, p. 1021.
80. Art. 1096 (3) provides: "If the obligor should default on his obligation, or should have undertaken to deliver the same thing to two or more different persons, he shall be liable for any fortuitous events until delivery thereof."
81. ICC Award No. 8873, *supra* note 67, p. 1021.
82. ICC Award No. 8873, *supra* note 67, p. 1022.
83. See, e.g. the ICSID Award *RSM Production Corporation v Central African Republic* , *supra* note 19, p. 45, para 211 stating that the notification requirement does not mean that the force majeure events need to be specified in detail in the notification letter sent to the other side, as long as the letter describes "in a sufficient manner" the actual atmosphere in the country at the moment of notification, in particular the political and military disturbances there on which the force majeure defence is based.
84. ICC Award No. 8873, *supra* note 67, p. 1021; see also Plate, *supra* note 4, p. 163; see for the various types of notification requirements and rules following from their violation used in international contract practice Brunner, *supra* note 2, p. 342 *et seq.*
85. ICC Award No. 8873, *supra* note 67, p. 1022 *et seq.*
86. ICC Award No. 8873, *supra* note 67, p. 1024.
87. Fontaine/de Ly, *supra* note 1, p. 427.
88. Phelps Dodge International Corp. v Iran, Iran-US C.T.R. 1986 I, p. 157, 173; see also Computer Sciences Corp. v Iran, Iran-US C.T.R. 1986 II, 269, 289; Schmitz, Allgemeine Rechtsgrundsätze in der Rechtsprechung des Iran-US Claims Tribunal, 1992, 171 *et seq.*
89. See for the various standard form contracts published by the Fédération Internationale des Ingénieurs Conseil (International Federation of Consulting Engineers, FIDIC) http://fidic.org/bookshop/about-bookshop/which-fidic-contract-should-i-use.
90. See for the various standard form contracts published by the Engineering Advancement Association of Japan (ENAA) http://www.enaa.or.jp/EN/activities/model.html.
91. ICC Award No. 8873, *supra* note 67, p. 1018.
92. See for this narrow understanding of usages in the context of international arbitration *Gaillard* in Études offertes à Pierre Bellet 1991, 204 *et seq.*; Gaillard, World Arbitration & Mediation Review 2011, 161 *et seq.*; see for a critical analysis of this narrow understanding of trade usages, favouring a broad notion of trade usages as directly applicable primary rules of law which are part of an independent theory of legal sources of the transnational law of business contracts, Gélinas, *supra* note 70, p. 257 *et seq.*
93. Jolivet/Marchisio/Gélinas, *supra* note 10, p. 216 *et seq.* with reference to ICC Awards Nos 14748, 13139, 10977, 14988, 13834 and 12788.
94. See Hascher, *supra* note 67, p. 1026.
95. ICC Award No. 8873, *supra* note 67, p. 1020.
96. Jolivet/Marchisio/Gélinas, *supra* note 10, p. 219 *et seq.*; Derains, *supra* note 10, 123 *et seq.*; see also Fouchard, *L'Arbitrage Commercial International*, 1965, p. 409 *et seq.*, 412: "All these documents reveal, confirm or fix a certain number of international commercial usages which can be applied in a more general manner to this or that category of international commercial operations; we have shown how they 'articulate' themselves to form customary norms which are more and more universal in nature" (Translation from French by the author).
97. See Nassar, *supra* note 26, p. 96 *et seq.*, 105: "Parties to private law disputes do not acquire rights directly from such instruments, which only affect contractual undertakings insofar as they represent settled international practice."
98. Bühler/Webster, *supra* note 73, No. 21-74.
99. See for ICC awards in which the tribunals, while rejecting the force majeure defence, nonetheless excused performance based on their findings that performance, under the circumstances of the cases before them, would have been unreasonably difficult: Nassar, *supra* note 26, p. 227 *et seq.*
100. See for this approach to the application of the UPICC Brödermann, *supra* note 8, Preamble, Nos. 8, 12.
101. See ICC Award No. 8873, *supra* note 67, p. 1020.
102. See for this problematic view that ignores that general principles of law as rules of law must be distinguished from fact-driven trade usages, Jolivet/Marchisio/Gélinas, *supra* note 10, p. 228.
103. ICC Award No. 8873, *supra* note 67, p. 1019; see also Hascher, *supra* note 67, p. 1026.

104. See the quote from the Award in Jolivet/Marchisio/Gélinas, *supra* note 10, p. 229: "... the hardship rules, as articulated in the UNIDROIT Principles, or the Lando Principles, are not accepted in all legal systems and may therefore hardly be regarded as a typical, universally applied trade usage".

105. ICC Award No. 7375, 11, Mealey's Int'l. Arb.Rep. 1996, A-1; Bonell, *An International Restatement of Contract Law*, 3rd ed. 2005, p. 286, n. 78, available at https://www.trans-lex.org/100800.

106. See *supra* note.

107. Brödermann, *supra* note 8, Art. 6.2.1, Nos. 1, 2.

108. See, e.g. *The Ministry of Defense and Support for Armed Forces of the Islamic Republic of Iran v Cubic Defense Systems, Inc.*, 29 F.Supp. 2d 1168 (S.D. Cal. 1998): "Under the laws of contract in all municipal legal systems exceptions to the basic notion of *pacta sunt servanda* have been developed on the ground that in particular circumstances fairness and justice require the making of legal excuse for non-performance of contractual promises. While the excuse concepts in different countries vary to a great extent, they are all based on largely the same premise; namely that some unforeseen development has occurred affecting the contractual performance without fault and beyond the control of the parties ... it is widely regarded as a general principle of law"; Berger, *supra* note 1, p. 222; Brunner, *supra* note 2, p. 418: "The hardship exemption as provided for in the UPICC/PECL may be regarded as an expression of a generally recognized principle"; Fontaine, in: *UNIDROIT Principles of International Commercial Contracts, Reflections on their Use in International Arbitration*, ICC International Court of Arbitration Bulletin Special Supplement 2002, p. 95, 97 *et seq.*, hinting at the fact that 42% of international contracts contain hardship clauses.

109. See ICC Award No. 1512, Yearbook Commercial Arbitration 1976, p. 128, 129: "The principle *rebus sic stantibus* is universally considered as being of strict and narrow interpretation, as a dangerous exception to the principle of sanctity of contracts."

110. Brunner, *supra* note 2, p. 36 *et seq.* emphasizing that this approach must be distinguished from the technique of using general contract principles as a means to interpret the applicable law or the terms of the contract; see for the "internationally useful" construction of domestic law, Berger, *The Concept of the "International Useful" Construction of Domestic Law*, https://www.trans-lex.org/5.

111. Brunner, *supra* note 2, p. 29 *et seq.*

112. Plate, *supra* note 4, p. 148, 187.

Chapter 7

Economic Sanctions, Force Majeure and Hardship[1]

by Dr Mercédeh Azeredo da Silveira*

INTRODUCTION

Half way between diplomatic protest and military action, economic sanctions are tools used for the achievement of political goals. Their primary purpose is coercive: they are designed to lead their target to refrain from engaging in activities in breach of international laws or standards or to renounce further wrongdoing.[2] In past instances, economic sanctions have been imposed, for instance, to bring a target state accused of human rights violations to alter certain features of its domestic or foreign policy,[3] to impair a target state's military potential, bring hostilities to a halt and secure the restoration of peace,[4] to prevent the development of weapons of mass destruction,[5] to secure the withdrawal of a target state's troops from an invaded territory,[6] and to destabilize foreign regimes or induce a target state to reinstate a legitimate government.[7] The purpose of economic sanctions is usually also symbolic, as the imposition of such measures constitutes an avenue to denounce the actions or policies of their target. Finally, some sanctions programmes have even been considered to serve a punitive purpose.

To achieve such goals, economic sanctions programmes are designed to deprive their targets of critical imports and/or export markets, and/or to curtail the flow of finance from which targets may benefit. To this end, two types of measures are regularly taken as part of economic sanctions programmes: first, measures—sometimes referred to as 'trade sanctions'—that are used to limit the flow of services and commodities (goods, technologies and capital) towards or from a target; second, measures—sometimes referred to as 'financial sanctions'—that provide for an interruption or reduction of financing, order the freezing of assets and/or prohibit the transfer of funds to the order or to the benefit of a target. Typically, economic sanctions programmes prohibit new trade and/or financial agreements and paralyse the performance of pre-existing ones. Contracts among private operators (individuals and corporate entities), which are used as instruments for the implementation of economic sanctions,[8] are thus most directly impacted.

Sanctions may be imposed spontaneously by states acting individually (unilateral sanctions) or by states acting jointly under the auspices of a regional organisation such as the EU (autonomous Community sanctions),

* Dr Mercédeh Azeredo da Silveira is an attorney-at-law specialising in international arbitration. She represents corporate entities and governments before arbitral tribunals in both commercial and investment arbitration proceedings. She is also the author of a series of publications in the areas of international arbitration, international trade, contracts, economic sanctions, and mediation.

or they may be imposed as state or Community measures of implementation of resolutions adopted by the United Nations Security Council under Chapter VII of the United Nations Charter (UNC) (multilateral sanctions).

In addition to the prohibitions they lay down, economic sanctions programmes may establish investigation and enforcement procedures. They usually specify penalties that may be imposed in case of breach. Property involved in, and proceeds obtained through, a transaction may be seized and subjected to forfeiture proceedings, existing authorisations may be cancelled, export privileges may be denied, civil and/or criminal monetary penalties may be imposed, and individuals may even be sentenced to imprisonment.

Typically, the party prohibited by an economic sanction from performing a transaction withholds performance, even if the contract which generated its obligations was validly entered into prior to the imposition or the entry into effect of the sanction.[9] In response, its contractual partner may launch judicial proceedings, seeking performance in kind and/or damages.

Today, the prevailing view is that, as a matter of principle, domestic courts and arbitral tribunals have the authority to give effect to measures, such as economic sanctions, which serve public interests, whether the measures under consideration have been imposed by the forum state (in the case of a dispute decided by a domestic court), by the state of the applicable law or by yet another state.[10] In particular, disputes involving economic sanctions are deemed to be arbitrable:[11] the competence to rule on such disputes is not retained exclusively by domestic courts.[12] Two questions, however, remain to be addressed whenever a party claims, in court or arbitral proceedings, that it should be freed from pre-existing obligations on the ground that their performance is now prohibited by an economic sanctions programme: should the sanction be taken into account for the resolution of the dispute and, if so, how does the sanction affect the contract and the parties' rights and obligations?

Section I. of this contribution focuses on the question of the characterisation of economic sanctions from a private law perspective. This question must be delved into to allow an identification, in Section II., of economic sanctions that may—perhaps must—be taken into account by a domestic court or an arbitral tribunal. Section III. is dedicated to the substantive effects of economic sanctions on pre-existing contracts between private operators.

I. CHARACTERISATION OF ECONOMIC SANCTIONS FROM A PRIVATE LAW PERSPECTIVE

To this day, the characterisation of economic sanctions from a private law perspective has been cause for debate. Is the prohibition against performing certain transactions, laid down in a sanctions programme, to be regarded as a legal rule that may have a claim to limit the parties' contractual freedom along with other possible limitations posed by the applicable law, or is it to be regarded as a factual element, a *datum*, with which the parties are confronted in the performance of their agreement?

I.A. The Traditional *Datum* Approach

On various grounds—such as the fact that economic sanctions are behaviour rules rather than decision rules,[13] the fact that economic sanctions typically prohibit all transactions falling within their scope irrespective of the law governing these transactions, and perhaps also the fact that economic sanctions do not form part of the law of contracts—it has traditionally been argued that from a private law perspective, an economic sanction imposed by a state other than the state of the applicable law must be regarded as a *datum*, that is, as an element of fact.[14]

For proponents of the traditional *datum* approach, it is the injunction's efficacy, its power to compel a party to withhold performance, through threats of penalty and of enforcement measures, which justifies taking into account the prohibition in order to determine the fate of a disputed transaction.[15] This position implies that irrespective of its origin and of its underlying purpose, a sanction that is foreign to the applicable law but deemed to be effective will be taken into account as a relevant fact and it will affect the parties' rights and obligations to the extent that the applicable law ascribes consequences to its existence or to the situation it has created.[16]

Under the traditional *datum* approach, foreign sanctions are thus given effect strictly through the prism of the *lex contractus*, which remains the sole set of legal provisions governing the parties' rights and obligations.[17] Swiss courts,[18] French courts,[19] German courts[20] and English courts,[21] among others, have relied on this approach to determine whether a contract concluded despite the existence of a foreign trade prohibition was to be considered illegal, immoral or contrary to public policy under the provisions of the *lex contractus*. In these cases, the relevant 'facts' were the existence of a foreign prohibition in force at the time of the conclusion of the contract and the parties' disregard thereof. Arbitral tribunals have also relied on the *datum* approach,[22] either to assess the validity of contracts or to determine whether a foreign prohibition imposed after the conclusion of a contract could be regarded, under the provisions of the *lex contractus*, as an event of force majeure or the like.[23]

I.B. The Legal Norm Approach

Today, the *datum* approach is no longer an inevitable course to ensure that a sanction bear due consequences on the parties' contractual relationship.

With the emergence of private international law, not only is a court ruling on a dispute governed by rules of private law no longer bound to disregard a substantively relevant provision merely because of its public law characterisation,[24] but it is even empowered to give effect to provisions (whether of a public or of a private law nature) that are external to the applicable law.[25] An 'overriding mandatory rule',[26] that is, a rule that purports to respond to essential needs and therefore proclaims itself applicable to all situations falling within its purview irrespective of the applicable law,[27] may be given effect as a legal norm even if it is external to the applicable law, provided that certain restrictive conditions be satisfied (these conditions are discussed below in section II.A.).

Regulation (EC) 593/2008 of the European Parliament and of the Council of 17 June 2008 on the Law Applicable to Contractual Obligations (Rome I

Regulation)—the governing text for all EU member states with respect to the identification of the law applicable to contracts concluded after 17 December 2009 (Article 28)—defines overriding mandatory rules as:

> provisions the respect for which is regarded as crucial by a country for safeguarding its public interests, such as its political, social or economic organisation, to such an extent that they are applicable to any situation falling within their scope, irrespective of the law otherwise applicable to the contract under this Regulation (Article 9(1)).

The Rome I Regulation further provides that:

> [e]ffect may be given to the overriding mandatory provisions of the law of the country where the obligations arising out of the contract have to be or have been performed, in so far as those overriding mandatory provisions render the performance of the contract unlawful (Article 9(3)).

The Rome I Regulation's predecessor, the Rome Convention on the Law Applicable to Contractual Obligations (80/934/EEC) of 19 June 1980 (Rome Convention),[28] also provided that:

> [w]hen applying under this Convention the law of a country, effect may be given to the mandatory rules of the law of another country with which the situation has a close connection, if and in so far as, under the law of the latter country, those rules must be applied whatever the law applicable to the contract (Article 7(1)).[29]

Economic sanctions fit into the category of overriding mandatory rules.[30] Indeed, as noted above, a distinctive feature of sanctions is that they strive to prohibit the performance of all transactions falling within their scope, irrespective of the law governing these transactions.[31] Many trade sanctions prohibit, for instance, trade-related transactions between individuals located in, citizens of, and corporate entities incorporated under the laws of, the sanctioning state, on the one hand, and individuals and entities located in the target state, on the other hand, irrespective of the law applicable to these transactions. Accordingly, today, economic sanctions may be taken into account in the context of disputes between private operators, as legal norms, notwithstanding the fact that they serve public interests and even if they are external to the applicable law, provided they satisfy the conditions that must be met for an overriding mandatory rule to be given effect.[32] In a 2010 decision, the French *Cour de cassation* held that Article 7(1) Rome Convention was to be relied upon to determine whether a unilateral Ghanean 'embargo' prohibiting imports of French beef into Ghana was to be taken into consideration for the resolution of a dispute pertaining to a contract (concluded in 2007) governed by French law, which provided for the transportation, from France to Ghana, of frozen beef.[33]

If the conditions, discussed below, of provisions such as Article 7(1) Rome Convention or Article 9(3) Rome I Regulation are satisfied, the court ruling on the dispute has the authority—though in principle no duty[34]—to give effect to a sanction that is foreign to the applicable law, irrespective of the content of this law, irrespective of contractual clauses that may collide with the sanction, and even irrespective of an agreement between the parties to exclude the application of the sanction.[35]

The same applies in the case of disputes heard by an arbitral tribunal.[36] Indeed, although arbitrators are not bound *a priori* by any set of rules of private international law and therefore provisions such as Article 7(1) Rome

Convention and Article 9(3) Rome I Regulation are not directly applicable to arbitration, they are applicable by analogy; at the very least, arbitrators should be guided by their underlying principles.[37] Accordingly, as early as in 1973, an arbitral tribunal took into account Lebanese import restrictions—which it characterised as overriding mandatory rules—in the context of a contract between a Japanese seller and a Lebanese importer, governed by general principles and usages of international trade and to be performed in Lebanon, Syria and Jordan.[38]

In light of the above, proponents of the legal norm approach maintain that nothing justifies that sanctions be relegated to the sphere of *data* and assert that their legal nature ought to be acknowledged. Accordingly, they maintain that a sanction should be regarded as an impediment to the performance of contractual obligations only if the party required to withhold performance is legally bound to comply with it, that is, if the sanction has a valid claim under rules and/or principles of private international law to limit the parties' contractual freedom, either as an element of the applicable law or as an overriding mandatory rule external thereto.[39]

II. APPLICATION OF ECONOMIC SANCTIONS BY DOMESTIC COURTS AND ARBITRAL TRIBUNALS

In many case scenarios, the *datum* approach and the legal norm approach lead to the same outcome, in particular if the performance of the contract requires the obligor to take steps within the sanctioning state. In this case, possible enforcement measures or threats of penalty will usually weigh heavily against a decision to disregard the sanction, and whether the latter be characterised as an element of fact or as an element of law ultimately matters primarily for procedural purposes. However, as shown in the present section, one cannot exclude the possibility that the two approaches lead to different results in certain situations, notably in the case of unilateral sanctions and autonomous Community (or, more generally, autonomous regional) sanctions. Indeed, under the legal norm approach, mechanisms of private international law afford arbitrators and judges the ability to disregard sanctions programmes that do not meet certain narrowly defined conditions.

II.A. Unilateral and Autonomous Community Sanctions

It may be tempting to argue that whenever the *lex contractus* provides that exemption may be granted in situations of factual impediment (including situations in which performance has become excessively difficult or unreasonably onerous), a defaulting party may be exempted irrespective of the sanctioning state's authority to proscribe the disputed transaction, if that state has the power to prevent the performance of this transaction. One may indeed be tempted to opine that a defaulting party should be denied exemption from liability for non-performance only if it failed to perform a contract that it could have performed, hence that it should be exempted if the sanctioning state would in any event have had the power to prevent its performance, irrespective of any other consideration including the sanction's purpose.

Such an approach—which is in line with the *datum* approach—may, however, amount to an unsatisfactory shortcut if the measure under consideration is a unilateral or a Community autonomous sanction.[40] Indeed, relying primarily, if not solely, on the factual circumstances created by sanctions and disregarding the fact that these constitute deliberate instructions issued by one or several states, directed to the achievement of a political purpose, detrimental to one of the contractual partners, and that have at times been condemned by states if not by the international community at large, may lead to undesirable results.[41]

As shown below, by relying on the *datum* approach, a domestic court may run the risk of giving effect to a sanction that the forum state has refused to condone,[42] perhaps to a sanction that the forum state has forthrightly condemned, perhaps even to a prohibition directed against the forum state. By relying on the *datum* approach, a deciding domestic court or arbitral tribunal may also run the risk of giving effect to extraterritorial sanctions (that is, sanctions that prohibit persons and entities located outside the sanctioning state from dealing with a target[43]) against which blocking statutes have been adopted (possibly by the forum state itself in the case of a dispute litigated before a domestic court).[44] The deciding court may even run the risk of giving effect to sanctions programmes that violate international law.

In addition and as a matter of principle, if the contract or the *lex contractus* does not itself address the relevance of, or allocate the risk associated with, foreign prohibitions,[45] one may question whether a court should subject parties to a prohibition that is external to the applicable law merely on the ground that this prohibition proclaims itself applicable to their transaction, without first ascertaining the reasons justifying that it be taken into consideration and limit the parties' contractual freedom.[46]

Finally, one ought to pay heed to the fact that in cases (discussed in Section III. below) in which a sanctions programme contains prescriptions governing its impact on contractual relationships, the traditional *datum* approach may entail an unwarranted limitation or alteration of the consequences of this programme on private operators.[47]

In light of the above, it is arguable that, at least as far as unilateral and Community (or other regional) autonomous sanctions are concerned, domestic courts and arbitral tribunals called to rule on contractual disputes should refrain from relying on the *datum* approach and rather examine whether the sanction under consideration has a valid claim, as a legal norm, to be given effect.[48]

Given that economic sanctions fall into the category of overriding mandatory rules, domestic courts are bound, as state officers, to give effect to substantively relevant economic sanctions imposed by the forum state, even if the law of the forum is not the applicable law (see Article 7(2) Rome Convention and Article 9(2) Rome I Regulation).[49] By contrast, a domestic court may, by virtue of the public policy exception,[50] disregard a sanction (foreign to the law of the forum) imposed by the state of the applicable law if giving it effect would lead to an outcome which would be in conflict with the forum's international public policy (see Article 16 Rome Convention and Article 21 Rome I Regulation[51]), that is, with fundamental principles and essential values that the forum state considers inviolable.[52] Similarly, an arbitral tribunal may disregard a sanction imposed by the state of the applicable law if giving it effect would lead to an outcome which would be in conflict with principles of transnational public policy,[53] that is, with universally recognised principles of justice.[54]

A domestic court may thus, for instance, disregard sanctions imposed by the state of the applicable law that are directed against the forum state[55] or sanctions against which the forum state has enacted a blocking statute. Both domestic courts and arbitral tribunals may also disregard sanctions imposed in breach of customary or conventional public international law binding on the sanctioning state,[56] for instance sanctions imposed in breach of the United Nations Charter (in particular the principle of non-intervention rooted in Article 2(1) UNC), of the General Agreement on Tariffs and Trade (GATT) (in particular its provisions aiming at the liberalisation of international trade, such as Article XI(1)),[57] of bilateral agreements, or of international human rights law.[58] Domestic courts and arbitral tribunals may also refuse to give effect to unilateral sanctions programmes that strive to be applied extraterritorially in breach of public international law.[59]

As to economic sanctions that are external to the applicable law, as mentioned above, under the legal norm approach, the deciding court must examine whether the sanction has a valid claim, as an overriding mandatory rule, to be given effect. In this respect, Article 7(1) Rome Convention provides the following:

> When applying under this Convention the law of a country, effect may be given to the mandatory rules of the law of another country with which the situation has a close connection, if and in so far as, under the law of the latter country, those rules must be applied whatever the law applicable to the contract. In considering whether to give effect to these mandatory rules, regard shall be had to their nature and purpose and to the consequences of their application or non-application.

Article 9(3) Rome I Regulation, in turn, reads as follows:

> Effect may be given to the overriding mandatory provisions of the law of the country where the obligations arising out of the contract have to be or have been performed, in so far as those overriding mandatory provisions render the performance of the contract unlawful. In considering whether to give effect to those provisions, regard shall be had to their nature and purpose and to the consequences of their application or non-application.

Thus, to determine whether effect ought to be given to a sanction that is external to the applicable law, the deciding court must ensure that the following conditions are met: first, that the sanction serves interests so commanding that it should not be disregarded in a situation that falls within its scope; second, that a close connection exists between the disputed contract and the sanctioning state; and third, that the benefits of a decision to give effect to the sanction outweigh those of a decision to disregard it.

The first condition (sometimes referred to as the 'application-worthiness' condition[60]) requires courts to weigh the ethical essence and importance of the policy underlying a foreign prohibition.[61] They will thus determine whether they should contribute to the achievement of the purpose of the prohibition, even though the latter is foreign to the applicable law. Domestic courts generally rely on domestic and/or EU standards.[62] Arbitral tribunals, on the other hand, must examine whether the sanction's purpose is considered by the international community to be legitimate (even if the achievement of this purpose is not essential to the international community[63]) and whether there is an agreement at the international level, be it implicit, that this purpose mandates that the sanction be given effect.[64] In this respect, it should be noted that the international community may recognise the legitimacy of a sanction imposed by a single state, considering that other states may have refrained from imposing the same sanction for contingent reasons while being in agreement with its underlying purpose.[65] One must bear in mind that a binding resolution of the Security Council is the outcome of an affirmative vote of nine members (out of the 15 members), including the concurring votes of the five permanent members (Article 27(3) UNC),[66] each of which has its own interests to safeguard. Furthermore, multilateral sanctions have, in some instances, followed unilateral measures, the legitimacy of which was thus subsequently validated.[67] Arbitrators should therefore not assume that because a sanction is unilateral, it does not serve a legitimate purpose. In each case, they must consider the context in which the sanction was imposed and determine whether its purpose mandates that it be given effect.[68]

By way of example, unilateral and autonomous Community sanctions imposed following, and in accord with, a non-binding resolution of the UN Security Council[69] ought to be regarded as serving a legitimate purpose.[70] The deciding court may also recognise the legitimacy of, and therefore 'take into account economic sanctions of foreign governments which promote mutually accepted policies or prevent a mutually recognized evil',[71] and sanctions programmes that are intended to protect the sanctioning state's vital interests or national security and that are not in conflict with the interests of the forum state.[72] This being said, it should be emphasised that courts should always ponder on the purpose of unilateral and autonomous regional sanctions rather than be influenced by pure considerations of reciprocity or international comity.

In this respect, the following may be noted. Today's broad conventional and treaty obligations protecting freedom of trade circumscribe the latitude of states to impose limits on the exchange of goods and services for reasons other than national and international peace and security. While it is true that, as noted above, in the absence of a conventional or treaty obligation of one state towards another to maintain trade relations, the use of trade sanctions is not to be considered intrinsically in breach of public international law, these conventional and treaty prescriptions may be regarded as guidelines in the assessment of the application-worthiness of a given sanctions programme, even where the sanctioning state is not bound by any such convention or treaty. Thus, for instance, considering provisions of the GATT (in particular Article XXI) and NAFTA (in particular Article 2102(1)) regarding the imposition of restrictive measures, a ban on arms exports to a state which is suspected of engaging in the development of weapons of mass destruction will likely be considered to serve a legitimate purpose, even if the sanctioning state has not sustained any direct injury and its interests have not been directly threatened.[73]

By contrast, it is hardly conceivable that a domestic court would consider legitimate a sanction that is directed against the forum state[74] or a sanction against which the latter has enacted blocking statutes.[75] Furthermore, sanctions based, for instance, on racial, religious or gender discrimination should never be considered legitimate and should therefore not be given effect.[76] An extraterritorial sanction imposed by a state other than the state of the applicable law may also have to be disregarded[77] if its scope is unjustifiable under principles of public international law[78] or, in the case of a dispute litigated before a domestic court, if the forum state has enacted a blocking statute[79] or its interests are adversely affected by the sanction.[80] The existence of a blocking statute must also be weighed against a finding of legitimacy by arbitral tribunals, given that, as noted above, arbitral tribunals ought to give effect to measures whose legitimacy has been acknowledged by the international community, rather than assist one state in the pursuance of an extraterritorial policy that others have opposed.

Regarding the second condition, namely that a close connection exist between the disputed contract and the sanctioning state, pursuant to Article 9(3) Rome I Regulation, domestic courts in EU member states may only give effect to sanctions imposed by the state where contractual obligations under the disputed contract have to be or have been performed.[81] Thus, in a decision rendered on 25 February 2015, the *Cour d'appel* of Paris refused to take into account US (extraterritorial) sanctions against Iran in the context of a dispute related to a contract governed by French law between a French company and an Iranian company.[82]

Arbitral tribunals, which are not bound by this limitation,[83] may consider the close connection requirement satisfied, for instance, if the disputed contract (or part of it) is to be performed within the territory of the sanctioning state,[84] if it involves prohibited imports into and/or exports from that territory, or if one of the parties must take some measures within that state to carry out its performance. The close connection requirement may also be deemed to be satisfied if the disputed contract involves prohibited transactions by nationals (or permanent residents) of the sanctioning state, or if the prohibited transactions threaten the sanctioning state's national security.

With respect to the third condition, namely that the benefits of a decision to give effect to the sanction outweigh those of a decision to disregard it, the deciding court may consider several variables. It ought to examine whether the sanctioning state has the power to enforce the sanction through material measures and thus prevent the performance of the contract[85] and whether penalties could be imposed by the sanctioning state against a party that would perform the contract in breach of the sanction.[86] The deciding court may also have to consider the foreseeable financial repercussions of a decision to give effect to a sanction.[87] In addition, an arbitral tribunal must weigh the risk that an award taking into account or disregarding a sanction be set aside or that enforcement of the award be refused.[88] Finally, in its assessment of the consequences of a decision to disregard or give effect to a sanction that has an extraterritorial scope, the deciding court should pay heed to decisions issued and legislation enacted to thwart the operation of the sanction or 'neutralise' its effects. Indeed, the deciding court should consider blocking statutes threatening persons and entities under the enacting state's jurisdiction with penalties[89] and prohibiting courts from recognising or enforcing judicial and administrative decisions giving effect to the sanction.[90] It should also examine possible clawback provisions granting persons and entities under the enacting state's jurisdiction the right to recover damages (including legal costs) caused by the application of the sanction or by actions based thereon or resulting therefrom.[91]

II.B. Multilateral Sanctions—Sanctions Adopted under Chapter VII of the UN Charter

The situation of UN sanctions is different.

UN Security Council mandatory resolutions on sanctions emanate from an international organisation acting on behalf of all its member states. They are adopted under Chapter VII of the UN Charter,[92] in pursuance of the Charter's goals, in situations in which the Security Council has determined the existence of a breach of the peace, an act of aggression, or a threat to the peace (Article 39 UNC).[93] UN Security Council mandatory resolutions not only are deemed to serve a purpose that the international community considers to be worthy of protection, but in fact form part of transnational public policy,[94] and are accordingly binding on domestic courts and arbitral tribunals.[95] In other words, the latter must give effect to any relevant domestic and Community measure implementing UN Security Council mandatory resolutions without calling into question the legitimacy of their purpose[96] (even if, in the case of a dispute brought before a domestic court, the forum state has not yet enacted domestic implementation measures).

Accordingly, arbitral tribunals and domestic courts are bound, rather than just authorised, to give effect to any domestic or Community measure which implements a UN Security Council sanction and is relevant to the case at hand (that is, a measure in the scope of which the disputed contract falls), even if this measure is external to the applicable law[97] and foreign to the law of the forum state (in the case of a dispute brought before a domestic court).[98] The prohibition laid down in this piece of legislation must have on the targeted transaction the impact intended by the Security Council. Therefore, the characterisation of such a measure, as an element of fact (*datum*) or as an element of law, is not as relevant in the case of multilateral sanctions as it is in the case of unilateral and autonomous Community sanctions:[99] measures implementing UN Security Council mandatory resolutions ought never to be disregarded on the purported ground that they do not serve a legitimate purpose, that they do not present a close connection to a given transaction that they prohibit, or that the benefits of a decision to disregard them outweighs those of a decision to give them effect.[100]

Most importantly, in the unlikely event that a UN Security Council mandatory resolution has not been transposed into Community or domestic law, either as a result of an omission or of a political choice of the state concerned, it is satisfactory to take into consideration the prohibition laid down in the resolution itself as a relevant *datum* for the settlement of the dispute.[101] A UN Security Council mandatory resolution—which typically requires member states to take all necessary measures to give effect to its operative paragraphs notwithstanding pre-existing contracts and prior licences—itself does not create rights and obligations for private operators.[102] It does, however, affect their contractual relationships, even if it has not been translated into state or Community legislation, to the extent that individuals and corporate entities may legitimately consider themselves bound not to overlook the content of such resolutions. Therefore, where a resolution has not been transposed into Community or domestic law, taking into account as *data* the prohibitions laid down in the resolution itself allows the deciding court to make up for a state's failure to meet its international implementation obligation.[103] Accordingly, in *Etat irakien v SA Dumez GTM*, the French *Cour de cassation* stated that 'si les résolutions du Conseil de Sécurité des Nations Unies s'imposent aux Etats membres, elles n'ont, en France, pas d'effet direct tant que les prescriptions qu'elles édictent n'ont pas, en droit interne, été rendues obligatoires ou transposées', but added that 'à défaut, elles peuvent être prises en considération par le juge en tant que fait juridique.'[104]

In sum, the *datum* approach appears to be satisfactory in the case of multilateral sanctions as well as in the case of UN Security Council resolutions that have not been translated into domestic or Community legislation.

III. EFFECTS OF ECONOMIC SANCTIONS ON THE RIGHTS AND OBLIGATIONS OF PRIVATE OPERATORS UNDER INTERNATIONAL LAW INSTRUMENTS

Whereas section II. above focussed on the question of whether a given economic sanctions programme ought to be taken into account by a domestic court or an arbitral tribunal for the resolution of a contractual dispute, the present section addresses the substantive effects of a sanctions programme on pre-existing obligations, during the sanction's term and after it is lifted. In essence, this section explores the tension between the principle of sanctity of contracts, on the one hand, and the need to adapt the parties' obligations in situations of subsequent alteration of circumstances such as the types of alteration that result from the imposition of economic sanctions, on the other hand.

In this context, the terms and breadth of a sanctions programme invoked by the defaulting party to justify its non-performance or delayed performance must be carefully examined to identify which transactions are actually prohibited. Does the sanction invoked by a defaulting seller only prohibit shipments from the sanctioning state (directly and indirectly) to the target state? Does it also prohibit nationals of the sanctioning state from making goods available to nationals of the target state, even within the sanctioning state? Does it prohibit any action ultimately intended to allow imports or exports, direct or indirect, from or to the target state?

If a sanction prohibits shipments from the sanctioning state (directly and indirectly) to the target state, it may well constitute an impediment to a seller's obligation to deliver the goods at the port of shipment (for instance under a CIF contract[105]) or in the country of destination.[106] By contrast, such a sanction is no impediment to the seller's obligation to deliver the goods by making them available on its own premises[107] (for instance under an EXW contract[108]). A sanction prohibiting persons and entities within the sanctioning state from making goods available to nationals of the target state or prohibiting any transaction aimed at the export of goods to the target state may, on the other hand, constitute an impediment to a seller's obligation to make goods available to the buyer inside the sanctioning state. A buyer may, in turn, invoke as an impediment to performance an import prohibition preventing it from taking delivery of the goods at the port of destination.[109] By contrast, a sanction prohibiting imports to a location other than the one where the buyer must take delivery is no impediment to the performance of its obligations, unless the contract clearly stipulates that the buyer must transport the goods to the location which is now under prohibition.[110]

If the performance of a party's obligations is indeed prohibited under a given sanctions programme, it must be determined whether the prohibition amounts to an exonerating impediment. In this context, section III.A. and section III.B. below address two different types of situations.

Section III.A. focuses on situations in which the deciding court has resolved to take the sanction into account for the resolution of the dispute. The deciding court may have followed the *datum* approach (discussed in section I.A. above) and come to the conclusion that the sanction (or the situation created by it) constitutes a relevant factual element to be taken into account for the resolution of the dispute. The deciding court may, alternatively, have followed the legal norm approach (discussed in section I.B. above) and reached the conclusion that the relevant sanctions statute is to be given effect either as part of the law applicable to the disputed contract or as a foreign overriding mandatory rule (see section II.A. above). Section III.A. examines how the sanction affects the rights and obligations of the parties during the sanction's term (section III.A.1.) and after it has been lifted (section III.A.2.). Both situations in which the sanction plainly prohibits performance by the obligor (section III.A.1.a.) and situations in which performance by this party is subject to a regime of authorisation (section III.A.1.b.) are analysed.

Section III.B. deals with situations in which the ruling court, having followed the legal norm approach, has come to the conclusion that even though the contract falls within the scope of a sanction prohibiting its performance, this prohibition, as such, is not to be taken into account for the resolution of the dispute. That is, on grounds of a private international law nature (discussed above in section II.A.), the deciding court has determined that the sanction is not to be given effect, be it as an element of the applicable law or as an overriding mandatory rule, and that the prohibition, in itself, can therefore not justify the obligor's failure to perform its obligations. In this context, the question arises whether any kind of relief is nevertheless available to the obligor, considering not the prohibition itself (the deciding court having resolved that the statute must be disregarded) but rather solely the factual risk of penalty that the obligor would run if it were to perform the transaction. Should this party be compelled to perform its obligations despite the risk of penalty, on the ground that performance is not illegal in the eyes of the ruling court? Should the obligor be compelled to choose between being liable to the obligee for breach of the contract and being penalised by the sanctioning state for breach of the sanction? Or does the risk of penalty constitute a valid ground for some kind of relief, considering that the environment in which the contract must be performed differs from the one in which, at the time of the conclusion of the contract, the parties assessed their risks, costs, and benefits? Section III.B. below is devoted to the examination of these questions.

III.A. Economic Sanction as a Ground for Exemption from Liability for Non-Performance

Only a few sanctions programmes address (sometimes implicitly or indirectly) the question whether the prohibition against performing pre-existing obligations amounts to an exonerating impediment. Some sanctions stipulate that targeted persons and entities or persons and entities of the target state are precluded from seeking compensation for non-performance of contracts affected by these sanctions.[111] They thus make such claims inadmissible (*irrecevables*)[112] before both domestic courts and arbitral tribunals. Other sanctions programmes provide that no claims filed in connection with contracts or transactions the performance of which was affected by these sanctions shall be satisfied.[113] Under such sanctions programmes, no judicial authority—be it domestic or arbitral—may hold liable a party that has withheld performance of its contractual obligations.

Most sanctions programmes are, however, silent as to the rights and obligations of the parties to contracts whose performance is prohibited. Typically, the UN Security Council calls upon states to act in accordance with its resolutions 'notwithstanding the existence of any rights or obligations conferred or imposed by any international agreement or any contract entered into or any licence or permit granted prior to the date of adoption of [the] resolution [in question]'.[114] Accordingly, domestic rules implementing UN resolutions most often prohibit the performance of such agreements and contracts or of actions they involve, without addressing the fate of these agreements or that of the parties' rights and obligations. The same is true of unilateral sanctions. A unilateral sanction is typically silent, for instance, on the question of whether a pre-existing contract falling within its scope 're-lives' after the sanction is lifted, whether a party that withholds performance of its contractual obligations in order to comply with the sanction is exempted from liability for non-performance, and whether any remedy is available to the other party. As a result, relying solely on the terms of a sanction prohibiting a party from performing its contractual obligations often does not allow the deciding court to rule on the parties' claims. The deciding court must turn to the contract if it contains a clause dealing with occurrences that may prevent a party from performing its obligations.[115] In the absence of such a contractual clause, it must look into the applicable law.

III.A.1. Exemption from Liability for Non-performance While the Sanction Is in Force

a. Economic sanction plainly prohibiting the performance of a transaction

Under general principles of law, international law instruments and domestic laws, primary economic sanctions (commonly simply referred to as economic sanctions)—namely sanctions that prohibit persons and entities under the prescriptive jurisdiction of the sanctioning state from performing certain transactions—are deemed to constitute some form of exonerating obstacle, even if they do not make performance technically impossible.[116]

In an International Chamber of Commerce arbitral award rendered in 1974 regarding a dispute between a French buyer and a Romanian seller, the arbitral tribunal stated that the annulment of export authorisations constituted an event of force majeure, both under general principles of law and under the disputed contract.[117]

Several awards were also rendered in the context of disputes governed by the United Nations Convention on Contracts for the International Sale of Goods (CISG), whose Article 79(1) reads as follows:

> A party is not liable for a failure to perform any of his obligations if he proves that the failure was due to an impediment beyond his control and that he could not reasonably be expected to have taken the impediment into account at the time of the conclusion of the contract or to have avoided or overcome it, or its consequences.

In a 1996 Bulgarian Chamber of Commerce and Industry award, a prohibition on exports imposed by the Ukrainian Government was found to constitute an impediment, under Article 79(1) CISG, to the delivery of coal by the seller.[118] In a Hungarian Chamber of Commerce and Industry award, rendered that same year, the arbitral tribunal also held that UN sanctions in force against Yugoslavia constituted, under Article 79(1) CISG, an impediment to the payment, by a Hungarian buyer, of the portion of the price that was due after the sanction had come into effect.[119]

As to decisions issued under domestic law, in 1992, a final award was made under the Rules of the Milan Chamber of National and International Arbitration, in which the sole arbitrator found that a contract between an Italian main contractor and an Italian subcontractor, governed by Italian law, was 'affected by the impossibility to perform, ensuing from [EU and Italian] embargo legislation' in force against Iraq.[120] One may also refer to judgments of US courts regarding disputes involving trade restrictions. Relying on para 2-615(a) of the Uniform Commercial Code (UCC)—which provides that discharge can result from 'compliance in good faith with any applicable foreign or domestic governmental regulation or order whether or not it later proves to be invalid'—US courts have granted discharge on grounds of 'commercial impracticability' in cases of governmental prohibitions,[121] as well as in cases of informal governmental pressure[122] and informal governmental restrictions.[123] Under French law, a party that withholds performance of its obligations in order to comply with a sanctions programme may invoke Article 1148 of the French Civil Code, which provides that '[d]amages are not due when, because of a force majeure or a fortuitous event, the obligor-debtor either was prevented from giving or doing what he was obligated to give or did what he was forbidden to do'.[124]

As noted above, for proponents of the traditional *datum* approach (discussed in section I.A.), it is the situation created by a primary sanction (hence its compelling power over private operators) that is deemed to constitute a factual impediment. For proponents of the legal approach (discussed in section I.B.), a primary economic sanction may only give rise to an impediment of a legal nature. Accordingly, the prohibition laid down in a sanctions programme may be deemed an impediment to performance only if the conclusion was first reached that the sanction must be given effect in the context of the dispute at hand, either as a legal prescription that is part of the applicable law or as an overriding mandatory rule external thereto.

It is questionable whether measures known as secondary and tertiary sanctions may be deemed to constitute exonerating impediments to performance. Secondary and tertiary sanctions are measures used by some states to increase the efficiency of their primary sanctions programmes through the exertion of pressure (for instance, by way of threats of penalties, trade restrictions or denial of loans or credit from financial institutions of the sanctioning state) on foreign persons and entities which are not under the jurisdiction of the sanctioning state, to induce them to sever their ties with target states.[125] These measures do not amount to legal impediments to performance given the absence of prescriptive jurisdiction of the sanctioning state,[126] which can only threaten with penalties persons and entities that would maintain commercial and/or financial ties with the targets of a primary sanctions programme.[127] It has also been argued that, in principle, secondary and tertiary sanctions cannot justify an exemption from liability on grounds of factual impediment to performance, considering, *inter alia*, that the risk of future adverse measures taken by a sanctioning state often only makes the performance of the contract indirectly more onerous through a possible subsequent deprivation of certain advantages related to other transactions (for example, the denial of export licences or export financing),[128] and that secondary and tertiary sanctions are generally not insurmountable.[129]

In the case of primary economic sanctions which, as mentioned above, may amount to impediments to performance, exemption from liability for non-performance is subject to a number of conditions.

Under international law instruments and uniform projects such as the CISG and the 2016 UNIDROIT Principles of International Commercial Contracts (UNIDROIT Principles), a compilation 'set[ting] forth general rules for international commercial contracts',[130] a party prevented by an impediment from performing its obligations may be granted exemption from liability for damages and its duty to perform in kind may be considered unenforceable, provided that the impediment was beyond the defaulting party's control and this party could neither reasonably be expected to have taken the impediment into account at the time of the conclusion of the contract nor reasonably be expected to avoid or overcome the impediment.[131] Article 79(1) CISG indeed provides that:

> [a] party is not liable for a failure to perform any of his obligations if he proves that the failure was due to an impediment beyond his control and that he could not reasonably be expected to have taken the impediment into account at the time of the conclusion of the contract or to have avoided or overcome it, or its consequences.

Article 79(5) CISG further specifies that

> [n]othing in this article prevents either party from exercising any right other than to claim damages under this Convention.[132]

Article 7.1.7(1) UNIDROIT Principles, in turn, provides that:

> [n]on-performance by a party is excused if that party proves that the non-performance was due to an impediment beyond its control and that it could not reasonably be expected to have taken the impediment into account at the time of the conclusion of the contract or to have avoided or overcome it or its consequences.

Article 7.1.7(5) UNIDROIT Principles then clearly adds that

> [n]othing in this article prevents a party from exercising a right to terminate the contract or to withhold performance or request interest on money due.

With respect to the condition that the impediment be beyond the defaulting party's sphere of control, state interventions in general (such as the imposition of quotas, import and export restrictions, blockades, boycotts, exchange controls and closing of traffic routes) are in principle deemed to lie beyond the control of private operators, in the same way as wars, civil strife, riots, terrorist acts, industrial disasters and man-made catastrophes (such as prolonged breakdowns of transport or electricity), natural catastrophes or disasters (such as earthquakes, storms, fire, floods and epidemics), and tortious acts of third parties (such as robberies, explosions and the destruction of machines).[133]

Prohibitions on transfer of funds and import and export prohibitions, in particular, constitute impediments beyond the control of private parties.[134] Such was the arbitral tribunal's finding in a 1985 Final Award on Force Majeure in a case opposing National Oil Company (NOC) to Libyan Sun Oil Company (Sun Oil). The tribunal held that US government orders issued in 1981 and 1982 declaring that US passports were no longer valid for travel to Libya, banning imports of Libyan oil into the US and subjecting exports of goods and technical information to the delivery of licences, 'were acts of Government and thus clearly beyond the control of the Parties'.[135] Similarly, in a dispute, governed by the CISG, opposing a US seller of chicken leg quarters to a Romanian buyer, the ruling arbitrator held that '[t]he Romanian government's decision to stop all chicken imports on virtually no notice to the industry was certainly beyond Seller's control'.[136] Thus, an economic sanction prohibiting the sale or purchase of goods or services to or from a given target may constitute an impediment beyond the seller's or the buyer's control to deliver the goods or to accept delivery and/or pay for the goods, respectively.

The situation is different if a party to the disputed contract withholds performance not on the ground that it is itself prohibited by an economic sanction, but because of its supplier's default resulting from a sanction prohibiting the supplier from performing its obligations. Such a situation may arise, for instance, if the seller's supplier is prohibited from exporting goods to the seller or if the buyer's financial institution is ordered to freeze the buyer's assets or is prohibited from making funds available to the buyer or from transferring funds upon this party's order or to the seller's benefit. Regarding such situations, the following must be noted.

As a general rule, the seller bears the 'acquisition risk' (or 'procurement risk').[137] The acquisition of the goods is considered within its sphere of risks and responsibilities. Accordingly, if it has sold goods that are only generically defined in the contract,[138] it cannot invoke its supplier's non-performance as a ground for exemption,[139] even if the supplier's non-performance results from a sanction. The seller must acquire the goods from another available source, even a more expensive one,[140] and may only be excused for the unavoidable delay that this may cause. Similarly, the buyer is deemed to guarantee its financial capacity.[141] It is therefore liable for the price even if it is denied access to the sum due by a newly imposed sanctions programme (or any impediment beyond its control) and must therefore seek funds elsewhere.

The impediment can only be deemed beyond the seller's or the buyer's sphere of risks and responsibilities if it is insurmountable.[142] This is the case, for instance, if the contract provides expressly or implicitly that the seller must deliver goods from the very supplier that is now affected by the sanction, if the seller promised to deliver the goods 'provided that' he receive the necessary deliveries from his supplier (in which case the seller's obligation is in fact conditional), if the sanction has led to the goods' unavailability on the international market[143] or if, although the goods are still available on the international market, their price has risen so steeply as a result of the sanction that the acquisition of substitute goods may not reasonably be expected from the seller.[144] In turn, the buyer may be deemed to be facing an impediment beyond its control if, for instance, all of its assets have been frozen pursuant to a UN Security Council mandatory resolution.[145]

As noted above, the second condition for an exemption from liability for non-performance is that the defaulting party could not reasonably be expected to have taken the impediment into account at the time of the conclusion of the contract. Whether this condition is satisfied must be determined on a case-by-case basis[146] considering, in particular, the relevant trade area or industry.

One may indeed more easily expect a company involved in the nuclear or military sector, than a manufacturer of agricultural equipment or educational material, to have taken into account the risk of future sanctions.[147] In all instances in which, at the time of the conclusion of the contract, the United Nations Security Council had already passed a resolution for the imposition of sanctions, the impediment must be deemed to have been reasonably foreseeable even if domestic (and EU) implementation measures were adopted only after the conclusion of the contract.[148] Similarly, an impediment resulting from the imposition of economic sanctions must be considered to have been reasonably foreseeable if, by the time of the conclusion of the contract, the target state had been threatened with sanctions or the UN Security Council had on its agenda to address a situation in reaction to which sanctions could be imposed.

The third condition mentioned above, namely that the impediment be reasonably unavoidable and insurmountable, implies that it must have become impossible for the defaulting party to lawfully perform the transaction.[149] Exemption must be denied if the defaulting party could have performed its obligations without breaching or evading the sanction,[150] be it at greater cost and with more extensive efforts than anticipated at the time of the conclusion of the contract.[151]

If, for instance, a sanction grants a period of time for the performance of pre-existing contracts (before the sanction comes into effect), the defaulting party will not be granted exemption if it could have performed its obligations during that time-period.[152] Exemption will also be denied if the defaulting party could have avoided the consequences of a sanction by delivering the goods at a location other than the agreed one (without, of course, defeating the sanction's purpose), or if the goods could have been channelled through a different route from the one envisaged in the contract so as to avoid a prohibited transit through a certain state,[153] even if this were to entail additional costs.[154] This being said, a defaulting party cannot reasonably have been expected to channel the goods through an alternative route if the itinerary specified in the contract was critical,[155] in particular if the goods would have perished or if they would not have reached their destination by a compulsory date had they been shipped via an alternative route.[156]

Also, if a trade sanction prohibits a seller from using a specific carrier for the transportation of the goods to the buyer, the seller may be expected to overcome the impediment by using an alternative means of transportation to carry out its delivery obligation.[157]

Finally, the obligor may be expected to tender a 'commercially reasonable substitute' (that is, a substitute that departs only from 'non-exclusive' or 'non-essential' specifications laid down in the contract[158] and one that can 'satisfy the purpose of the contract just as well'[159]) in order to overcome the consequences of a sanction prohibiting, for instance, exports of goods originating in or manufactured through technology developed in the sanctioning state, or containing materials, parts or components originating in that state.[160]

In this respect, the above-mentioned 1985 Final Award on Force Majeure rendered in a case opposing NOC to Sun Oil[161] is relevant. In 1980, the parties had entered into an Exploration and Production Sharing Agreement (EPSA), whereby Sun Oil was to undertake, finance and carry out an oil exploration programme in Libya. In March 1982, however, the Reagan administration banned imports of Libyan oil into the US and subjected exports of goods and technical data to the delivery of licences. On 21 April 1982, Sun Oil informed NOC that pursuant to this new regulation, it had to obtain an export licence in order to continue its operations in Libya and that this constituted an event of force majeure until it obtained such licence. On 23 June 1982, Sun Oil advised NOC that the licence had been denied and that it continued to invoke the force majeure excuse. The tribunal interpreted the contractual clause on force majeure (Article 22 EPSA) in light of Article 360 of the Libyan Civil Code (the applicable law) to conclude that:

> under the meaning of Art. 22, non-performance by a party or delay in performing contractual obligations is excused when an unforeseen circumstance beyond the control of the parties occurs, which circumstance constitutes an obstacle such that an obligor, normally diligent, having the same obligations and placed in the same situation, could not have overcome it.[162]

The tribunal found that it was not an essential condition under the EPSA that Sun Oil use its own technological resources to perform the contract, and that Sun Oil did have the possibility to fulfil its undertakings by resorting to resources other than its own (other parties engaged in similar exploration operations had been able to overcome the supervening obstacle). The tribunal concluded that the 1982 US Export Regulations did not constitute, for Sun Oil, an event of force majeure excusing the discontinuance of exploration.[163]

If all of the conditions enunciated above are met, the universally recognized principle of sanctity of contracts or *pacta sunt servanda*[164]—according to which a contract validly entered into is binding upon the parties and must be observed—may be circumvented and the defaulting party may be exempted from liability for non-performance.

b. **Economic sanction subjecting performance to a regime of authorisation**

Certain sanctions programmes do not prohibit performance altogether but rather subject the performance of certain transactions to a regime of authorisation (or of 'specific licence').

In most instances, the party that needs an authorisation to perform its obligations undertakes to seek such authorisation[165] and to take all the required steps in view thereof, but does not guarantee that it will be successful.[166] Accordingly, its duty is a duty of 'best efforts' (or of 'diligence') and its obligation to perform is conditional upon the delivery of the necessary authorisation. Therefore, to be discharged from its obligations, this party needs to apply for the required authorisation in due time and in compliance with the applicable procedure, unless it is clear that, under the relevant sanctions programme, no authorisation will be granted (in which case, it need not even apply for an authorisation).[167] If, despite this party's best efforts, authorisation is denied, it is not bound to perform and there is therefore no reason to seek an exemption from liability for non-performance.[168]

The situation is different if it may be inferred from the contract that the obligor has committed itself to obtaining the required authorisations, and must accordingly be deemed to have assumed a 'duty of result' (also sometimes referred to as an 'absolute duty' or as a 'duty to achieve a specific result').[169]

In this case, if the sanction was already in force or had at least already been adopted at the time of the conclusion of the contract, the party that committed itself to obtaining all required authorisations may reasonably be deemed to have implicitly assumed the risk that the authorisation be denied.[170] Consequently, if the authorisation is eventually denied, it cannot successfully invoke the existence of an exonerating impediment or event of force majeure. 'Where the obligor has contractually assumed a particular risk and therefore a "greater obligation", there may be—strictly speaking—no impediment in the first place'.[171] The risk of authorisation denial 'is actually within the sphere of control of the relevant party, since, before accepting the obligation to clear the goods for export or import, the seller or buyer should ascertain that the regulations in the relevant country do not prevent them from obtaining the required permits under the circumstances'.[172]

In light of the above, in order to avoid a finding that a party assumed an absolute duty to obtain an authorisation despite denial being reasonably foreseeable, and the ensuing finding that it assumed the risk of authorisation denial, this party would be well-advised to make a contractual reservation to the effect that it does not guarantee its ability to perform if authorisation is denied.[173]

The situation is different with respect to licences or authorisations that are made necessary by a subsequent economic sanctions programme (or any subsequent change of legislation or policy), that is, by a sanctions programme imposed after the conclusion of the contract and which was reasonably unforeseeable at the time of the conclusion of the contract.

In this case, the defaulting party cannot be deemed to have assumed the risk that the authorisation be denied, even if it assumed, for instance, the risk of import or export clearance, unless there is clear evidence that it assumed the risk of legislation or policy changes (or assumed unconditionally the risk of authorisation denial).[174] Indeed, the obligor cannot be considered to have assumed the risk that an authorisation be refused following unforeseeable legislation or policy changes.[175] Thus, even if the parties have incorporated into their contract a term (for instance, an Incoterm) to the effect that a party must obtain the required licences or authorisations 'at its own risk', this party does not automatically assume the risk of reasonably unforeseeable changes in law, regulations or practices making new licences or authorisations necessary. 'The same principle applies when an export license is first granted but then indirectly annulled by a general export ban'.[176]

In such circumstances, the defaulting party may be granted exemption from liability for non-performance if it is able to prove that under the relevant sanctions programme, no authorisation would possibly be granted or if authorisation was denied although duly applied for.[177]

III.A.2. Adaptation of the Contract in Situations of Hardship Once the Sanction Has Been Lifted

International law instruments and uniform projects such as the CISG and the UNIDROIT Principles suggest that the existence of the contract is not affected by the occurrence of an impediment justifying an exemption from liability for non-performance. In accordance with the principle of *favor contractus*, Article 79(3) CISG stipulates that '[t]he exemption provided by this article has effect for the period during which the impediment exists'. Thus, in principle, performance must be resumed by the defaulting party, and its contractual partner must accept performance and carry out its own counter-performance when the consequences of the impediment no longer prevent performance.[178] Article 7.1.7(2) UNIDROIT Principles seems to offer greater flexibility, as it provides that '[w]hen the impediment is only temporary, the excuse shall have effect for such period as is reasonable having regard to the effect of the impediment on the performance of the contract'.

Like wars and strikes, economic sanctions are temporary by nature. Some sanctions are imposed for a predetermined period of time (with possible extensions), as in the case of UN sanctions against Eritrea and Ethiopia,[179] Sierra Leone,[180] Afghanistan/the Taliban,[181] Liberia,[182] the Democratic Republic of the Congo[183] and Ivory Coast.[184] Even in the more frequent case in which sanctions are imposed for an unspecified period of time,[185] they are not intended to remain permanently in effect, but rather to be lifted once they have successfully achieved their purpose, most often of a coercive nature.[186]

When performance of a contractual obligation is prevented by an economic sanction, the impediment is thus known from the outset to be temporary. It is only if timely performance is of the essence and if the sanction prevents performance from taking place on the agreed date[187] that a sanction may arguably be deemed a definitive impediment and the defaulting party may accordingly be considered to be permanently exempted from liability.[188]

If timely performance is not of the essence, the temporary nature of economic sanctions cannot be overlooked, which is why it is often said that performance must be resumed once the sanction or ban is lifted.[189] Accordingly, in the 1996 Hungarian Chamber of Commerce and Industry award referred to above, the arbitral tribunal held that United Nations sanctions against Yugoslavia constituted a temporary impediment under Article 79 CISG to the payment, by the Hungarian buyer, of the portion of the price due after the sanctions had come into effect.[190] UN sanctions had become effective in Hungary on 3 June 1992 (by virtue of Government Order 91/1992) and were effectively suspended on 22 November 1995 at 12 am (UN Security Council Resolution 1022 (1995)). The tribunal held that from 23 November 1995, the buyer was in default of the payment of the said portion of the purchase price and interest ran until the sum was paid.[191]

In an ICC award rendered in 2002, the sole arbitrator handed down a similar decision in a case opposing an Italian company to a Yugoslavian company.[192] The Italian company argued that the UN sanctions against the Socialist Federal Republic of Yugoslavia made the performance of its obligations impossible and justified termination of the contract. On the ground that the sanctions had been lifted by the time the dispute was brought to arbitration, the arbitrator rejected the Italian company's argument, found that the parties were no longer prevented from performing their obligations, and ordered the payment of sums due by the Italian company to the Yugoslavian company.[193]

This being said, it must be conceded that most sanctions remain in effect for years, some even for decades. Furthermore, a sanction's term typically depends on the sanctioning state's discretionary decision to lift the sanction once its coercive purpose has been achieved. Parties may therefore find themselves in a difficult situation if they are bound to perform obligations contracted for in entirely different circumstances, years or decades before. This is why one may question whether the rule that instructs parties to resume performance under the initially agreed terms need not be adapted when the impediment is a sanction.

In this respect, one can hardly dispute the emergence of a general principle (to be interpreted narrowly[194]) according to which a party should not be held to its contractual obligations if circumstances have changed so radically and unforeseeably that the contract's implications, at the time of performance, are entirely different from what was anticipated at the time of the conclusion of the contract.[195]

Many civil law jurisdictions have endorsed the principle and consequences of changed circumstances (also referred to as the *clausula rebus sic stantibus*), either statutorily[196] or in case-law,[197] empowering the disadvantaged party to request renegotiation or seek a court-ordered adaptation of the contract, sometimes even its termination. As noted by Brunner, 'the more modern civil codes in many Arab countries have also imported European civil law notions of "rebus sic stantibus"'.[198] In the US common law system, discharge may be granted to a party that faces 'commercial impracticability', that is, to a party that can perform its obligation(s) though only with extreme and unreasonable difficulty, expense, injury or loss, as a result of unexpected supervening events the non-occurrence of which was a basic assumption of the contract.[199] In some cases, the party that faces commercial impracticability may seek an adaptation of the contract.[200] Under US law, discharge may also be granted in cases of 'frustration of purpose', that is, if a party's principal purpose is substantially frustrated after the conclusion of the contract, due to an event the non-occurrence of which was a basic assumption on which the contract was made.[201] Under English law, although no relief is available in situations of impracticability, the doctrine of frustration recognises, in addition to physical and legal impossibility, frustration of purpose as a ground for automatic discharge, bringing the contract to an end (termination *ex nunc*).[202]

International law instruments and uniform projects also deal with situations of 'hardship', that is, situations in which a dramatic change in circumstances leads to a fundamental disruption of the contractual balance by making performance radically more onerous or radically less profitable for one of the parties. Article 62 of the 1969 Vienna Convention on the Law of Treaties, applicable to treaties between sovereign states, addresses instances of 'fundamental changes of circumstances' (following Article 61 which deals with situations of 'supervening impossibility of performance'). Articles 6.2.1 through 6.2.3 UNIDROIT Principles also offer remedies to a party disadvantaged by a fundamental alteration of the contractual equilibrium[203] (alongside Article 7.1.7, which deals, as explained above, with force majeure). Finally, the ICC Model Clauses include both a force majeure clause (2003) and a hardship clause (2003).

Impossibility of performance is usually not required for a finding of hardship.[204] What is critical is that the distortion of the contractual equilibrium could not reasonably have been taken into account by the disadvantaged party at the time of the conclusion of the contract; that is, the distortion did not constitute a normal risk associated with the kind of contract under consideration[205] or a risk that this party agreed to assume.

The rationale of provisions on hardship is that good faith prevents the obligee from seeking performance under the original terms if the circumstances differ fundamentally from those that were in place when these terms were agreed upon, considering that the obligor (which may well still be capable of performing the contract) might not have consented to the contract had the surrounding conditions been—or had this party foreseen that they would become—radically different.[206].

The UNIDROIT Principles grant the disadvantaged party the right to request renegotiation (Article 6.2.3(1) and (2)[207]) in derogation of the general principle of *pacta sunt servanda* (Article 6.2.1[208]) and, if an attempt to renegotiate fails, the right to seek a court-ordered adaptation or the termination of the contract (Article 6.2.3(3) and (4)[209]). Thus, in a dispute between Cubic Defense Systems, Inc. (a US corporation) and the Iranian Air Force with respect to two contracts for the sale and installation of military equipment, the deciding arbitral tribunal, relying on the UNIDROIT Principles, found that the Islamic Revolution justified a unilateral request for an adaptation or the termination of the contracts.[210] The contracts had been only partially performed when the Revolution broke out. The parties entered into a series of negotiations but were unable to reach an agreement. The arbitral tribunal held that considering the events preceding and following the 1979 Revolution and the consequences on the political relationship between Iran and the US, each party was entitled to unilaterally request, if not the termination of the contracts, at least an adaptation of their terms, in particular the postponement of the performance dates by a reasonable period of time.[211] Referring explicitly to Article 6.2.3(4) of the 1994 edition of the UNIDROIT Principles,[212] the arbitral tribunal based its conclusions on the following considerations, among others:

> [F]rom the covenant of good faith and fair dealing which is implied in each contract follows that in a case in which the circumstances to a contract undergo... fundamental changes in an unforeseeable way, a party is precluded from invoking the binding effect of the contract. The idea that a change in circumstances may affect the binding force of a contract is known under the maxim *clausula rebus sic stantibus*: the contract remains binding provided that things remain unchanged. It is understood, however, that due to the fundamental principle of *pacta sunt servanda* not any change of circumstances can be sufficient. Due to its exceptional character, its application is only justified if the change in circumstances was fundamental and unforeseeable.[213]

As to the CISG, while it does not explicitly authorise a party to request renegotiation or to seek a court-ordered adaptation of the contract in situations of hardship, a historical interpretation of the Convention suggests that this may be interpreted as an internal gap, to be filled by inferring a solution from general principles on which the CISG is based (Article 7(2) CISG).[214] The right to request a renegotiation of the contract may be derived from a combination of five general principles underlying the CISG, namely the principle of good faith, the principle of reasonableness, the general duty to cooperate, the principle of *favor contractus* and, finally, the parties' duty to mitigate losses.[215] In other words, an adaptation of the contract may need to be considered in situations in which performance has not necessarily become impossible or unreasonably difficult, but in which an unforeseeable change in circumstances leads to a fundamental disruption of the contractual balance, making performance for one party either radically more onerous or radically less profitable.[216] The right to seek a court-ordered adaptation of the contract following an unsuccessful attempt to renegotiate its terms may be inferred from Article 50 CISG applied by analogy.[217]

It is therefore arguable, at least under general principles of law, the UNIDROIT Principles and the CISG, that if circumstances surrounding performance, once the sanction is lifted, have drastically changed, renegotiation may be requested on grounds of hardship. If renegotiation fails, the disadvantaged party may seek a court-ordered adaptation of the contract. In amending the contract, the court should strive to adapt it to the new set of circumstances, without neglecting the original explicit or implicit risk allocation by the parties.[218] A change of circumstances that does not exceed the ultimate limit of sacrifice is part of the risk implicitly assumed by the relevant party.

Alternatively, the party whose performance has become radically more onerous may seek a new (definitive) exemption, this time on grounds of economic impediment to performance.[219] All the conditions for an exemption from liability for non-performance must, however, be satisfied to justify an exemption on economic grounds. In particular, the cost increase must be such that the obligor could not reasonably be expected to have taken it into account at the time of the conclusion of the contract—a condition that will often not be satisfied in the case of market fluctuations.[220] It must also be such that the obligor cannot reasonably be expected to overcome it.

Finally, it may be observed that if the provisions of a sanction themselves address the fate of contracts falling within its scope, including after the sanction is no longer in force, these provisions may have to be taken into account irrespective of the solutions provided in the *lex contractus*. Relying on the terms of certain economic sanctions, some courts have indeed felt bound to declare terminated contracts affected by these sanctions. In particular, tribunals have declared terminated contracts affected by the UN sanctions against Iraq. They relied primarily on Community legislation implementing Security Council Resolutions 661 (1990) and 687 (1991). In paragraph 29 of the latter resolution, the Security Council had decided that:

> all States, including Iraq, shall take the necessary measures to ensure that no claim shall lie at the instance of the Government of Iraq, or of any person or body in Iraq, or of any person claiming through or for the benefit of any such person or body, in connection with any contract or other transaction where its performance was affected by reason of the measures taken by the Security Council in resolution 661 (1990) and related resolutions.[221]

To implement this provision, the Council of the European Communities adopted Council Regulation (EEC) 3541/92 of 7 December 1992 prohibiting the satisfying of Iraqi claims with regard to contracts and transactions, the performance of which was affected by United Nations Security Council Resolution 661 (1990) and related resolutions. Considering claims filed by non-Iraqi parties, courts held that in order to comply with the above sanctions legislation and not to impair the sanctions' purpose,[222] they were bound to declare contracts affected by the sanctions against Iraq terminated rather than merely suspended for the duration of the sanctions.[223]

III.B. For Proponents of the Legal Norm Approach, the Risk of Penalty for Breach of a Sanction as Ground for an Adaptation of the Contract

As explained above, a prohibition against performing a certain transaction, laid down in an economic sanctions programme which the deciding court has resolved to take into account for the resolution of a dispute, may constitute an exonerating obstacle—an event of 'force majeure' under the UNIDROIT Principles or an 'impediment' in CISG parlance—to the performance of contractual obligations.

According to proponents of the legal norm approach (discussed above in section I.B.), there is, *a contrario*, no exonerating obstacle if the sanction invoked by the defaulting party is declared inapplicable to the contract or if it is disregarded on the ground that the conditions (of a private international law nature) to give it effect as an overriding mandatory rule are not satisfied. Indeed, proponents of the legal norm approach contend that if the ruling court has decided not to give effect to the sanction itself, that is, if there is no legal impediment to performance, exemption may not be granted merely on the ground that performing the contract would involve a risk of penalty,[224] even if the penalty that could be imposed would exceed the boundaries of a 'reasonable sacrifice'.[225] They opine that given that the risk of penalty is one of the factors considered to determine whether a sanction that is external to the applicable law should be given effect as an overriding mandatory rule (see the discussion in section II.A. above), then the very same risk of penalty cannot, on its own, justify the obligor's exemption if the sanction is disregarded despite this risk (and if the existence of a legal impediment is therefore denied). Similarly, if an economic sanction imposed by the state of the applicable law is disregarded on the ground that giving it effect would lead to an outcome which would be in conflict with principles of international public policy of the forum (or principles of transnational public policy, if the dispute is heard by an arbitral tribunal) and the deciding tribunal has therefore reached the conclusion that there is no exonerating legal impediment to performance, measures adopted by the sanctioning state to increase the efficiency of the sanction—hence to favour the achievement of its underlying purpose—cannot justify an exemption of the defaulting party.

Overall, according to proponents of the legal norm approach, a decision not to take a sanction into account despite the risk of penalty strongly suggests that the downsides of giving effect to the sanction outweigh the inconvenience of a penalty for the obligor. Logically, therefore, a tribunal that has decided not to give effect to a sanction despite the risk of penalty cannot hold that this risk alone bears the same consequences on the performance of the contract as those that would have resulted from the sanction itself being taken into consideration,[226] knowing, in particular, that by granting a party exemption, the deciding court will contribute to the achievement of the sanctioning state's purpose.

Thus, for proponents of the legal norm approach, notwithstanding the risk of penalty, exemption from liability for non-performance is not justifiable if, for instance, the sanction is disregarded on the ground that it is directed against the forum state, on the ground that it was imposed in violation of public international law, or yet on the ground that the connection between the sanctioning state and the disputed contract is not sufficiently close.

This being said, knowing that the threat of penalty for breach of a sanction imposed after the conclusion of the contract[227] implies an alteration of the risks involved in the performance thereof,[228] proponents of the legal norm approach concede that it may be unreasonable to disregard altogether such threat.[229]

The question indeed arises whether any kind of relief is available despite the prohibition itself being disregarded by the deciding court. Should the obligor be compelled to perform its obligations despite the risk of penalty, on the ground that performance is not illegal in the eyes of the ruling court? Should the obligor be compelled to choose between acting in breach of the contract or acting in breach of the sanction?

The same questions may be posed if the obligor is the object of a secondary or a tertiary sanctions programme. As noted earlier, these are measures used by some states to increase the efficiency of their primary sanctions programmes through the exertion of pressure on foreign persons and entities, to induce them to sever their ties with a target state. While these persons and entities, which are not under the jurisdiction of the sanctioning state, are not prohibited from trading with the target state, they are under threats of penalties (such as the denial of future exports from the sanctioning state or of loans or credit from financial institutions of that state, or the blocking of property interests subject to the sanctioning state's jurisdiction) if they maintain direct or indirect ties, in particular commercial ties, with a target state.

As noted above, parties that have validly entered into a contract remain in principle bound to perform their obligations according to the terms of the contract, even in case of evolution of the surrounding circumstances. This is the 'basic and universally accepted principle'[230] of *pacta sunt servanda* (or sanctity of contract) which 'places the burden of such a change of circumstances upon the party on which it falls'.[231] 'That rule, however, may prove too harsh in cases where completely unexpected and unforeseeable events prevent performance of one's contractual obligations'.[232] This is why the principle of *pacta sunt servanda* may suffer limited exceptions. As explained in section III.A.1. above, there is one such exception, under international law instruments, if, as a result of a reasonably unforeseeable, unavoidable, and insurmountable impediment beyond the obligor's control, performance has become impossible or so excessively difficult that it may no longer reasonably be expected from that party; the latter may therefore be exempted from liability for non-performance. In addition, as explained in section III.A.2. above, international sets of principles and rules authorise a party deemed to be facing 'hardship'—i.e. a party for which performance has become either dramatically more onerous or dramatically less profitable than anticipated at the time of the conclusion of the contract—to seek renegotiation of a contract, possibly even its adaptation or termination by way of court order.

The risk of penalty that the obligor incurs if it performs a contract in breach of a sanction may precisely give rise to one such situation of hardship.[233] Irrespective of a finding of inapplicability of the sanction by the deciding court, penalties may be imposed by the sanctioning state. Accordingly, the balance of risks, costs, and benefits assessed by the parties at the time of the conclusion of the contract is often altered by the subsequent imposition of a sanction.[234]

According to Article 6.2.2 UNIDROIT Principles, '[t]here is hardship where the occurrence of events fundamentally alters the equilibrium of the contract either because the cost of a party's performance has increased or because the value of the performance a party receives has diminished, and (a) the events occur or become known to the disadvantaged party after the conclusion of the contract; (b) the events could not reasonably have been taken into account by the disadvantaged party at the time of the conclusion of the contract; (c) the events are beyond the control of the disadvantaged party; and (d) the risk of the events was not assumed by the disadvantaged party', whether expressly or implicitly. The cause of the alteration may be factual or legal.[235] It is, however, required that the event be 'beyond the control of the disadvantaged party' (*lit.* c), which is the case—at least as far as contracts among private operators are concerned—of 'acts of rulers and governments'.[236] Furthermore, as per *lit.* b, only an event that is 'so outside the bounds of probability that reasonable parties would not provide for it' may lead to hardship.[237] The risk of penalty for breach of a primary economic sanction may be deemed to have been reasonably unforeseeable only if the imposition of the sanction itself was reasonably unforeseeable at the time of the conclusion of the contract. As noted above, the reasonable unforeseeability condition is less likely to be satisfied if the parties are involved in a sensitive trade area, such as the nuclear or military sector. Finally, knowing that a party may be deemed to be facing hardship only if performance has become excessively onerous, not merely more onerous than anticipated,[238] the party that runs the risk of incurring penalties for breach of a sanctions programme may only be considered to be facing hardship if these penalties exceed a 'reasonable limit of sacrifice'.[239]

In this respect, while it is undeniable that legal certainty and the parties' need for predictability would be served by the identification of a general benchmark below which an increase in onerousness could not, in principle, allow hardship, whether the 'excessive onerousness' requirement is met can only be determined on a case-by-case basis.[240] Various critical parameters, specific to each case, must be considered, such as the cost increase in percentage,[241] the value of the counter-performance to be received by the obligor, the obligor's financial situation,[242] the number of other contracts concluded by this party that are affected by the same sanction, the nature of the contract, in particular whether it is a long-term instalment contract, and the often decisive specifics of any possible explicit or implicit risk allocation by the parties.[243]

Provided that the obligor did not explicitly or implicitly assume the risk of the imposition of an economic sanction, that the hardship threshold is met, and that an adaptation of the contract is conceivable to restore the contractual equilibrium, the obligor may request renegotiation. Should the parties fail to reach an agreement on amended terms within a reasonable time frame,[244] the obligor may seek a court-ordered adaptation of the contract (possibly the termination thereof).

It is reasonable to expect that a court will more readily conclude that a seller threatened with penalties for breach of an export prohibition is facing hardship than a buyer threatened with penalties for breach of an import prohibition. In the latter case, indeed, a court could find that although penalties would make the buyer's performance more onerous, this party is less prone to face hardship if the value of the goods purchased has risen as a result of the imposition of the sanction.[245]

CONCLUDING REMARKS

This contribution, which has dealt with the effects of economic sanctions on contractual relationships between private operators, suggests that a pre-existing contract may be affected by an economic sanction even if the sanction was imposed by a state other than the state of the applicable law and, in the case of a dispute litigated before a domestic court, even if the sanctioning state is not the state of the forum. This study also suggests that the outcome of the dispute may vary depending on the sanction's characterisation, from a private law perspective, as a factual element—a *datum*—whose effects on pre-existing contracts is to be examined solely through the prism of contract law, or as a legal norm whose effects on pre-existing contracts must be addressed pursuant to both rules of conflict of laws and rules of substantive law.

Multilateral sanctions imposed by way of mandatory resolutions of the United Nations Security Council are compulsory for all member states, and even non-member states may be invited to comply with them. These sanctions, which belong to the realm of transnational public policy, are binding on domestic judicial authorities around the globe as well as on arbitral tribunals. A party prohibited from performing pre-existing obligations, by a domestic or Community piece of legislation implementing a UN Security Council mandatory resolution, will invariably be deemed to be facing an impediment justifying its exemption from liability for non-performance, whether the sanction be regarded as a factual element (a *datum*) or as a legal element.

If the traditional *datum* approach is followed, the imposition of unilateral economic sanctions and Community autonomous sanctions are also often regarded as events of force majeure that may justify that a party's non-performance be excused. Such a general statement cannot, however, be made if unilateral and Community autonomous economic sanctions are regarded as legal norms. Indeed, as such, a sanction may be (or may have to be) disregarded on grounds of a private international law nature, in which case the prohibition laid down in the sanction cannot be deemed to constitute an exonerating impediment to performance. This being said, the risk of penalty involved in a prohibited transaction, which signals an alteration of the circumstances in which the contract must be performed, may nonetheless justify an adaptation of the contractual terms on grounds of hardship.

The above analysis thus shows that whether economic sanctions be regarded as *data* or as legal norms, the mere fact that private operators face certain risks in the performance of their agreement once a sanction has been imposed calls for some form of relief.

Furthermore, because of the uncertain and often lengthy term of economic sanctions, parties that were exempted from liability for non-performance while a sanction was in force may be prevented from resuming performance under the contractually agreed terms even after the sanction has been lifted. Indeed, despite the temporary nature of economic sanctions, resuming performance under the initially agreed terms may not be possible if, as a result of changes in market conditions, performance has become radically more onerous or dramatically less profitable for one of the parties. The tension between the principle of sanctity of contracts, on the one hand, and the need to adapt the parties' obligations in situations of subsequent alteration of circumstances, on the other hand, may thus persist after the sanction has been lifted: a sanction, intrinsically temporary, may lead to a permanent disruption of the contract.

While the effects of economic sanctions on the fate of contracts falling within their scope often depend directly upon solutions provided in each contract and in the law governing it, it is safe to conclude that the longer a sanction remains in force, the more efficient it is, if not in achieving its ultimate political goal, certainly in preventing the performance of contracts under the initially agreed terms, perhaps even altogether.

NOTES

1. This contribution is partly based upon material discussed in my chapter 'Economic Sanctions and Contractual Disputes Between Private Operators' in Larissa van den Herick (ed), *Research Handbook on UN Sanctions and International Law* (Edward Elgar Publishing 2017) 330, and contains sections already published therein

2. See, among others, C Lloyd Brown-John, *Multilateral Sanctions in International Law—A Comparative Analysis* (Praeger Publishers, Inc 1975) 17; Geneviève Burdeau, 'Le gel d'avoirs étrangers' (1997) 1 *Journal du Droit International* 5, 10, n 7; Sandra Szurek, 'Le recours aux sanctions' in Habib Gherari and Sandra Szurek (eds), *Sanctions unilatérales, mondialisation du commerce et ordre juridique international—A propos des lois Helms-Burton et d'Amato-Kennedy* (Montchrestien 1998) 19, 24; Robin Renwick, *Economic Sanctions* (Center for International Affairs, Harvard University 1981) 89.

3. Sanctions against South Africa, for instance, which were in force between 1977 and 1994, were intended, *inter alia*, to bring about the elimination of the policy of apartheid and racial discrimination, as well as the establishment of equal rights for all South African citizens (see UNSC Res 418 (1977), preambular para 1; UNSC Res 473 (1980), preambular para 7, paras 4 and 7; UNSC Res 569 (1985), preambular para 5; UNSC Res 591 (1986), preambular para 7; UNSC Res 765 (1992), para 7). In 1978, the US Congress imposed a general ban on all imports from, and exports to, Uganda, in reaction to Idi Amin's genocidal regime (Pub L No 95-435, Sec 5(c)–(d), 92 Stat 1051 (1978)). UN sanctions against the Federal Republic of Yugoslavia, imposed in 1998 following the build-up of tension between Serbian authorities and the Kosovar Albanian community, were intended, *inter alia*, to induce the Federal Republic of Yugoslavia to cease all action by security forces affecting the civilian population, to withdraw security units used for civilian repression (UNSC Res 1160 (1998), para 16b; UNSC Res 1199 (1998), para 4a), to enable the safe return of refugees and displaced persons, and to allow the free access of humanitarian organizations and supplies to Kosovo (UNSC Res 1199 (1998), para 4c). In 2004 and 2005, the UN Security Council passed mandatory sanctions resolutions directed against non-governmental and governmental actors in the Darfur region of Sudan, to address the unfolding humanitarian crisis, and in particular to disarm the Janjaweed militias and prevent further human rights violations and other atrocities (see, for example, UNSC Res 1556 (2004), para 6). Over the years, multilateral and unilateral sanctions have also been imposed against Libya, Iraq, Cuba, North Korea, Iran, Sudan and Afghanistan on account of their support of terrorist activities (see, for example, UNSC Res 748 (1992) against Libya, paras 2 and 3, and UNSC Res 1054 (1996) against Sudan, para 1b).

4. The establishment of peace and stability in general was one of the objectives explicitly articulated in UN mandatory resolutions imposing sanctions against former Yugoslavia in 1991 (UNSC Res 713 (1991), para 6), against Somalia in 1992 (UNSC Res 733 (1992), para 5), against Liberia in 1992 (UNSC Res 788 (1992), para 8), and against the Federal Republic of Yugoslavia in 1998 (UNSC Res 1160 (1998), para 8), among others. UN sanctions have been imposed in an effort to disarm and demobilize rebel groups or government-sponsored militias in several instances (see, e.g., UN sanctions against Sierra Leone (UNSC Res 1171 (1998), para 7), against the Democratic Republic of the Congo (UNSC Res 1493 (2003), para 22), against Liberia (UNSC Res 1521 (2003), para 5) and against Sudan (UNSC Res 1556 (2004), para 6)). For example, in September 1993, during the civil war in Angola, UN sanctions were imposed which prohibited the supply of arms and petroleum products to the National Union for the Total Independence of Angola (UNITA), the rebel group acting against the country's recognized government (UNSC Res 864 (1993), para 17; UNSC Res 1127 (1997), paras 2 and 3; UNSC Res 1173 (1998), para 3; UNSC Res 1295 (2000), preambular para 5). In 2000, the Security Council imposed sanctions against Eritrea and Ethiopia, so as to induce both countries to cease hostilities and engage in a peace process (UNSC Res 1298 (2000), para 17). In March 2001, the UN Security Council imposed arms, diamond and timber sanctions, among others, against Liberia, to prevent the Liberian government from providing support to the Revolutionary United Front, a Sierra Leonean rebel group (UNSC Res 1343 (2001), preambular para 9; UNSC Res 1408 (2002), preambular para 11; UNSC Res 1478 (2003), preambular para 13).

5. See, for example, UNSC Res 687 (1991) against Iraq and UNSC Res 1718 (2006) against the Democratic People's Republic of Korea (North Korea). Multilateral, Community, and unilateral sanctions against Iran are prominent examples of sanctions intended to prevent the development of a weapons programme.

6. This was the purpose of measures affecting, *inter alia*, strategic goods and grain exports to the USSR, decided by President Carter on 4 January 1980 after the invasion of Afghanistan by the USSR. Coercing Iraq into renouncing occupation was also one of the initial goals of UN Security Council sanctions against Iraq, following its invasion of Kuwait in 1990 (see UNSC Res 661 (1990), para 2).

7. During the Cold War, the US imposed unilateral sanctions against some Latin American countries in an effort to destabilize governments that it viewed as tilting towards the Soviet Union (see Gary Clyde Hufbauer, Jeffrey J Schott, Kimberly Ann Elliott and Barbara Oegg, *Economic Sanctions Reconsidered* (3rd edn, Peterson Institute for International Economics 2009) 13 and 52). The very first UN Security Council mandatory non-military sanctions, in force from 1966 until 1979, were imposed against the white minority regime in Southern Rhodesia following the Unilateral Declaration of Independence in 1965. These sanctions were intended to bring the illegal minority regime to an end (UNSC Res 232 (1966), preambular para 2; UNSC Res 253 (1968),

preambular para 3; UNSC Res. 277 (1970), in general; UNSC Res 288 (1970), para 2; UNSC Res 326 (1973), para 4; UNSC Res 423 (1978), in general) and to enable the self-determination and independence of all of the Southern Rhodesian people (UNSC Res 232 (1966), para 4; UNSC Res 253 (1968), preambular paras 7 and 8, para 2; UNSC Res. 277 (1970), para 4; UNSC Res 288 (1970), preambular para 4, para 2; UNSC Res 318 (1972), paras 1 and 2; UNSC Res 326 (1973), preambular para 3; UNSC Res 328 (1973), preambular para 7, para 3; UNSC Res 386 (1976), preambular para 4; UNSC Res 403 (1977), preambular para 3; UNSC Res 424 (1978), preambular para 4; UNSC Res 445 (1979), preambular para 8; UNSC Res 448 (1979), preambular para 7; UNSC Res 460 (1979), para 1; UNSC Res 463 (1980), para 1). Several unilateral and multilateral sanctions programmes, intended to facilitate the reinstatement of a legitimate government, followed. After the rise of Fidel Castro to power and Cuban expropriation without compensation of American property and the imposition of discriminatory taxes on American products, US sanctions were imposed against Cuba in 1962. One of the stated goals of these sanctions was to compel the adoption of democratic reforms (see, among other acts, Presidential Decree 3447 of 3 February 1962; the Cuban Asset Control Regulations of 1992 (31 CFR 515); and the Cuban Liberty and Democratic Solidarity (LIBERTAD) Act of 1996 (Pub L No 104-114, 110 Stat 785 (1996), codified at 22 USC paras 6021–6091)). The reinstatement of the democratically elected government of Haitian President Jean-Bertrand Aristide was also the purpose of the 1993 UN sanctions against Haiti (UNSC Res 841 (1993), para 16; UNSC Res 917 (1994), preambular para 8; UNSC Res 940 (1994), preambular para 8). Similarly, the 1997 UN sanctions against Sierra Leone were intended to induce the military junta, which had come to power by means of a *coup d'état*, to relinquish power and allow the restoration of the democratically elected government and a return to constitutional order (UNSC Res 1132 (1997), paras 1 and 19; UNSC Res 1171 (1998), para 7).

8. See Abdoullah Cissé, 'Les effets des sanctions économiques de l'Organisation des Nations Unies sur les contrats' in Laura Picchio Forlati and Linos-Alexandre Sicilianos (eds), *Economic Sanctions in International Law* (Martinus Nijhoff 2004) 683, 684, n 2; Jacques Périlleux, 'L'embargo et le droit des obligations' in *L'embargo—Actes de la journée d'études du 1er décembre 1995 organisée par l'Association Européenne pour le Droit Bancaire et Financier—Belgium* (Bruylant 1996) 169, 171.

9. An obstacle to the performance of a pre-existing contract may indeed arise if the sanction stipulates (or its wording or purpose suggests) that it applies to all pre-existing contracts that have not yet been fully performed or to pre-existing contracts concluded after a specified date. In such cases, the prohibitions laid down in the sanction may apply with immediate effect or after the expiration of a 'grace period'. A prohibited contract concluded while a sanctions programme is in force will usually be deemed null and void under the applicable domestic law, on grounds of illegality or the like. For an overview and a comparative law analysis of this question, see Aurore Marchand, *L'embargo en droit du commerce international* (Larcier 2012) 247 and following. See also Elliott Geisinger, Philippe Bärtsch, Julie Raneda and Solomon Ebere, 'Les conséquences des sanctions économiques sur les obligations contractuelles et sur l'arbitrage commercial international' (2012) *Revue de droit des affaires internationales/International Business Law Journal* 405, 410 and following.

10. See Mercédeh Azeredo da Silveira, *Trade Sanctions and International Sales—An Inquiry into International Arbitration and Commercial Litigation* (Kluwer Law International 2014) chapter 4.

11. See, for example, *Belship Navigation, Inc v Sealift, Inc*, in which the US District Court for the Southern District of New York granted Belship's motion to compel arbitration of a dispute involving the Cuban Assets Control Regulations (1995 US DIST LEXIS 10541, 1996 AMC 209 (SDNY 1995)). See also Azeredo da Silveira, *Trade Sanctions and International Sales* (n 10) §4.02[A][1]; Jean-Baptiste Racine, 'L'arbitrage commercial international et les mesures d'embargo—A propos de l'arrêt de la Cour d'appel du Québec du 31 mars 2003' (2004) *Journal du Droit International* 89, 95, n 8; Matthias Scherer, 'Swiss Embargos and their Impact on Contracts Governed by Swiss Law Illustrated by the Swiss Sanctions against Iran' (5 April 2011) *Kluwer Arbitration Blog* available at <http://kluwerarbitrationblog.com/2011/04/05/swiss-embargos-and-their-impact-on-contracts-governed-by-swiss-law-illustrated-by-the-swiss-sanctions-against-iran/>. In particular, the fact that an agreement may be null and void, under a given sanctions programme, does not imply that the arbitration clause is null and the dispute inarbitrable. The arbitration clause is considered 'severable' from the rest of the contract (it is a contract of its own), and it is therefore generally admitted that the nullity of the contract does not entail the nullity of the arbitration clause. On the doctrine of severability (or autonomy) of the arbitration agreement, see, *inter alia*, Gary B Born, *International Commercial Arbitration* (2nd edn, Wolters Kluwer 2014) Vol I, 349 and following; Emmanuel Gaillard and John Savage (eds), *Fouchard, Gaillard, Goldman on International Commercial Arbitration* (Kluwer Law International 1999) 198, n 389 and following; Gabrielle Kaufmann-Kohler and Antonio Rigozzi, *Arbitrage international—Droit et pratique à la lumière de la LDIP* (2nd edn, Weblaw 2010) 75, n 148; Christophe Seraglini, *Lois de police et justice arbitrale internationale* (Dalloz 2001) 443, n 939. Furthermore, the fact that some sanctions programmes provide that persons and entities

of the target state are precluded from seeking compensation for non-performance of contracts affected by these sanctions (see, for example, para 29 of UNSC Res 687 (1991) against Iraq, implemented by Council Regulation (EEC) 3541/92 of 7 December 1992; para 8 of UNSC Res 757 (1992) against Yugoslavia, implemented by Council Regulation (EC) 1733/94 of 11 July 1994; para 8 of UNSC Res 883 (1993) against Libya, implemented by Council Regulation (EC) 3275 of 29 November 1993; and para 11 of UNSC Res 917 (1994) against Haiti, implemented by Council Regulation (EC) 1264/94 of 30 May 1994) has an impact on the admissibility (*recevabilité*) of such claims, not on their arbitrability (see the decision of the Cour supérieure de Montréal in *Air France v Libyan Airlines*, quoted in the decision of the Cour d'appel du Québec, 31 March 2003, *Rev arb* 2003 1365, 1371, n 25; unpublished ICC Award in Case 7698 of 24 May 2006, cited in Marchand (n 9) 118, n 102).

12. On the notion of arbitrability, see Kaufmann-Kohler and Rigozzi (n 11) 101–102, nn 190–193a.

13. Economic sanctions indeed prohibit certain transactions usually without addressing their impact on the parties' rights and obligations.

14. See Marchand (n 9) 169–171, nn 167–169 and 224, nn 243 and following. Van Hecke explains, in this respect, that '[s]ince the foreign law [is] not the law governing the contract, it [is] not applicable as law but [is] merely a fact to be taken into account in assessing the morality of the conduct of the parties' (Georges van Hecke, 'The Effect of Economic Coercion on Private Relationships' in *Les moyens de pression* économiques *et le droit international—Actes du colloque de la SBDI, 26-27 octobre 1984* (1984–1985) *Revue belge de droit international* 113, 116).

15. See, for example, Vincent Heuzé, 'Communication' in Gherari and Szurek (n 2) 103, 109; Marchand (n 9) 228, n 250 and 230, nn 251–252; Estelle Fohrer-Dedeurwaerder, *La prise en considération des normes* étrangères (LGDJ 2008) 88 and following; Patrick Kinsch, *Le fait du prince* étranger (LGDJ 1994) 157, n 133 and 198 and following, nn 166 and following, in particular his conclusions at 229–231, n 186.

16. See Mercédeh Azeredo da Silveira, 'Economic Sanctions and Contractual Disputes Between Private Operators' in Larissa van den Herick (ed), *Research Handbook on UN Sanctions and International Law* (Edward Elgar Publishing 2017) 330, 335.

17. This may, of course, influence the parties in their selection of the applicable law.

18. In a 1968 decision, the Commercial Court of the canton of Zurich declared contrary to *bonos mores* and consequently null and void under the Swiss Code of Obligations (SCO), a contract the purpose of which was to smuggle goods in breach of an Italian law (RSJ 1968 354 and following).

19. See *Spitzer v Amunategui*, in which a French court held the following: '[S]i les juges français n'ont pas à réprimer devant les tribunaux français les atteintes portées en pays étranger, à l'ordre public national propre à ce pays, du moins doivent-ils considérer comme illicites et dépourvues d'effet de ce chef, les opérations de contrebande qui, faites en fraude des lois étrangères portent … atteinte à la conscience publique et à l'ordre public international' (4 January 1956, (1956) *Revue Critique de Droit International de la Haye* 679, 680).

    The Second Chamber of the *Cour d'Alger* had taken a similar stance in a judgment rendered on 20 February 1925 in *Garau v Lambert* (1926) *Journal du Droit International* 701, 702.

20. In 1960, the German Supreme Court declared immoral and void under the German Civil Code a contract governed by German law, between two German companies, for the delivery of 100 tons of borax to be produced in Germany from raw material imported from the US but which the parties knew to be ultimately destined for Rostock, East Germany, at a time when export licences were granted by the US on condition that no borax be shipped to any socialist country (21 December 1960, BGHZ 1961 169 and following, NJW 1961 822 and following). A similar decision was rendered on 24 May 1962 (NJW 1962 1436 and following). In 1972, the German Supreme Court declared null and void, pursuant to German law, an insurance contract concerning the transportation of cultural goods of national interest from Nigeria to Germany, on the ground that exports of such goods were strictly prohibited under Nigerian law (22 June 1972, BGHZ 1972 82, NJW 1972 1575).

21. See *Foster v Driscoll and Others* [1929] 1 KB 470, [1928] All ER 130, in which the King's Bench declared contrary to public policy and consequently void an agreement to load a ship with a cargo of whisky to be carried across the Atlantic and sold, if possible, in the US, and if not, in Canada or on the high seas at a location sufficiently close to the territory of the US, to facilitate its smuggling into the US in violation of the laws of that country. See also *Regazzoni v K.C. Sethia* [1958] AC 301, [1957] 3 All ER 286, in which the House of Lords declared unenforceable on the basis of international comity a contract governed by English law for the sale of jute bags to be shipped from India to Genoa, which both parties contemplated would subsequently be resold to a South African buying agency, notwithstanding an order of the Indian government prohibiting the taking out of British India of any goods destined directly or indirectly for the Union of South Africa.

22. See Gaillard and Savage (n 11) 849, n 1518; Hans van Houtte, 'Trade Sanctions and Arbitration' (1997) *International Business Lawyer* 166, 167; Hans van Houtte, 'Les effets des sanctions économiques sur les contrats transnationaux' in *L'embargo—Actes de la journée d'études du 1er décembre 1995 organisée par l'Association Européenne pour le Droit Bancaire et Financier—Belgium* (Bruylant 1996) 191, 194 and 196; Klaus Peter Berger, 'Acts of State and Arbitration: Exchange Control Regulations' in Karl-Heinz Bockstiegel (ed), *Acts of State and Arbitration* (C Heymann 1997) 99, 116–117.

23. See *In the Matter of the Arbitration Between Triad International Marketing, SA, et al v Northrop Corporation*, American Arbitration Association arbitration taking place in California, award reported in *Northrop Corp v Triad Int'l Marketing SA*, 593 F Supp 928 (CD Cal 1984), rev'd, 811 F 2d 1265 (9th Cir 1987), cert denied, 108 S Ct 261 (1987). In this case, the arbitral tribunal had to rule on the duty of Northrop Corporation (Northrop), a Californian seller of fighter aircraft and related equipment, to pay commissions to Triad International Marketing, SA (Triad), a Saudi Arabian sales representative, based on a 'Marketing Agreement' governed by California law, following the issuance of a Saudi Arabian decree prohibiting the payment of commissions in connection with armament contracts and requiring that existing obligations for the payment of commissions be suspended. The arbitral tribunal concluded that only a factual impossibility would justify non-performance, pointing out that decisions interpreting para 1511 of the California Civil Code did not look to the law of the foreign jurisdiction to determine whether performance was unlawful but instead examined the legal action the foreign jurisdiction had taken, to determine whether, in fact, it prevented performance of the contract. Noting that despite the issuance of the said decree, Northrop could still pay Triad the commissions the Marketing Agreement called for, and Triad could still give advice, translate documents, make local arrangements and perform the other services the Agreement required, the arbitral tribunal refused to excuse Northrop's failure to perform. The US District Court of the Central District of California vacated the award, but the US Court of Appeals for the 9th Circuit reversed and thus reinstated the arbitral award, noting that '"[i]mpossibility based on foreign law does not fall within the same class as that occasioned by domestic law, and it has generally been held no excuse for breach of contract." ... Such impossibility is not treated as impossibility of law, but as impossibility of fact.' (811 F 2d 1265, 1270, footnote 7).

24. In the 1975 Resolution on the Application of Foreign Public Law, the International Law Institute stated: 'The public law character attributed to a provision of foreign law which is designated by the rule of conflict of laws shall not prevent the application of that provision, subject however to the fundamental reservation of public policy' (para AI1) ((1975) *Annuaire de l'Institut de droit international* 550 and following, (1976) *Revue Critique de Droit International de la Haye* 423 and following (official text in French)). The purpose of this Resolution was to clarify once and for all that the understanding that mechanisms of conflict of laws pertain exclusively to the identification of rules of private law is outdated (see Giuseppe Sperduti, 'Les lois d'application nécessaire en tant que lois d'ordre public' (1977) *Revue Critique de Droit International de la Haye* 257, 263–264).

25. See Azeredo da Silveira, *Economic Sanctions and Contractual Disputes Between Private Operators* (n 16) 337.

26. Overriding mandatory rules are often also referred to as *lois de police* or as *lois d'application immédiate*.

27. On the definition of overriding mandatory rules, see Phocion Francescakis, 'Quelques précisions sur les "lois d'application immédiate" et leurs rapports avec les règles de conflit de lois' (1966) *Revue Critique de Droit International de la Haye* 1; Andrew Barraclough and Jeff Waincymer, 'Mandatory Rules of Law in International Commercial Arbitration' (2005) *Melbourne Journal of International Law* 205, 206; George A Bermann, 'Mandatory Rules of Law in International Arbitration' (2007) *American Review of International Arbitration* 1, 1; Marc Blessing, 'Impact of the Extraterritorial Application of Mandatory Rules of Law on International Contracts' in N. Vogt (ed), *Swiss Commercial Law Series* (Helbing & Lichtenhahn 1999) Vol 9, 1, 5; Thomas G Guedj, 'The Theory of the *Lois de Police*, a Functional Trend in Continental Private International Law—A Comparative Analysis with Modern American Theories' (1991) *American Journal of Comparative Law* 661, 662 and 664–665; David Jackson, 'Mandatory Rules and Rules of "Public Order"' in p. North (ed), *Contract Conflicts—The EEC Convention on the Law Applicable to Contractual Obligations: A Comparative Study* (North-Holland 1982) 59, 66; Kaufmann-Kohler and Rigozzi (n 11) 423, n 658; Pierre Mayer, 'Les lois de police étrangères' (1981) *Journal du Droit International* 277, 284; Nathalie Voser, 'Mandatory Rules of Law as a Limitation on the Law Applicable in International Commercial Arbitration' (1996) *American Review of International Arbitration* 319, 321.

28. The Rome Convention still provides the relevant rules of conflict of laws with respect to contracts concluded up to 17 December 2009.

29. Article 7(1) Rome Convention was applicable in all Contracting States except those that had reserved the right not to apply this provision, in accordance with Article 22(1). The Rome I Regulation contains no provision equivalent to Article 22(1) Rome Convention, and all member states are thus bound by Article 9(3) of the Regulation.

30. See Azeredo da Silveira, *Trade Sanctions and International Sales* (n 10) § 3.02[B]; Francois Knoepfler, Philippe Schweizer and Simon Othenin-Girard, *Droit international privé suisse* (3rd ed., Staempfli Editions SA 2005) 190–191, n 378; Bernard Dutoit, *Commentaire de la loi fédérale du 18 decembre 1987* (4th ed., Helbing & Lichtenhahn 2005 and Supplement 2011) 77, n 1 ad Article 19; Catherine Kessedjian, 'Mandatory Rules of Law in International Arbitration: What Are Mandatory Rules?' (2007) *American Review of International Arbitration* 147, 148; Bernard Audit, 'How Do Mandatory Rules of Law Function in International Civil Litigation?' in George A Bermann and Loukas A Mistelis (eds), *Mandatory Rules in International Arbitration* (JurisNet 2011) 53, 54; Barraclough and Waincymer (n 27) 207; Berger (n 22) 100; Andrea K Bjorklund, 'Investment Arbitration' in Bermann and Mistelis (n 30) 233, 239; Blessing, 'Impact of the Extraterritorial Application of Mandatory Rules of Law on International Contracts' (n 27) 13; Andrea Bonomi, 'Overriding Mandatory Provisions in the Rome I Regulation on the Law Applicable to Contracts' (2008) *Yearbook of Private International Law* 285, 291; Bernard Grelon and Charles-Etienne Gudin, 'Contrats et crise du Golfe' (1991) *Journal du Droit International* 633, 651; Trevor C Hartley, 'Mandatory Rules in International Contracts: The Common Law Approach' in *Recueil des cours*, Academie de droit international de La Haye (Martinus Nijhoff 1997) 341, 346; Daniel Hochstrasser, 'Choice of Law and "Foreign" Mandatory Rules in International Arbitration' (1994) 1 *Journal of International Arbitration* 57, 68; Bernd von Hoffmann, 'Internationally Mandatory Rules of Law before Arbitral Tribunals' in Bockstiegel (n 22) 3, 4; Kaufmann-Kohler and Rigozzi (n 11) 424, n 660; Laurence Landy-Osman, 'L'embargo des Nations Unies contre l'Irak et l'exécution des contrats internationaux' (1991) *Droit et pratique du commerce international* 597, 607–608, nn 24–25; Munir Maniruzzaman, 'International Arbitrator and Mandatory Public Law Rules in the Context of State Contracts: An Overview' (1990) 3 *Journal of International Arbitration* 53, 57–58; Marchand (n 9) 150–151, n 145; Pierre Mayer, 'Le rôle du droit public en droit international privé français' in F. Klein (ed), *Basel Symposium on the Role of Public Law in Private International Law* 20–21 March 1986 (Helbing & Lichtenhahn 1991) 63, 81; Loukas A Mistelis, 'Mandatory Rules in International Arbitration: Too Much Too early or Too Little Too Late?' in Bermann and Mistelis (n 30) 291, 292; Racine (n 11) 102, n 19; Voser (n 27) 349.

31. Economic sanctions prohibit the performance of specific actions (for instance, imports from a target state or exports thereto) by designated persons and entities (for instance, those located within the territory of the sanctioning state or nationals thereof, wherever located), without necessarily making an explicit reference to the contracts (for instance, sales contracts) they may affect. It remains, however, clear from their object that economic sanctions strive to apply to all contractual relationships involving the performance of a prohibited action (perhaps even of any action that would defeat the sanction's purpose), irrespective of the law applicable to these contractual relationships, whether selected by the parties or identified through mechanisms of conflict of laws.

32. See Azeredo da Silveira, *Trade Sanctions and International Sales* (n 10) § 3.02[B]; Azeredo da Silveira, 'Economic Sanctions and Contractual Disputes Between Private Operators' (n 16) 339.

33. *Moller Maersk Company v Viol Company and Fauveder Company*, *Cour de cassation*, n 08-21511, 16 March 2010, Bulletin 2010 IV n 54.

34. Article 7(1) Rome Convention and Article 9(3) Rome I Regulation are indeed permissive (see Guedj (n 27) 675; Daniel Gutmann, *Droit international privé* (6the edn, Dalloz 2009) 61, n 53 and 228, n 240; Mayer, 'Les lois de police étrangères' (n 27) 306–307 and 326; Allan Philip, 'Mandatory Rules, Public Law (Political Rules) and Choice of Law in the EEC Convention on the Law Applicable to Contractual Obligations' in North (n 27) 81, 87, n 19; Richard Plender and Michael Wilderspin, *The European Contracts Convention—The Rome Convention on the Law Applicable to Contractual Obligations* (Sweet & Maxwell 2001) 333, n 12-001 and 343, n 12-018). Domestic courts and arbitral tribunals are, however, bound to give effect to overriding mandatory rules that incorporate a recognized principle of transnational public policy, as is the case of sanctions implementing UN Security Council mandatory resolutions (multilateral sanctions)—see section II.B. below.

35. Azeredo da Silveira, *Trade Sanctions and International Sales* (n 10) § 4.01[C].

36. ibid. § 4.02[C]. See, however, George A Bermann, 'Mandatory Rules of Law in International Arbitration' in Franco Ferrari and Stefan Kroll (eds), *Conflict of Laws in International Arbitration* (Sellier European Law Publishers 2011) 325, 327 and 338.

37. See, *inter alia*, Kaufmann-Kohler and Rigozzi (n 11) 425, n 661; Knoepfler, Schweizer and Othenin-Girard (n 30) 201, n 397c; Voser (n 27) 329–330. Considering the core purpose of these provisions, arbitrators cannot be deprived of the authority to take into account overriding mandatory rules enacted by a state other than the state of the applicable law (see François Knoepfler, 'L'article 19 LDIP est-il adapté à l'arbitrage international?' in Christian Dominicé, Rob-

ert Patry and Claude Reymond (eds), *Etudes de droit international en l'honneur de Pierre Lalive* (Helbing & Lichtenhahn 1993) 531, 531-541; Laurence Shore, 'Applying Mandatory Rules of Law in International Commercial Arbitration' in Bermann and Mistelis (n 30) 131, 134-135 and 145).

38. ICC Award n 1859 of 1973 (excerpts in Yves Derains, 'Le statut des usages du commerce international devant les juridictions arbitrales' (1973) *Rev arb* 122, 134, and in Yves Derains, 'L'ordre public et le droit applicable au fond du litige dans l'arbitrage international' (1986) *Rev arb* 375, 408, n 54).

39. See Azeredo da Silveira, *Trade Sanctions and International Sales* (n 10) §3.02 and §7.01[A]; Azeredo da Silveira, 'Economic Sanctions and Contractual Disputes Between Private Operators' (n 16) 340.

40. EU sanctions are imposed (either autonomously or to implement Security Council mandatory resolutions) pursuant to Article 29 of the Treaty on European Union and Article 215 (and possibly Article 75) of the Treaty on the Functioning of the European Union. EU sanctions are self-executing within member states and may be invoked by individuals and corporate entities in judicial proceedings (see Vera Gowlland-Debbas, 'Implementing Sanctions Resolutions in Domestic Law' in Vera Gowlland-Debbas (ed), *National Implementation of United Nations Sanctions—A Comparative Study* (Martinus Nijhoff 2004) 33, 38; Rusen Ergeç, 'L'embargo et les droits nationaux' in *L'embargo—Actes de la journée d'études du 1er décembre 1995 organisée par l'Association Européenne pour le Droit Bancaire et Financier—Belgium* (Bruylant 1996) 125, 131, n 18; Grelon and Gudin (n 30) 640; Marchand (n 9) 79, n 58).

41. Azeredo da Silveira, 'Economic Sanctions and Contractual Disputes Between Private Operators' (n 16) 341-342. For an in-depth analysis of the rationale and weaknesses of the *datum* approach, see Azeredo da Silveira, *Trade Sanctions and International Sales* (n 10) §3.01[B].

42. For instance, '[i]n the Borax case [discussed above in n 20] the court respected the American embargo prescriptions although the German Government, which had previously co-operated with the United States within the Consultative Group and the COCOM, did not adopt the particular embargo in question. The judicial appreciation of foreign State interests led to the undesirable discrepancy that the court denounced as immoral the parties' conduct in a transaction which was approved by the executive authorities of the same forum State' (Frank Benedict Vischer, 'General Course of Private International Law' in *Recueil des cours*, Académie de droit international de La Haye (Martinus Nijhoff 1992) 9, 175).

43. For instance, a sanction has an 'extraterritorial scope' if it seeks compliance from nationals abroad or from subsidiaries of domestic entities incorporated in states other than the sanctioning state, or if it prohibits foreign individuals and entities that have imported goods from the sanctioning state or made use of technologies developed inside the territory of the sanctioning state from exporting to the target state these goods or technologies. For a definition of the concept of 'extraterritorial laws', see Paul Demaret, 'Les affirmations de compétence extraterritoriale des Etats-Unis' in *L'application extraterritoriale du droit économique—Troisième journée d'actualité internationale du CEDIN* (23 April 1986) (Montchrestien 1987) 41, 41; Jean-Michel Jacquet, 'La norme juridique extraterritoriale dans le commerce international' (1985) *Journal du Droit International* 327, 347, n 34; Patrick Juillard, 'L'application extraterritoriale de la loi économique' in *L'application extraterritoriale du droit économique—Troisième journée d'actualité internationale du CEDIN* (23 April 1986) 13, 20; Brigitte Stern, 'L'extraterritorialité revisitée—Où il est question des affaires Alvarez-Machain, Pâte de bois et de quelques autres' (1992) *Annuaire français de droit international* 239, 244. An example of an extraterritorial sanctions programme was the so-called 'pipeline controls' decided by US President Reagan in December 1981 and reinforced in June 1982, following the institution of martial law in Poland on 13 December 1981. In order to obstruct the Soviet construction of the Yamal natural gas pipeline to Europe, President Reagan prohibited, *inter alia*, the following: exports of foreign-origin goods (oil and gas equipment) and technologies (even of entirely foreign origin) by foreign subsidiaries of US companies; exports and re-exports, to the Soviet Union, by foreign purchasers not owned or controlled by US entities, of products containing US-origin parts and of US-origin oil- and gas-related machinery, even if the said machinery was already located abroad by the time the sanctions were imposed; and exports by foreign companies of foreign-produced commodities utilizing US technical data, if these foreign companies had agreed not to re-export US technology to the USSR, had agreed to comply with US legislation or were bound by a licence agreement to a person under US jurisdiction (47 Fed Reg 27250 (1982); see also Bernard Audit, 'Extra-territorialité et commerce international—L'affaire du gazoduc sibérien' (1983) *Revue Critique de Droit International de la Haye* 401, 403-404, n 3). Regarding the pipeline controls, which gave rise to an international controversy, see, for instance, Barry E Carter, *International Economic Sanctions—Improving the Haphazard US Legal Regime* (CUP 1988) 83; Kathleen Hixson, 'Extraterritorial Jurisdiction under the Third Restatement of Foreign Relations Law of the United States' (1988-1989) *Fordham International Law Journal* 127, 143 and following; J Brett Busby, 'Jurisdiction to Limit Third-Country Interaction with Sanctioned States: The Iran and Libya Sanctions and Helms-Burton Acts'

(1998) *Columbia Journal of Transnational Law* 621 and following; Daniel Marcus, 'Soviet Pipeline Sanctions: The President's Authority to Impose Extraterritorial Controls' (1983) *Law & Policy in International Business* 1163 and following.

44. Blocking statutes are counter-measures adopted by states for the purpose of preventing an extraterritorial sanction from producing effects within these states' territories. For examples of blocking statutes, see n 79 below.

45. A contract may, for instance, contain a clause such as the 2003 ICC Force Majeure Model Clause, under which the following, *inter alia*, constitute exonerating impediments: 'act of authority whether lawful or unlawful, compliance with any law or governmental order, rule, regulation or direction' (third paragraph, d). The applicable law may also provide, for instance, that any foreign or domestic governmental regulation or order may justify the obligor's discharge. Article 501(4) SCO, for instance, provides that '[i]f the duty to perform of a principal obligor who is domiciled abroad is barred or restricted by foreign legislation, as, for example, provisions relating to clearing systems or prohibitions on currency transfers, a guarantor domiciled in Switzerland may also invoke this legislation unless he has waived such defense' (translation of the Swiss-American Chamber of Commerce).

Paragraph 2-615(a) of the United States Uniform Commercial Code, in turn, stipulates that discharge may be granted in case of non-performance of actions that are prohibited by a regulation or an order (that is, actions that fall within the scope of application of a regulation or an order), whether domestic or foreign. Under this provision, discharge can result from 'compliance in good faith with any applicable foreign or domestic governmental regulation or order whether or not it later proves to be invalid'. By providing that any foreign or domestic governmental regulation or order may justify the defaulting party's discharge, the applicable law simply allocates the risks associated with any subsequent prohibition: the defaulting party is discharged not on the ground that it is legally bound to comply with any and all such measures, but because its contractual partner assumes the risk that a subsequent regulation prohibit the performance of the transaction.

46. The absence of an assessment of the purpose of sanctions that are external to the applicable law explains why the existence of a territorial link with the sanctioning state or concerns of comity or public policy are usually raised by courts relying on the traditional *datum* approach.

47. See, in general, Knoepfler, Schweizer and Othenin-Girard (n 30) 199, n 393; Voser (n 27) 323.

48. Azeredo da Silveira, 'Economic Sanctions and Contractual Disputes Between Private Operators' (n 16) 343-344.

49. Van Houtte, 'Les effets des sanctions économiques sur les contrats transnationaux' (n 22) 194, n 4; Marchand (n 9) 144, n 136; Landy-Osman (n 30) 608, n 25. Thus, whenever the disputed contract provides for the performance of an action that is prohibited by an economic sanction imposed by the forum state, domestic courts of that state must give effect to the sanction, unless the legislation of that state itself authorises its courts to examine the sanction's legality, constitutionality, and/or conformity with international law. By contrast, as arbitral tribunals are neither officers nor organs of any state, they have no duty to ensure compliance with the laws of a particular state or to act as a guardian of its public policy (see Christoph Brunner, *Force Majeure and Hardship under General Contract Principles—Exemption for Non-Performance in International Arbitration* (Wolters Kluwer 2009) 265; Andreas Bucher and Pierre-Yves Tschanz, *International Arbitration in Switzerland* (Helbing & Lichtenhahn 1988) 104; Pierre Mayer, 'Mandatory Rules of Law in International Arbitration' (1986) *Arbitration International* 274, 277; Voser (n 27) 338). Given the absence of forum in arbitration, all laws (and all overriding mandatory rules) including those enacted by the state of the seat of the arbitration, are foreign laws for the arbitrators (see, *inter alia*, ICC Award 6294 rendered in 1991, (1991) *Journal du Droit* 1050, 1051; Gaillard and Savage (n 11) 848, n 1517; Maniruzzaman (n 30) 56, 63; Lambert Matray, 'Embargo and Prohibition of Performance' in Bockstiegel (n 22) 69, 88).

50. The exception of public policy enunciates a general principle of law, according to which courts may disregard a specific provision of the governing law if its application would lead to an unacceptable outcome in the instance at hand (see, for instance, *C v C-E*, 4 July 2000, Swiss Federal Tribunal, 126 III 327; Andreas Bucher, 'L'ordre public et le but social des lois en droit international privé' in *Recueil des cours*, Académie de droit international de La Haye (Martinus Nijhoff 1993) 9, 76, n 39; Henri Batiffol and Paul Lagarde, *Traité de droit international privé* (8th edn, LGDJ 1993) Vol I, 575–576, n 358; Plender and Wilderspin (n 34) 363, n 12-055).

51. According to Article 16 Rome Convention and Article 21 Rome I Regulation, the application of a provision of the law of any country specified by the Convention or Regulation may be refused only if such application is manifestly incompatible with the public policy (*ordre public*) of the forum.

52. Regarding the concept of public policy (*ordre public*), see *inter alia* Bucher (n 50) 25; Joost Blom, 'Public Policy in Private International Law and its Evolution in Time' (2003) *Netherlands*

International Law Review 373, 385; Phocion Francescakis, 'Y a-t-il du nouveau en matière d'ordre public?' in *Travaux du Comité français de droit international privé, 1966–1969* (Dalloz 1970) 149, 154–155.

53. Although provisions such as Article 16 Rome Convention and Article 21 Rome I Regulation are not directly applicable to arbitration, it is today unquestionable that arbitrators must ensure the safeguarding of universal principles of justice (see Batiffol and Lagarde (n 50) 588, n 365; Kaufmann-Kohler and Rigozzi (n 11) 423, n 657; Matray (n 49) 71–72).

54. See, among others, Berthold Goldman, 'Les conflits de lois dans l'arbitrage international de droit privé' in *Recueil des cours*, Académie de droit international de La Haye (Martinus Nijhoff 1963) 347, 432, n 44; Kaufmann-Kohler and Rigozzi (n 11) 422–423, n 657; Pierre Lalive, 'Ordre public transnational (ou réellement international) et arbitrage international' (1986) *Rev arb* 329, 364; Serge Lazareff, 'Mandatory Extraterritorial Application of National Law' (1995) *Arbitration International* 137, 139; Sperduti (n 24) 269.

55. Van Houtte, 'Les effets des sanctions économiques sur les contrats transnationaux' (n 22) 194–195.

56. Trade and financial sanctions are not altogether prohibited by international laws and standards and are therefore not considered intrinsically unlawful measures. Rather, they are regarded by most as measures of retorsion, that is, measures which, albeit unfriendly, remain within the ambit of each state's sovereign and discretionary competence. Regarding trade restrictions, see, *inter alia*, Louis Dubouis, 'L'embargo dans la pratique contemporaine' (1967) *Annuaire français de droit international* 99, 108 and references cited therein at 108–110; Denis Alland, *Justice privée et ordre juridique international—Etude théorique des contre-mesures en droit international public* (A Pedone 1994) 152–155, n 106; Dominique Carreau, 'Les moyens de pression économique au regard du FMI, du GATT et de l'OCDE' (1984-1985) *Revue belge de droit international* 20, 20; Charles Leben, 'Les contre-mesures inter-étatiques et les réactions a l'illicite dans la société internationale' (1982) *Annuaire français de droit international* 9, 14, n 7. Regarding asset freezes, see, *inter alia*, Charlotte Beaucillon, 'Crise ukrainienne et mesures restrictives de l'Union européenne: quelle contribution aux sanctions internationales à l'égard de la Russie?' (2014) *Journal du Droit International* 787, 803, n 41. However, customary and conventional international obligations (such as conventional provisions that guarantee freedom of trade) may limit a state's latitude to impose economic sanctions. Sanctions that are in breach of such customary or conventional obligations will be considered in conflict with principles of transnational public policy. Indeed, as noted by Racine, 'le droit international public, en ce qu'il exprime des valeurs reflétées dans la légalité internationale, est une composante de l'ordre public transnational' (Racine (n 11) 104, n 24).

57. The GATT governs trade relations among over 150 member states of the World Trade Organization and lays down a 'general elimination of quantitative restrictions' (Article XI). It liberalises trade and allows restrictive measures only in certain specific circumstances. Article XXI(b) allows restrictive measures that are 'necessary [according to the enacting state] for the protection of its essential security interests (i) relating to fissionable materials or the materials from which they are derived; (ii) relating to the traffic in arms, ammunition and implements of war and to such traffic in other goods and materials as is carried on directly or indirectly for the purpose of supplying a military establishment; (iii) taken in time of war or other emergency in international relations'. In addition, Article XXI(c) allows restrictive measures taken 'in pursuance of [the enacting state's] obligations under the United Nations Charter for the maintenance of international peace and security'. The North American Free Trade Agreement (NAFTA) contains a clause (Article 2102(1)) very similar to Article XXI GATT.

58. See, among others, Marchand (n 9) 186–187, n 191 and 214, n 229; Jean-Hubert Moitry, 'L'arbitre international et l'obligation de boycottage imposée par un Etat' (1991) *Journal du Droit International* 349, 363 and 365; Emmanuel Gaillard, 'Trente ans de Lex Mercatoria—Pour une application sélective de la méthode des principes généraux du droit' (1995) *Journal du Droit International* 5, 21, n 27. The Swiss Federal Tribunal lays down, among other principles of transnational public policy, 'la prohibition des mesures discriminatoires ou spoliatrices' (13 November 1998, (1999) *ASA Bulletin* 529, 533, c. 1.b.aa).

59. See Hans van Houtte, 'The Impact of Trade Prohibitions on Transnational Contracts' (1988) *Revue de droit des affaires internationales/International Business Law Journal* 141, 150. Public international law dictates that a state's prescriptive jurisdiction must be based on criteria that are neither superficial nor arbitrary. A country's prescriptive jurisdiction may be based on criteria such as the following: a 'territoriality' criterion (a state has jurisdiction over situations that occur on its territory); a 'nationality' criterion (a state has jurisdiction over its nationals); a 'protection' criterion (a state has jurisdiction over situations that threaten its own national security, integrity or vital economic interests). Some states also rely on an 'effects criterion' (a state has prescriptive jurisdiction over foreign persons and entities located outside its territory if their behaviour produces effects inside that territory). If the sanction strives to be applied extraterritorially, based on a criterion that is either superficial or arbitrary, it may have to be disregarded even if

it is part of the applicable law. Furthermore, even if the scope of an extraterritorial sanction is considered by the deciding court to be in accordance with public international law, it may have to be disregarded if giving it effect extraterritorially would clearly not contribute to the achievement of the sanction's stated foreign policy or national security goal.

60. See Blessing, 'Impact of the Extraterritorial Application of Mandatory Rules of Law on International Contracts' (n 27).

61. See van Hecke (n 14) 118.

62. EU domestic courts may wish to rely on the European Union's 'Basic Principles on the Use of Restrictive Measures (Sanctions)' (Council document 10198/1/04). According to these Principles, sanctions may serve to maintain and restore international peace and security in accordance with the principles of the UNC and of the EU's common foreign and security policy, to fight terrorism and the proliferation of weapons of mass destruction, and to uphold respect for human rights, democracy, the rule of law and good governance.

63. As rightly noted by Seraglini, 'la fin poursuivie peut non seulement être contingente, mais ... elle n'a par ailleurs pas besoin d'être partagée par une majorité d'Etats pour voir sa légitimité reconnue. En d'autres termes, si la légitimité s'impose s'agissant d'intérêts contingents "généralement protégés par la communauté internationale" ..., elle peut également être reconnue à des intérêts contingents qui ne bénéficient pas de la même généralité mais qui peuvent être considérés comme "généralement acceptés par la communauté internationale"' (Seraglini (n 11) 377–378, n 784).

64. On the applicable standard in international arbitration, see Azeredo da Silveira, *Trade Sanctions and International Sales* (n 10) 141–142, nn 226–227; Voser (n 27) 351; Berger (n 22) 113; Kaufmann-Kohler and Rigozzi (n 11) 426, n 663.

65. See Seraglini (n 11) 377–378, n 784.

66. These are China, France, Russia, the United Kingdom and the United States (Article 23(1) UNC). The international community may well also be of the opinion that unilateral sanctions are sufficient measures against the target state.

67. For instance, after Iraq's invasion of Kuwait, France, the US and the UK were first to impose sanctions against these countries and only subsequently did the UN Security Council pass Resolution 661 on 6 August 1990.

68. See Karl M Meessen, 'Extraterritorial Jurisdiction in Export Control Law' in Karl M Meessen (ed), *International Law of Export Control—Jurisdictional Issues* (Graham & Trotman/Martinus Nijhoff 1992) 3, 10–11; Seraglini (n 11) 385, n 801.

69. For example, on 20 November 1965, the Security Council passed Resolution 217, calling upon all states 'to refrain from any action which would assist and encourage the illegal regime and, in particular, to desist from providing it with arms, equipment and military material, and to do their utmost in order to break all economic relations with Southern Rhodesia, including an embargo on oil and petroleum products' (para 8).

70. Domestic courts of member states of regional organizations may also be expected to consider that sanctions imposed further to a recommendation issued by these organizations serve a legitimate purpose. See, for instance, the 1991 and 1992 Resolutions passed by the Organization of American States (OAS)—following the overthrow of President Aristide by the Haitian military under the command of General Cedras—recommending its member states to impose trade sanctions against Haiti on all but humanitarian goods (OAS Res 1/91, OEA/SerJ/VI MRE/RES1/91 (1991); OAS Res 2/91, OEA/SerF/V1 MRE/RES2/91 (1991); OAS Res 3/92, OEA/SerF/VI MRE/RES3/92 (1992)).

71. Van Houtte, 'The Impact of Trade Prohibitions on Transnational Contracts' (n 59) 149. See also Van Houtte, 'Les effets des sanctions économiques sur les contrats transnationaux' (n 22) 197–198; Marchand (n 9) 211–212, n 225.

72. Marchand (n 9) 212, n 226.

73. For a discussion of the distinction to be drawn between sanctions serving a coercive purpose (possibly combined with a symbolic and/or punitive purpose) and sanctions that serve an exclusively punitive purpose, see Azeredo da Silveira, *Trade Sanctions and International Sales* (n 10) 157 and following, nn 252 and following.

74. Marchand (n 9) 211, n 224.

75. See Bernardo Cortese, 'International Economic Sanctions as a Component of Public Policy for Conflict-of-Laws Purposes' in Picchio Forlati and Sicilianos (n 8) 717, 745.

76. See Andreas Bucher, in Andreas Bucher (ed), *Commentaire romand—Loi sur le droit international privé Convention de Lugano* (Helbing Lichtenhahn 2011) 273–274, n 43 ad Article 19 LDIP; Marchand (n 9) 210–211, n 224; Seragini (n 11) 385, n 800.

77. Article 9(3) Rome I Regulation provides a clear-cut solution in situations in which the sanction strives to apply extraterritorially. Under this provision, effect may only be given to overriding mandatory provisions of the law of the state where the obligations arising out of the contract have to be or have been performed. In other words, Article 9(3) Rome I Regulation explicitly requires the existence of a territorial nexus between the sanctioning state and the disputed contract. See the decision of the *Cour d'appel* of Paris, dated 25 February 2015, discussed below.

78. See *Compagnie Européenne des Pétroles SA v Sensor Nederland BV, Arrondissementsrechtbank*, The Hague, 17 September 1982 (1983) ILM 66 and following, (1983) *Revue Critique de Droit International de la Haye* 473 and following. See also Bucher, *Commentaire romand—Loi sur le droit international privé* (n 76) 274, n 48 ad Article 19 LDIP. A state may be deemed to have a legitimate interest in enacting extraterritorial legislation only if there is a reasonable connection between this state and situations affected by this legislation. See, in this respect, n 59 above.

79. Several countries as well as the EU have adopted blocking statutes to prevent US extraterritorial sanctions from producing effects within their territories. For instance, in reaction to the pipeline sanctions described above in n 43, the UK government issued an Order under the Protection of Trading Interests Act as well as directions addressed to four UK companies (three of which were subsidiaries of US companies) prohibiting compliance with US measures intended to obstruct the construction of the Siberian gas pipeline (see the Protection of Trading Interests (US Re-export Control) Order 1982 (Statutory Instrument 1982 n 885), *British Yearbook of International Law* 1982 452–453). The European Community also responded to these US measures (see, for instance, the European Communities' Comments on the US Regulations Concerning Trade with the USSR of 11 August 1982, Europe-Documents n 1216, 12 August 1982, reprinted in ILM 1982 891 and following). As to US extraterritorial sanctions against Cuba, Canada (see the Order of 9 October 1992 (Foreign Exraterritorial Measures (United States)), Statutory Orders and Regulations 92-584, Canada Gazette Part II 4048) and the UK (see the Statutory Instrument of 14 October 1992, Order n 2449 (Protection of Trading Interests (US Cuban Assets Control Regulations))), among others, reacted to the breadth of the Cuban Democracy Act and issued blocking orders prohibiting US-owned or -controlled Canadian and UK companies, respectively, from complying with this Act. In 1996, the European Union also adopted a regulation in response to US extraterritorial and secondary sanctions laid down in the Cuban Democracy Act, the Cuban Assets Control Regulations, the Helms-Burton Act, and the Iran and Libya Sanctions Act (ILSA) (see Council Regulation (EC) 2271/96 of 22 November 1996 Protecting Against the Effects of the Extra-Territorial Application of Legislation Adopted by a Third Country, and Actions Based Thereon or Resulting Therefrom (OJ L309 of 29 November 1996, ILM 1997 125)).

80. See Bernard Audit, *Droit international privé* (Economica 2010) 118, n 123.

81. This limitation—which did not exist under the Rome Convention—is unfortunate if one considers that a sanctioning state may, for instance, have a legitimate interest in prohibiting exports to a target state, even if the delivery of exported goods takes place outside the sanctioning state. In Audit's opinion, 'le véritable critère devrait être de savoir si les intérêts généraux de cet Etat sont ou non engagés' (Audit, *Droit international privé* (n 80) 740, n 840).

82. *Cour d'appel* of Paris (pôle 5, ch 4), Decision 12/23757, 25 February 2015. In the words of the *Cour d'appel*: 'Considérant qu'en application de l'article 9 du Règlement "Rome I" il ne peut être donné effet à une loi de police étrangère que s'il s'agit d'une loi de police du lieu d'exécution du contrat et si cette loi de police rend illégale l'exécution du contrat; qu'en l'espèce, sans avoir à se prononcer sur la qualification de loi de police des dispositions du Code des Réglementations Fédérales, "CFR", instituant un embargo sur les exportations à destination de l'Iran, la Cour ne peut donner d'effet à la loi américaine, qui n'est ni une loi de police française, ni une loi de police iranienne'.

83. An application by analogy of Article 9(3) Rome I Regulation should indeed not limit the authority of arbitral tribunals to give effect to overriding mandatory rules enacted by states other than those where contractual obligations have been or have to be performed. As noted earlier, arbitral tribunals are not directly bound by provisions such as Article 7(1) Rome Convention and Article 9(3) Rome I Regulation. Rather, they must be guided by principles inferred therefrom. It is therefore suggested that prior to giving effect to a sanction external to the applicable law, arbitral tribunals should simply verify the existence of a close connection between the sanction and the disputed contract.

84. See ICC Award 1859 of 1973 (excerpts in Derains, 'Le statut des usages du commerce international devant les juridictions arbitrales' (n 38) 134, and in Derains, 'L'ordre public et le droit applicable au fond du litige dans l'arbitrage international' (n 38) 408, n 54), discussed above, in which Lebanese import restrictions were taken into account in the resolution of a dispute pertaining to a contract between a Japanese seller and a Lebanese importer, governed by general principles and trade usages and to be performed in Lebanon (where the goods were to be delivered).

85. Ole Lando, 'The Conflict of Laws of Contracts—General Principles' in *Recueil des cours*, Académie de droit international de La Haye (Martinus Nijhoff 1984) 225, 405.

86. Cortese (n 75) 729.

87. In the well-known *Fruehauf* decision of 22 May 1965, the *Cour d'appel* of Paris pointed to 'the catastrophic results which would have been produced, on the eve of delivery date, and which would be felt even today, if the contract had been breached', and refused to apply a US trade sanction against the People's Republic of China, to a sales contract between two French companies providing for the supply of vans destined to be ultimately delivered to the People's Republic of China (*Fruehauf Corporation v Massardy*, *Cour d'appel*, Paris, 22 May 1965, *Gaz Pal* 1965 86 and following, ILM 1966 476).

88. See Azeredo da Silveira, *Trade Sanctions and International Sales* (n 10) § 4.02[C][3] and 163–164, n 264.

89. See, for instance, Article 9 of Council Regulation (EC) 2271/96 of 22 November 1996.

90. See, for instance, Article 4 of Council Regulation (EC) 2271/96 of 22 November 1996.

91. See, for instance, Article 6 of Council Regulation (EC) 2271/96 of 22 November 1996.

92. According to Article 24(1) and (2) UNC, '[i]n order to ensure prompt and effective action by the United Nations, its Members confer on the Security Council primary responsibility for the maintenance of international peace and security, and agree that in carrying out its duties under this responsibility the Security Council acts on their behalf. In discharging these duties the Security Council shall act in accordance with the Purposes and Principles of the United Nations. The specific powers granted to the Security Council for the discharge of these duties are laid down in Chapters VI, VII, VIII, and XII'.

93. Pursuant to Article 39 UNC, the Security Council 'shall [then] make recommendations, or decide what measures shall be taken in accordance with Articles 41 and 42, to maintain or restore international peace and security'. As per Article 41 UNC, measures not involving the use of armed force include 'complete or partial interruption of economic relations'.

94. See, *inter alia*, Racine (n 11) 101, n 18 and 104, n 23; Nabil Ferjani and Véronique Huet, 'L'impact de la décision onusienne d'embargo sur l'exécution des contrats internationaux' (2010) *Journal du Droit International* 737, 755; Gaillard and Savage (n 11) 853, n 1522; Landy-Osman (n 30) 609, n 28; Marchand (n 9) 68, n 42 and 104–105, n 88.

95. Marchand (n 9) 97–98, n 80, 106, n 90, and 104–105, n 88. In the same vein, domestic 'counter-legislation' enacted by the target state to thwart the effects of a multilateral sanction must be disregarded. See, for instance, the 1990 Law for the Protection of Iraqi Property, Interests, and Rights in and outside Iraq (or 'Law no 57' available in *Yearbook of Islamic and Middle Eastern Law* 1994 519–520) enacted by Iraq to thwart the effects of UN Security Council Resolution 661 passed after the invasion of Kuwait by Iraq (Grelon and Gudin (n 30) 661; Jean Matringe, 'Problèmes et techniques de mise en œuvre des sanctions économiques de l'Organisation des Nations Unies en droit interne' in Picchio Forlati and Sicilianos (n 8) 637, 668).

96. Azeredo da Silveira, *Trade Sanctions and International Sales* (n 10) 63, n 101 and 147–148, n 240. For situations in which several implementation measures purport to apply to the disputed contract (that is, several states claim to have jurisdiction over the same parties and transactions), see Azeredo da Silveira, *Trade Sanctions and International Sales* (n 10) 149–150, nn 241–242.

97. In the case of UN sanctions against the Democratic People's Republic of Korea, for instance, one may imagine a scenario in which the disputed contract was entered into by a French entity and a North Korean entity and was governed by Swiss law. Unless otherwise specified, Swiss sanctions (including measures of implementation of UN Security Council mandatory resolutions) only apply territorially, that is, they apply to individuals and corporate entities located in Switzerland and/or engaged in commercial activities in Switzerland (Mathias-Charles Krafft, Daniel Thürer and Julie-Antoinette Stadelhofer, 'Switzerland' in Gowlland-Debbas (n 40) 523, 548). Swiss sanctions against North Korea (implementing UN Security Council mandatory resolutions) therefore likely do not prohibit the performance of the disputed contract between the French entity and the North Korean entity. EU and/or French sanctions (implementing UN Security Council mandatory resolutions), on the other hand, may prohibit the transaction and may therefore have to be given effect despite being external to the applicable law.

98. A failure to give effect to a domestic or an EU measure implementing a UN Security Council binding resolution would fall within the category of instances in which, according to Mistelis, 'failure to [apply an overriding mandatory rule is] inconsistent with international public policy, e.g. where an element of illegality or immorality is asserted' (Mistelis, 'Mandatory Rules in International Arbitration' (n 30) 299).

99. According to Bismuth, 'si les résolutions du Conseil de sécurité ne bénéficient pas nécessairement d'un effet direct devant les juges internes ou les arbitres, ceux-ci peuvent en tenir compte en tant que fait juridique ... (par exemple au titre de la force majeure) ou comme un élément d'un "ordre public réellement international"' (Régis Bismuth, 'Odyssée dans le conundrum des réactions décentralisées à l'illicite' (2014) *Journal du Droit International* 719, 729, n 14).

100. See Azeredo da Silveira, *Trade Sanctions and International Sales* (n 10) §3.02[C]; Azeredo da Silveira, 'Economic Sanctions and Contractual Disputes Between Private Operators' (n 16) 353.

101. See Azeredo da Silveira, *Trade Sanctions and International Sales* (n 10) §3.02[C]; Azeredo da Silveira, 'Economic Sanctions and Contractual Disputes Between Private Operators' (n 16) 353.

102. UN Security Council mandatory resolutions are directed to, and binding on, states only, and must therefore be translated into domestic or EU legislation to be effective. See *Etat irakien v SA Dumez GTM*, *Cour de cassation*, n 02-17344, 25 April 2006, JCPG 2006 II 10179, p 2058; *Affaire pénale Barcot et Trojić*, Trieste Tribunal, 24 December 1993, (1998) *Journal du Droit* 441, 441–442; *Bradley v The Commonwealth of Australia and the Postmaster-General*, High Court of Australia, 10 September 1973 (1974) *Journal du Droit International* 865, 867; Burdeau (n 2) 43, n 67; Cissé (n 8) 685, n 6 and 701, n 38; Ergeç (n 40) 130–131, nn 15–17; Grelon and Gudin (n 30) 639; Gilbert Guillaume, 'L'introduction et l'exécution dans les ordres juridiques des Etats des résolutions du Conseil de sécurité des Nations unies prises sur le fondement du chapitre VII de la Charte' (1998) *Revue internationale de droit comparé* 539, 546 n 15; Landy-Osman (n 30) 602, n 11 and 604, n 15; Marchand (n 9) 73, n 51 and 92, n 73; Matringe (n 95) 643, 644, 646–647 and 656–657; James AR Nafziger and Edward M Wise, 'The Status in United States Law of Security Council Resolutions under Chapter VII of the United Nations Charter' (1998) *American Journal of Comparative Law* Supplement 421, 424 and 431; Saber Salama, *L'acte de gouvernement—Contribution à l'étude de la force majeure dans le contrat international* (Bruylant 2001) 32, n 25. A minority of authors, however, maintain that UN Security Council mandatory resolutions are self-executing within member states. For a detailed discussion of the controversy regarding the direct applicability of Security Council mandatory resolutions (including French case-law and further references to scholarly writing dealing with this question), see Marchand (n 9) 81–89, nn 61–69.

103. See Azeredo da Silveira, *Trade Sanctions and International Sales* (n 10) §3.02[C].

104. *Etat irakien v SA Dumez GTM*, *Cour de cassation*, n 02-17344, 25 April 2006, JCPG 2006 II 10179, 2058. See also Giuseppe Cataldi, 'L'application des décisions du Conseil de sécurité en droit interne' in Rafaa Ben Achour and Slim Laghmani (eds), *Droit international et droits internes, développements récents* (Pedone 1998) 205, 221; Marchand (n 9) 90, n 70 and 95, n 78.

105. Under C-term contracts, delivery must be made on board the vessel at the port of shipment (Incoterms 2010, CFR and CIF terms) or by handing the goods over to the carrier (Incoterms 2010, s 4A of the CPT and CIP terms). Under F-terms, the delivery may also have to be made alongside the ship (Incoterms 2010, s 4A of the FAS term) or on board (Incoterms 2010, s 4A of the FOB term) at the port of shipment. C-term and F-term contracts are therefore often characterised as 'shipment contracts'.

106. Under D-term contracts, the seller's delivery obligation is extended to the port or place of destination (see Incoterms 2010, s 4A of the DAT, DAP, and DDP terms). These contracts are therefore often characterised as 'arrival contracts'.

107. In this case, the buyer may, however, attempt to argue that because the sanction prohibits the shipment of the goods to the target state, the contract's purpose is frustrated.

108. Under the term EXW ('Ex Works ... named place'), the seller fulfils its delivery obligation by making the goods available to the buyer at the named place of delivery in the seller's own country (Incoterms 2010, s A4 of the EXW term).

109. Brunner (n 49) 134.

110. ibid.

111. See UNSC Res 687 (1991) against Iraq, para 29 (implemented by Council Regulation (EEC) 3541/92 of 7 December 1992) and other Security Council resolutions referred to in n 11 above.

112. See *Air France v Libyan Airlines*, *Cour d'appel du Québec*, 31 March 2003, (2003) *Rev arb* 1365, 1371, n 25, (2003) *ASA Bulletin* 630, 636; unpublished ICC Award in Case 7698 of 24 May 2006, quoted in Marchand (n 9) 118, n 102. See also Racine (n 11) 99–100, nn 13–14; Alain Prujiner, 'Note—Cour d'appel du Québec, 31 mars 2003: Canada: Le refus des juges québécois d'intervenir dans un arbitrage international avant la sentence finale' (2003) *Rev arb* 1385, 1389; Philippe Pinsolle, 'Note following *CA Quebec, 31 March 2003, Air France v Libyan Arab Airlines*' (2003) *ASA Bulletin* 649 and following.

113. See, for example, Article 38 of Council Regulation (EU) 267/2012 of 23 March 2012 concerning restrictive measures against Iran and repealing Regulation (EU) 961/2010, and Article 11 of Council Regulation (EU) 833/2014 of 31 July 2014 concerning restrictive measures in view of Russia's actions destabilising the situation in Ukraine, according to which '[n]o claims in connection with any contract or transaction the performance of which has been affected, directly or indirectly, in whole or in part, by the measures imposed under this Regulation, including claims for indemnity or any other claim of this type, such as a claim for compensation or a claim under a guarantee, notably a claim for extension or payment of a bond, guarantee or indemnity, particularly a financial guarantee or financial indemnity, of whatever form, shall be satisfied ...' See

also UNSC Res 418 (1977) imposing a mandatory arms embargo against South Africa, which 'call[ed] upon all States to review ... all existing contractual arrangements with and licenses granted to South Africa relating to the manufacture and maintenance of arms, ammunition of all types and military equipment and vehicles, with a view to terminating them' (para 3).

114. This phrase appears in most resolutions of the United Nations Security Council imposing trade sanctions. See, for instance, UNSC Res 864 (1993), para 20, UNSC Res 1127 (1997), para 10, and UNSC Res 1173 (1998), para 17 (Angola); UNSC Res 232 (1966), para 2 and UNSC Res 253 (1968), para 7 (Rhodesia); UNSC Res 661 (1990), para 5, UNSC Res 670 (1990), para 3, and UNSC Res 687 (1991), para 25 (Iraq); UNSC Res 757 (1992), para 11 and UNSC Res 1160 (1998), para 10 (Yugoslavia); UNSC Res 748 (1992), para 7 and UNSC Res 883 (1993), para 12 (Libya); UNSC Res 841 (1993), para 9 and UNSC Res 917 (1994), para 12 (Haiti); UNSC Res 1132 (1997), para 11, UNSC Res 1306 (2000), para 9, UNSC Res 1298 (2000), para 9, UNSC Res 1267 (1999), para 7 and UNSC Res 918 (1994), para 15 (Sierra Leone); UNSC Res 1333 (2000), para 17 (Afghanistan); UNSC Res 1343 (2001), para 22 (Liberia); UNSC Res 1298 (2000), para 9 (Erythrea and Ethiopia).

115. While the parties may not exclude by contract the application of an economic sanction, they may agree on the sanction's impact on their rights and obligations, provided that their agreement neither is in conflict with, nor defeats the purpose of, the sanction.

116. See, *inter alia*, Cissé (n 8) 702, n 40; Xavier Dieux, 'Questions relatives aux effets de la contrainte étatique sur les contrats économiques internationaux—Un point de vue belge' (1987) *Revue belge de droit international* 184, 201; Ferjani and Huet (n 94) 758, n 28; Saber Salama, 'Le sort des contrats conclus avec des opérateurs irakiens à la suite de la levée de l'embargo' (2003) *Revue de droit des affaires internationales/International Business Law Journal* 887, 888, n 2.

117. ICC Award in Case 2478, 1974, (1975) *Journal du Droit International* 925, 926.

118. Bulgarian Chamber of Commerce and Industry Award 56/1995, 24 April 1996, CISG-online 435. Exemption was, however, denied on the ground that the prohibition was already in force at the time of the conclusion of the contract and was therefore foreseeable.

119. Hungarian Chamber of Commerce and Industry Award, 10 December 1996, CISG-online 774.

120. Final Award in Case 1491, 20 July 1992, (1993) *Yearbook of Commercial Arbitration* 80, 87, n 22. The contract, under which the subcontractor had agreed to supply to the main contractor parts of a plant to be built in Iraq, was considered to fall within the purview of the EU and Italian sanctions against Iraq.

121. See *McDonnell Douglas Corp v Islamic Republic of Iran*, 591 F Supp 293 (ED Mo 1984), in which a military aircraft builder was excused from performance on the ground that a US federal government order prohibited the transfer of all Iranian property back to Iran.

122. See *Eastern Air Lines, Inc v McDonnell Douglas Corp*, 532 F2d 957 (5th Cir 1976), in which the US Government's informal military priorities policy was found to excuse the delayed performance of an aircraft seller.

123. See *Harriscom Svenska, AB v Harris Corp*, 3 F3d 576 (2nd Cir 1993), in which a seller was excused on the ground that uncontradicted evidence showed that the government would not have authorised the seller to continue to sell products to Iran, and that the government had the power to compel compliance.

124. Translation available at <http://www.legifrance.gouv.fr/Traductions/en-English/Legifrance-translations>. The original text reads: 'Il n'y a lieu à aucun dommages et intérêts lorsque, par suite d'une force majeure ou d'un cas fortuit, le débiteur a été empêché de donner ou de faire ce à quoi il était obligé, ou a fait ce qui lui était interdit'.

125. 'Secondary sanctions' are directed against persons and entities located outside the sanctioning and the target states but which have ties with the target state. 'Tertiary sanctions' are directed against persons and entities located outside the sanctioning and the target states and which have ties with persons or entities, also located outside the target state, which themselves have ties with the latter state. The first serious case of secondary sanctions was associated with the Arab-Israeli conflict, during which the Arab League imposed secondary sanctions on foreign firms which maintained commercial ties with Israel (see Mahmood Bagheri, *International Contracts and National Economic Regulation—Dispute Resolution through International Commercial Arbitration* (Kluwer Law International 2000) 85). The 'boycott of Israel' organized by the Arab League required foreign firms dealing with Arab countries to refrain from using a subcontractor, supplier, bank, shipper or insurer that had been blacklisted as a result of commerce with Israel, and to terminate existing contracts with any such subcontractor, supplier, bank, shipper or insurer. As part of its sanctions programmes against Cuba, Iran, and Libya, the United States threatened to impose penalties on foreign firms which would not refrain from doing business with these countries (see the Helms-Burton Act signed by President Clinton on 12 February 1996 following the downing of two private US planes by the Cuban government (Pub L No 104-114, 110 Stat 785 (1996) codified at 22 USC paras 6021–6091), and the ILSA signed by

President Clinton on 5 August 1996 to 'help deter Iran and Libya from supporting international terrorism or acquiring weapons of mass destruction' (Pub L No 104-172, 110 Stat 1541 (1996)); the ILSA was replaced by the Iran Sanctions Act (ISA) (50 USC para 1701 note) in 2006 and reinforced by the Comprehensive Iran Sanctions, Accountability, and Divestment Act (CISADA Pub L 111-195) in 2010 as well as by the Iran Freedom and Counter Proliferation Act (IFCA 22 USC Ch 95) in 2013).

126. Indeed, these sanctions do not prohibit the performance of transactions with the target, but rather threaten with penalties and/or denial of privileges individuals and entities that would fail to comply with these sanctions' terms.

127. See Bruno Leurent, 'Les implications des législations de sanction et de blocage sur les relations juridiques privées internationales' in Gherari and Szurek (n 2) 277, 283. From a prescriptive jurisdiction standpoint, secondary and tertiary sanctions differ from extraterritorial sanctions (defined above), under which the sanctioning state prohibits individuals and entities that are purportedly under its prescriptive jurisdiction from carrying out business with certain targets. This being said, one must acknowledge that secondary and tertiary sanctions are used as a tool to coerce foreign persons and entities into severing their commercial and/or financial ties with the target state and thus into complying with the terms of a sanctions programme, just like persons and entities that are under the jurisdiction of the sanctioning state, which explains why secondary and tertiary sanctions are often discussed by authors in the context of extraterritorial sanctions.

128. Azeredo da Silveira, *Trade Sanctions and International Sales* (n 10) 319, n 480.

129. See Leurent (n 127) 283.

130. See the Preamble to the UNIDROIT Principles.

131. These conditions are mirrored in the first paragraph of the 2003 *ICC Model Clause on Force Majeure*, and often in standard contractual clauses. The first paragraph of the 2003 *ICC Model Clause on Force Majeure* reads as follows: 'Unless otherwise agreed in the contract between the parties expressly or impliedly, where a party to a contract fails to perform one or more of its contractual duties, the consequences set out in paragraphs 4 to 9 of this Clause will follow if and to the extent that that party proves: (a) that its failure to perform was caused by an impediment beyond its reasonable control; and (b) that it could not reasonably have been expected to have taken the occurrence of the impediment into account at the time of the conclusion of the contract; and (c) that it could not reasonably have avoided or overcome the effects of the impediment'.

132. On the suspension of the obligation to perform in kind under Article 79 CISG, see Azeredo da Silveira, *Trade Sanctions and International Sales* (n 10) §8.02.

133. See the illustrative lists of impediments typically beyond the control of the parties, laid down in Brunner (n 49) 206-207; Dionysos P Flambouras, 'The Doctrines of Impossibility of Performance and *Clausula Rebus Sic Stantibus* in the 1980 Convention on Contracts for the International Sale of Goods and the Principles of European Contract Law: A Comparative Analysis' (2001) *Pace International Law Review* 261, 267 available at <http://www.cisg.law.pace.edu/cisg/biblio/flambouras1.html>; Pascal Pichonnaz, *Impossibilité et exorbitance—Etude analytique des obstacles à l'exécution des obligations en droit suisse (art. 119 CO et 79 CVIM)* (Press Universitaire de Fribourg 1997) 392, n 1693.

134. See, *inter alia*, Brunner (n 49) 207 and 264; Flambouras (n 133) 267; Pichonnaz (n 133) 392, n 1693. An economic sanction may be considered an impediment within the obligor's control if the latter is a governmental or administrative entity or a state instrumentality (company owned or run by the sanctioning state). On this question, see Marchand (n 9) 292-298, nn 349-355. See also Cissé (n 8) 704, n 43; Dieux (n 116) 203 and following; Landy-Osman (n 30) 621-622, nn 63-65 and references cited therein; Ingeborg Schwenzer, in Ingeborg Schwenzer (ed), *Schlechtriem & Schwenzer: Commentary on the UN Convention on the International Sale of Goods (CISG)* (3rd edn, OUP 2010) 1071, n 17 ad Article 79 and references cited therein.

135. *National Oil Company v Libyan Sun Oil Company*, Case 4462, Final Award on Force Majeure, 31 May 1985, (1991) *Yearbook of Commercial Arbitration* 54, 61, n 18.

136. *Macromex Srl v Globex International Inc*, American Arbitration Association Interim Award of 23 October 2007, CISG-online 1645.

137. See Brunner (n 49) 171; Yesim M Atamer, in Stefan Kröll, Loukas A Mistelis and Maria del Pilar Perales Viscasillas (eds), *UN Convention on Contracts for the International Sale of Goods (CISG)* (CH Beck Hart Nomos 2011) 1063, n 22 ad Article 79; Schwenzer (n 134) 1079, n 37 ad Article 79; Ingeborg Schwenzer, Pascal Hachem and Christopher Kee, *Global Sales and Contract Law* (OUP 2012) 661, n 45.51. The failure of a supplier is always within the range of foreseeable occurrences, and if the seller can reasonably be expected to overcome the supplier's failure to deliver the goods, the latter's non-performance must be considered to be within the seller's sphere of risks and responsibilities.

138. The parties' agreement determines the goods' 'degree of genericity'.

139. Nor can a seller claim exemption if its supplier's default resulted from the seller's failure to apply for the necessary import or export authorisations.

140. See Brunner (n 49) 322; Schwenzer (n 134) 1074, n 27 ad Article 79.

141. The ability to perform financial obligations is a prerequisite to all sales contracts and therefore falls within the buyer's sphere of risk and responsibility. See Brunner (n 49) 167–170; Joseph Lookofsky, *Understanding the CISG—A Compact Guide to the 1980 United Nations Convention on Contracts for the International Sale of Goods* (3rd edn, Wolters Kluwer 2008) 140, n 6.19 and 154, n 6.32; Ulrich Magnus, 'Force Majeure and the CISG' in Petar Šarčević and Paul Voken (eds), *The International Sale of Goods Revisited* (Kluwer Law International 2001) 1, 16; Joseph M Perillo, 'Force Majeure and Hardship under the UNIDROIT Principles of International Commercial Contracts' in *Contratación internacional—Comentarios a los Principios sobre los Contratos Commerciales Internacionales del UNIDROIT* (Universidad Nacional Autónoma de México/Universidad Panamericana 1998) 111, 121–122; Jan Kleinheisterkamp, in Stefan Vogenauer and Jan Kleinheisterkamp (eds), *Commentary on the UNIDROIT Principles of International Commercial Contracts (PICC)* (OUP 2009) 773, n 18 ad Article 7.1.7.

142. See Fritz Enderlein and Dietrich Maskow, *International Sales Law: United Nations Convention on Contracts for the International Sale of Goods* (Oceana 1992) 327, n 7.3 ad Article 79; Peter Schlechtriem, *Uniform Sales Law—The UN-Convention on Contracts for the International Sale of Goods* (Manz 1986) 104.

143. 'For example, if a specific type of oil was only produced in Iraq and was not obtainable due to the international embargo, a seller would not bear the risk of procurement' (Flambouras (n 133) 268, footnote 20).

144. See Brunner (n 49) 432–433; Schwenzer, Hachem and Kee (n 137) 661, n 45.51.

145. In the case of an asset freeze, however, it may be difficult for the buyer to establish that the impediment was reasonably unforeseeable, considering that a freeze of assets is a measure often imposed directly in reaction to the actions and conduct of the individual or entity targeted by the measure. Whether a buyer will be exempted from liability for failure to make a payment following an asset freeze will therefore depend on the circumstances surrounding the imposition of the measure, considering that 'an act of public authority making performance impossible is not beyond the obligor's control if its issuance was caused by the obligor's conduct' (Brunner (n 49) 168).

146. In an arbitral award regarding a dispute opposing a US seller of chicken leg quarters to a Romanian buyer, the sole arbitrator held that '[t]he Romanian government's decision to stop all chicken imports on virtually no notice to the industry … would not have been reasonably contemplated as a risk assigned to the Seller at the conclusion of the contract, as no prior ban experienced by either party was taken as precipitously' (*Macromex Srl v Globex International Inc*, American Arbitration Association Interim Award of 23 October 2007, CISG-online 1645). Regarding the question of the foreseeability of sanctions by state instrumentalities, see Marchand (n 9) 282, n 331.

147. In this respect, it is interesting to note that in a 1985 decision, the Swiss Federal Tribunal refused to discharge a Swiss company (T. AG) under Article 119 SCO following this company's failure to build and deliver a nuclear installation ('Mini 8067') to Pakistan. The Federal Council had prohibited the export of another installation ('Makro 8062'), not the export of Mini 8067, and it was therefore not established that performance of the contract regarding Mini 8067 had become impossible. Furthermore, the Federal Tribunal held that even if the export of Mini 8067 had been prohibited, discharge would have been denied given that export prohibitions in the nuclear sector are foreseeable. The Tribunal explained: 'Le débiteur répond de l'impossibilité juridique si, lorsqu'il a promis la prestation, il savait – ou devait savoir en faisant preuve de la diligence nécessaire – que les circonstances pourraient l'empêcher de s'exécuter. … L'art. 8 al. 2 [Loi fédérale sur l'utilisation pacifique de l'énergie atomique] dispose ce qui suit: Le Conseil fédéral et les organes désignés par lui sont autorisés, dans l'exercice de leur surveillance, à ordonner en tout temps les mesures qui s'imposent pour assurer la protection des personnes, des biens d'autrui et de droits importants, pour sauvegarder la sûreté extérieure de la Suisse et garantir le respect de ses engagements internationaux; ils sont également compétents pour veiller à l'exécution de ces mesures. … [P]our l'entrepreneur, il était prévisible que de telles interventions étaient possibles. La disposition précitée porte expressément que les autorités peuvent ordonner "en tout temps" les mesures qui s'imposent. Un contractant engagé dans la technologie nucléaire doit toujours s'attendre à d'éventuelles mesures destinées à permettre au Conseil fédéral de faire face aux développements parfois imprévus de la politique internationale en matière d'énergie. T. AG est incontestablement spécialisée dans le secteur de la technique nucléaire. Elle était au courant de la législation fédérale en la matière et des mesures d'application que les autorités fédérales pourraient prendre. Elle pouvait en tenir compte en négociant le contrat et stipuler des réserves ad hoc pour le cas où la livraison n'aurait pas lieu. En l'espèce,

elle n'a rien fait de tout cela; elle répond donc de l'inexécution consécutive à une interdiction d'exporter' (*Bank K und T AG v M Co.*, 3 September 1985, Swiss Federal Tribunal, 111 II 352, c 2a, JdT 1986 I 73, 74–75).

148. Some may even contend that in cases in which a UN Security Council mandatory resolution for the imposition of sanctions is adopted before the conclusion of the contract, the impediment already exists at that time. Considering that such resolutions are directed to states and do not create rights or obligations for private operators, this view is not compelling: private operators face an impediment from the moment the said resolution has been transposed into domestic or Community legislation. In any event, in neither case should the defaulting party be granted exemption, given that in both cases the impediment is reasonably foreseeable at the time of the conclusion of the contract.

149. See Matray (n 49) 94, who refers to ICC Award no 1782, 1973 (1975) *Journal du Droit International* 923 and following. The dispute pertained to a contract between a German company and a Yugoslavian company, under which the former had agreed to deliver trucks and ensure their maintenance on three construction sites located in an Arab country. The German company failed to carry out the maintenance part of the deal and invoked force majeure, alleging that its representatives, of Israeli origin, could not obtain the necessary visas to enter the said country. The arbitrators ruled that this did not make performance impossible as the German company could have made other arrangements so as to carry out its obligation. See also *National Oil Company v Libyan Sun Oil Company* (n 135) 54 and following. In this award (discussed above and below), one of the issues examined by the tribunal was whether the US government's 1981 order declaring that US passports were no longer valid for travel to Libya constituted, under the force majeure excuse, a ground for the suspension of Sun Oil's performance under an Exploration and Production Sharing Agreement (EPSA) entered into with NOC. The tribunal interpreted the contractual clause on force majeure (Article 22 EPSA) in light of Article 360 of the Libyan Civil Code (the applicable law) to conclude that 'under the meaning of Art. 22, non-performance by a party or delay in performing contractual obligations is excused when an unforeseen circumstance beyond the control of the parties occurs, which circumstance constitutes an obstacle such that an obligor, normally diligent, having the same obligations and placed in the same situation, could not have overcome it' (*National Oil Company v Libyan Sun Oil Company* 60–61, n 16). The tribunal held that the above-mentioned 1981 US Government order did not constitute one such circumstance, given *inter alia* the following: it could not be inferred from the EPSA that the only commonly envisaged mode of performing the EPSA by Sun Oil was one involving the use of Sun Oil personnel with US passports (*National Oil Company v Libyan Sun Oil Company* 63, n 28), and Sun Oil had failed to provide evidence that it was impossible for it to hire non-US personnel (*National Oil Company v Libyan Sun Oil Company* 63, n 27).

150. See ICC Award 5864, 1989 (1997) *Journal du Droit International* 1073 and following. Under the disputed contract, a US company was acting as a consultant for a Libyan company. In 1986, the US President prohibited US nationals from carrying out activities in Libya. The US company was, however, authorised to pursue its activities provided that they be completed within a few months. The tribunal granted the US company exemption on grounds of force majeure, holding that beyond the allocated time-frame, the US company could not have been expected to overcome the prohibition by hiring another company or by delegating its work to a foreign daughter company, as this would have contravened the US prohibition and the terms of the authorisation.

151. See Brunner (n 49) 322; Pichonnaz (n 133) 402, n 1742; Ingeborg Schwenzer and Christiana Fountoulakis, *International Sales Law* (Routledge-Cavendish 2007) 567.

152. If performance was due before the prohibition became effective, the defaulting party cannot be granted exemption given that, in this case, it simply faced no impediment to performance.

153. In *Macromex Srl v Globex International Inc* (discussed above), the arbitrator found that by shipping the goods to an alternative port proposed by the buyer, the seller could reasonably have avoided a ban imposed by the Romanian government on all chicken imports not certified as of 7 June 2006. Thus, even though the ban imposed by the Romanian government was considered an impediment beyond the seller's control and one that the latter could not reasonably be expected to have foreseen at the time of the conclusion of the contract, the unavoidability condition was not satisfied and the seller was denied exemption under Article 79 CISG (American Arbitration Association Interim Award of 23 October 2007, CISG-online 1645; this interim award was fully integrated in a Final Award dated 12 December 2007 (CISG-online 1647), confirmed by the US Federal District Court of the Southern District of New York on 16 April 2008 (CISG-online 1653), and subsequently by the US Court of Appeals, 2nd Cir, on 26 May 2009 (CISG-online 1837)).

154. In past cases in which as a result of the closing of traffic routes a different itinerary had to be selected, the impediment was often considered reasonably surmountable despite the additional costs that this would entail. In cases decided under American and English law, carriers (in charter contracts) and sellers (in sales contracts) who were to bear cost and freight were therefore often denied discharge. One may refer to the cases related to the closing of the Suez Canal

following hostilities in the Middle East in 1956 and 1967. No discharge was granted despite the fact that ocean carriers and sellers were compelled to take a longer route around the Cape of Good Hope and consequently bear costs that largely exceeded the agreed price. See, for instance, *American Trading & Production Corp v Shell International Marine Ltd*, 453 F2d 939 (2nd Cir 1972); *Transatlantic Financing Corp v United States*, 363 F2d 312 (DC Cir 1966).

155. As noted by Brunner, '[t]he fact that both parties contemplate a particular method of performance does not in and of itself mean that the method should be exclusive' (Brunner (n 49) 325; emphasis omitted). Whether a method of performance expressly or implicitly agreed upon by the parties is exclusive (or of fundamental importance) must be determined based on both the terms of the contract and the circumstances.

156. See Brunner (n 49) 327.

157. Schwenzer (n 134) 1069, n 14 ad Article 79.

158. Whether a specification is non-essential or non-exclusive is to be determined 'by way of contract interpretation in the light of all relevant circumstances' (Brunner (n 49) 324).

159. Hans Stoll, in Peter Schlechtriem (ed), *Commentary on the UN Convention on the International Sale of Goods (CISG)* (2nd edn, Clarendon Press 1998) 612, n 24 ad Article 79. See Brunner (n 49) 323 and 367.

160. Van Houtte, 'The Impact of Trade Prohibitions on Transnational Contracts' (n 59) 146; Van Houtte, 'Les effets des sanctions économiques sur les contrats transnationaux' (n 22) 203–204, n 17; Matray (n 49) 95.

161. *National Oil Company* v *Libyan Sun Oil Company* (n 135).

162. ibid. 60–61, n 16.

163. See also the observations above on this case.

164. As stated by the sole arbitrator in *Sapphire International Petroleums Ltd v National Iranian Oil Company* (15 March 1963), 'it is a fundamental principle of law, which is constantly being proclaimed by international courts, that contractual undertakings must be respected. The rule pacta sunt servanda is the basis of every contractual relationship' (ILR 1967 136, 181).

165. The party responsible for obtaining, for instance, import or export authorisations may be explicitly designated in the contract (Brunner (n 49) 127). Alternatively, the party that is responsible for import or export clearance may be identified by reference to, or incorporation in, the contract of an 'International Commercial Term' or 'Incoterm' ('Incoterms' being commercial terms published by the ICC, which lay down duties of exporters and importers regarding the handling of the goods (transportation and delivery) and allocating to each of them certain costs and risks). The Incoterms 2010 (effective since 1 January 2011) typically provide that each party bears the risk of obtaining those public authorisations that are necessary for the performance of its obligations. Under the 2016 UNIDROIT Principles, the duty to apply for a public permission affecting the performance of the contract rests on the party that has its place of business in the state whose permission is required, provided that the other party does not also have a place of business in the state in question (Article 6.1.14(a)). In all other instances (that is, if neither party has or both parties have a place of business in that state), the party whose performance requires permission shall take the necessary measures (Article 6.1.14(b)). In other words, each party must procure those authorisations that are necessary for the performance of its contractual obligations. According to Brunner, '[t]hat principle may be considered to constitute an international trade usage in the form of a supplementary rule to be applied when neither the contract nor the law requiring the permission or the circumstances clearly specify which party is under an obligation to apply for the required public authorisation' (Brunner (n 49) 128, footnote 662).
For a discussion of situations in which the obligee must assist the obligor in the authorisation application process and situations in which the obligee is in charge of seeking the authorisation, see Azeredo da Silveira, *Trade Sanctions and International Sales* (n 10) 238-240, nn 378–380.

166. This is the case under Article 6.1.14 UNIDROIT Principles; see Brunner (n 49) 130; Perillo, 'Force Majeure and Hardship under the UNIDROIT Principles of International Commercial Contracts' (n 141) 126.

167. See Azeredo da Silveira, *Trade Sanctions and International Sales* (n 10) 230, n 364; Brunner (n 49) 140-141.

168. See Azeredo da Silveira, *Trade Sanctions and International Sales* (n 10) 230-231, n 364; Brunner (n 49) 141 and 165.

169. If the contract allocates the duty to apply for the necessary authorisations without specifying whether this duty is one of specific result or one of best efforts, 'the standard of duty depends on the construction of the relevant term or terms of the contract' (Brunner (n 49) 136). As noted by Brunner, 'elements such as the (actual or constructive) knowledge of the party in charge of the necessity to obtain a public permit, its position in the industry, the knowledge of the oth-

er party or explicit or implicit representations to the other party that there would be no problem obtaining permits may be relevant in determining that the obligor assumed the risk of obtaining a particular permit' (ibid. 290-291).

170. Brunner (n 49) 129 and 264. More generally, a party that guarantees its ability to perform notwithstanding the need to obtain an import or export authorisation, must be considered to have assumed the risk that the authorisation be denied. Also, reference to or incorporation of a 2010 Incoterm in the contract implies that the party responsible for the goods' import or export clearance must obtain, at its own risk, the necessary authorisation.

171. Brunner (n 49) 112.

172. Brunner (n 49) 132.

173. See the CIETAC Award, 7 August 1993, CISG-online 1060, ruling on a dispute that arose from a contract for the sale of guns and the buyer's failure to pay the purchase price following a denial of US 'import approval' due to the design of the guns. The tribunal held that 'the necessity of getting import approval could have been foreseen by [Buyer], because the law has been in effect for many years in the U.S.' and that '[Buyer] shall be liable and take the risk for getting the import approval'.

174. Azeredo da Silveira, *Trade Sanctions and International Sales* (n 10) 230, n 363.

175. Brunner (n 49) 132-133, 165 and 264; Hans Stoll and Georg Gruber, in Peter Schlechtriem and Ingeborg Schwenzer (eds), *Commentary on the UN Convention on the International Sale of Goods (CISG)* (2nd edn, OUP 2005) 828, n 37 ad Article 79; Stoll (n 159) 611, n 21 ad Article 79. Contra: Atamer (n 137) 1085, n 73 ad Article 79, according to whom 'if the duty is an absolute one, *i.e.* the attainment of permission is guaranteed, ... the relevant party must also assume the risk of any rejection after such changes to the law'.

176. Brunner (n 49) 133.

177. If performance is authorised, the defaulting party may be granted exemption from liability for the delay caused by the authorisation procedure.

178. See Brunner (n 49) 247 and 363; Vincent Heuzé, *La vente internationale de marchandises—Droit uniforme* (LGDJ 2000) 430, nn 475 and 476; Niklas Lindström, 'Changed Circumstances and Hardship in the International Sale of Goods' (2006) *Nordic Journal of Commercial Law*, n IV.2.2; Lookofsky (n 141) 143, n 6.19 and 155, n 6.32; Magnus (n 141) 21; Schwenzer (n 134) 1080, n 41 ad Article 79.

179. UNSC Res 1298 (2000), para 16: sanctions were established for a 12-month period, at the end of which the Security Council decided not to extend the sanctions, which therefore expired.

180. UNSC Res 1306 (2000), para 6: diamond sanctions were imposed for an initial period of 18 months.

181. UNSC Res 1333 (2000), para 23: measures against the Taliban, decided in December 2000, were imposed for an initial period of 12 months.

182. UNSC Res 1343 (2001), paras 9 and 10: arms sanctions were established for an initial period of 14 months, while diamond and travel sanctions were established for an initial period of 12 months. UNSC Res 1478 (2003), para 17: timber sanctions were established for an initial period of ten months. UNSC Res 1521 (2003), para 18: arms, travel, diamond and timber sanctions were established for an initial period of 12 months.

183. UNSC Res 1493 (2003), para 20: arms sanctions were established for an initial period of 12 months.

184. UNSC Res 1572 (2004), paras 7, 9 and 11: arms sanctions were established for an initial period of 13 months, while travel and financial sanctions were imposed for an initial period of 12 months.

185. The UN Charter does not provide for an automatic expiration of sanctions after a given period of time or after the occurrence of a given event.

186. See Alexander Kern, *Economic Sanctions—Law and Public Policy* (Palgrave Macmillan 2009); Geisinger, Bärtsch, Raneda and Ebere (n 9) 419-420; Grelon and Gudin (n 30) 655.

187. To determine whether timely performance by one party is of the essence to the other, the terms of the contract must be considered as well as the nature and purpose of the contract, the branch of activity the latter party is involved in, and possible contractual commitments towards third parties.

188. In this case, it is not commercially sound to compel the defaulting party to remain ready to resume performance at whatever time the sanction is lifted, since its contractual party has lost interest in that performance.

189. See Atamer (n 137) 1092, n 87 ad Article 79; Brunner (n 49) 246-247; Magnus (n 141) 21; Pichonnaz (n 133), 389, n 1680; Peter Schlechtriem and Petra Butler, *UN Law on International*

Sales—The UN Convention on the International Sale of Goods (Springer 2009) 201, footnote 547 and 207–208, n 295; Peter Schlechtriem and Claude Witz, *Convention de Vienne sur les contrats de vente internationale de marchandises* (Dalloz 2008) 258, n 381; Grelon and Gudin (n 30) 655.

190. Hungarian Chamber of Commerce and Industry Award of 10 December 1996, CISG-online 774.

191. ibid. n 11.

192. ICC Award in Case 7575, 2002 (2010) *Journal du Droit International* 1378 and following.

193. In the words of the arbitrator: 'Dès lors qu'il est constaté que des livraisons de marchandises ont bien eu lieu, on ne peut qu'en déduire que si un cas de force majeure s'est produit, il n'est intervenu qu'en cours d'exécution du contrat et ne pourrait donc affecter que les obligations contractuelles non encore exécutées. ... Aujourd'hui, les sanctions internationales prise [*sic*] à l'encontre de la République socialiste fédérative de Yougoslavie ayant été levées, l'arbitre ne voit aucun élément permettant d'étayer l'existence d'une quelconque cause de force majeure relativement au lieu d'exécution du contrat' (ibid. 1380).

194. See, for example, ICC Award 1512, 1971 (1976) *Yearbook of Commercial Arbitration* 128 and following; ICC Award no 6281, 26 August 1989 (1990) *Yearbook of Commercial Arbitration* 96 and following, (1991) *Journal du Droit International* 1054 and following, CISG-online 8.

195. See, for instance, ICC Award in Case 2291, 1975 (1976) *Journal du Droit International* 989 and following, in which the tribunal stated that '[i]t is a rule of the lex Mercatoria that the performances on the financial plane stay in equilibrium and that is why in almost every international contract "the price is determined according to the conditions which exist in the moment of the conclusion of the contract and it will vary according to the parameters, which reflect the variations of values of the different elements that compose the product or the performance"' (ibid. 989).

See also the 20 September 1985 decision of the Iran-US Claims Tribunal, which stated that the 'concept of changed circumstances, also referred to as clausula rebus sic stantibus, ... has in its basic form been incorporated into so many legal systems that it may be regarded as a general principle of law' (*Questech Inc v The Ministry of National Defence of the Islamic Republic of Iran*, Iran-US CTR 1985 107, 122). See also, *inter alia*, the arbitral award of 5 May 1997 in *Islamic Republic of Iran v Cubic Defense Systems, Inc* (ICC Case 7365/FMS, ULR 1999 796 and following), in which the tribunal held that '[u]nder the laws of contract in all municipal legal systems exceptions to the basic notion of pacta sunt servanda have been developed on the ground that in particular circumstances fairness and justice require the making of a legal excuse for non-performance of contractual promises. ... Moreover, from the covenant of good faith and fair dealing which is implied in each contract follows that in a case in which the circumstances to a contract undergo ... fundamental changes in an unforeseeable way, a party is precluded from invoking the binding effect of the contract' (ibid. 797–798).

For scholarly writing on this question, see, *inter alia*, Brunner (n 49) 413; James Gordley, 'Impossibility and Changed and Unforeseen Circumstances' (2004) *American Journal of Comparative Law* 513, 525; Hans Van Houtte, 'Changed Circumstances and *Pacta Sunt Servanda*' in Emmanuel Gaillard (ed), *Transnational Rules in International Commercial Arbitration* (ICC Publication 1993) 105, 115 and following and references cited therein; Nagla Nassar, *Sanctity of Contracts Revisited: A Study in the Theory and Practice of Long-Term International Commercial Transactions* (Martinus Nijhoff 1995) 201; Perillo, 'Force Majeure and Hardship under the UNIDROIT Principles of International Commercial Contracts' (n 141) 119; Joseph M Perillo, 'Hardship and its Impact on Contractual Obligations: A Comparative Analysis' in *Saggi, Conferenze e Seminari 20* (Centro di studi e ricerche di diritto comparato e straniero 1996) 1, 13.

196. See, for instance, Article 1198 of the Argentine Civil Code, Articles 478–480 of the 2002 Brazilian Civil Code, Article 868 of the Colombian Commercial Code, para 313 of the German Civil Code, Articles 1467–1469 of the 1942 Italian Civil Code, Article 6:258 of the 1992 Dutch Civil Code, Articles 1440–1446 of the Peruvian Civil Code, Article 437 of the Portuguese Civil Code, and Article 451 of the 1994/1995 Civil Code of the Russian Federation.

197. In Austria, Spain and Switzerland, for instance, courts have endorsed the possibility of contract adaptation on grounds of changed circumstances.

198. Brunner (n 49) 404. See the references in Schwenzer, Hachem and Kee (n 137) 668, footnote 188.

199. See para 2-615 UCC and Section 261 Restatement (Second) of Contracts.

200. Official comment no 6 on para 2-615 UCC provides that '[i]n situations in which neither sense nor justice is served by either answer when the issue is posed in flat terms of "excuse" or "no excuse", adjustment under the various provisions of this Article is necessary, especially the sections on good faith, on insecurity and assurance and on the reading of all provisions in the light of their purposes, and the general policy of this Act to use equitable principles in furtherance of commercial standards and good faith'.

201. See Section 265 Restatement (Second) of Contracts.

202. See the Law Reform (Frustrated Contracts) Act 1943.

203. According to Article 6.2.2 UNIDROIT Principles, '[t]here is hardship where the occurrence of events fundamentally alters the equilibrium of the contract either because the cost of a party's performance has increased or because the value of the performance a party receives has diminished, and (a) the events occur or become known to the disadvantaged party after the conclusion of the contract; (b) the events could not reasonably have been taken into account by the disadvantaged party at the time of the conclusion of the contract; (c) the events are beyond the control of the disadvantaged party; and (d) the risk of the events was not assumed by the disadvantaged party'.

204. Tom Southerington, 'Impossibility of Performance and Other Excuses in International Trade' in Tuula Ämmälä (ed), Publication of the Faculty of Law of the University of Turku (Private law publication series B:55 2001), n 2.4 available at <https://www.cisg.law.pace.edu/cisg/biblio/southerington.html>.

205. See Anja Carlsen, 'Can the Hardship Provisions in the UNIDROIT Principles Be Applied When the CISG Is the Governing Law?' (1998) n III available at <https://www.cisg.law.pace.edu/cisg/biblio/carlsen.html>.

206. On the question of lasting consent as the foundation of contractual liability, see Perillo, 'Force Majeure and Hardship under the UNIDROIT Principles of International Commercial Contracts' (n 141) 118-119; Perillo, 'Hardship and its Impact on Contractual Obligations' (n 195) 13.

207. Article 6.2.3(1) and (2) UNIDROIT Principles reads as follows:

> In case of hardship the disadvantaged party is entitled to request renegotiations. The request shall be made without undue delay and shall indicate the grounds on which it is based. The request for renegotiation does not in itself entitle the disadvantaged party to withhold performance.

208. Article 6.2.1 UNIDROIT Principles stipulates that '[w]here the performance of a contract becomes more onerous for one of the parties, that party is nevertheless bound to perform its obligations subject to the following provisions on hardship'. This provision 'acts as a reminder that the general duty is to perform and that relief is very much the exceptional case' (Ewan McKendrick in Vogenauer and Kleinheisterkamp (n 141) 716, n 4 ad Article 6.2.1; emphasis omitted).

209. Article 6.2.3(3) and (4) UNIDROIT Principles reads as follows:

> Upon failure to reach agreement within a reasonable time either party may resort to the court. If the court finds hardship it may, if reasonable, (a) terminate the contract at a date and on terms to be fixed, or (b) adapt the contract with a view to restoring its equilibrium.

210. *Islamic Republic of Iran v Cubic Defense Systems, Inc.*, ICC Award of 5 May 1997 in Case 7365/FMS, ULR 1999 796 and following (confirmed on 7 July 1998 by the United States District Court, SD California, 29 F. Supp. 2d 1168).

211. ibid. 797 (summary of the award).

212. The contracts contained a choice-of-law clause designating the law of Iran, but the parties eventually agreed to the complementary and supplementary application of general principles of international law. The tribunal held that '[a]s to the contents of such rules, the Tribunal shall be guided by the Principles of International Commercial Contracts, published in 1994 by the UNIDROIT Institute, Rome' (ibid. 797).

213. ibid. 797-798.

214. Azeredo da Silveira, *Trade Sanctions and International Sales* (n 10) §11.01[B][1].

215. For a thorough discussion of the remedies available under the CISG in situations of hardship, see Azeredo da Silveira, *Trade Sanctions and International Sales* (n 10) §11.01[B][2].

216. In Kessedjian's opinion, if performing the contract, once an impediment is lifted, would entail 'adverse consequences' for one of the parties, one should 'use Article 7 and the good faith requirement to say that, in such a case, parties are under an obligation to adapt the contract ... since it is difficult to imagine that the force majeure event[,] however ... temporary it may be, would have no impact on the initial equilibrium of the contract' (Catherine Kessedjian, 'Competing Approaches to Force Majeure and Hardship' (2005) *International Review of Law and Economics* 415, 418). Also, without dealing specifically with the CISG, Blessing suggests that if a certain time has elapsed, '[o]nce the intervening trade sanction is lifted, ... the parameters of the resurrecting contract might have to be renegotiated in good faith, since the resuming of the performance might have become substantially more onerous to the aggrieved party (typically for the party that will have to resume its works). Thus, an Arbitral Tribunal might have to consider carefully the impact of such sanctions ... It might have to declare the contract terminated or extinct due to its suspension over a longer period of time, and determine the consequences thereof' (Blessing, 'Impact of the Extraterritorial Application of Mandatory Rules of Law on

International Contracts' (n 27) 67; see also Marc Blessing, 'Mandatory Rules of Law *versus* Party Autonomy in International Arbitration' (1997) 14(4) *Journal of International Arbitration* 23, 34–35).

217. See Peter Schlechtriem, in H Flechtner (ed), 'Transcript of a Workshop on the Sales Convention: Leading CISG Scholars Discuss Contract Formation, Validity, Excuse for Hardship, Avoidance, Nachfrist, Contract Interpretation, Parol Evidence, Analogical Application, and Much More' (1999) 18 *Journal of Law and Commerce* 191, 237. Article 50 CISG reads: 'If the goods do not conform with the contract and whether or not the price has already been paid, the buyer may reduce the price in the same proportion as the value that the goods actually delivered had at the time of the delivery bears to the value that conforming goods would have had at that time. However, if the seller remedies any failure to perform his obligations in accordance with article 37 or article 48 or if the buyer refuses to accept performance by the seller in accordance with those articles, the buyer may not reduce the price'.

218. Azeredo da Silveira, 'Economic Sanctions and Contractual Disputes Between Private Operators' (n 16) 374.

219. Azeredo da Silveira, *Trade Sanctions and International Sales* (n 10) 299–300, n 456.

220. In a decision rendered in 1995, the *Rechtbank van Koophandel* of Hasselt, Belgium, held price fluctuations to be foreseeable events in international trade and to result in an economic loss included in the normal risks of commercial activities (*Vital Berry Marketing v Dira-Frost, Rechtbank van Koophandel*, Hasselt, Belgium, 2 May 1995, CISG-online 371).

In a case decided in 1997, the Oberlandesgericht of Hamburg denied the seller's exemption claim following its supplier's failure to deliver the goods and a tripling of the market price for the goods. The Court held that '[t]he Seller is also not exempted by the fact that acquiring the goods elsewhere would have led to considerable financial loss because it would have had to pay a higher price. The Seller generally bears the risk of considerable extra expenses in connection with acquiring the goods elsewhere, even the loss of transactions, as it has accepted the risk of acquiring the goods and the risk that they cannot be acquired at a certain price'. The Court added: 'Despite of the triplication of market price that had to be paid ... an excess of the absolute limit of sacrifice is not given ... For parties doing business in a sector that has a very speculative aspect the limits of reasonability are very high' (*Oberlandesgericht*, Hamburg, Germany, 28 February 1997, CISG-online 261). A similar opinion was handed down by the *Cour d'appel* of Colmar, France, on 12 June 2001, in which the Court held that in a long-term contract like the one between the buyer and the seller, 'price fluctuations, even sudden and significant, are not exceptional and, a fortiori, are not unforeseeable. Besides, when becoming involved in such a long and restrictive supply agreement ... the [Buyer], an experienced professional acting in the international market, should have arranged either guarantees of performance of the contractual obligations entered into in respect of the [Seller], or means of revision of these obligations. Otherwise, it should bear the risk of non-performance' (*Société Romay AG v SARL Behr France*, *Cour d'appel*, Colmar, France, 12 June 2001, CISG-online 694; confirmed by the *Cour de cassation* on 30 June 2004, CISG-online 870).

See also Bulgarian Chamber of Commerce and Industry Award of 12 February 1998 in Case 11/1996, CISG-online 436; and ICC Award in Case 6281, 26 August 1989 (1990) *Yearbook of Commercial Arbitration* 96 and following, (1991) *Journal du Droit International* 1054 and following, CISG-online 8.

221. Similar clauses were incorporated in other Security Council resolutions. See n 11 above.

222. The requirement laid down in the quoted portion of Security Council Resolution 661 (1990) was intended to permanently protect the contractual counterparts of Iraqi parties from being held liable after having complied with the UN sanctions programme, and to prevent the performance of transactions affected by the sanctions, considering the seriousness of Iraq's behaviour.

223. See Blessing, 'Impact of the Extraterritorial Application of Mandatory Rules of Law on International Contracts' (n 27) 67, footnote 75; Van Houtte, 'Les effets des sanctions économiques sur les contrats transnationaux' (n 22) 207–208, n 21 and references cited therein; Landy-Osman (n 30) 630–631, nn 83–85. An often-cited decision is the 1990 decision *SA Lesieur International v Société Norasia Line, LPA* (*Tribunal de commerce*, Nanterre, 31 October 1990, Les Petites Affiches, 28 December 1990, n 156-21). The dispute pertained to a sales contract between SA Lesieur International and a Kuwaiti buyer, the performance of which was affected by the sanctions against Iraq. The *Tribunal de commerce* of Nanterre ratified the parties' agreement regarding the contract's termination and authorised SA Lesieur International to regain possession of the goods. It is noteworthy that in this case, the buyer and the seller had agreed on the termination of the contract.

224. See Azeredo da Silveira, *Trade Sanctions and International Sales* (n 10) §7.01[A][2] and §10.02.

225. See, however, van Houtte, 'The Impact of Trade Prohibitions on Transnational Contracts' (n 59) 147, who argues that '[t]he substantial threat of punishment by a foreign government ... can constitute "*force majeure*"'; van Houtte, 'Les effets des sanctions économiques sur les contrats

transnationaux' (n 22) 205, n 18; Matray (n 49) 95, according to whom 'the risk of a foreign accusation can render the performance of an agreement dangerous to the extent that one cannot reasonably require its performance. The serious threat of a foreign sanction can therefore constitute a case of *force majeure*'; Pichonnaz (n 133) 404, n 1753, for whom '[o]n peut ... imaginer que les sanctions en cas de violation d'un embargo rendent généralement l'obstacle insurmontable'.

226. According to proponents of the legal norm approach, if the risk of penalty could lead to an exemption of the defaulting party despite the sanction itself being disregarded, mechanisms of private international law discussed earlier would lose their *raison d'être*. Irrespective of any potential conflict with principles of public policy or of the stringent conditions that ought to be satisfied for an overriding mandatory rule to be taken into account, economic sanctions would be given effect on the sole ground that the sanctioning state may impose penalties. Thus, the efficiency of economic sanctions would be directly and solely dependent on the severity of penalties that the sanctioning state would threaten to impose in case of non-compliance. It would be unnecessary to examine whether the prohibition itself is to be taken into account and constitutes a legal impediment. This would arguably encroach on the principle of party autonomy, under which the parties' freedom to agree on contractual terms and to select the applicable law should in principle only be limited by overriding mandatory rules. See Azeredo da Silveira, *Trade Sanctions and International Sales* (n 10) 209, n 337.

227. In addition to forfeiture proceedings against property involved in a violation, penalties for breach of a sanction typically include fines.

228. It is noteworthy that although a state cannot enforce its laws through material means of coercion on foreign territory, it may threaten to impose penalties on all those—whether located within the enacting state or within the territorial jurisdiction of another state—that would fail to comply with these laws (Juillard (n 43) p. 26).

229. In some of its resolutions, the Security Council itself has called upon states to enact domestic legislation providing for the imposition of penalties and to bring proceedings against those that would act in violation of domestic measures implementing these resolutions. See, for instance, UNSC Res. 333 (1973), para 4; UNSC Res. 820 (1993), para 19; UNSC Res. 841 (1993), para 12; UNSC Res. 864 (1993), para 21; UNSC Res. 1267 (1999), para 8; UNSC Res. 1295 (2000), paras 16 and 27; and UNSC Res. 1306 (2000), para 17. If penalties are imposed by one state against individuals located or entities incorporated in another state, the latter state's assistance will be necessary for the enforcement of these penalties.

230. Joern Rimke, 'Force Majeure and Hardship: Application in International Trade Practice with Specific Regard to the CISG and the UNIDROIT Principles of International Commercial Contracts' (1999-2000) *Pace Review of the Convention on Contracts for the International Sale of Goods* 197, 197 available at <https://www.cisg.law.pace.edu/cisg/biblio/rimke.html>. The principle is spelt out, for instance, in Article 1.3 UNIDROIT Principles, which provides that '[a] contract validly entered into is binding upon the parties. It can only be modified or terminated in accordance with its terms or by agreement or as otherwise provided in these Principles'.

231. Ingeborg Schwenzer, 'Force Majeure and Hardship in International Sales Contracts' (2008) *Victoria University of Wellington Law Review* 709, 709.

232. Magnus (n 141) 1.

233. The situation may be compared to the one in which a party is compelled by the courts of one state to provide information that is confidential under the law of another state, and this law is not taken into account by the deciding court in the context of proceedings carried out in the former state. '[F]oreign secrecy laws often carry penal sanctions for disclosure of confidential information. Thus, an American discovery order requiring confidential information subject to the foreign law would create hardship against the party having knowledge of the information' (Bernhard Grossfeld and Paul C. Rogers, 'A Shared Value Approach to Jurisdictional Conflicts in International Economic Law' (1983) *International and Comparative Law Quarterly* 931, 945).

234. Even though penalties could possibly be imposed only after the contract is performed, the contractual equilibrium must be considered disrupted from the moment the sanction is in force and the obligor is under threat of penalty. Arguably, the same cannot be said with respect to threats of penalties under secondary and tertiary sanctions, such as future denial of exports from the sanctioning state or loans from financial institutions of that state.

235. See McKendrick in Vogenauer and Kleinheisterkamp (n 141) 718, n 3 ad Article 6.2.2. See also van Houtte, 'Changed Circumstances and *Pacta Sunt Servanda*' (n 195) 117; ICC Award in Case n 9479 (1999), in which the arbitral tribunal asserted that 'a change in the law [can] be the source of hardship. It may well be the case, when a new law makes the performance of the contractual obligations of a party more onerous or when the value it receives from the performance of the other party is severely reduced' ((2001/2) *ICC Bull*. 67, 70).

236. McKendrick in Vogenauer and Kleinheisterkamp (n 141) 721, n 14 ad Article 6.2.2.

237. Perillo, 'Force Majeure and Hardship under the UNIDROIT Principles of International Commercial Contracts' (n 141) 128-129. See also Jennifer M. Bund, 'Force Majeure Clauses: Drafting Advice for the CISG Practitioner' (1997-1998) *Journal of Law and Commerce* 381, 391. In particular, risks that are commonly associated with a given type of contract cannot give rise to hardship.

238. See Brunner (n 49) 214; Schwenzer, 'Force Majeure and Hardship in International Sales Contracts' (n 231) 714-715.

239. Based on a comparative law analysis, Brunner has suggested that in 'standard situations' (that is, situations where there is no specific risk assumption by the parties and the existence of the obligor would not be seriously and effectively endangered if it were to perform the contract under its original terms), the contractual equilibrium must be altered by at least 100 percent to be deemed fundamentally altered (Brunner (n 49) 428-435). Others concur when discussing specifically the requirements of Article 79 CISG (Enderlein and Maskow (n 142) 325, n 6.3 ad Article 79; Klaus Peter Berger, *Private Dispute Resolution in International Business—Negotiation, Mediation, Arbitration* (Kluwer Law International 2006), Vol. II, 491, n 24-66). For one author, '[a] 150-200 per cent margin seems to be advisable' (Schwenzer, 'Force Majeure and Hardship in International Sales Contracts' (n 231) 717) given that '[t]he suggested '100 per cent threshold' seems to be based upon considerations of domestic markets[,] [whereas] ... [i]n an international market, one may expect the potentially aggrieved party to insist on incorporating terms for a possible adjustment in the contract or otherwise assuming the risk for higher fluctuations than usually occur on domestic markets' (ibid. 716-717; see also Schwenzer (n 134) 1076, n 30 ad Article 79).

240. See Brunner (n 49) 426 and 427; Pichonnaz (n 133) 408-409, n 1778; Schwenzer (n 134) 1076, n 30 ad Article 79; Schwenzer, 'Force Majeure and Hardship in International Sales Contracts' (n 231) 716; Stoll (n 159) 618, n 40 ad Article 79.

241. Fines for breach of a sanction are typically a fixed amount or a multiple of the amount involved in the transaction.

242. An increase in the costs of performance that would otherwise not be considered beyond the limit of sacrifice may be considered reasonably insurmountable if performance would cause the obligor's ruin. As suggested by Schwenzer, 'in cases where the financial ruin of the obligor is imminent, the threshold for allowing hardship may be lowered' (Schwenzer, 'Force Majeure and Hardship in International Sales Contracts' (n 231) 716). See also Stoll (n 159) 618, n 40, footnote 135 ad Article 79.

243. Azeredo da Silveira, *Trade Sanctions and International Sales* (n 10) 347-348, n 525.

244. As noted by Brunner, '[t]he "reasonable" time period during which renegotiations can be held should [indeed] be limited in order to avoid dilatory tactics by a party' (Brunner (n 49) 489). This time period will depend on 'the particular circumstances of the case, including the nature of the dispute, any risk of prejudice for either party caused by the delay in setting up and attending the renegotiation process, and the reasonable prospects of success' (ibid. 490).

245. Azeredo da Silveira, *Trade Sanctions and International Sales* (n 10) 348, n 526.

Conclusion

The contributions contained in this XVII Dossier of the ICC Institute of World Business Law clearly show the importance and actuality of the subject matter of force majeure and hardship. Finding a fair compromise between the principle of *pacta sunt servanda* and the need to take into account unforeseen circumstances which make performance impossible or too onerous, remains a basic issue for legislators, contract negotiators, as well as judges and arbitrators in case of dispute.

Parties involved in international commercial contracts need updated information about developments in recent years in order to face the problems which may arise due to unforeseen events which make performance impossible or excessively onerous. They need in particular to deal with these problems when drafting their contracts by providing clauses which regulate these issues according to their needs.

The articles collected in this volume offer an updated view of the various issues arising in this context: an indispensable tool for those who need to understand and manage these complex issues. Those who draft and negotiate contracts will find useful information about contractual clauses and in particular about the recent developments of the ICC force majeure and hardship clauses. Those who are involved in litigation (counsels, judges, arbitrators) will find updated information about the approach followed by arbitrators and courts with respect to the main issues arising in this context.

We believe that this dossier will be an essential tool for a more in-depth understanding of force majeure and hardship and for approaching possible future problems through an accurate drafting of appropriate clauses or, at least, if this is not possible, through the use of well-drafted standard clauses.

Fabio Bortolotti and Dorothy Ufot, SAN

Contributors

About the Authors

Pascale Accaoui Lorfing

Ph.D. International Law (Paris II-Assas)

She is a researcher in International and Investment Contracts & Arbitration. She is an Associate to Lamy International Contracts (Investment Contracts, Contractual provisions on hardship, equilibrium provision and Force Majeure). She is a member of Groupe de Travail sur les Contrats Internationaux (G.T.C.I.), member of la Société de Législation Comparée and member of Paris MENA Legal Club. She is the author of *La renégociation des contrats internationaux*, Editions Bruylant, 2011. Among her publications, "The Evolution and Current Status of the Concept of Indirect Expropriation in Investment Treaties and Arbtitration", *Indian Journal of Arbitration Law* (IJAL), 2017 vol. 6, no. 2, pp. 98-137 (co-authored with Maria Beatriz Burghetto); "The Evolution of State Contract till the 1960s", *International Business Law Journal (IBLJ)*, no. 5, 2017, pp. 393-430; "L'obligation de renégociation: étude de droit comparé", *Revue de Droit International et de Droit Comparé (RDIC)*, 2015/2, pp. 233-277. (The Obligation of renegotiation in comparative law).

Latest article "Article 1195 of the French Civil Code on Revision for Hardship in light of Comparative Law", *International Business Law Journal*, no. 5—2018, pp. 449-464.

"The contractually unforeseen renegotiation", *International Business Law Journal*, no. 1, 2010, pp. 35-55.

Fluent in French, English and Arabic.

Mercédeh Azeredo da Silveira

Attorney-at-Law, Baer & Karrer SA

Dr Mercédeh Azeredo da Silveira is an attorney-at-law with fifteen years of experience in international arbitration. She is acting as arbitrator in international commercial arbitration proceedings and represents individuals, corporate entities and governments before arbitral tribunals in both commercial and investment arbitration proceedings. She has acted as counsel in the context of commercial disputes related, *inter alia*, to international engineering and construction contracts, sales contracts, distribution agreements and share purchase agreements, as well as in the context of investment disputes in the mining, telecommunications and energy sectors. Dr Azeredo da Silveira also acts as counsel before the Swiss Supreme Court in proceedings related to challenges of international arbitral awards, including sports-related awards. Finally, she regularly advises clients and serves as legal expert on issues pertaining to economic sanctions.

Dr Azeredo da Silveira has an academic expertise in the field of economic sanctions. She is the author of *Trade Sanctions and International Sales—An Inquiry into International Arbitration and Commercial Litigation*, which was awarded the Professor Walther Hug Prize in 2015. She is also the author of numerous publications in the areas of international arbitration, international trade, contracts, economic sanctions and mediation. Her academic research has been funded by the Swiss National Science Foundation and three renowned Swiss private foundations (*Société académique de Genève, Fondation Boninchi, Fondation Schmidheiny*).

She has taught at the European Law Students' Association's Summer Law School on Arbitration (2017), given guest lectures at the University of Geneva Law School (2013-2014), at Fordham University School of Law (2010) and at Columbia Law School (2009), and is regularly invited to speak at conferences. Dr Azeredo da Silveira is fluent in French, English and Persian.

Klaus Peter Berger, LL.M.

Klaus Peter Berger is professor of domestic and international business and banking law, comparative and private international law at the University of Cologne, director of the Institute for Banking Law and the Center for Transnational Law (CENTRAL) at the Cologne law faculty. He has been Honorary Lecturer and Member of the Global Faculty at the Centre for Energy, Petroleum and Mineral Law and Policy, University of Dundee (2000-2012), and visiting professor at the University of Virginia School of Law, Charlottesville (1999), Asser Institute, The Hague (1997-2004), and at Columbia Law School, New York City (2014).

Professor Berger is a practicing international arbitrator and member of the panel of arbitrators of the China International Economic Trade Arbitration Commission (CIETAC, Beijing, China), ICDR, International Arbitration Centre of the Austrian Federal Economic Chamber, Dubai International Arbitration Centre (DIAC), Hong Kong International Arbitration Centre (HKIAC) Panel of Arbitrators for Financial Services Disputes, P.R.I.M.E. Finance, and Driver Contract Recognition Board (CRB, Formula 1), Fédération Internationale de l'Automobile (FIA).

Professor Berger is author of more than 200 publications on domestic and international arbitration, contract law, trade law, comparative law, M&A, banking and finance. See for a full list www.klauspeterberger.de. He is the inventor and operator of the TransLex-web-platform on transnational law, www.trans-lex.org, and the Director of the annual "Cologne Academies" on International Arbitration & International Business Mediation (www.cologne-academies.com).

Professor Berger is past President and member of the Board of the German Arbitration Institute (DIS). He is also member of the Council of the ICC Institute of World Business Law and co-editor of Arbitration International.

Christoph Brunner

Peter & Partners International Ltd, Switzerland

Christoph Brunner has been practising dispute resolution for over 20 years. He has acted as counsel, presiding arbitrator, sole arbitrator, co-arbitrator and legal expert in more than 80 international commercial arbitrations governed by various procedural and substantive laws, including Swiss, California, English, French, German, Italian, Spanish, Turkish and UAE law (among others).

His range of expertise covers in particular M&A, joint ventures, construction/infrastructure projects, sales and distribution and agency contracts. He is recommended for arbitration and litigation in Who's Who Legal since 2013 and is considered by clients and his peers as an "excellent, knowledgeable and fair" lawyer (WWL, 2017).

LL.M. (Berkeley); PhD, Titular professor for commercial law and arbitration (University of Bern); member of the Court of the Swiss Chambers Arbitration Institution (SCAI); member of various arbitration institutions; author of several books and numerous articles on commercial law and international arbitration, in particular the treatise "Force Majeure and Hardship under General Contract Principles" and a Commentary on the CISG.

Filip De Ly

Filip De Ly teaches private international law, comparative law, international business law and international arbitration law and is doing research on international business law and international commercial arbitration.

Professor De Ly has written 5 books (including his dissertation *International business law and lex mercatoria*, Amsterdam, North Holland 1992 and his inaugural address in Dutch on the European Union and private law harmonization) and co-authored/edited 6 books including a book on *The place of arbitration*. He published some 110 articles in the field of international business law, international commercial arbitration, conflict of laws, comparative law and EC business law. Also, he published 16 case notes and some fifty reports and book reviews.

He is frequently retained as counsel, expert witness or arbitrator in international commercial arbitrations and often gives legal opinions with regard to international business law problems. He acted in more than two hundred arbitrations in the capacity of expert witness, sole arbitrator (50 cases), co-arbitrator (69 cases) or chairman of the arbitral tribunal (61 cases).

Filip De Ly studied at Ghent Law School (Belgium) and obtained a LL.M. degree from Harvard Law School in 1983. He has worked for the US-law firm Cleary, Gottlieb, Steen & Hamilton in Brussels (1983-1986) and as a Associate Professor at Utrecht Law School (The Netherlands) before becoming a professor at the Law Faculty of Erasmus University in 1992. He is a Belgian citizen who has been working and living in The Netherlands for the past twenty-nine years.

Prof Dr H. Ercüment Erdem

Prof Dr H. Ercüment Erdem is the Founder and Senior Partner of Erdem&Erdem. He has more than 30-year experience in arbitration, international commercial law, competition and antitrust law, mergers and acquisitions, privatizations and corporate finance. He serves international and national clients in a variety of industries including energy, construction, finance, retail, real estate, aerospace, healthcare and insurance.

He has acted as chairman and sole or party-appointed arbitrator in many international and national arbitrations under different rules including International Chamber of Commerce (ICC) Arbitration, Swiss Arbitration, Moscow Arbitration, United Nations Commission on International Trade Law (UNCITRAL) Arbitration, Tehran Arbitration, and ad hoc arbitrations and is, furthermore, distinguished in this field.

He is a commercial law professor lectured in leading universities such as Galatasaray University in Turkey and Fribourg University in Switzerland. He has over 30 year experience as a scholar and his research contains arbitration, competition and antitrust, international commercial law, M&A, corporate law etc.

Prof Erdem is a member of International Bar Association, Istanbul Bar Association, Co-chair of ICC CLP Commission and member of ICC Arbitration Commission, ICC Court of Arbitration, ICC Institute Counsel, ICC Turkish National Committee Arbitration, Istanbul Arbitration Centre (ISTAC) and Association Suisse de l'Arbitrage (ASA).

Marcel Fontaine

Marcel Fontaine is Professor emeritus at the University of Louvain at Louvain-la-Neuve (Belgium). He has also taught as a guest professor or lecturer in numerous other universities. His main legal fields of expertise are the law of contracts and the law of insurance, domestic, international and comparative.

He has been the reporter for several chapters in the working group of UNIDROIT in charge of drafting *Principles for International Commercial Contracts*. He was the expert in charge of drafting a Uniform Act on the Law of Contracts for the 17 African countries of *OHADA*. He has chaired the *Working Group on International Contracts* for 17 years. He has advised governements of several countries of Central and Eastern Europe, as well as Central Asia, on preparing insurance legislation, and he has written the draft of the Luxembourg law on insurance contracts. He is Honorary President of the *International Insurance Law Association (AIDA)*. He has been a member, for 22 years, of the Council of the *ICC Institute of World Business Law*. He regularly serves as an arbitrator in domestic and international disputes, both ad hoc and institutional (*ICC, LCIA, CEPANI*), mostly concerning contracts, insurance and reinsurance disputes (over 150 cases, most often as chairman of the Tribunal). He is the author of several books and over 260 articles. He is doctor *honoris causa* of the Universities of Montpellier, Bourgogne, Paris I Panthéon-Sorbonne et Geneva.

Contributors

About the Editors

Fabio Bortolotti

For more than 40 years Fabio Bortolotti has been dealing with international contracts, not only as professor of International Commercial Law at the University of Torino, but also as counsel assisting companies in negotiating and drafting international transactions and in dealing with possible disputes before courts and arbitral tribunals.

He is founding partner of the law firm Buffa, Bortolotti & Mathis, Torino. He has acted and is at present engaged as arbitrator or counsel in several international and domestic arbitrations. He is an accredited mediator, Center for Dispute Resolution (CEDR).

Fabio Bortolotti is co-chair of the Commission on Commercial Law and Practice (CLP) of the International Chamber of Commerce and has chaired various task forces which have drafted the major ICC model contracts (e.g. commercial agency, distributorship, sale, occasional intermediaries, turnkey, M&A, trademark license).

He is member of the council of the ICC Institute of World Business Law, of the ICC Commission on International Arbitration, of the ICC Commission on Competition and vice-chair of ICC Italy. He is member of various associations: "Associazione Italiana per l'Arbitrato (AIA), "Deutsche Institution für Schiedsgerichtsbarkeit E.V." (DIS); "Union Internationale des Avocat" (U.I.A.); "Association Suisse de l'Arbitrage" (A.S.A.). He is founder and chairman of the International Distribution Institute.

He is the author of numerous books and articles in the field of the international commercial contracts, contract law, distribution law, conflict of laws, international litigation and arbitration.

Dorothy Ufot, SAN

Mrs Ufot is the founding partner of Dorothy Ufot & Co, a leading law firm in Nigeria since 1994, where she heads the international arbitration and litigation departments of the firm.

Dorothy specialises in international arbitration, litigation and other forms of dispute resolution, including investment treaty arbitration, enforcement of foreign arbitral awards, investment consulting, corporate and commercial law.

Dorothy was elevated to the prestigious rank of Senior Advocate of Nigeria (SAN), the equivalent of the English Queen's Counsel, in April 2009, in recognition of her vast work in commercial litigation.

Dorothy is a fellow of the Chartered Institute of Arbitrators UK and a chartered arbitrator. She is a former member of the Court of Arbitration of the International Chamber of Commerce (ICC) Paris

(2006 -2018) and a member of the Court of Arbitration of the Casablanca International Mediation and Arbitration Centre (CIMAC) Morocco (2016).

Dorothy was designated to serve a six-year term on the panel of arbitrators of the International Centre for the Settlement of Investment Disputes (ICSID) in February 2017 and she is currently on her third ICSID case, pursuant to her appointment as a member of the panel of Arbitrators by ICSID.

Index

Cases

ICC Dispute Resolution Bulletin

The ICC e-Bulletin is published 4 times a year. It includes sections on Doctrine, Case Decisions (Awards, Procedural Orders), Global Developments, ICC Activities, Book Reviews and ICC Dispute Resolution Practice and Procedure. An editorial board of twenty arbitration and dispute resolution specialists from all parts of the world work on the content of the Bulletin.

> ICC Members: free of charge

> Non members: €180 yearly subscription

International Commercial Mediation Training Role-Plays

ICC Pub. No. 765E, €99

A compilation of 21 of the best role-plays written for the ICC International Mediation Competition. The role-plays address a range of issues including contractual and quality disputes, cases in intellectual property rights, disputes in the construction industry and cases involving personal conflict in close international partnerships. Each case includes general information for both parties and confidential information for each party. Expert commentary is provided on each role-play from business, legal and training perspectives. The book is an indispensable resource for mediation students and trainers.

Expedited Procedures in International Arbitration

Dossier XVI of the ICC Institute of World Business Law

Edited by Laurent Lévy and Michael Polkinghorne
ICC Pub. No. 793E, €75

The amended ICC Rules of Arbitration entered into force on 1 March 2017. They include an ICC expedited procedure automatically applicable to cases with an amount in dispute below USD 2 million unless expressly excluded by the parties. This Dossier explores some of the ways and means to conduct proceedings in a reasonable time without jeopardizing due process.

Dispute Prevention and Settlement through Expert Determination and Dispute Boards

Dossier XV of the ICC Institute of World Business Law

Edited by Filip De Ly, Paul-A. Gélinas
ICC Pub. No. 792E, €75

Thirteen international experts share their knowledge and their experience on the impact of applicable law, contract law issues, procedural issues and the relationship between Expert Determination or Dispute Boards on the one hand and litigation and arbitration on the other.

Specific topics include the challenges of Expert Determination in M&A transactions, Expert Determination by Accounting firms including real-life examples, the settlement of disputes including under the FIDIC forms of contract and recent case law on Dispute Boards.

Class and Group Actions in Arbitration

Dossier XIV of the ICC Institute of World Business Law

Edited by Bernard Hanotiau and Eric Schwartz
ICC Pub. No. 771E, €75

Is there a place for such proceedings within the framework of the arbitration process? Class action procedures, as developed in the United States court system and more recently in Canada, are almost nonexistent in Europe. The book highlights the lessons learned from cases in the US and in Europe.

Addressing Issues of Corruption in Commercial and Investment Arbitration

Dossier XIII of the ICC Institute of World Business Law

Co-editors: Domitille Baizeau, Richard H. Kreindler
ICC Pub. No. 768E, €67.50 (e-book only)

The topics covered include the impact of corruption on "gateway issues" of arbitrability, jurisdiction, admissibility and procedure; the arbitrator's rights and duties to investigate and report corruption. It also addresses the most recent thinking and case law on the burden and standard of proof for allegations of corruption as well as the consequences and effects of allegations or positive findings of corruption on the dispute on the merits and the enforceability of the award respectively.

Jurisdictional Choices in Times of Trouble

Dossier XII of the ICC Institute of World Business Law

Co-editors: Georges Affaki, Horacio Grigera Naon
ICC Pub. No. 755E, €75

Written by arbitrators, academics and practitioners, this Dossier addresses the multiple challenges facing the jurisdiction such as Unilateral Dispute Resolution Clauses, Asymmetrical Arbitration Clauses, Hague Convention on choice of court agreements and other arbitration and court proceedings.

The Application of Substantive Law by International Arbitrators

Dossier XI of the ICC Institute of World Business Law

ICC Pub. No. 753E, €75

This book examines issues that can arise when international arbitrators apply the rules of a national legal system. It provides a thorough picture of the practical issues raised when there is contradiction between the applicable law and the needs of international business.

Third-party Funding in International Arbitration

Dossier X of the ICC Institute of World Business Law

ICC Pub. No. 752E, €75

This publication gives an overview of the various funding techniques specific to international arbitration. It also analyzes some of the legal issues raised by such funding and the reactions it may arouse amongst practitioners. To give you a complete picture of challenges and opportunities of third-party funding, this vital reference for any practitioner and academic includes points of view of financiers, funders, arbitrators and counsel.

Players' Interaction in International Arbitration

Dossier IX of the ICC Institute of World Business Law

ICC Pub. No. 737E, €75

Arbitral procedures are becoming longer, costlier and more complex. How can the different 'players' involved in a case ensure that the proceedings remain efficient, harmonious and at the same time respectful of the parties' rights? Some of today's leading experts discuss this and other questions, taking into account the points of view of all 'players' concerned: arbitrators, counsel, corporate lawyers and arbitral institutions. A must-read for anyone involved in international arbitration.

Is Arbitration Only as Good as the Arbitrator?

Dossier VIII of the ICC Institute of World Business Law

ICC Pub. No. 714E, €67.50 (e-book only)

Invaluable companion for practitioners and scholars alike, this publication looks at the relationship between the qualities of the arbitrators and the arbitrators' "work-products", namely the award and the arbitral process itself. Leading experts discuss issues such as clashes between arbitrator and litigants, arbitral discrimination under English and EU law or the arbitrator's relation with third parties.

Multiparty Arbitration

Dossier VII of the ICC Institute of World Business Law

ICC Pub. No. 701E, €75

Arbitral procedures are becoming more complex as commercial transactions begin to take place in an ever-increasing interdependent world. How can the several parties involved in multiparty contracts and proceedings be harmonized and handled in the interests of the best administration of justice? This Dossier seeks to encourage reflection on complex multiparty, multicontract arbitrations.

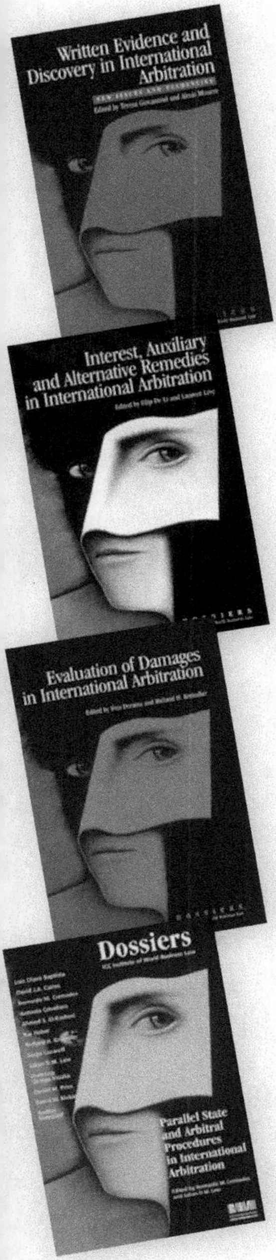

Written Evidence and Discovery in International Arbitration

Dossier VI of the ICC Institute of World Business Law

ICC Pub. No. 698E, €67.50 (e-book only)

This Dossier seeks to encourage reflection on future practice in relation to documentary evidence in international arbitration, looking for transnational solutions capable of striking a proper balance between efficiency and fairness. It tackles relevant issues including fraud, forgery, confidentiality and privilege.

Interest, Auxiliary and Alternative Remedies in International Arbitration

Dossier V of the ICC Institute of World Business Law

ICC Pub. No. 684E, €75

How can the quick and effective enforcement of awards be guaranteed in arbitral practice? The aim of this publication is to provide the reader with solutions on how to control the impact of time between the occurrence of the damage and its full compensation. Renowned arbitration professionals Antonias Dimolitsa, John Beechey, Andrea Giardina, John Yukio Gotanda, Grabrielle Kaufmann- Kohler, Alexis Mourre and V.V. Veeder, amongst others, give their own perspective on a wide range of topics related to remedies (contractual remedies, judicial penalties, specific performance) and interest (issue of applicable law, comparative approaches, interest in arbitration practice).

Evaluation of Damages in International Arbitration

Dossier IV of the ICC Institute of World Business Law

ICC Pub. No. 668E, €67.50 (e-book only)

This publication provides the reader with a comprehensive overview of the difficulties encountered by arbitrators, governments and international organizations in calculating the amounts of recoverable damages in cases of international arbitration. Written by expert arbitrators and practitioners, the book covers vital issues arising from determining recoverable damages and proposes practical solutions for resolving them.

Parallel State and Arbitral Procedures in International Arbitration

Dossier III of the ICC Institute of World Business Law

ICC Pub. No. 692E, €67.50 (e-book only)

This Dossier gives the reader a thorough picture of the practical issues raised by the conflicts arising when there is more than one arbitration and when commercial arbitrations run in parallel with state legal procedures. This indispensable guide for arbitrators, lawyers and anyone with an interest in arbitration procedures includes points of view of expert arbitrators and practitioners.

Notes

www.ingramcontent.com/pod-product-compliance
Lightning Source LLC
Chambersburg PA
CBHW071244230926
51849CB00001B/221
9789403514635